PSYCHOLOGICAL REPORT WRITING SECOND EDITION

NORMAN TALLENT

Prentice-Hall, Inc., Englewood Cliffs, New Jersey 07632

Library of Congress Cataloging in Publication Data

TALLENT, NORMAN, (date)
  Psychological report writing.

  Bibliography.
  Includes index.
  1. Clinical psychology. 2. Report writing. I. Title.
[DNLM: 1. Psychology 2. Writing. WZ 345 T147p]
RC467.T34 1983   808'.066616021   82-9132
ISBN 0-13-732511-8   AACR2

© 1983, 1976 by Prentice-Hall, Inc., Englewood Cliffs, N.J. 07632

Printed in the United States of America

10 9 8 7 6 5 4 3 2 1

Editorial/production supervision:
Jeanne Hoeting
Cover design: Ray Lundgren
Manufacturing buyer: Ron Chapman

ISBN 0-13-732511-8

Prentice-Hall International, Inc., *London*
Prentice-Hall of Australia Pty. Limited, *Sydney*
Editora Prentice-Hall do Brasil, Ltda, *Rio de Janeiro*
Prentice-Hall of Canada Inc., *Toronto*
Prentice-Hall of India Private Limited, *New Delhi*
Prentice-Hall of Japan, Inc., *Tokyo*
Prentice-Hall of Southeast Asia Pte. Ltd., *Singapore*
Whitehall Books Limited, *Wellington, New Zealand*

This book is lovingly dedicated to Shirley,
who suggested that I write it.

CONTENTS

PREFACE

The development, communication, and adaptation of knowledge are basic across the spectrum of organized endeavor. The process of disseminating that knowledge, generally through written reports, has not always been recognized as a problem area by those psychologists who engage in *clinical* assessment functions, such as are carried out to help resolve questions in therapy, rehabilitation, school psychology, consultation, or private practice. Many of those served by these specialists, such as mental health workers (including psychologists who write reports for their own use), educators, and administrators, share an awareness, often enthusiasm, of the great contribution that the psychological report can make to the successful performance of their duties. Many "consumers" of the psychologist's assessment efforts also share frustration over the quality of the product with which they are presented. All is not well with many psychological reports.

The first edition of *Psychological Report Writing* developed from the author's felt need for an approach to developing reports that are effective, optimally useful, and responsible. This edition continues to work toward such a goal and builds on this motif of the well-received earlier work.

Since publication of the first edition significant material has appeared in the literature, much of it perhaps not specifically addressed to the topic of psychological report writing but nevertheless germane to our purpose. It is now imperative to deal more explicitly with the topic of therapy—although assessment concerns in most settings are never really far from issues of remediation. Behavioral assessment needs are burgeoning, cognitive assessment is a growing area, and neuropsychological assessment has become a solid specialty. Family therapy is becoming professionally prominent in response to the high incidence of family disharmony. Psychodynamic orientations continue to be ever present; psychoanalysis lives and indeed is experiencing a decided resurgence.

Beyond the obvious need to recognize and deal with all of these facets of our clinical psychological pluralism, we also find a compelling need to focus on ethical issues and professional standards—long matters of concern to psychologists. Ethics codified into law and lawful constraints define yet another technical area where the psychological report writer had better master a level of expertise.

Considering the scope of topics and issues relevant to psychological report writing, we well might have yielded to the temptation to develop a multikilogram tome. We chose, rather, to aim for an integrated, logically sequential approach that might better meet the needs of students, instructors, supervisors, and practitioners. Thus we have sought to hit hard on both broad and specific issues and topics, some of them presented here for the first time, and to amplify, clarify, and reconceptualize some of the content from the first edition. The reader might find particularly helpful the new schema of the psychological assessment process in Chapter 5 and the approach to the supervisory practicum of psychological report writing in Chapter 8.

I want to thank Professor Joel Schorr of Alfred University and Professor Douglas Strohmer of State University of New York at Albany for their helpful comments during the preparation of this manuscript.

N.T.

1

THE PSYCHOLOGICAL REPORT
Purpose and Context

The psychological report may be likened to an individual. It too reveals a continuity with the past, an ongoing process of change, and an evolution toward the future. Neither has the role of the psychologist remained static. Now psychologists are firmly established as professionals: they are not the "testers" or technicians of the past, and their scope of functions seems to be steadily increasing. The psychological report can be instrumental in this process.

TODAY, EVEN MORE SO THAN IN RECENT YEARS, a person in need of psychological help must be understood, particularly in terms of the areas that need changing and how the change can be brought about. Such understanding is the substance of the psychological report, a powerful and proximate instrument that is used in planning and effecting such change. Typically reports are the psychologist's conclusions and reflect the outcome of tests, direct observations of behavior, other inputs of information, or a combination of these. Similarly when therapy is conducted the therapist's initial notes plus subsequent progress notes are psychological reports. How effectively a psychological report is written may be of great consequence for the individual who is the subject of the report.

MISSION

The psychological report, then, is seen as an active contribution to a broad mission. Whether in a private or an institutional context, the purpose of that mission may be summarized by such terms as *therapy, growth, remediation, skill acquisition,* or *jurisprudence.*

The purpose of schools is to educate and to enhance the quality of life of their students. Hospitals and clinics deal broadly with problems of health—physical, mental, or emotional. Juvenile training schools are charged with rehabilitating youthful offenders. Courts are concerned with dispensing justice. Psychologists in private practice deal with a wide range of issues centering about personal problems.

Subsumed under such general missions are the specific missions with which a psychologist must deal. Each mission generally involves an individual, although groups and the interaction of individuals may also be proper topics of concern. Whatever the problem, the psychologist brings to bear the resources that are available and delivers needed information in the form of a psychological report—written, oral, or a combination of the two.

The question with which the psychologist is asked to deal may necessarily be quite general. What is wrong? A child is doing poorly in school. Why? Is there an intellectual problem? Brain damage? A personality disorder? Autism? Excessive anxiety? Lack of goals or interests? A problem with authority figures? Situational stress in the home? An abnormally high intellect to which the curriculum does not cater? And so on. Or the psychologist may be asked to deal with an employee who is in frequent conflict with superiors, performs poorly on the job, and is prone to absenteeism. What is the problem? Can the employee be salvaged? How?

A commonly occurring problem is the diagnosis of a patient newly admitted to a mental hospital. The general problem areas must be identified. Does the patient suffer from a borderline personality disorder or from a schizophrenic disorder? Or perhaps the problem is sufficiently vague to render an early differential diagnosis impossible. Beyond general definition of the problem, as required by a formal diagnosis, much specific information is needed. Answers may be sought to such questions as a person's problems in living, inner conflicts, major defenses and how effective these are, the extent to which depression may be present, the possible existence of acting-out tendencies, and whatever else would appear to be of practical significance.

In various settings, as the individual is better understood, increasingly specific questions may arise. Thus, "There is reason to suspect that this student's intellectual level as established by group testing is not representative of his true abilities. Please evaluate individually." "From what sort of therapy is this person most likely to benefit?" "The patient's family indicates that a suicidal threat was made prior to admission. Are there any further indications that he might be potentially suicidal?" "Six months ago the psychological examination showed disturbances of the formal thought processes. The patient has since improved considerably. Are the thinking disturbances noted still present?"

Beyond generating descriptive material on an individual, the possible decision implications of the data must always be kept in mind and may be transmitted in the form of recommendations. These may be entirely implicit, such as when the psychologist reports to a somatically oriented physician on the presence of a generalized anxiety disorder, a dysthymic disorder, or a schizophreniform disorder. The accepted chemotherapeutic options for treating each of these conditions are limited, and the competent physician will prescribe accordingly. On the other hand, where psychotherapy is available, the psychologist may judge a person a suitable candidate for such therapy, and it is important to spell out what sort of therapy is most likely to be helpful. Will the patient probably do best in group or in individual therapy, or should both be considered? Is a behavioral strategy indicated, or should we go the insight route? Should efforts be primarily supportive, or is the essential need of the person practical guidance? How should staff react to the individual? To what extent, for example, should a student be coached, or to what extent should the youngster be encouraged to remedy educational deficiencies through personal initiative? Should staff listen one-sidedly to a person's marital difficulties? Might this reinforce some unconstructive viewpoints and help to rationalize self-defeating behaviors? Might this approach keep the person from seeking competent marriage counseling with his or her spouse?

A variation of mission exists in the case of screening or routine evaluation. Here the report may be based on impressions gained from group testing, individual testing, or both. The goal is to generate a data base and to identify salient features such as problem areas, intelligence level, insight, and motivation for change. These data may then suggest the need for further evaluation. Subsequent events may also give rise to specific questions that require answers.

The behavior therapist may approach the mission by listing target symptoms or other behaviors to be changed and the treatment strategy to be followed. A bioenergetic therapist may take a similar tack. A humanistic-existential approach may include a report to be shared with the client as a vehicle of interaction between therapist and client.

In the community mental health movement, naturalistic observation can be more important than testing. Concern is likely to center about environmental rather than intrapsychic forces, since a community model of psychopathology stresses etiological factors that are "outside" rather than "inside" the individual. Although testing may not be central to a mission—it may in fact be eliminated or minimized, especially when the psychologist's clinical assessment skills are high—psychological instruments are typically a valuable resource. The competent psychologist, of course, can never overlook social and cultural factors and must be wary that what is derived from psychological instruments does not lead us to neglect the individual's unique situation.

Not to be overlooked is the teaching value of the psychological report. Every report written should add to the psychologist's skill and knowledge. A well-written, well-conceptualized report, depicting a person in his or her individuality, similarly enriches the serious reader of the report. When psychological reports are prepared for a case conference, and especially for a training seminar, the teaching mission of the report is even more important.

Psychological reports, then, may be designed to contribute to various outcomes. Considering that therapy is a major activity of large numbers of psychologists, psychological reports in the form of *progress notes* should be specially commented on. The following observations are adapted from Mosak.[1]

Purpose of Progress Notes

The purpose of progress notes varies with the mission. We may think in terms of an institutional mission, when the psychologist is a member of an organization such as a school, hospital or clinic, and the responsibility for the mission is shared by the staff. Notes written in such a context may variously

[1] Harold H. Mosak, Personal Communication

emphasize administrative content or therapeutic matters. Other notes, often written by a therapist for personal use, are structured as therapeutic tools.

First, let us consider institutional notes. These are of two sorts, the *status documentation* note and the *administrative note*. The status documentation note records the client's condition, progress, or course of illness. Typical statements are of the sort "Patient continues to hallucinate," "The client is appreciably less depressed than she was at intake," or, simply, "No change." The administrative note documents actions that have been taken or are contemplated. Thus, "Psychological assessment completed," or "The patient will probably be ready for transfer to an open ward in a few days."

Progress Notes as Therapeutic Tools

Mosak identifies centers of emphasis in progress notes that may be helpful to the conduct of therapy. These notes may be identified by their differing contents. The centers of emphasis are:

Topics Discussed   The purpose is to serve as a reminder of the most recent topics of therapy, or, "What's going on now." Example: "Parents asked John to move out of the house. Most of the session spent discussing feelings and options."

Topics to be Discussed or Other Reminders   Here the therapist wishes to have a reminder so that there will be continuity between the previous session and the next. Example: "Discuss marital relations next week." Important intervening events or developments in the client's situation may, of course, lead the therapist to ignore such entries. The therapist may also want to have a reminder on points to be made, conclusions to be "tied up," questions to be asked, or tasks to be set for the client, "homework."

Behavior   Behavior, in or out of the therapy situation, may command interest as a record of progress or lack of progress, or as a matter of future concern. Examples: "The client is more assertive this week," "Beatrice still wanders in her communication," "Ms. F. relates a dream about me, emphasizing a scene in which I scolded her," "Bill promised himself and me that he will stop drinking, attend A.A. regularly, and control his destructive behaviors."

Dynamics   It frequently is helpful to record an impression of a client's dynamics as these have implications for treatment. For example, what might be the implications of the analysis of transference? Or, can a knowledge of a client's dynamics be of value in dealing with his or her maladjustive behaviors? At times a note about dynamics may indicate a therapist's uncertainty at the stage of therapy when it is written. Thus, "I can't understand the patient's reluctance to talk about his aunt during the early years of his life when she cared for him. Watch for clues."

Summary/Overview An inclusive impression of the client and therapeutic parameters typically is of value both at the initiation and the termination of contacts, and may serve an administrative as well as a therapeutic function. An initial note might be concerned with such topics as an impression of the nature of a presenting problem, including prognosis, the possible need for additional early assessment, the client's expectations of therapy and motivation for change, initial goals discussed with the client, and the therapeutic strategy that is contemplated. A final note might review the highlights of treatment, record a reassessment of the client's psychological status, including the gains made during therapy, and make an estimate of the outlook.

INITIATION OF PSYCHOLOGICAL ASSESSMENT

Psychological reports are the product of an assessment procedure. Individuals become involved with psychological assessment in various ways, commonly on the basis of a referral to the psychologist from another professional person. The manner in which the request for assessment is made might well be a potent factor in the quality of the psychological report that will be received by the referral source.

As we have seen, in many settings some sort of routine initial workup is requested. In a school it is often a teacher, counselor, or principal who feels the need for psychological information. In a hospital or a clinic it may be a nurse, a social worker, or a therapist. A psychologist who functions as a hopsital ward administrator may decide which patients are to be assessed. In traditional psychiatric settings psychological assessment (probably called *psychological testing*) typically has been initiated at the request of a psychiatrist.

In many instances the psychologist initiates psychological assessment, as in routine screening or in the practice of behavior therapy. When such is not the case, the mechanics of referral, the manner in which requests for evaluation are made, may have much bearing on the usefulness of the psychological report. The request for evaluation is the means, or should be the means, by which the psychologist is charged with a mission. When the psychologist understands the specific problem to be dealt with and can choose the most relevant and economical approach, the person making the referral will be most likely to benefit from the psychologist's efforts. In turn, the psychologist must know well the mission of the referring person and also the general mission of that person's profession. In an institutional context the psychologist must have a comfortable knowledge of the workings of the institution.

Often the request for psychological assessment comes in general terms when the raising of specific questions would be more appropriate. The overly general referral may come from psychologically unsophisticated personnel who have difficulty pinpointing the individual's problems and possess inadequate knowledge of the psychologist's skills and procedures. Such a referral may read "psychological examination," "For psychological testing," "Psychological survey," "Have the psychologist test this patient," or "Give this patient a Rorschach and see what you get." On the other hand, the psychologist is likely to be displeased with certain requests for specific information. Not welcome may be requests for formal diagnoses to be used largely for administrative record keeping rather than as a basis for treatment; equally unwelcome, in a psychiatric setting, are requests for IQ determinations, particularly when such information is asked for on a recurring basis or is the only sort of information requested.

When the psychologist receives a request for assessment in terms that are inappropriately general, several options are available. The psychologist may simply ask the person who initiates the request for assessment for more specific information on the problem. Or the psychologist may try to guess what is needed or wanted, with unpredictable results. Some psychologists prepare a general report that is likely to be both stereotyped and inclusive, hoping somehow that one or more of the statements will hit the mark. Such documents commonly are referred to as "shotgun reports," with pejorative meaning intended. When the reason for referral is not well formulated, it is difficult for the psychologist to be on target.

In sharp contrast to such reports, we advocate *case-focused* reports. Case-focused reports start with case-focused questions and attempt to reveal the unique aspects of persons, hence the psychologist tries to avoid stereotypes, theory-dictated and test-dictated statements. Statements in the report are interrelated, just as personality features in an individual are interrelated. Uppermost, the focus is on the mission; the client's problem(s) and the helping measures that should be taken are spelled out as recommendations or are clearly implied. In most situations recommendations should be explicit. The advice for which the psychologist in a school setting, for example, is consulted is far more important than are general statements about the child. In a psychiatric situation, however, where the psychologist and the psychiatrist are in a close working relationship and there is good mutual understanding and frequent contact, specific statements of recommendation can often be redundant. The options for treatments are broadly implicit.

The development of case-focused reports is illustrated in Chapter 5. Examples of this approach are presented in Chapter 6.

The psychologist should encourage the making of specific referrals, when these are appropriate, and discourage those that do not seem to define a mission, especially those requesting that a certain procedure be carried out. If such a request is made, the reason should be stated. A general request may simply be an example of poor communication—that is, the writer fails to express the underlying thoughts that prompted the referral. Several surveys (Lacey & Ross, 1964; Tallent & Rafi, 1965; Tallent & Reiss, 1959a, 1959b) indicate that many clinical workers have definite ideas of what sort of information they wish to receive through psychological assessment. Perhaps they assume psychologists know how they can best render services to their associates.

Although we stress the value of the specific referral, cases definitely exist where a referral cannot be based on a circumscribed problem. Sometimes not enough is known about a person to raise specific questions. Or circumstances may reveal an *apparently* clear-cut problem. "Is this patient homicidal, suicidal, depressed, likely to act out antisocially?" "Is his conduct attributable to mental deficiency; to brain damage?" "Is he ready for discharge from a hospital or clinic or from office treatment?" "Can he be rehabilitated, and to what extent?" "Will he profit from psychotherapy; if so, from what approach?" Often, however, the problem is not as specific.

An example of a nonspecific problem may be presented by a patient who appears anxious, depressed, or schizophrenic. She evidences certain deviant behavior. It is too early to crystallize definite problem areas. Is it not legitimate in such a case to refer the patient for psychological assessment? Implicit are a number of questions about the patient concerning, perhaps, relevant history, the dynamics of the situation, or defenses, ego strength, reality perception, thought organization, severity of the condition, impulse control, central conflicts, goals, fantasies, interpersonal relationships, the psychoeconomic value of symptoms, probable outcome, and indications for various sorts of intervention. If the psychologist is personally aware that the referring person has such questions in mind, we have a broad but definite mission. Such an assignment will be more of a challenge than a general referral that appears to represent a lack of reflection or acumen.

Daigle (see reference to Vernon, 1955) suggests that the emphasis should be away from *what* is to be known about a person and in the direction of *why* certain information is important. He refers to the first as charging the psychologist with "testing for areas," the second with "testing for alternative means of management." The suggestion appears to have merit. It is important that the psychologist know the alternative procedure that might stem from assessment so that the pertinent information can be specifically sought and the conclusions be presented so as to be most meaningful practically. Of course, this does not mean that "testing for areas" should or can be abandoned. The point Daigle makes has to do with emphasis. Often the test battery may be modified only partly, or not at all, because of an awareness of why certain information is needed. Daigle's recommendation applies partly to how the request for referral should be made and partly to how the findings should be presented by the psychologist.

From the foregoing it should be evident that the psychologist and the person who refers cases to the psychologist must make a special effort, when necessary, to "educate" one another. Smith and Gabbard (1980) point out that "a common frame of reference with the same language concepts and views about treatment is an enormous asset." Along with such abstractions there are some very mundane issues, such as what the psychologist can and cannot do. What constitutes a proper referral is a related matter.

The referring person must be cognizant of some very practical clinical realities that although they might seem trivial, are important. For example, a student or a patient is often referred to a psychologist with no idea of why the referral is being made. To explain why it is a good idea to "see" a psychologist might help to set the person at ease and to facilitate the establishment of rapport. In an institutional setting it is all too common for a patient to arrive for an appointment, only for the psychologist to find that testing cannot be done because the patient has inadequate vision and lacks corrective lenses. Another problem that can be nipped in the bud by the referral source stems from sending medicated patients for psychological assessment. It is well known that psychoactive medication frequently modifies behaviors of concern to the referring person (as they are supposed to do!)—for example, the extent and effects of anxiety and depression that typically characterize a patient. When possible, it is generally a good idea to withhold psychoactive medication until the psychologist's assessment has been completed.

Request for psychological evaluation may be made with various degrees of formality. In private practice and in many institutions, a phone call or direct personal contact is often most expeditious. The important thing is that the needs of the referring person be set forth clearly. This objective can best be accomplished when there is a close working relationship between the person referring the case and the psychologist, whether referral is in writing or transmitted orally. Ideally all cases should be discussed prior to evaluation. In this way the points to be explored can be jointly developed and differences in understanding the nature of the problem(s) can be resolved.

A written referral form may be most appropriate in a large setting or when there is a forensic aspect. In many institutions requests for specialized evaluations, medical or psychological, for example, are by regulation printed on standard consultation forms on which the report may be typed. Many such forms are extant. A sample, "homemade," form (from a medical setting) on which psychological evaluation may be requested follows on page 10. No particular claim is made for its merit: changes would perhaps have to be made in terms of the mission of any particular setting. The main consideration for a referral form is the conscientiousness with which it is used. Most important is the detail and explicitness with which the nature of the problem is stated.

Request for Psychological Evaluation

To:_____
Name of Patient: _____
Age:_____Sex:_____
Provisional or Established Diagnoses: _____
Nature of Problem: _____
(Reason for Referral) _____

Special Characteristics:

Psychological

Untestable _____
Poor Cooperation _____
Assaultive _____
Unduly Suspicious _____
Mute _____
Aphasic _____
Poor Understanding of
Language _____
(Why?)
Other _____

Physical

Limitation of Movement Which
Might Hinder Testing _____
(Specify)
Hearing Loss _____
(How Serious?)
Poor Vision _____
(How Serious?)
Is Visual Defect Properly
Compensated? _____
Speech Impediment _____
(Specify)
Other _____
Patient is Ambulatory _____
               In a Wheel Chair _____
               Confined to Bed _____

"TYPES" OF PSYCHOLOGICAL REPORTS

Both the content and the format of the psychological report change in response to new concepts and tools. In the early days of Binet testing the emphasis was on recording a child's IQ and a listing of the subtests or items that were passed and failed and their year levels. Psychologists also began to determine whether the IQ was representative or optimal and gave reasons for making such judgments based upon the cooperativeness and motivation of the child or upon such detracting factors as poor hearing or faulty vision. These "results" were regarded as directly useful for understanding the child in a school situation.

There appeared to be some slippage of rationale when psychologists became IQ testers in mental hospitals, since there was little correlation between a patient's IQ and the treatment prescribed for him or her. The same may be said of the psychologist's diagnoses and dynamics, the latter probably following a Freudian orientation. (This writer's early reports "out-Freuded" Freud, and the reader would be in line for laughs as well as instruction if any could be located.) Many fine dynamic reports were produced to no particular purpose, however. "They all get shock anyway" was the cynical but accurate observation.

Dynamics, an understanding of the motivations of the individual, became increasingly important (in the opinion of many) as psychotherapies multiplied and psychotherapy became widely practiced. However, the decision on whether to test depended, and still does, on the orientation of the therapist. There is similar disagreement on the matter of diagnosis. We are among those who insist that diagnosis often does make a difference. It makes a difference to know if a child's school deportment is related to a brain dysfunction or to something else. It makes a difference to know whether a person is suffering from schizophrenia or whether others are suffering because of his or her histrionic personality. Misdiagnosed people are likely to receive faulty treatment. Diagnosis in the broad sense of making descriptive statements about a person routinely enters decisions made about a person. Most psychological reports today consist largely of such descriptive statements.

In recent years psychological reports increasingly reflect a rationale. Many reports now are sharpy focused and highly prescriptive. What is the problem, and what can we do about it? In this tradition the behavior-oriented report is strictly a no-nonsense, businesslike approach. Psycho-pathologically oriented reports increasingly reflect the fact that certain classes of medication target certain behavior symptoms.

It is because the need for a guiding rationale for psychological reports is widely recognized that psychological reports now are seen in protean form, and properly so. Their content and organization obviously reflect the orientation of the writer and the use to which the report will be put. Thus a behavioral report would be quite beside the point for a psychoanalyst, and an analytically oriented report would probably not be acceptable to a humanistic therapist. Early Binet and psychoanalytically oriented reports were about the individual—what is "inside" the person, so to speak. Current reports may heavily emphasize social and cultural factors in a person's life, and personal circumstances.

Reports also vary in the degree to which they are "traditional"—that is, built on early school and mental hospital models that stressed matters of the intellect or dynamics and pathology. The case-focused report may be regarded as a refinement of the traditional report based on explicit rationale. Behavioral reports generally differ from the traditional report according to the specific understanding of the therapeutic approach. Humanistically oriented reports may also depart from tradition for different but equally valid reasons. Because narrative, case-focused reports are highly flexible, they can accommodate both behavioral and humanistic orientations.

In general the psychological report may be defined as a document written as a means of understanding certain features about a person and current life circumstances in order to make decisions and to intervene positively in a problem situation. Commonly the reports are prepared by a psychologist for others, such as a teacher, a psychiatrist, or a court, but a psychologist—a behavior therapist, for example—might prepare a report for personal use in outlining a treatment approach. Subsequently, for the same client, the psychologist may record changes in the person and in the treatment approach in progress notes.

Originally the psychological report was a vehicle to transmit test findings. In many current reports information gained from testing is minimal or absent. Originally the psychological report took the form of a narrative. Now reports may consist of a terse listing of problems and proposed solutions. Computer-derived reports may consist of sequential statements or a profile of characteristics. Checklists of statements or adjectives are a form of report. Clinical notes are reports. The oral relating of impressions also constitutes a report. A physician may ask a psychologist who has just completed two hours of testing, "Do you think he can make it?", to which the psychologist may respond with a nod, a horizontal shake of the head, or a gesture of uncertainty. Such is also a report.[2]

Custom-written narrative reports probably continue as the single most-used form. Most typically they are written by a psychologist for others.

THE TEAM APPROACH: FROM "TEAM" OF ONE TO TEAM OF N

Team is a loosely structured concept that ordinarily refers to the multiple input and interaction of two or more persons who share responsibility in dealing with clinical-type problems. There is no immutable definition of what personnel constitute a team, their roles, specific functions and interrelationships, or the power structure of the group. Teams may appear to have a central core composed of key, highly active, influential workers, plus a more peripheral membership, some of whom become involved in specific cases and absent themselves from others. A diagnostician-therapist may carry out the functions of a team.

A psychologist serving as a team member is commonly expected to play a key role through contributing a report, observations, and other inputs. She or he may be "teamed up"—permanently or on an ad hoc basis with teachers or with a counselor, lawyer, probation officer, psychiatrist, or pediatrician. In a mental health clinic the core team may consist of a psychiatrist, a clinical psychologist, a social worker, and perhaps one or more nurses. In a psychia-

---

[2]The expression psychological report *writing* is retained in a generic sense. Most still appear in that form.

tric hospital the team is likely to be rather extended, consisting of a psychiatrist, a clinical psychologist, a psychiatric social worker, one or more nurses, one or more nursing assistants, and various counselors and therapists. This by no means exhausts the list. A parent or spouse may be asked to participate, and the patient (or in a school situation, the child) may also be regarded as a team member actively participating with staff in deliberating on remediation and plans for the future. (The role of parents and child on the student study team in special education is discussed in Tallent, 1980.) In special instances an internist or a dietitian may be brought in by a team that normally is not directly concerned with the contributions of these professionals.

One of the most unusual teams coming to the author's attention is known as the *Forensic Psychiatry Clinic*. Based at the University of Virginia, its staff includes three psychiatrists, a psychologist, two members of the law faculty, a psychiatric social worker, researchers, and students. With a total input of about 20 to 30 hours per case, citizens involved in both civil and criminal law actions are evaluated. The team is available to courts and lawyers in Virginia and neighboring states.

Another team format, a psychodiagnostic-therapeutic team, has been developed by the author in collaboration with nursing colleagues (Tallent, Kennedy, Szafir, & Grolimund, 1974). Situated in a psychiatric setting, the essence is to involve in the diagnostic process the nurses and the nursing assistants who are in daily therapeutic interaction with patients. Conceived as an expanded role for nurses, in accordance with evolving nursing concepts, all test administration and initial interviewing is carried out by nurses and assistants trained in these functions. This accomplished, the psychologist meets with the nursing staff, the test protocols and other inputs are collaboratively evaluated, and tentative conclusions are reached. The patient is next interviewed by the team. Then, in further discussion, conclusions are reached on the nature of the patient's problems, indicated treatment, and plans for the future. These are immediately incorporated in the nursing care plan and are orally transmitted to the psychiatrist and discussed before the report is written.

The roles that the various team members play, the power structure of the team, the interpersonal dynamics of the team members, and personality features of the psychologist and the nursing staff, all help to determine the quality of the psychological report and how effectively it and other of the psychologist's inputs will be used. Teams that function in psychiatric settings are particularly instructive in these regards.

Such teams have traditionally been headed by a psychiatrist member—the captain of the team, as this clinician has sometimes been called. Traditionally medicine has had an authoritative role, particularly with nonmedical associates—so-called ancillary persons. The former practice of a well-known and respected setting is illustrative. Here a rigid seating arrangement was enforced at staff meetings. The senior physician occupied the chair at the head of the conference table, with physicians of lesser rank arranged in order, toward the far end. Next were seated the various ancillary personnel, by profession (from the highest on "down") and by rank within profession; the individuals at the far end of the table could thus entertain few illusions about their status.

Such hierarchical team structure is now largely in disrepute. A more democratic arrangement is widely endorsed and operates to a greater or lesser degree in many settings. It is sometimes referred to as a *wagon wheel*, because all members occupy a comparable position, and none is more distant from the hub of power than any other. In reality the dominance, other personality features, or qualifications of the persons involved come into play, and regardless of discipline, some are closer to the power center than others. Only in the sense of the lip service to the democratic ideal do all have equality. If the truth be known, a psychologist, a social worker, or a nurse in a medical setting may wield more power than does the physician in reaching some sort of group consensus on the nature of the problem and the treatment indicated. A determined physician sometimes falls back on the legal aspects of responsibility for making a "medical" diagnosis and prescribing treatment.

ROLE OF THE PSYCHOLOGIST

The role of the psychologist has evolved considerably since the emergence of the "testing movement," the high-water mark of the 1920s. At that time the psychologist, identified with an oversold IQ, was commonly known as a *mental tester*. Even when projective techniques had well overshadowed psychometrics in many settings, Schafer (1954), writing from a psychodynamic perspective, persisted in referring to the psychologist as the *tester,* a term also retained by Rosenwald (1963) and Appelbaum (1970), both psychodynamically oriented psychologists.

The proper role for today's psychologist, when functioning as a professional who provides information to others, is that of consultant, as explicated by Towbin (1960), formulated by Matarazzo (1965), and endorsed by Holt (1967). This is in sharp contrast to the role of tester, who is on a par with a laboratory technician. There are a number of distinguishing features.

The laboratory technician functions in a limited, circumscribed role for which the formal and practical preparation is much less lengthy and rigorous than that required for full professional functioning at the Ph.D., Psy.D., Ed.D., or the M.D. level, for example. The training of the technician is always in accordance with the principles and needs of a professional group, and the parent group, through various direct and indirect means, influences the training program: the students are trained explicitly to serve the group. The technician is asked to make a particular determination; the procedure will be the same regardless of the purpose. The technician does not interpret findings, make a judgment on which findings are relevant and which are not, or make recommendations. The technician is not sought out by the person who made the referral to discuss possible implications of findings or the need for additional tests or subsequent retests. It is sufficient that the technician gives results along with some indication of their reliability. The report of a psychological technician may contain such material as an IQ, various other requested scores, ratios, profiles, psychographs, or whatever raw responses might be requested by a supervisor.

The consultant, by contrast, is a product of advanced scientific and professional education designed to prepare an individual for high-level, responsible functioning. The consultant must have a grasp of both broad and specific knowledge and the ability to reach decisions that may be of major importance. Such training is under the sponsorship and direction of the discipline of the consultant, who claims a unique role. Thus the psychologist is thoroughly familiar with concepts of human personality, carries out psycholgical techniques with expertise, and works from a background of relevant research orientation. He or she must be familiar with the nature and the background of the problem at hand and the alternative decisions that might be influenced by the psychological report. On this basis the consultant must then decide on what kind(s) of data to seek, which findings have relevance, and how these can be most effectively presented.

The distinction between professional, or consultant, and technician is sometimes unclear to the psychologist's associates. One reason is that some continue to perceive the psychologist as a "tester." Another is the notion of test objectivity, where even psychometric instruments may be lacking; the scores obtained on these tests need at least some interpretation. Tests can't think, as Schafer (1954) points out. In problems involving disorders of personality, we do not have instruments that can be routinely administered and interpreted by subprofessionally trained personnel.

In the clinical-type situation both the objectivity and validity of our tools have meaning as they relate to specific problems and to the confidence the psychologist is able to place in the relevant conclusions that can be drawn from them. Published indexes of validity for particular research strategems are but rough guides, for the psychologist must make judgments of clinical validity and meaningfulness in each particular case. Many tests, particularly tests of personality, are subjected to interpretive procedures that yield information not available from standard usage of the instrument. Both knowledge and clinical acumen enter all phases of the assessment process and, inevitably, some psychologists tend to be more effective than others in their clinical judgments (see Thorne, 1960, 1961). How does one assess validity of a test when even superficial familiarity with the process suggests that the individual is evaluated not by tests alone, nor by tests and interview data alone, but by psychologist-test data–interview data (test data typically referring to the information deriving from administration of a battery)? The input of other team members must also be taken into account. It is a meaningless abstraction in the individual case to speak of the validity of (for example) the Rorschach, the TAT, or the Affective Adjective Check List. Evaluation more reasonably involves the basic assessment units of "Rorschach-Psychologist A," "TAT-Psychologist B," "SOMPA-Psychologist C," "Neuropsychological Questionnaire, Luria-Neraska-Psychologist D," and more typically, such units as "Rorschach, TAT, AACL, Interview, Staff Input-Psychologist E."

PERSONAL AND
INTERPERSONAL DYNAMICS
OF THE STAFF

Schafer (1954) discusses at length the dynamics of the psychologist and how these bear on relationships both with the person who is being assessed and with the psychologist's colleagues. He lists no fewer than eight "types" of psychologists, types in the sense of salient personality failings. He discusses, for example, the psychologist with a defective self-concept, the rigidly intellectualistic psychologist, the psychologist with unresolved dependency needs, the masochist, and the sadist. All of these failings influence the sort of report produced. The sadist, for example, is a "chief inquisitor" who concentrates on the shortcomings and weaknesses of the subject and whose report reads like an "exposé" or a "denunciation," what is called in this book "the prosecuting attorney brief." This is discussed more fully on pages 73–74.

Although the personality of the psychologist has frequently been emphasized as a factor in his or her ability to function as a therapist, in our preoccupation with tests and our zeal to establish their validity, too little has been written on the psychologist's personality as a significant factor in assessment. One of the greater concerns with the psychologist's personality has been with the tendency of some examiners to confuse their own problems with their clients'.

Perhaps an even greater source of difficulty is the confusion of the self-needs of a psychologist, particularly role needs, with the needs of the task. It is readily acceptable that one's occupation be a factor in bringing about a sense of personal fulfillment. However, in dealing with people who have major problems, who perhaps find themselves in a life-crisis situation, the psychologist must avoid intruding personal adjustment problems. Typical are difficulties with the self-concept; this may become evident in role aspirations that are hardly compatible with the specialized, technical functions of psychology. The psychologist may step outside the role of professional psychology. Sometimes this sort of problem detracts from effective contribution because the psychologist encroaches on the prerogatives of others rather than gathering the sort of information the team needs.

There are various other problems that seem to detract from the psychologist's function. These include attempts to seek insight through clients and thus effect self-therapy; the opportunity to try, at some level of consciousness, to work through personal conflicts; the opportunity to see oneself as superior to another (the client); and the opportunity for catharsis, voyeurism, exhibitionism, or hostile expression. Sometimes the problem may be an ineptitude for psychological diagnostic work; sometimes the difficulty is one of lack of personal integrity. These latter deficiencies could go hand in hand, since the psychologist who cannot produce what is required may try to conceal inabilities as an assessor. One often effective maneuver is to slant the report in a manner designed to please the individual who has referred the case. Klopfer (1960) refers to such a document as the "Madison Avenue Report."

Any of these personality difficulties may find its way into, and be readily identified in, the psychological report. Often the report reflects self-conflict. Sometimes there is an expression of interpersonal or interprofessional conflict, with the report itself serving as a battleground. Both offensive and defensive maneuvers will be evident, but the aggressiveness is called up by defensive needs. Thus the report that is exhibitionistic and authoritative in tone, displaying apparent knowledge of words and theory, may be a way of saying, "I am as good as you, even better." (It has also been suggested that words and theory may be used to hide ignorance.) But defensiveness in other respects may be even more obvious. The excessively detailed omnibus personality description ("shotgun report") is an example, as is the heavily hedged report.

Needless to say, the mission is best advanced when team members are comfortable with themselves and with one another. There should be mutual respect and compatibility (obviously only a goal in many settings), and each should have a good understanding of the function of the others. Even under favorable conditions, the psychologist needs to interact with colleagues in a persuasive manner. The psychologist is often able to make highly confident statements that are at variance with the impressions of other team members who operate without the benefit of psychological tools. Because of this the psychologist has a selling job to do in the interest of the client. Appelbaum (1970) suggests that a psychologist must also be a sociologist, a politician, a diplomat, a group dynamicist, a salesperson, and, if you please, an artist. Sales ability Appelbaum advises, ". . . may denote high pressure, 'activity,' hucksterism; and, indeed, there may be clinical situations that do require some of this. Usually, however, the test report is more akin to institutional advertising, a low key presentation of evident factualness."

CONTINUITY, CHANGE, AND EVOLUTION IN THE PSYCHOLOGICAL REPORT

Today's psychological *Zeitgeist* is quite different from that of the early years of Binet testing. Many of our key instruments, however, have shown no particular evolution. The newer Wechsler scales, for example, are built essentially as was the Wechsler-Bellevue of 1939, and the standard Rorschach cards are identical to those that Hermann Rorschach bequeathed to us in 1922. Our understanding and use of these instruments have undergone a veritable revolution, however. The Rorschach *experiment,* for example, is now conceived as the *Rorschach systems* (Exner, 1969), systems that have traveled far from Rorschach's own modest estimate of the worth of his blots. The most obvious addition to the current assessment scene is the vast interest in, and proliferation of, behavioral and cognitive approaches. Also widespread is the adaptation of older instruments to computer interpretation and the development of new instruments specially designed for computer analysis. The uses of assessment and how the psychologist's mission may be conceptualized have also undergone vast change. It should be instructive to note Wechsler's (1944) view of the first duty of a psychologist in a psychiatric hospital: ". . . to define, as an expert, the patient's intellectual level and to indicate whether the I.Q. obtained represents the true or merely the present level of functioning."

In just one 11-year period, Dollin and Reznikoff (1966) noted a decline in interest in formal diagnostic labels. In 1956 some 64 percent of the referrals received requested that a diagnosis be made, whereas in 1966 only 29 percent of the referrals asked for a label. In another study of referral questions Korner (1962) found that over an eight-year period requests to clarify diagnosis dropped by some 60 percent, while questions pertaining to ego functioning and defenses increased by 50 percent and requests to assess organic deficit quadrupled. Studying the topics discussed in psychological reports, Korner noted many changes. Discussion of ego defects climbed from 30 to 72 percent, evidently in response to the changes in referral questions just noted. Discussion of diagnosis dropped by a factor of five and anxiety by a factor of two. Talk of aggression dropped from 42 percent to 18 percent, and discussion of sexuality fell from 48 percent to 12 percent. Since we may assume that eight years could not possibly make much difference in how aggressive or sexual people are, we might conclude that the interests of the psychologists who wrote the reports had changed. In 1950 clinical psychology was a rather new profession with a preponderance of youthful practitioners. Perhaps, as practitioners mature, they become more mellow and less voyeuristic. However, an alternate explanation might emphasize change in both the general and the psychological culture. Freudian concepts, in many settings, have yielded to other interests. Sex has lost much of its glamour, and aggression is all too prominent in our awareness.

In this context of flux there remain a number of persistent, nagging problems, among them the questions of validity and of the utility of psychological assessment. The latter pops up occasionally in the literature and continually in some settings where such assessment is carried out. The question concerns not only the utility of psychological reports for traditional psychotherapists but also their utility for some of the newer therapies, particularly the behavior therapies and the humanistic therapies. These questions are addressed shortly.

Modern economics being what they are, the cost of preparing a psychological report—from the initial handshake to the last period of the report—is an increasingly important, if underdiscussed, problem. As a specific example, we may read with nostalgia Odom's (1950) paper on the time required to do a Rorschach examination and be transported back to that halcyon era when a psychologist's time was not worth very much, a fact confirmed by his or her income. Odom concludes: "The consensus is that the average test requires a little more than four hours, but that the total time required will sometimes be less than two hours, and at other times over eight hours." Even a leading practitioner like Beck spent at that time, ". . . on the average, from three and one half hours at the minimum to about nine hours at the maximum in completing a Rorschach test." As an exercise, let's translate that into today's costs. And remember that, typically, the Rorschach is only part of a battery. We could just price ourselves out of the market.

Utility of Psychological Reports in Making Clinical Decisions

Let us consider the matter of utility, for if psychological reports are not useful, or cannot be made useful, we need not continue our discussion. There is a dearth of studies on this important topic, and the limited evidence available is contradictory and can be interpreted in various ways. It also appears that the methods of study need to be evaluated, for the obtained results differ widely, evidently as a result of differences in research design. Note the varied conclusions that derive from representative studies on utility.

Dailey (1953) reported that psychological reports contributed to clinical decisions in 26 percent of the cases referred for psychological evaluation. Cole and Magnussen (1966) state: "Traditional diagnostic procedures are only loosely related, if at all, to disposition and treatment." Breger (1968), examining psychological testing in clinical settings "in terms of its history and underlying assumptions," concludes: "Serious questions are raised about the clinical usefulness, logic and validity of practice." He refers here to the notion that diagnosis is a valid prerequisite to treatment and to psychology's emphasis on assessment and selection. Hartlage, Freeman, Horine, and Walton (1968) found that a sample of psychological reports ". . . was evidently of little value in contributing toward any treatment decisions for the patient." However, these studies also concur that this state of affairs is remediable and make suggestions accordingly.

Studies by Dana, Hannifin, Lancaster, Lore, and Nelson (1963), Affleck and Strider (1971), and Hartlage and Merck (1971) reach quite encouraging conclusions. Studying routine psychological diagnosis and treatment planning in a juvenile probation department, Dana et al. report as follows:

"Predictions of prognosis were made from psychological reports with 80.5% accuracy. When recommendations contained in these reports were followed, 82.5% accuracy of predictions was obtained." The Affleck-Strider study also revealed high utility of psychological reports. The authors observe: "About two-thirds of the requested items of information were seen as either providing new and significant information or as providing information which confirmed information previously suspected, but which was not well-established." Further, ". . . it was found that 52% of the reports altered management in some manner, 24% had a minimal effect or confirmed current thinking, 22% had no effect, and 2% were felt to have an erroneous or detrimental effect."

The study by Hartlage and Merck is particularly instructive. It is not, these authors find, a basic lack of interpretive skills that detract from the utility of reports. It is nothing more profound than a lack of reflection by report writers on what might be useful to report readers, a simple failure to use common sense. They note ". . . reports can be made more relevant to their prospective users merely by having the psychologists familiarize themselves with the uses to which their reports are to be applied." And, "It appears that merely having the psychologists who write reports to consider the value to users of some of the statements that they commonly make in their reports can have a significant salutary effect on the value of these reports." Also, ". . . psychologists learn to test and write reports in an academic setting and that in the absence of any external stimulation they tend to persevere in a somewhat theoretical, non-decision-oriented approach to handling test data." Accordingly, they advise that psychologists need ". . . to evaluate their own reports in terms of what these reports contribute to the operation of their unique settings rather than to continue to grind out reports with good theoretical consistency but little decisional value." We agree. Case-focused reports are tailored to the setting as well as to the personal parameters of a case.

With the exception of the studies by Dana et al. and Hartlage and Merck, all of these studies were either done in or had reference to a psychiatric setting. One way to evaluate their significance, then, is to compare their findings against what little data are available on the utility of other diagnostic procedures in such settings. These are entirely impressionistic; the practical utility of such inputs as the anamnesis recorded by the psychiatrist, the mental status examination, the social history, and nursing notes have not been systematically studied and established. But even if only 26 percent of psychological reports make a difference in patient management and disposition, we might regard the psychological report as a very effective instrument indeed. Most of the diagnostic procedures done in psychiatric hospitals, although expensive, have in most cases little bearing on treating the mental or emotional problem for which the patient was admitted to the hospital.

Utility of Psychological
Reports for Psychotherapy

Another way to evaluate the utility of psychological findings is to note the extent to which they are an adjunct to psychotherapy, to some degree still an open question. Many therapists psychologically assess or request assessment on their clients; some do not. Meehl (1960), on the basis of a survey of 168 therapists, disclosed that only 17 percent of the sample believed that the information provided by testing was of much value to them. Kelly (1961) reported that only half of his therapist sample always or commonly relied on psychological diagnoses. Hinkle, Nelson, and Miller (1968) found that approximately two-thirds of the respondents used tests, and those reporting frequency of usage indicated that they resorted to testing in 50 percent or more of their cases.

Mintz (1968) found that the then-upcoming crop of new therapists shared the beliefs of those practicing therapists inclined against evaluation. In rating items having to do with the usefulness of psychological reports, on the average, 65 to 75 percent of the respondents said "not at all." To the item "In sum, how valuable to you as a therapist were the reports," the overall view was just below "slightly." Mintz concludes: "Thus, the reports seem to have little significant impact on therapy (other than confirmatory, at least)." He notes further: "Once therapy had begun, ratings of value of specific reports were largely a function of general attitudes to diagnostics. Overall ratings were so low that the general utility of such work may well be questioned."

In a later study Wiedemann and Mintz (1974), surveying student therapists (psychologists, psychiatrists, and social workers) report that "in general the respondents indicated psychodiagnostics could be of significant utility." Other views give support to this contention. De Courcy (1971) and Lambley (1974), in case presentations, demonstrate how psychotherapy without assessment can present a distinct hazard. Appelbaum (1977), reporting on a large-scale study of the effects of psychotherapy, noted that those psychiatrists who ignored the content of psychological reports prior to beginning therapy were at the greatest risk for being in error. Cerney (1978) presents case material to illustrate the use of the psychological report in therapy and discusses the use of the report both to predict outcome and to understand "the progress of psychotherapy and to alert the therapist of potentially very critical and delicate situations." A survey of counseling psychologists found that 35.9 percent of clients had been given objective testing and 11.4 percent were tested with projective instruments, the chief item of information being sought pertaining to personality structure (Fee, Elkins, & Boyd, 1982). Klopfer (1964) goes so far as to state: "To deliberately blind himself and handicap himself as the psychotherapist by refusing to use the tools of assessment available to him, would seem a practice so questionable as to border on the unethical."

Allen (1942) regards as a "false belief" ". . . that if enough can be learned about situations and happenings and motives, change will take care of itself. Or they [some child guidance clinics] believe that a person can be changed by the 'complete understanding' a therapist acquires through having all these facts." In this regard it should be noted that many therapists, especially psychoanalysts, who routinely seek psychological assessment have little interest in the bulk of the content that finds its way into psychological reports but seek primarily information on the patient's ego strength. It is important to assess the possibility that the client will decompensate in intensive, uncovering therapy.

Rogers' (1942) early position is that

> . . . the place of tests in counseling treatment is not nearly so clear-cut. The disadvantage of using tests at the outset of a series of therapeutic contacts are the same as the disadvantages of taking a complete case history. If the psychologist begins his work with a complete battery of tests, this fact carries with it the implication that he will provide the solution to the client's problems. The point of view consistently maintained throughout this book is that such "solutions" are not genuine and do not deeply help the individual, but tend to make him either resentful or overdependent.

On the other hand, in the same work he sees a definite place for assessment

> with some individuals . . . handicapped in fundamental ways by their own inadequacies or the destructive quality of their environment. . . . In such cases to initiate psychotherapy without a diagnostic study may only plunge the client further into hopelessness as his own lacks are brought into greater prominence by his increasing insight. Consequently, even though the diagnostic study may interfere somewhat with a counseling process, it is definitely advisable here.

In his later *Client-Centered Therapy*, Rogers (1951) retains and strengthens his negative position. It is the client who must be the "diagnostician"—that is, experience a change in perception. The therapist's intellectual knowledge of the client is for nought, since only self-knowledge can effect change. Rogers views it as a net therapeutic loss if the client sees judgment and responsibilities as the prerogative of the therapist (the expert). Further, the client's feeling that an individual cannot know oneself—only the expert can—leads to ". . . a degree of loss of personhood. . . ." Rogers even postulates dire social implications in the use of psychological assessment: it may lead to the control of the many by a few experts.

The advent of the behavior therapies and the humanistic therapies would appear to raise fresh questions about what the psychological report can contribute to therapy, or whether indeed it might detract from the process or even damage the therapist-client relationship. Rogers' position would appear to anticipate the sort of arguments that some therapists in the humanistic-existential orientation might advance (pp. 27–29). As far as the behavior therapists are concerned, an early a priori guess that this group would have little use for psychological reports seemed to be substantiated in numerous instances. Yates' (1970) double-barreled blasting of psychodynamics and psychological evaluation is a good case in point. Greenspoon and Gersten (1967) observe: "The behavior therapist is generally as unsympathetic to the use of psychological tests as his nondirective colleagues, though for markedly different reasons." There are other considerations, however, and many early behavior therapists did, in fact, see merit in psychological assessment. Along with considerations of hard data, very human elements have entered the development of positions on this matter, as observed by Ciminero, Calhoun, and Adams (1977).[3]

> Although behavior therapy has shown tremendous advances over the past 15 years, behavioral assessment has lagged behind in its development. This delay may have been due to a negative reaction exhibited by many behavior therapists to the word *assessment*. Prior to the 1960s assessment was often associated with testing procedures (e.g., the Rorschach, TAT, and MMPI) that were frequently criticized for their lack of reliability, validity, and clinical utility (Kanfer & Phillips, 1970). Goldfried and Pomeranz (1968) suggested that the avoidance of assessment may have been due to additional factors such as the professional status of psychometricians, the dynamic or trait conceptualization of personality that generally went along with traditional methods of assessment, and the lack of a systematic relationship between the assessment strategies and treatment. Fortunately many of us by this time have been desensitized to the word *assessment,* and preceding *assessment* with the word *behavioral* makes us feel even more relaxed. The legitimate concern with behavioral assessment over the past few years suggests that this topic has literally begun to flourish in the 1970s.

The earliest endorsement is perhaps that of Wolpe (1958) who found it useful to assess the degree of neuroticism in those he treats. Since then other

---

[3]*Handbook of Behavioral Assessment,* Ciminero, A.R. Chapter 1, "Behavioral Assessment: An Overview" in Ciminero, A.R., Calhoun, K.S., & Adams, H.E. (New York: John Wiley), 1977.

behavior therapists have affirmed the value of assessment, and the need for research to link psychological findings to behavioral therapy has been pointed out by a number of workers. Greenspoon and Gersten (1967) set forth a basic position:

> It is our contention that psychological tests should be of value to provide the behavior therapist with information that should be of value in doing behavior therapy. This contention is based on the assumption that the behavior on any psychological test should be lawful. We believe this assumption of the lawfulness of any behavior is necessary in a science of behavior, but it is an explicit assumption made by the behavior therapists. Having accepted the assumption of lawfulness of test behavior, we have proceeded to assume that the behavior on a test should be related to behavior emitted by the test taker outside the testing situation. The important issue is the basis of the relationship. We propose to look for this relationship in a realm that is considered critical in behavior therapy, sources of control of behavior. In other words, we believe that it may be possible to determine sources of control of the patient's behavior outside the test situation from his performance on psychological tests. Control is the essence of behavior therapy. That is, the behavior of the patient must be brought under the control of the therapist and/or others who are working with him. To effect this control the behavior therapist manipulates the consequences of a behavioral act of the patient. These consequences may be called contingencies or contingent stimuli.

Goodkin's (1967) position is:

> Before employing any of a variety of efficient techniques, the therapist must determine what behavior he wishes to change. . . . Surely, the question of diagnosis is an important one. In discussing various aspects of the patient's life, there may emerge a considerable number of behaviors, which the therapist sees as maladaptive. Which ones are most relevant in aiding the patient? Which should receive attention first? Which should be left alone?

Dengrove (1972) emphasizes the need to identify target symptoms:

> All behavioral therapies must be preceded by proper behavioral diagnosis. The application of behavioral principles is so precise that without a proper delineation of the "target" symptoms one can go astray. It is worth emphasizing that target behaviors involve the identification of "emotional habits" and faulty cognitions. "Symptoms" merely denote the patient's awareness of the reactions that go on within him.

Fensterheim (1972), in speaking of diagnosis, includes the establishment of a formal diagnosis. Thus,

> A differential diagnosis between a character disorder and a neurosis is often important. Neurotics tend to have anxiety and guilt connected with crucial problem areas and the treatment of choice usually centers around some form of desensitization and tension reduction. Character disorders, when they do

show anxiety, usually experience it as a consequence of the symptom rather than as a cause of the symptom. Desensitization may be difficult because of the inability to experience anxiety when picturing scenes or even in the actual situation. At best, the desensitization procedures lead only to peripheral changes in that the patient becomes more comfortable with an inadequate mode of life. The treatments of choice for character disorder usually center around a combination of operant methods, aversive techniques, assertive training, education and guidance.

Similarly he points out differences between the hysterical and the obsessive-compulsive neuroses, and the implications these have for behavioral treatment—a new discovery of the value of old-fashioned psychodiagnostics.

Cautela (1968) is convinced that "there is a widespread misunderstanding about assessment in Behavior Therapy." This misunderstanding has contributed in turn to a belief that training in assessment techniques is not needed by the behavior therapist. But, "The first task of the behavior therapist is the identification of the specific maladaptive behavior or behaviors and any relevant antecedent conditions which might be maintaining that behavior." Cautela and Upper (1973) have in this regard introduced a behavioral coding system and also present a comprehensive position on assessment (1974).

Goldfried and Pomeranz (1968) present some very incisive reasoning on the relationship of assessment to behavior modification. They assert that

> . . . one topic which has been conspicuously neglected by behavior therapists is that of assessment. . . . Indeed, our thesis is that assessment procedures represent *a most crucial and significant* step in the effective application of behavior therapy. . . . As we see it, the two most significant potential clinical uses of assessment material for therapy are (1) to delineate those target areas where the change should take place and (2) to offer some information about the specific therapeutic technique which would be best suited for bringing about such change with this particular individual. In practice, assessment procedures have served neither of these two purposes in traditional therapy.

This latter assertion perhaps rests on the commonly held belief that the treatment a client in psychotherapy usually receives is more a function of the therapist's orientation than of the client's problem.

> In the practice of traditional, insight-oriented psychotherapy, we would tend to agree that the need for detail and comprehensive assessment information prior to the treatment itself may exist minimally—if at all. From the viewpoint of the contemporary, behaviorally oriented attempts to *understand* and change human behavior, on the other hand, the development and utilization of appropriate assessment techniques is crucial. (emphasis supplied)

They quote with approval from Paul (1967); "*What* treatment, by *whom*, is most effective for *this* individual with *that* specific problem, and under *which* set of circumstances." A lofty goal indeed. The ideal case-focused report would address itself to all of these issues, together with *understanding* of the individual, the *why* of the recommendations.

Goldfried and Pomeranz give little attention to the sort of content the behavior therapist needs to fulfill a mission. They do identify thoughts and feelings as the sort of target behaviors that may be in need of direct modification. In presenting a hypothetical case, they indicate that assessment procedures point up a person who might "become anxious in unfamiliar situations" as "the type of person who would prefer to have other people look after and care for him" (a dependent personality). Thus, although the report writer might have to adjust the focus to meet the needs of the behavior therapist, it appears that the sort of content the behavior therapist seeks is not unfamiliar to the traditional personality assessor. Ritchie (1968), for example, shows how conventional psychological evaluation may be used in the successful treatment of a case by behavior therapy.

Mischel's (1968) approach to assessment as a precondition for effecting behavior change is most precise. First, he defines "with *clear* behavioral referents" ". . . the problem behaviors and the desired objectives." His next concern is with ". . . the *exact* circumstances provoking the problem behaviors and to identify the conditions maintaining them. In light of this information the *particular* behavior change operations most likely to produce the desired objectives must be *selected.*" His view ". . . presupposes that different problems require different treatment and that *specific* treatments can be *designed* to fit them—an assumption that is basic to social behavior theory." (emphasis supplied)

The idea of specificity is also uppermost in the view of Goldfried and Kent (1972) who largely reject traditional personality assessment in favor of behavioral assessment—that is, an approach that favors samples over signs and selects items from such sources as direct observation, from role playing, and self-report. They distinguish between "traditional" and "behavioral" approaches to assessment as follows:

> Although the ultimate goal of both procedures may be essentially the same (e.g., the prediction of human behavior), the general approach which has been employed in the pursuit of this goal has differed. The traditional approach to personality assessment has been directed primarily toward an understanding of the individual's underlying *personality characteristics* or *traits* as a means of predicting behavior. This general approach to assessment is reflected in most of our currently available personality tests—both projective techniques (e.g., Rorschach, TAT, Draw-A-Person, etc.) as well as objective personality inventories (e.g., MMPI, California Psychological Inventory, etc.). The behavioral approach to personality assessment, by contrast, involves more of a direct measurement of the individual's *response to various life situations.* The techniques associated with behavioral assessment include the observation of individuals in naturalistic situations, the creation of an experimental analogue of real-life situations via role-playing, and the utilization of the individual's self-reported responses to given situations.

Serious differences between the aims of behavior modifiers and those who focus on intrapsychic factors may be more apparent than real. Many observers attribute differences in theories in large part to differences in terminology and emphasis. Among those who focus on the similarities between psychoanalytic and behavioral theories are French (1933), Kubie (1934), Shaw (1946), Dollard and Miller (1950), Shoben (1949), Alexander (1963), Weitzman (1967), Woody (1968,1969) who published an integrated therapeutic approach that he called *psychodynamic counseling and therapy,* Sloane (1969), Marmor (1971), Rhoads and Feather (1974) who coined the term *psychodynamic behavior therapy,* Abel and Blanchard (1974), and a task force of the American Psychiatric Association (APA, 1973), the latter calling for "cross-fertilization" of viewpoints rather than parallel development and wasteful duplication of effort. The most ambitious attempt to integrate the concepts of psychoanalysis and behavior therapy appears to be that of Wachtel (1977). Nevertheless, the view persists that "behavior therapy and psychodynamic therapy (including psychoanalysis) are and must remain irreconcilable" (Yates, 1981).

From a historical perspective, Kubie's (1959) account of the views of Pavlov and Freud makes interesting reading. The information is from Ralph W. Gerard, who visited Pavlov in 1935 and then later carried Pavlov's opinion to Freud:

> They [Gerard and Pavlov] were discussing his [Pavlov's] work on condititioning and especially the production of experimental "neuroses" in dogs by present-ing them with a task of discrimination which was too difficult. To Dr. Gerard's surprise, Pavlov said with a twinkle that he was led to try these experiments by reading some of Freud's work. He then proceeded to speak of his indebtedness to Freud for stimulating his thoughts and his experiments into this productive channel, and added that he anticipated that deeper understanding of behavior would come from a fusion of the concepts of the conditioned reflex and of psychoanalysis. Subsequently, Dr. Gerard related this conversation to Freud during the course of a visit to him in Vienna. Freud was impressed and then said ruefully, "It would have helped if Pavlov had stated that publicly a few decades ago."

Currently humanistic therapists differ on the value of psychological assessment to the therapist. There are polarized positions, both for and against assessment, intermediate positions, and positions polarized against assessment that nevertheless allow for exceptions. Part of the disagreements noted seems to center about what underlying assumptions are made about assessment methods and psychological reports, and how such instruments are actually used.

Rogers' (1942, 1951) assumptions about assessment—that, generally, it impairs the therapeutic relationship, sets up unrealistic understandings on the part of the client, and compromises the client's responsibility for personal growth—anticipate later views of May (1958), Bugental (1963, 1964), Brown (1972), and Hacker, Gaitz, and Hacker (1972).

May (1958), however, seeks to make it clear that "Nothing we are saying here in the slightest deprecates the importance of gathering and studying seriously all the specific data we can get about the given person." He then gives specific examples of the sort of content that enters psychological reports. But such material, he indicates, is *about* the person, not *of* the person. Whether material *of* the person can be committed to words and to paper is not clear. By *of,* May seems to mean the configuration of psychological facts grasped about an individual in person-to-person encounter; this is a very valuable datum but less complete than the configuration that also incorporates material gained from the use of psychological instruments.

Bugental (1963) seeks to explode as a fallacy that diagnosis is basic to treatment. He regards diagnostic information as deindividualizing[4] the person, as "part-function" information. With May, he characterizes assessment information as *about* rather than *of* the person. In a later paper (1964) he writes of testing as depersonalizing the relationship and as taking responsibility from the patient. He regards testing as making the patient an object of study, as fostering dependency on the therapist, and as creating (unrealistically) a sense of certainty outside oneself—the "certainty" of the one who applied diagnostic instruments or relayed conclusions gained by the use of these instruments. Further, he believes testing takes time from the therapeutic task, interferes with encountering the patient as a total human being, and "the therapist may unwittingly use the test information to bulwark his own resistance to confronting his unsureness concerning the relationship with the patient." Bugental does, however, find a use for tests on some occasions. Such occasions may arise when it is necessary either for the therapist or the patient to reach a decision on whether psychotherapy is indicated, or perhaps whether some other service might be more desirable.

Hacker et al. (1972) are concerned with the effect of testing on the test *users.* They feel that using instruments ". . . themselves encouraged a dehumanizing orientation toward the people we had tested." Brown and Smith (1968), using Kotchen's (1960) 27-item self-report, questionnaire-type rating scale sought to measure existential mental health in Kotchen's terms that ". . . a mind is healthy when it has achieved a sufficient store of 'meaning' to enable it to master suffering and to direct daily action." Nevertheless, Brown (1972) ultimately concludes that ". . . to proceed psychometrically violates

[4]An etymological note is in order. Tracing *diagnosis* back to its Greek root, the *Oxford English Dictionary* lists such meanings as to discern, to distinguish, to learn, to know, to perceive. ("Perception is essentially a diagnosis," Herbert Spencer, *Principles of Psychology,* 1872). We know more about A to the extent we distinguish A from B, C, D, and E. Each increment of knowledge about A enables us to know A *more* as an *individual* and renders us less likely to confuse A with B, C, D, and E.

the major tenets of humanistic psychology." Specifically he is concerned that psychometrics violates "the *image of man,* and the image of human relationship." This view is challenged by Craddick (1972) who argues that the ". . . separation of man into parts is antithetical to *both* the humanistic tradition *and* to personality assessment." (emphasis supplied) Craddick often shares his test protocol with the testee (his term), or with the testee and therapist simultaneously, as implementation of an ethical, humanistic viewpoint. He concludes: "I feel that each of Brown's demands for humanism could be met in testing." At the same time, publications emerge seeking to establish the value of psychometric instruments for gauging humanistic attributes such as self-actualization (Bonjean & Vance, 1968), [the Personal Orientation Inventory (POI) and the Comrey Personality Scales (CPS)] (Anon. EITS Research and Development, 1973). A mixed bag.

Fischer (1970) advocates psychological assessment but notes that the client must be a coevaluator of the protocol for ". . . to understand his past behavior, predict his future behavior, or identify feasible possibilities, the client's perspectives must be understood." Mosak and Gushurst (1972) follow a similar procedure. They regard psychological testing as helping to establish a therapeutic relationship rather than hampering. They emphasize the humanistic concept of openness: "Psychologic testing can be used very fruitfully as an introduction to the therapeutic process. This is often conducted most effectively in a 'double interview' where the major therapist presents his findings to a second therapist who serves as a consultant. The cards are placed on the table: the therapist says what he thinks, and the client is encouraged to respond with a similar openness. . . ." Mosak and Gushurst see this approach as opening a relationship on an honest footing and as engendering in the client confidence in the therapist. They believe that the psychological report ". . . can be used in a number of ways to encourage a patient and arouse hope for the future."

In a comprehensive dialectic Sugarman (1978) examines five allegations gleaned from various sources, allegations that alienate some psychologists from the psychodiagnostic process. They are

Assessment is reductionistic.
Assessment is artificial.
Assessment does not pay attention to the examiner-patient relationship.
Assessment judges the patient.
Assessment is too intellectual.

After examining these positions he concludes, "An emphatic yes is the only logical response to 'Is Psychodiagnostic Assessment Humanistic?' That as, if the assessment process and philosophy follow the model proposed herein, then it is incomprehensible to state that it is not humanistic."

Assessment in the Eighties
. . . and Beyond?

Fein (1979), in an overview article, comments on recent setbacks in training students in psychological assessment:

> . . . directors of mental health delivery agencies discovered that the post-doctoral applicants for staff positions in psychology lacked even minimal skills in psychodiagnostic testing and personality assessment. In dismay these employers warned of the incipient demise of psychodiagnostic testing and personality assessment skills in training programs at the universities, a trend that was creating an ever widening gap between the mental health delivery systems and graduate training in psychological assessment.

In the same article, however, she presents "evidence that reports of demise of testing are premature."

Psychological assessment today is alive and well. A letter from the president of the Society for Personality Assessment (Jones, 1978) advises, "The membership . . . continues a slow but steady upward trend, indicating a continued growth of interest in the field, a clear reversal of the declining trend of the '60's." Similarly Cleveland (1980) notes a reversal of trend in Veterans Administration psychology:

> . . . psychological assessment remains an important activity within VA psychology. While it is true that psychological testing was viewed with disfavor and often assigned a lowered priority a few years ago, a shift in attitude has occurred more recently and the contribution to diagnosis, treatment, planning and rehabilitation . . . is once again recognized. Where psychology interns once arrived protesting assignment of assessment duties they now clamor for didactic courses and practical clinical experience in psychological testing.

In addition to this new emphasis on assessment, qualitative changes are also of great importance for psychological report writing. We may exemplify by noting new foci of concern in various areas of psychological activity.

In Behavior Therapy   Thus in the behavioral area Hersen (1981) calls for more training in psychopathology, in general, and in the etiology of symptoms.

> We all know a great deal about the presenting symptoms of the major disorders . . . but woefully little about *their birth and progression.* If the behavioral therapies are to be at the forefront of the field in the next few decades, our ability to practice preventive therapeutics will need to be enhanced. Thus, again, a clearer understanding of the genesis of psychopathology would seem mandatory.
>   More generally, I am very concerned that in our graduate seminars we have not dealt sufficiently with the varied issues of psychopathology. In our zeal to teach students how to pinpoint and consequate, I am afraid that, quite often,

we have not devoted sufficient time or space for them to develop a thorough understanding of *the more subtle ramifications of psychopathology*. This, unfortunately, is most apparent when these students make their appearance in the psychiatric setting . . . during the course of their internships. Here we have seen some gaping holes in their training. Very often, they simply are unable to distinguish between, say, depression and schizophrenia. And they do not have at their disposal the needed *theoretical and empirical underpinnings* for making that distinction. Despite many of our concerns about the psychiatric method of classification, it does appear that the DSM system is alive and well and here to stay. . . . Moreover, if in the future we expect to have greater impact in influencing the basis for arriving at a diagnostic appraisal, it is my contention that our students should be made aware of both the advantages and flaws of the existing nomenclature. Simply ignoring the issue, in this instance, will not lead to its behavioral extinction. (emphasis supplied)

Wolpe (1979) illustrates with the diagnostic concept of depression how similar presenting symptom patterns can have different origins and require different treatment approaches. Distinguishing among four kinds of neurotic depression, he recommends specific methods for dealing with each.

Type 1. Neurotic depression as a consequence of severe directly conditioned anxiety.
Treatment. Reactive depression of this type responds well to the deconditioning of anxiety.

Type 2. Neurotic depression as a consequence of anxiety based on erroneous self-devaluative cognitions.
Treatment. The treatment is, of course, cognitive correction.

Type 3. Neurotic depression due to failure to control interpersonal situations.
Treatment. As might be expected, assertive training figures largely in the treatment of depression of this kind.

Type 4. Reactive depression based on exaggeration of normal reaction to loss.
Treatment. When the investigation of the base suggests an endogenous element, the appropriate drug or hormonal treatment should be administered.

In Psychoanalysis   In psychoanalysis a rethinking of the parameters of treatment may have implications for psychological assessment, particularly on the focus of the content that is to be reported. Thus Paolino (1981) observes, "It is now widely recognized that the alliance and transference are not the only meaningful relationships in psychoanalysis." Rather than being exclusively concerned with these two important variables, Paolino suggests that it is important to assess the patient's *analyzability* as a contribution to making a decision on whether the prospective analysand is a suitable candidate for psychoanalysis. By analyzability he means that the patient experiences ". . . a state of readiness that involves the capacity to cognitively and emotionally understand psychoanalysis plus the capacity for constructive psychological and behavioral change as a result of that understanding." From his discussion of this position the following requirements for analyzability of prospective patients are abstracted.

A "need" for analysis in the sense that symptoms are sufficiently troublesome to warrant the sacrifices that analysis entails.

A good "fit" between the patient and the particular analyst who is involved.

An intact ego that will not be overwhelmed and still be able to maintain trust and a therapeutic alliance in the face of crises.

A close relationship with one who is sufficiently supportive and flexible to adjust to the personality changes that result from a successful analysis.

A skeptical attitude that is based on a relative lack of knowledge of psycho-analysis, this skepticism later to give way to an attitude of trust in the analyst and in analytic methods (Freud, 1913).

The quality of "psychological mindedness" (Appelbaum, 1973).

The capacity for insight, a quality related to psychological mindedness.

An understanding of the harmful role of symptoms (not just that they are painful) and the holding of a realistic view on ridding onself of them.

The capacity to experience [painful] feelings [and thoughts] within the session rather than just describe them.

The ability . . . to bear . . . painful feelings and thoughts without acting them out.

To be able to supply such information demands considerable flexibility and skill on the part of the psychological assessor. Most test data cannot directly be translated into these variables. It is expected that interview data, thorough knowledge of the analytic process, and considerable clinical skill would be necessary to make the sort of judgments that are required by Paolino's criteria.

In Individual, Group, and Couples Therapy   Clinicians have long used psychological reports in the conduct of psychotherapy. A commonly used format is the feedback to clients of selected data (test responses, for example), their significance as they relate to aspects of the client's personality then becoming a matter of joint interpretation by therapist and client—very much as analysts or analytically oriented therapists might jointly interpret dreams with a patient. In recent years along with an increase in the number of clinicians who endorse the sharing of test protocols and reports with clients (p. 29), we must presume that such sharing takes place in a thera-peutic context of ethical necessity (pp. 63–65). A report that was prepared for such use is presented on pages 202–203. Discussion of such sharing of reports is presented by Fischer (1970, 1972). The approaches of Craddick (1972, 1975) and Mosak and Gushurst (1972) (p. 29) further contribute to an understanding of how psychological reports may be used in the therapeutic process.

A variation of the therapeutic use of psychological reports has been designed for use in group therapy (Yalom, Brown, & Bloch, 1975). A number of gains for patients and therapists stemming from this approach are reported by the authors. These are listed on pages 234–235 together with samples from reports as entered by participating therapists.

The current use of psychological reports, whether in the form of oral or written feedback, is an approach that is based on historical support (Harrower, Vorhaus, Roman & Bauman, 1960). The application of the technique by Roman and Bauman to marriage therapy is of particular recent interest. The introduction by Harrower et al. of the concept that each marriage has a "personality" defines a rich source of diagnosable material that can profitably be examined. The observation that what the different partners contribute to a marriage by virtue of the fact that each has "a different 'way of looking at the world' can be presented in *projective counseling* [their expression] through the study of a single Rorschach card by both partners simultaneously" focuses an approach to studying the interaction in the nuptial dyad. Many instruments, however, can yield data to study personality and the interaction of persons in an intimate relationship. These include projective techniques, standardized psychometric instruments, and forms for observation by self and others.

Dorr (1981) builds on such approaches, citing specifically the work of Loveland, Wynne, and Singer (1963), Levy and Epstein (1964), Willi (1969), Araoz (1972), Floyd (1974), and Williams (1974). His own procedure consists of three phases. The initial phase is given to the administration of a comprehensive battery of five instruments. Each marriage partner completes the examination independently, following which a "consensus Rorschach" is administered. The major feature here is the offering of joint responses by the couple, these coming into being on the basis of the partners' agreement on what are the "best" responses.

The psychological report is presented to the couple in the next two phases. In the first, an oral report is given by the therapist in the context of a give-and-take conversation with some of the interpretations reached being developed by the couple with the therapist's guidance. In the final phase a written psychological "report letter," a rather lengthy document of five to eight pages, is prepared and sent to the couple, with provision made for continuing therapy with the examiner or elsewhere. Dorr notes that "the follow-up letter encapsulates what has transpired and provides an opportunity for me to clarify any errors or ambiguous interpretations that I may have made." He explains further that "the couple cannot possibly absorb all that is said in the feedback session, much less metabolize it effectively."

A number of advantages are claimed for this procedure. Testing is seen as cutting through defenses that are destructive to the therapeutic process and that have also created tensions in the marriage. The contributions of testing to the therapist's understanding of the case is seen as even greater than the gains that accrue from more typical examination: "The abundance of information yielded by a full, individual battery is geometrically expanded when integrated with an identical battery administered to the marital partner." Dorr observes further that in the procedure described the tests may "take on the quality of a separate therapeutic agent," an agent that "paradoxically fosters both objectivity and extreme emotionality." And finally, although exercising a therapeutic function, the clients cannot develop a transference to the tests nor can the tests develop a countertransference to the clients!

The preceding are examples of an increasing emphasis on the use of assessment approaches for direct remediation, an evident trend but a trend that appears to be in the early stages. Glaser (1981), commenting on the use of diagnostic test batteries in schools, observes, "It appears that tests continue the *tradition* of identifying particular symptoms of learning disability or inexperience and then using this information for classification and differential assignment." (emphasis added) In contrast to this purpose, "Teachers and schools need information that is oriented toward instructional decision rather than prediction." But, on what he perceives as a brighter note, "There is now less emphasis on selecting individuals for available educational opportunities and more on helping them to succeed in these opportunities."

In Neuropsychology   In the case of neuropsychological assessment, it is not tradition that is slowing the application to remediation; it is the current state of our knowledge and of the art. "This work is at an early stage and it would be premature to expect proof of clinical effectiveness whilst techniques are still in an early stage of development" (Miller, 1980). Goldstein (1981) holds what might be a dimmer view: "The area of rehabilitation of brain damaged patients represents a controversy within a controversy."

Be that as it may, he sees promise in the joining of forces of neuropsychologists and behavior therapists. One legitimate goal would be to minimize performance decrements in the presence of irreversible brain dysfunction: "Some behaviors may be maintained by environmental contingencies and are therefore modifiable even if the behavioral deficits produced by the brain damage cannot be changed." With this behavioral orientation Goldstein proposes that we train concrete deficits rather than more abstract "disabilities." Quite succinctly, in the case of a patient who is lacking in eating skills he would "treat the patient in the dining room rather than in the laboratory."

Others also hold viewpoints on skill retraining—for example, Carter, Caruso, Languirand, and Berard (1980) have published a workbook of exercises to be performed with a therapist for the treatment of thinking skills and Farber (1982) has contributed to the theory and practice of sensorimotor integrative therapy. In today's clinical pluralism, therapists of various persuasions have a role. Small's (1980) orientation considers the relationship of brain damage to significant personality processes, and his therapeutic approach heavily incorporates dynamic factors as these relate to typical issues that he has discerned in brain dysfunctional patients. Note the following:

> A primary goal with many MBD patients is to break through denial in order to improve reality perception and testing. Care is necessary to test the patient's

ego strength, and his willingness and ability to tolerate this process without undue intensification of anxiety and threat of regression, both of which induce resistance. When the parents foster the denial, work with them is a necessary prelude or accompaniment to the patient's therapy. This may require some sessions with the parents alone, and then together with the child, or the parents may require individual treatment by other therapists.

Improved reality perception and testing here center on the patient's dysfunctions, their possible causes, and, above all, the many steps the patient can take to circumvent or remedy his dysfunction, and the assets he has available to help him in the effort. Chess recommends giving the child a clear concept of his handicap in age-specific terms. The child is helped to recognize situations in which he competes on an equal basis with peers and those in which he can participate only partially. For some children there may be activities that are best avoided altogether.

The Evolving Zeitgeist

The role of the *Zeitgeist* is evident in the forms and the applications of current assessment activities. Nowhere is this fact more evident than in the use of computers to interpret raw data and to write reports; we are in an age of computers. Only a few years ago "testing" was a "dying" activity. Today psychological instruments are being put to uses that were not even imagined when they were developed.

2

PITFALLS
IN REPORTING

Psychological assessment, the results of which are formulated and conveyed in the psychological report, is widely accepted and sought as a contribution to the case study. In the opinion of many, however, psychological evaluation frequently could be of more value were the psychological report made a more effective practical document. There are many ways in which the report can fall short of its potentialities. Although these pitfalls are a hardy breed, most can be corrected. A first step in the right direction is to examine the criticisms commonly made of reports. Simultaneously, however, we must recognize that some of the problems in report writing stem from limitations in the field of behavorial science itself, and from shortcomings in our knowledge of how to apply it to practical issues.

WITH A POSITIVE PURPOSE, this chapter discusses the negative aspects that are extant in many psychological reports. The concentration of negative comments that follows shortly is an artifact of presentation, and the reader should not reach a pessimistic conclusion about psychological reports, which are widely regarded as doing a needed and valuable job. Rather, the purpose is to highlight those difficulties, often unrecognized, that many psychologists incorporate in their reports and that might be eliminated.

The categorized problems in psychological reporting presented in this chapter are based on returns from a large-scale survey of clinical workers in interdisciplinary settings that resulted in an unusually high rate of response—97.7 percent of psychologists, 81.2 percent of psychiatrists, and 97.2 percent of social workers, a rate achieved with the help of two follow-up mailings (Tallent & Reiss, 1959c; 1960). Of slightly more than 1,400 workers who returned the form, over 700 completed an appended "optional" sentence (or paragraph) root "The trouble with psychological reports is . . . ." The product of this invitation to tell what is wrong is now in the author's files—118 single-spaced pages of pitfalls, which, to be sure, contain numerous instances of overlap. Interestingly, even this slanted sentence completion item, designed to draw negative comments, resulted in a number of favorable, even laudatory observations from nonpsychologists. Mingling with critical, occasionally caustic remarks, are statements like "No trouble at all. They are useful and helpful," "I like 'em," "I find the psychological reports written at this hospital excellent," and "The trouble with psychological reports is . . . there are not enough of them." More neutral are comments that better approximate the author's outlook in that they recognize values, shortcomings, and greater potentialities: "A lot of work to be done, but still valuable," and "I appreciate whatever help they give and would allow their improvement to stem largely from the psychologist's own efforts." Perhaps the most favorable observation to be made is that, of those who contributed their time and thought to completing a lengthy form, almost half did not see fit to complete the sentence root that "pulled" for negative comments.

The primary purpose in trying to find out what writers and users of psychological reports think is wrong with such reports is to develop a rationale for practice. The gathering of such opinions is an example of searching for a rationale by means of the "popularity" approach (Tallent, 1956). This method has certain shortcomings. A compendium of opinions should not lead automatically to conclusions, and certainly not to a systematic approach to practical issues. Reflection on the overall problem of report writing and additional pertinent research are required. The major asset of the popularity approach is that numerous insights may be obtained by "talking" with hundreds of workers through a survey form. Yet, just as in talking face-to-face, the person seeking the benefits of the experience and observations of others must weight and measure the information received and act accordingly. In the present instance it is well not to be seduced by the expressions of praise for psychological reports, however well deserved. Several respondents who made favorable comments indicated that they had the good fortune to be associated with excellent psychologists. In other instances there was a suggestion that the respondents were not sufficiently versed in the methods of psychology; they assumed that psychologists know their work and are beyond criticism by members of other disciplines.

The hundreds of negative comments received are particularly interesting. They are a sample of impressions gained by practicing professionals who have had experience in variously constituted psychodiagnostic/treatment settings, and need to be seriously considered. Although much of the criticism may appear valid to many psychologists, some of it obviously stems from disparity in training and orientation among members of the team; solutions to the difficulties noted would appear to lie in the direction of greater interdisciplinary contact and understanding. It is also interesting that some of the comments are mutually contradictory; what are regarded as superior report-writing practices by some workers are seen as wretched by others. The solicited comments give much food for thought, and the reader of them must be the judge. Thus the author disagrees with some of the criticisms as suggesting practices contrary to the effectiveness of the mission. Indeed, whereas in our sample an appreciable number of workers, mostly psychiatrists, criticized the offering of diagnoses, prognoses, and recommendations, Siskind's (1967a) group of psychiatrists questioned whether such practice should be criticized. The justification for accepting, rejecting, or modifying any sincerely made criticism is to be sought in the implication it has for fulfilling the psychologist's mission, which itself is an evolving function.

A second purpose in studying what others have identified as shortcomings of pyschological reports is to gain a better understanding of the image the psychologist presents to associates. Indeed, as we would expect, some of the comments made about psychological reports reflect the psychologist's self concept. Such remarks bear on the entire groups of psychologists working in clinical-type settings and on the psychologist's role, attitudes, theories, and procedures, as well as on individual skills. They thus afford awareness of certain value judgments made about psychology and psychologists by their associates.

A number of respondents suggest or imply as a base issue the individual psychologist's personality or a conflict of personalities among staff persons: "The trouble with psychological reports is . . . psychologists," "The trouble with psychological reports is . . . they try hard to be an M.D.," and "The trouble with psychological reports is . . . many are influenced by psychiatrists' diagnoses and comments." In practice, relations between psychologists and team associates range from those characterized by cordiality, mutual respect, and interdependence, to hostility. A paper by Moore, Boblitt, and Wildman (1968) cites examples of the latter, more offensive (and amusing) than any received in the present survey. The authors report the following two examples: "[Psychologists] lack training in the basic sciences of medicine and Freudian psychology," and "Psychology is to psychiatry as astrology is to astronomy." (!) Many other illustrations suggesting personality shortcomings of a more serious nature will be found under various headings of criticism.

A comment offered by a number of workers made no reference to the quality of reports as such, but pointed out that they often arrive too late to be of maximum use (Mussman, 1964; Smyth & Reznikoff, 1971). This complaint should be borne in mind as the rationale of psychological reporting is studied. Might better practices allow the psychologist to deliver more punctual, and thus more practical, reports?

THE PERSISTENCE OF PITFALLS

The discussion starting on page 42 is a compilation of pitfalls the report writer should be wary of. (We believe the listing is rather complete but hope that our readers will inform us of any we have overlooked.) Although training may tend to reduce the incidence of errors in report writing, in general, available research suggests that errors are a hardy breed. Each generation of psychologists must be taught anew. Both human traits and the nature of language itself tend to perpetuate errors. Only by conscientious effort at avoiding them can they be reduced. Other pitfalls will tend to continue, minimized only by diligent concern with certain problem areas, until research provides better solutions.

Thus Lacey and Ross (1964), in a poll of workers in child guidance clinics, turned up a number of the same complaints noted in the Tallent and Reiss (1959c) study, although the percentages varied. Olive (1972) compared psychoanalysts' opinions of psychological reports in two different years, 1952 and 1970. Her general conclusion was that there is a disenchantment with the psychologist both as a tester and as a writer of reports. In both 1952 and 1970, the analysts' criticisms included "lack of clarity," "vagueness," "excessive use of jargon," "theoretical bias," "unreliability," and "overgeneralized." The 1970 survey revealed additional "bias to pathology" and "overlooking the patient's potential for change" (which is dealt with in the next chapter as the "prosecuting attorney brief" [Tallent, 1958]), "too pat," and "too intellectualized." Rosen (1973), in a delightful contribution entitled "Alice in Rorschachland," also points out psychologists' concern with pathology to the neglect of health factors. He also chides those psychologists who "restructure reality along Rorschach dimensions of personality and terminology."

One gets similar feelings about report shortcomings from reading Holzberg, Allessi, and Wexler (1951), Garfield, Heine, and Leventhal (1954), Cuadra and Albaugh (1956), and Smyth and Reznikoff (1971). Though differing in point of focus, the common denominator is the frequent occurrence of shortcomings in reports. All of these articles may currently be read with profit. Similarly Foster's (1951) succinct, half page of counsel to report writers is as pertinent today as when written. Just as teachers of rhetoric through the generations have been making the same corrections on their students' papers, so too has this writer noticed that students today tend to make the same errors as did students 20 years ago.

The persistence of pitfalls is well established in the faulty use of language. In 1950 Grayson and Tolman studied the definitions of clinical psychologists and psychiatrists for words that commonly appear in psychological reports. The first 20 words on the list were

Abstract	Bizarre	Defense	Father Figure
Affective	Bright Normal	Dependent	Hostility
Aggression	Compulsive	Depressive	Identification
Ambivalence	Constriction	Ego	Immaturity
Anxiety	Control	Emotional	Impulsive

The authors conclude that "the most striking finding of this study is the looseness and ambiguity of the definition of many of these terms." In a replication of this study 15 years later, Siskind (1967b) found that there was no decrease in the ambiguity of the same 20 terms. A study by Auger (1974) in which clinical personnel matched behavior descriptors with psychologists' definitions suggested that "either the behavior descriptors lacked specificity, the definitions were ineffective, or both."

Such problems are not limited to mental health concepts; they are present also in the practice of school psychology. Rucker (1967) and Shively and Smith (1969) reported poor agreement on the meaning of terms that are commonly used in reports. In Shively and Smith's study, teachers, counselors, and students, using a four-item, multiple-choice format, were asked to select the best definition for terms such as *aphasia, borderline intelligence, cortical involvement, neurological impairment,* and *perseverate.* Counselors tended to disagree significantly with both students and teachers, more than a third of the latter group failing to understand a number of terms that are presumably related to learning problems. Rucker's sample of teachers similarly showed poor agreement between school psychologists and teachers when they sought to define educational terms that appear in psychological reports.

Report stereotypy (pp. 69–74) continues to be a potent danger. This topic is discussed at length in Chapter 3. The psychologist needs to be vigilant in guarding against stereotyped material entering the report, and the psychologist's colleagues should be wary of accepting it.

That many psychological reports are written so as not to be very useful, so as not to contribute to decision making, is a complaint that just won't go away. Dailey (1953), Cole and Magnussen (1966), Breger (1968), and Hartlage, Freeman, Horine and Walton (1968) all conclude that many reports exhibit this deficiency and suggest solutions that are considered in the following three chapters.

Ziskin (1981), in a heavily documented work addressed to lawyer colleagues, seeks to spread an awareness of all of the preceding shortcomings to those in the legal profession who have occasion to cope with psychiatric and psychological testimony. Being at a disadvantage in contributing to the legal process is only one of the problems that saddle psychologists who ignore the perils of allowing pitfalls to find their way into reports.

But the ultimate problem is the limitations of the science and profession, aptly put by Holtzman (1964) in the title of his paper, "Recurring Dilemmas in Personality Assessment." His major points are (1) that personality assessment is hampered by lack of a clear, adequate, and consensual definition of personality; (2) that there is no agreement on what are the units and combinations of units needed to understand a person; (3) that personality variance and method variance are not readily separable; (4) that personality and personality assessment are overly culture-bound; and (5) that there are built-in moral dilemmas arising out of the individual's right to privacy and the investigative probing needed to (hopefully) understand the client's personality. The psychologist's awareness of such shortcomings might make for a more cautious approach to assessment.

Ziskin is particularly attuned to problems of science and profession, especially those having to do with such mundane issues as validity and reliability of tests, diagnoses and predictions, standardization, and practical usefulness.

PITFALLS BY CATEGORY

The solicited comments on "The trouble with psychological reports . . ." are classified under five major headings and numerous subheadings. The first four pertain specifically to the performance of the individual psychologist. Problems of science and profession (Category V) have to do with issues that psychology must identify and cope with. The matter of role conduct is particularly commented upon by psychiatrists, a reflection of a situation that can negatively affect treatment in some settings.

I. Problems of Content

The psychological assessor seeks to convey a body of information or content that will contribute to a mission. Study of the psychological report calls for the examination of a number of problem areas that are associated with the use of this tool, but all considerations are aimed toward delivering the content most likely to be helpful in individual case situations. It is therefore appropriate first to turn our attention there.

Raw Data   Whether or not the psychologist ought to include raw data in reports, or whether current reports contain too much or too little raw data, is an issue of major importance. To a large degree opinions on this matter are distributed along professional lines, the psychologists tending to be critical that there is overinclusion of such content, the psychiatrists being concerned that reports offer too little raw data, and the social workers being divided on this matter but perhaps siding somewhat with the psychiatrists. The way one views this issue is an individual matter, and there is widespread disagreement on whether the liberal quoting of clients' responses is a major asset or a distinct liability. From a plethora of comments, just a few are needed to capture three basic points of view. First consider these two opposing statements, reflecting as they do differing role concepts. They were written by a psychologist and a psychiatrist, respectively.

> They are too often descriptive rather than interpretive, leaving this job to the reader when really the psychologist is in the best position to interpret results.
> They do not contain enough selected raw material to permit the psychiatrist to draw his own conclusions.

A social worker pleads a lack of qualification to deal with data that are not meaningfully interpreted.

> Reference to specific psychological material in reports has little meaning to nonpsychologists.

And similarly, from another social worker—

> When reference is made to test cards, formulas, etc., the reader is often not familiar enough with the tests to understand what significance they have.

Improper Emphasis   Many workers, especially psychologists, criticize that reports are written with improper emphasis. The implications of such a shortcoming might be far reaching. It would seem to suggest, for example, that the report is not geared to the specific purpose(s) for which it is needed, a criticism mentioned many times and examined at greater length under another heading of this chapter ("Not practical or useful"). Improper emphasis may also suggest a faulty or incomplete knowledge of personality or behavior, and of clinical operations—for example, what sort of finding is likely to prove clinically rewarding and what sort is not. The occurrence of such errors might indicate a deficiency of clinical judgment. Some psychologists evidently do not discriminate among findings. The following comments show how report readers are likely to evaluate reports with regard to the appropriateness of emphasis.

> They seem to emphasize the personality state of an individual whereas I think more emphasis should be placed on the functioning of an individual in terms of what that person is doing to and with other people. If the patient is to be seen in psychotherapy, the psychological report should include some predictions about how he will probably act toward the therapist, how he will see the therapist, some goals for the therapist, and how the therapist might try to accomplish these goals and why he might do it in the way suggested. If the psychologist knows something about the limitations of the therapist who is to see the patient, then he should take these into consideration before he includes some of the goals of treatment.
>
> The report of dynamics and structure of the personality is very good. There should be more attention to the strength of defenses or pattern of adaptation, i.e., how well will a reaction formation stand up under stress, for example.
>
> Tendency to emphasize the unconscious to the neglect of the conscious goals and values.
>
> Not enough emphasis is given to conscious, practical controls.

And an impassioned protest—

> Too much pressure on sex. I know, I know, it is important, but, for heaven's sake, the world does not spin around the axis of . . . genitals.

Diagnoses, Prognoses, Recommendations   Offering a diagnosis, a prognosis, or recommendation in a psychological report seems to raise numerous objections, almost all of them from psychiatrists. In a sense this reaction is surprising, since many of this group actively seek such information from psychologists (Tallent & Reiss, 1959a, 1959b), but as already pointed out, preferences in psychological reports are an individual matter. The dissenting group evidently sees the offering of such content as an encroachment upon its role, although quite often this meaning was not spelled out. A few quotes are more than sufficient to clarify this position.

> In my opinion, the recommendation as to plan of treatment, chemotherapy, etc., is not appreciated.
>
> They try to diagnose.
>
> Recommendations should be excluded from psychological reports. It would seem more appropriate a function of a staff decision where other data can be considered.

Omission of Essential Information   Some readers and writers of psychological reports, particularly the latter, feel that reports omit essential information—that is, they evidently fall short of what is required for an effective psychological contribution. It is not certain whether this criticism is based chiefly on the supposition that a fixed body of content ought to be conveyed in reports, or whether reports tend not to have information necessary to specific cases. The following representative quotes, however, indicate what is meant as far as the individual respondents are concerned.

> They do not present specific and essential data which would be helpful to a team conference or individual attempting to formulate a plan of treatment and working diagnosis.
> They usually do not give any practical recommendations.
> Seldom do they make recommendations regarding treatment goals, nor do they specify areas of strength.

In view of the content of the previous section, the reader is probably wondering if it is possible to write a report to please everybody.

Minor Relevance   The problem of data selection seems to have arisen in any number of contexts. Some of the content of psychological reports is criticized as being not necessarily inappropriate, but of minor relevance. The flavor of such comments is captured by these statements.

> Our prejudices often lead us to make statements which are of little import to the recipient.
> They include data that I belive are not an essential part of the report, such as clinical description of the patient, social and medical data. This may be necessary to the examiner conducting the tests in evaluating the responses of the patient, but I do not believe this should be included as a routine procedure.

Unnecessary Duplication   The final criticism pertaining specifically to content, one made by a minority of workers, is that in some reports the same content tends to be repeated unnecessarily. There can be no dispute that where duplication occurs without good reason, such as to provide needed emphasis, its appearance is not defensible. Poor rhetoric can hardly be good psychology.

II. Problems of Interpretation

Irresponsible Interpretation   The psychological report frequently reveals weaknesses in various aspects of the assessment process. One of the more common of these evidently occurs before the psychologist begins to write the report. The phenomenon is that of eisegesis, faulty interpretation based on personal ideas, bias, and whatnot. It has frequently been noted in the misinterpretation of scripture. Dana (1966) urges that eisegesis be trained out of student psychologists and suggests a way of doing so.

Several meaningful patterns of criticism of data interpretation emerged in the analysis of negative comments made about reports. So many different kinds of alleged interpretive errors were pointed out that they are best summarized as "assorted irresponsible interpretations." Of the workers who made any sort of negative comments on psychological reports, no less than 41 percent of the psychiatrists, 27 percent of the psychologists, and 22 percent of the social workers made criticisms placed in this category. An examination of some of the criticism is informative.

> Clearly written to please the psychiatrist for whom it is being written, often interpreting data to fit his known pet theories and thus rendered unscientific.
> Tending to find more or less schizophrenia in every case.
> They sometimes seem to reflect the psychologist's feelings about the patient rather than the data revealed by the patient's responses to the tests.
> They draw conclusions from insufficient data, lack objectivity.
> They are frequently too arbitrary, expressing theory as fact.
> They are not sufficiently related to the tests they presumably are derived from.
> The referral question is frequently vague, and psychologists frequently hate to admit it when the tests don't give much information, and so overinterpret what they have.
> Too much "Barnum effort" (see pp. 71–73).
> Too much . . . (unquotable) . . . invalid statements, overgeneralizations, stereotypy and evidence of lack of reflection and integration of the material into a meaningful picture of the patient as a person.
> Just as the TAT reflects one's feelings, attitudes, desires, conflicts, etc., so do our psychological reports; We project ourselves. If we are integrated then so are our reports; if not—then?
> We read in the reports the examiner's own conflicts. These are usually discernible after seeing a few reports in which certain phrases and ideas repeatedly occur.
> Sometimes there is more of the psychologist than the patient in the test reports.
> People who write them frequently feel they have to say something about all areas of the client's life, even those about which they have little or no information.
> Occasionally they paint a darker picture than is true, possibly because not enough emphasis is given to conscious, practical controls.
> Sometimes sweeping pronouncements are made, and I doubt that the best tests can support such big conclusions.

Overspeculation   A specific type of irresponsible interpretation frequently mentioned is overspeculation. From reading the criticisms, it is somewhat difficult to know what all of the speculating is about, or why psychologists feel impelled to do so much speculating. There does seem to be definite opinion that many psychological reports are characterized by too much speculation, that this practice often irritates readers, and that in some instances it reduces respect for the psychologist's contribution. Just a few illustrations suffice.

> . . . speculative assertions beyond the realm of the testing results.
> Too theoretical and speculative.
> Too much speculation, reading between the lines, personal interpretation rather than reporting facts as observed.

Unlabeled Speculation   Many report readers are not particularly disturbed by speculation, provided that such interpretations are properly labeled. There do not seem to be group differences among the members of the team in this regard.

> Facts, inferences, speculations are often mixed and not labeled.
> The distinctions between reasonable deductions from the data, speculative extrapolations from the data, and the psychologist's clinical impression are not clear.
> If some indications were given for the bases for speculation and if clearly labeled as speculation.
> Many speculate and do not so indicate until questioned.
> Data is frequently overinterpreted. One can speculate but should label it as such.

Inadequate Differentiation   Another apparently frequent problem of interpretation is that psychological reports sometimes deal in generalities. It is charged that such reports do not differentiate among those who are assessed. Psychologists seem to be roughly three times more cognizant of this difficulty than are their psychiatric and social worker associates.

> Too little individuality of descriptions.
> All too often they don't present a comprehensive, logical picture of a unique individual.
> Very frequently they are made up of too many stock phrases which do not give any real feeling for the individual client.
> They frequently involve too many generalizations about human behavior and fail to describe the specific person who is involved.
> They tend to present generalizations that might apply to anyone rather than to the particular individual.
> Typically, they present a rather stereotyped picture into which any number of patients—or other people—might fit, rather than describing the individual.
> They report in broad generalizations that, although they sound quite profound, really would apply to nearly any patient.
> Too often the generalizations are so great that one could visualize the same report having been made on the preceding dozen persons seen at staff. Reaching for psychoanalytic concepts too often is the reason (and I am psychoanalytically oriented).
> They tend to rely on vague, psychoanalytically-oriented phrases which fail to convey an individualized picture of the client. Their vocabulary is excellent but what is lacking is a feeling for the client's individuality as a troubled human being.

III. Problems of Psychologist's Attitude and Orientation

A number of difficulties in the writing of psychological reports were singled out as more or less direct reflections of the psychologist's attitude and orientation. That is, many of the criticisms seemed more meaningful in terms of the ultimate improvement of reports when emphasis is related to certain personal features of the psychologist than to the end product.

Not Practical or Useful The most frequent criticism made of the psychologist's attitude or orientation is that the report is not written with a practical or useful purpose in mind. Psychologists identify the existence of such a deficiency far more frequently than do social workers and psychiatrists. The following examples reflect some of the more cogent observations regarding this difficulty.

> Our prejudices often lead us to make statements which are of little import to the recipient and to ignore or deal lightly with the objective reason for the referral.
> Their lack of function and value to the person.
> Often lack of comprehensibility in terms of a real-life treatment program.
> They are often written without a clear idea of the practical "users" or "consumers" on the receiving end.
> In my view we need to write more in the spirit of an operational approach.
> Many writers forget the purpose(s) of their reports and wander all over the psychic range, even when they are asked for a relatively clear-cut opinion.
> They're too sophisticated, too impractical for the people who rely upon the information they dispense.
> They are not pertinent to the purpose desired.
> They seem at times very professional but useless in terms of the personality of the patient.
> They are too often written to satisfy the interest of the psychologist rather than for the clinical application and understanding.

Exhibitionism That psychological reports are sometimes seen as exhibitionistic calls up a good deal of comment, especially from psychologists. A number of such comments refer to high-flown terminology in psychological reports but do not mention exhibitionism as such. Those so disposed should find it easy to interpret a prominent dynamic in a number of psychologists via the following remarks. In fact, gratuitous interpretations are already built into some of them.

> They are written in stilted psychological terms to boost the ego of the psychologist.
> They are attempts on the part of the examiner to show what he or she can do rather than what the patient is.
> Reports delight in including details of findings which are obviously comprehensible only to one who has made a study of psychological testing or is

versed in the finer significance of statistical research expressions. Such reports occasionally produce the feeling that words of less than four to six syllables and sentences with less than two thoughts will convince the reader that the writer is too simple.

It is not necessary to impress the reader with the psychologist's mentality. Their reports reflect their needs to shine as a psychoanalytic beacon in revealing the dark, deep secrets they have observed.

Reports should be concise and clear without an attempt to impress the reader with the erudition of the person who performed the test.

Too Authoritative   Reports that convey an authoritative stamp may have a motivation similar to those regarded as exhibitionistic. Their effect on the reader, however, seems to be different. Reports that pontificate tend to irritate the reader even more than those that are merely regarded as show-offy, perhaps because an authoritative report is likely to be perceived as an affront, whereas the defensive motive of the exhibitionistic report is more transparent. Psychiatrists evidently take more offense at, or at least are more aware of, overly authoritative reports than are other workers.

They are too positive, confident, assured, as though they were the last word, irrefutable, authoritative.

Many reports are much too opinionated and obviously reflect the author's own biased viewpoints.

Some are too dogmatic.

They often are too definite in their interpretations and assume to have all the answers.

The psychologist feels too superior and will generally write a short summary of his interpretation forgetting that a psychiatrist reading the report might differ in interpretation. This feeling of superiority on the part of the psychologist has alienated many intelligent psychiatrists.

A lack of humility, I never cease to be amazed by the confidence some psychologists have in their tests and in their own abilities to interpret them. To accept such reports the psychiatrist would have to lose what little intelligence he or she is supposed to have [a psychiatrist's comment].

I have seen some reports which affected me adversely because of a tendency to sound pompous with the implication "This is the final word!" rather than "This is an opinion which is intended to be helpful in understanding the whole" (and) to be all-inclusive to the point of excluding the specific contributions of other disciplines—a sort of "I can do everything approach" which sometimes results in the clouding of the most important observations. A second, though no less important result, is the impairment or even destruction of the team function.

Test Orientation vs. Client Orientation   It is perhaps suprising that psychologists complain more frequently than do other team members that clinical reports are too test-oriented rather than client-oriented. It may be that, since a number of workers from the other professional groups wish the inclusion of raw data, they do not find talk of tests offensive.

They usually talk about tests and test results rather than the client's personality.
Talking about the tests too much and the patient too little.
They often describe responses rather than people.
They are test centered too often rather than containing statements about behavior in the nontest environment.
Often the writers feel it necessary to include scoring and other quantitative detail at the expense of providing a useful and helpful picture of the person evaluated.
Psychological reports should reflect the judgment of the psychologist with all the limitations of maturity and experience. The psychologist should proceed as though he knows something about human behavior and tests are aids in his understanding. He should not act as though he is lost without his tests. I think other disciplines want us to give opinions which are free to open discussion and exchange.

Too Theoretical   Sometimes criticisms indicate or imply that reports are not useful or client-oriented because they are too theoretical.

In general, they are too theoretical.
They concern vague hypothetic properties of people.
They often are too theoretical or academic in language to be comprehensible or meaningful in terms of future treatment goals for the client. They occasionally give us the feeling that no client was present at the time.
At times one has the feeling he is reading a biological dissertation on protoplasm rather than about a flesh and blood person.
Sometimes I come across psychological reports which are loaded with textbook phrases, but giving very little clear picture of the particular individual involved.
We sometimes get bogged down in vague, theoretical terminology which has little direct relation to the actual behavioral dilemmas confronting the individual. Also, we employ theoretical concepts reflective of basic psychological processes (e.g., oral sadistic orientation) which are so general and so removed from the level of behavior that we write more like textbook theoreticians than as psychologists confronted with the task of making some sense out of a client's behavior.

Overabstract   Similar to the criticism that some psychological reports are too theoretical is the complaint that they are overabstract. Criticisms that reports are too theoretical and overabstract frequently occur in the same statement.

At times they become too difficult and abstract.
They are sometimes too theoretical and/or abstract; and on the other hand, too concrete—as reports of exact performance on tests as such. Ideally, there should be a happy medium.
They are too often lofty abstractions or concrete banalities. In either case, they fail to offer a meaningful, readily grasped, exposition of the subject's psychological condition.
The more abstract and/or intellectual the report is, the more likely the examiner is either defensive or projecting his own conflicts into the report.

Some are unnecessarily involved, technical and abstruse so as to be virtually useless in planning disposition of the subject.

Miscellaneous Deficiencies of Attitude and Orientation   There are a number of aspects of the psychologist's attitude and orientation we term "miscellaneous." Included are criticisms calling reports too intellectual, too academic, and too pedantic, comments which no doubt overlap those just quoted. Such features may stem from the transplantation of an earlier generation of psychologists from an academic to a clinical setting. At any rate the academic influence is noted by a number of observers who seem to feel it detracts from the practical utility of reports.

They are too studiously intellectual.
   Too pedantic—obscure to other professions.
   Usually too involved, pedantic.
   In many instances psychological reports have the tendency to be too academic.
   They are often esoteric to the practice of psychological testing.
   Esoteric reference to statistical mechanisms.

A reluctance on the part of some psychologists to take on the consultant role, or to prepare psychological reports, is suggested by some clinicians as an explanation for blameworthy reports. In individual instances this could be a lack of confidence in or confusion about psychological methods. Such criticism might be seen as part of the psychologist's role problem as discussed in the following.

Psychologists feel it is almost below their dignity to do them.
   (The trouble is) that you've got to write them.
   Psychologists appear to have lost confidence and/or interest in testing.
   I have a strong personal dislike for writing psychological reports, in spite of my recognition of their usefulness. Perhaps part of my feeling is due to the excessive length and detail of reports which are seldom read by anyone else, anyway. To me it is the most distasteful part of my job.

IV. Problems of Communication

Many of those concerned with psychological reports oversimplify the matter in terms of communication. The negative comments already made about psychological reports demonstrate clearly enough that report writing cannot be divorced from purpose or context or from the basic technical competence of the psychologist. The communication aspect is but one of the vital problems to be singled out for study.

Hundreds of workers had one or more negative comments to make about this pitfall. More respondents were concerned with this kind of difficulty than with any other aspect of psychological writing or consultation. Accordingly there is a tendency for overlap among the subcategories.

Word Usage   The worst offender, according to our sample, is what is classified here as "Word Usage"—really a variety of offenses against the King's English. Thirty-seven percent of psychiatrists, 45 percent of psychologists, and 65 percent of social workers making negative comments on psychological reports had something to say on this matter. Deficiencies of terminology and wordiness were mentioned with great frequency. Some may be surprised to learn that psychoanalytic terminology is singled out as an offender with great frequency.

> A good report writer uses the language of the novelist, not the scientist unless he's writing for another psychologist. Analytic language is a language of generalities and thus loses the uniqueness we should be striving for.
> Often padded with meaningless multisyllable words to lengthen report.
> Gobbledygook [this expressive term was used by numerous respondents].
> Too much jargon [also a *very* frequently used term of criticism].
> I don't like reports which contain jargon which I can't understand.
> They do not take advantage of simplicity and ordinary words.
> Semantics have a tendency to creep in, and the phenomenon of "verbal diarrhea" occurs too often.
> The appearance of stereotyped phrases.
> They are too often written in a horrible psychologese—so that clients "manifest overt aggressive hostility in an impulsive manner"—when, in fact, they punch you on the nose.
> Too much emphasis is placed on psychological phraseology and such when we could say the same thing quickly, efficiently, and simply.
> They are not frequently enough written in lay language. I belive it requires clear thinking to write without use of technical terms.
> What about describing the person's behavior in terms that one ordinarily uses in describing a person rather than a client?
> Their value depends on whether the psychologist talks English or a special language of his own.

Vague, Unclear, Ambiguous   Many clinical workers are critical that psychological reports are vague, unclear, or ambiguous. No doubt a good deal of this difficulty stems from expressive deficiencies, although there are apparently other ways of writing reports that cannot be understood. How this occurs is a matter about which many respondents are not clear.

> They sometimes are vague and unsubstantial.
> They tend to rely on vague, psychoanalytically oriented phrases.
> New words or new meanings to familiar words are used, leaving the reader confused as to what is meant.
> Excessive wordiness which clouds the findings.
> Perhaps some are a little "veiled" in meaning, so as to attempt to prove the psychologist is truly a professional.
> Oftentimes the psychologist has to be interpreted.

They contain too many ill-phrased, hard-to-understand sentences.
Often lack of comprehensibility in terms of real life treatment programs.
They are intellectual vagaries.
They are not clear enough to be wrong.
Statements are made which could have more than one meaning, or are difficult to understand.
They suffer mainly from vagueness, double-talk and universality without enough of an attempt being made to specify more precisely what sets this person off from other people (and what does not).
Scores have little meaning even to the psychologist who understands their rationale, unless he also knows how they fit together in terms of cause and effect regarding behavior. To cover up his ignorance he resorts to the reporting of percentages, ratios, etc., and overwhelms his reader with such technical language that little information is conveyed.

Length of Reports   The length of psychological reports comes in for a good deal of criticism. In general, the consensus is that they are too long, but some feel they are too short. The latter scourge does not yet seem to be pandemic.

They are too lengthy—should be concise and to the point.
Many are too long. This usually teaches the reader to look for a summary and ignore the rest.
Too often the completed report is too long. Often I might go to the summary to get the gist of the examination.
Most of them are too long. Few people, if any, will take the time to read them.
Psychological reports should present specific data and specific interpretation. Too many contain omnibus recommendations and universal statements which apply to most people. I'd rather see brief reports with relatively little said then lengthy stereotyped reports which also say little.
A good report should stop when it has run out of useful data.

And one unhappy psychologist is concerned with length for what appears to be good reasons, and therefore would prefer to lessen the burden.

They are:
Over-imaginative,
Over-academic,
Over-syllabic,
And not over soon enough!

Too Technical, Too Complex   A further plea for simplicity and straightforwardness is registered in comments that psychological reports are too technical and too complex.

The more simply the material is presented, the more useful it is.
I have made "Flesch counts" of quite a large number of reports and the level of difficulty tends to be much too high. Psychological reports should not be as

difficult to read as our professional papers, but often they are. Many reports of this type are actually meaningless—a kind of polysyllabic illiteracy.

Too technical or too esoteric.

Technical terminology, particularly Freudian or statistical language, where these do not serve as highly specific communications, which implies writing a report for another psychologist or analyst.

I think that it is important that the person write in such a way as to communicate to those who will read the report. In some cases this will require that he write in a much simpler and more descriptive manner.

Documentation makes reports too technical.

It appears that the psychologist prepares the report for one of his own group rather than the benefit of other members of the team.

Style   Although style is generally regarded to be a rather individual matter, a number of workers believe there are certain necessary style requirements for effective communication. Psychologists are evidently more concerned with this matter than are members of other groups.

The reports tend to sound very much alike—to represent a personal "style."

Style is a matter of choice, but since we are supposed to be literate people, we should have certain standards of excellence to meet—too often this is not the case.

Too concerned with literary style.

The art of report writing should be akin to caricature.

They become too "flowery."

They all sound too much alike, as though the writers are adhering to a standardized model instead of allowing the form of their reports to be determined by the individual subject and the circumstances.

Too many reports follow a stylized form without due consideration to the real needs of the patient for which psychological testing had been requested.

Too often they seem to satisfy the writer's literary, "expressive" needs rather than communicate adequate description.

They give one more the impression of poetry than of scientific writing.

Under the guise of "capturing the flavor of the patient," appropriate scientific writing is sacrificed for style.

Organization   Psychologists are evidently more prone to the belief that psychological reports are not well organized than are other members of the team.

Often they are not coherently organized in terms of a personality or psychoanalytic theory and hence become meaningless jumbles of bits of data and information.

Frequently they are not organized—thought out—before they are dictated.

Too often they are so poorly organized that the reader has a difficult time to get a clear psychological picture of the client.

The analysis is in fragmented form rather than being integrated.

Write-ups frequently are not really organized, but formulations are "faked" in a sense by the use of syntax and grammatical construction.

They are often not organized around a central pattern characteristic of a person. Each paragraph seems a separate, discrete, unrelated part which could be clipped out and inserted in any other report.

When several tests have been administered, many psychologists cannot integrate the findings without giving separate results for each test.

Hedging   The final elicited problem of communication is that of hedging. A number of workers feel the psychologist should commit himself or herself at one level or another, and not straddle the fence.

Some writers refuse to take a chance and say anything definite. They beat about the bush, include every possible descriptive or diagnostic phrase.

Psychologists seem too often to "play it safe" and include so much in their reports (or so little) that they can never be wrong, refuse to make specific predictions, and therefore can never really be right either.

They too often are riddled with qualifications—"it appears that," "it may well be," "the test reports indicate." This is fine when speculation is being introduced, but many reports merely convey the inadequacy and timidity of the writer.

We seem to be afraid to commit ourselves in a few words; using too many qualifying statements and thus avoiding ever being wrong, but never actually predicting anything at all.

Can't they be more confident in their findings, i.e., when it might appear from testing that the patient may be homicidal or suicidal and may act this out, to say so clearly? It's better to know before than later—or too late.

Often no definite conclusions are reached and the reader of the report is left as bewildered as he was prior to requesting psychological examination.

V. Problems of Science and Profession

Problems of Science   Our survey shows that it was primarily psychologists who made observations to the effect that the trouble with psychological reports is not entirely the fault of individuals. Rather, a number of respondents see the need for a number of basic advances in areas such as psychological theory and the validity and applicability of tests. This latter problem is of great moment to many of the psychologist's team associates.

There is too little research on effective report writing. This would make an excellent thesis topic. (emphasis supplied)

I suggest that a "sociologist from Mars" would find the test reporting behavior of psychologists quite as "weird" as any of the rituals and customs and beliefs of many so-called primitive societies.

There is lack of agreement, even among members of a small staff, as to how they should be written. Clinical psychology doesn't have an adequate basis, either in theory or tools, for writing simple, straightforward, meaningful reports.

Most people, including psychologists, don't know what they are for or how to use them once they are written.

It has never been convincingly shown that the type of information contained in a psychological report contributes information which can improve the validity of decisions beyond that possible on the basis of interview impressions and a good case history. The trouble does not lie so much with psychological reports as with the material we have to report.

Primarily that their utility is unknown and untested. Few encouraging reports of prediction studies have been noted lately. Assuming validity and reliability (mighty big assumptions) psychologists are still in doubt as to the purpose of their own diagnostic efforts—particularly in a team setting.

Their usefulness is limited by the validity of the inferences based upon test performance. Formulations of test findings in terms of some general conception of personality processes appropriate to the issues raised in the referral are always preferable in my mind to showing description of test responses and behavior in the test situation. Such formulations must, however, be explicitly tentative in the light of doubts one must entertain about the dependability of inferences drawn from test responses—especially in the area of projective techniques.

Interpretation is too often based on theories which are yet poorly validated.

Essentially the same trouble as is found with psychiatric and psychological theory and terminology in general. That is, theories and concepts are vague and of low reliability and validity.   We have too many concepts, none of which can be regarded as demonstrably fundamental. Thus we write confused reports which depend on literary excellence more often than scientific knowledge.

The greatest defect is inadequate and unsympathetic personality theory on which to hang our observations.

Problems of Role Conduct   An insight into psychological consultation, far broader in scope than the psychological report, is gleaned from an observation of comments classified as "Problems of Role Conduct." These relate to what is regarded as encroachment of psychology upon the functions or prerogatives of other professionals. It is the psychiatrists who feel most abused in this respect. An appreciable number of social workers also feel that the realm of the psychiatrist has been invaded by the psychologist, but some social workers see their own functions as assumed by the psychologist. Even more, a number of respondents are of the opinion that the psychological report encompasses the function of the entire team. None of the psychologist contingent indicated that they felt there was psychological encroachment upon the duties of any of their associates. The author disagrees with some of the following statements, but it is important to know how one's team associates might feel. A number of psychologists are concerned that their role is not adequately defined, and they do see their effectiveness as being compromised by their equivocal position.

Too enterprising, perhaps too flavored with clinical feeling.
Many psychologists tend to digress in other fields.
They frequently do not mind their own business and go beyond their ken—invading territory properly allocated to the M.D.

Some reports go to the extreme of becoming a clinical summary of the client, including social and personal history and mental status.

They often contain medical and/or psychiatric diagnoses, prognosis, and at times, treatment.

Some even suggest medical and other treatment.

They often try to give purely medical advice to physicians.

They make specific recommendations that an M.D. or a psychiatrist should do, and psychoanalytical insights or formulations that a psychoanalyst should do.

There is a tendency to avoid the very purpose for which psychological testing exists. Namely, to present laboratory data codified in its original terminology so that the physician who has requested such testing for his own purpose of treating the patient may add to his clinical estimate of the patient. In my opinion, the recommendation as to plan of treatment, chemotherapy, etc. is not appreciated. Psychological testing and reporting is certainly a highly specialized and technical field which adds a great deal to the doctor's knowledge of the patient and should confine itself to this area.

They tend to make diagnoses rather than furnish specific data supporting a certain diagnosis. They are requested by the M.D. to help him make the diagnosis, prognosis, etc. The M.D. is not interested in what the psychologist thinks but why he thinks so. History and behavior are already available on the patient. The skilled psychiatrist knows how to interpret the data. If the psychologist feels his M.D. does not know what all this means, he should first give the data and follow it with a polite interpretation beginning such as "This data suggests . . . etc. . . . ."

Some psychologists seem to take offense and think it too menial to perform I.Q. tests. Their reports reflect their needs to take over the functions of a psychiatrist.

The psychologist tries to do everything else but an evaluation of intelligence, which is what he is best equipped to do. I personally feel that psychiatric diagnosis does not fall within the realm of the psychologist.

They try to make psychiatric formulations instead of assist.

The frequency with which the psychologist attempts to be a psychiatrist and does not use his legitimate observations from his testing materials to provide a picture of one or more samples of behavior. Most psychiatrists feel psychologists and their tests have value as such. Why don't psychologists feel this way?

They are too much concerned with matters unfamiliar to the psychologist and familiar to the psychiatrist. Thus the reports are too often replete with amateur psychiatric data, and deficient in psychological data, which had been requested and presumably are needed by the physician. On several occasions, I have been surprised, if not shocked, to see included in psychological reports "Patients should be helped by E.C.T."

On the other hand, one psychiatrist sees the "trouble" as quite the opposite from that expressed by some of the psychiatrists quoted above. This is definitely a minority opinion.

Too many psychologists are afraid they'll tread on M.D.'s toes. The properly trained psychologist will prepare better psychological reports as soon as he is liberated from the fear of overstepping certain unwisely defined professional bounds. Once liberated, he will have no need to fill space with social data. His reports will then reveal his full understanding of the patient based on observation, experience, plus the skillful interpretation of special tests.

When social workers make comments on the psychologist's role conduct, they are likely to be concerned with the same matters which trouble many psychiatrists, or to have very similar feelings. They feel, for example, that an invasion of social work territory, the taking of social histories, has occurred. One social worker, however, sees a problem of role dissatisfaction which affects a number of groups:

> Our hospital has six psychologists and many student trainees. They have a wide range of duties and responsibilities but can't keep inside their own yard! Our staff has six social workers, one researcher, and an anthropologist.
> The social workers all want to be psychologists.
> The psychologists anthropologists.
> The anthropologists social workers.
> And only God knows what direction we are all going in.

A SUGGESTION
FOR AVOIDING PITFALLS

An awareness of the pitfalls discussed in this Chapter will become most useful as the reader searches them out in their native habitat—actual psychological reports. Those reports in Chapter 6 that we suggest are not to be emulated provide examples of a number of the problems just discussed. The Quality Check of the Psychological Report provided at the conclusion of this book can be useful to the reader in locating pitfalls in report writing as they occur in academic and practicum training and in the writing of reports in applied situations.

3

RESPONSIBILITY AND EFFECTIVENESS

The effectiveness of the psychological report may be enhanced by attention to a number of factors. Everything is subsidiary to the matter of the psychologist's understanding and fulfilling the mission of meeting responsibilities in the case. Matters of ethics and of legal constraint are of the greatest moment. The psychologist must provide an individualized report rather than one heavily saturated with some form of report stereotypy. Always important is the need to guard against personal factors compromising the value of the report. Responsibility also demands that the psychologist focus on practical requirements, carefully consider the use (or nonuse) of raw data, and decide on the proper terminology and report length. If the report is to be an effective instrument, the psychologist must even take into account its cost and its timeliness.

PRIMUM, NON NOCERE—FIRST, DO NO HARM. These words have been widely recognized as the sage admonition of Hippocrates to his medical students and they are equally applicable to psychologists today. Typically psychological assessment occurs when intervention in another's life is taking place or is contemplated, an awesome responsibility. The psychological report thus may be a powerful instrument for good or ill. The points that the psychologist makes and how effectively they are communicated may influence such decisions as the sort of school or vocation an individual is to enter, the treatment that will be offered, or the client's living conditions. In the formative years of childhood, the school psychologist's understanding of a child, together with the ability to effectively convey that understanding, may contribute importantly to shaping the child's future. At times an individual's very life may be at stake. It is a matter of some moment, for example, when a psychologist is able to identify a client who appears to have suicidal propensities and is able to relate this impression unambiguously and convincingly to colleagues. The currently accelerating concern with social accountability reflects in part a recognition of the need for psychologists to deal competently with such matters.

Principle 1 of the Ethical Principles of Psychologists (American Psychological Association, 1981), Paragraph f, reads in part, "As practitioners, psychologists know that they have a heavy social responsibility because their recommendations and professional actions may alter the lives of others." Having reference to assessment, and specifically to the assessment of intelligence, Matarazzo (1981) recounts the contributions of Binet and Wechsler thusly:

> . . . the fruit of their creative minds and the simplicity of the practical tools of measurement and assessment produced by Alfred Binet and David Wechsler would touch the lives and influence the careers of the majority of people who were born during the 20th century. Probably the work of no other psychologists, including Freud or Pavlov, has so *directly* impinged upon the lives of so many people.

In this chapter we deal with two rather basic issues: (1) the responsible development of data and (2) in an ethical, and perhaps also a legal context, the presentation of these data using the principles of sound rhetoric. There is a logical relationship between knowing what one means and saying what one means, as Flesch (1972) reminds us in his book *Say What You Mean.*

Knowing what one means must precede putting words on paper. In the course of recording what we mean, however, we also more fully develop the theme that we are setting forth, thus further clarifying for ourselves and for our readers what we do mean.

Style or rhetoric, then, contributes to (or detracts from) the psychological report. As a basic point, it is well to point out to the psychologist the words of Sydney Smith: *Everything which is written is meant either to please or to instruct. The second object is difficult to effect, without attending to the first.*

The psychologist who needs to improve writing skills, as many do, had better study the topic, perhaps from a good book on rhetoric. We are somewhat partial to Flesch's *Say What You Mean* and to his earlier work *The Art of Readable Writing* (1949/1974). What appeals most is the emphasis on simplicity, directness, and good common sense. Of particular interest in *The Art of Readable Writing* are scales for measuring the ease of reading and the level of interest of content.

Responsible interpretation, however, has many facets, the most basic being a well-trained, knowledgeable interpreter. The psychologist must understand the mission, colleagues, the client, the client's circumstances, and available resources for dealing with the client's needs. The psychologist must have a good grasp on theory of personality and behavior but not be ruled by it, must know what *can* be interpreted and what *should* be interpreted, and must be able to present the client as an individual—with individual needs and goals—and not travel the easy road of stereotypy.

ETHICAL AND LEGAL RESPONSIBILITIES

One might suppose that a definition of the assessment psychologist's responsibilities would be adequately covered by the ethical principles of scientific and professional associations and by the concern for ethics as enacted into law, and frequently this is so. However, Bersoff (1975) also points out that ". . . codes of ethics and the law may present competing demands" and that the onus for such incongruity lies with the ethical codes. He explains:

> 1. A basic reason for the failure of ethical codes to provide adequate bases for behavior is their ethnocentrism . . . codes represent the professional group's point of view and are rarely developed with help from the consumers who receive the professional's services. Psychologists may be living under the false presumption that their ethic is shared by the people they serve.
> 2. . . . ethical principles are formulated on such an abstract level that they merely provide general guides to actual behavior; practitioners rarely understand how those principles are to be applied in specific situations."
> 3. . . . the value of codes may be perceived solely as a means of providing practitioners with a symbol that they are truly professionals. . . .

Developing this position and pointing out some special vulnerabilities of school psychologists, Bersoff suggests that "it is apparent that psychology's codes are insufficient protections against increased scrutiny by the courts." And, ". . . while psychology may permit different interpretations of its ethical guidelines, the courts may not be so benevolent. They do not find it at all difficult to disregard a profession's claim to autonomy when the behavior of its practitioners is perceived to interfere with the rights of individuals or the public at large."

In formulating his thesis Bersoff quotes Principle II(c) of the ethical code of the National Association of School Psychologists (1974): (Regarding assessment) ". . . the emphasis is on the interpretation and organization rather than the simple passing along of test scores. . . ." To implement this abstract principle (in the sense of item 2 in the preceding list of ethical code shortcomings), much of the content of this book may be understood as offering practical explication and exemplification of the precept. Also following the theme of responsibility, Principle V(c) of the NASP code calls for getting the students' parents involved with their children's problems through ". . . frank and prompt reporting . . . of findings obtained in the evaluation of the student," an injunction that is paralleled in law (p. 65). *Effective* involvement requires that the parents understand the psychologist's conclusions.

In a related context there is a court ruling that requires that clinical records be written so that they be understandable and serviceable as guides to care providers (*Wyatt* v. *Aderholt,* 1974). In a suit brought in U.S. District Court for the Middle District of Alabama pertaining to the constitutional guarantee of the right to treatment of persons civilly committed (not committed on a criminal charge) to state mental institutions, the court found that "evidence established that the hospitals failed to meet the conditions of individualized treatment programs." The evidence referred to was expert testimony that ". . . the patient records kept at the hospital were wholly inadequate; that they were written in such a way as to be *incomprehensible* to the aide level staff that had prime responsibility for patient care; and that they were kept where they were not accessible to the direct care staff particularly in need of them." (emphasis supplied) Clearly both ethical and legal constraints are involved in the preparation and use of psychological reports; society is an interested consumer of our work.

In terms of the number of people affected—in excess of eight million at any given time—the Education for All Handicapped Children Act of 1975 (Public Law 94–142) sets a far-reaching precept for psychologists who are involved in the implementation of this act. For both educators and psychologists, the key term of this law is *individualized.* Calling for an "*individualized* education program" for each handicapped child, the psychologist's preparation of an *individualized,* case-focused report is most likely to be helpful in the preparation of an *individualized educational plan* to guide the course of instruction for each child. We submit that individualized, case-focused reports also are more effective than are reports written in general terms in contributing to effective (therefore ethical) psychotherapy and to management of clients. (emphasis supplied)

Sharing Reports with the Client and Other Persons

To share or not to share the psychological report with the client is a longstanding issue. Brodsky (1972) summarizes both sides thusly:

> Traditionally the sharing of a client's files with the client himself has been only minimally considered, and when discussed at all, the practice has been seen as unethical, irresponsible, or at least questionable. Contrary to such traditional views, we suggest here that specific ways of sharing results with a client are a means for effective involvement and the assumption of appropriate professional responsibilities and roles.

The traditional position is well set forth by B. Klopfer and Kelley (1946) and by W. G. Klopfer (1954). The earlier formulation reads:

> It should be considered an unalterable role of professional conduct *never* to give a written Rorschach interpretation to the subject himself, since psychological terminology is so readily misinterpreted even by persons who should be familiar with it. (emphasis supplied)
>
> [Also,] when the Rorschach expert deals directly with a subject without any professional intermediary, a completely new problem arises. No one should be permitted by his own professional conscience to give to another person as penetrating information about his personality as the Rorschach provides, unless he has specific psychotherapeutic training. Any person who violates this rule of professional conduct uses the Rorschach method in an irresponsible way.

In 1954 the topic continued to be approached with the greatest of caution:

> . . . if particular concern is expressed by the patient about test results it is best to give fairly superficial kinds of interpretation, which are apt to be consciously acceptable to the individual and not particularly anxiety provoking. In these cases it usually has been found that an emphasis on the intellectual aspects of the personality, thought contents, characteristic ways of reacting to stressful situations and the like can be discussed most easily. It should be kept in mind that some aspects of the Rorschach are apt to be of an unconcious nature, dealing with repressed material, and should not be brought out except in the context of intensive psychotherapy, and after the establishment of substantial rapport. It need hardly be stated that giving a written report to a patient is an extremely dangerous and harmful thing to do and may cause much grief, both to the patient and to the psychologist.

Proscription of sharing is a feature of a number of current approaches to reports, particularly of computer-generated reports that are widely available to professionals (Chapter 7). Here the concern stems from scientific caution and tentativeness rather than with explicit concern with possible harm to clients—although one might infer that the welfare of clients is also under consideration. Thus Western Psychological Services prefaces the Personality Inventory for Children (PIC) report with the statement "This report consists of a series of hypotheses that may serve to guide further investigation." The WPS MMPI report is similarly introduced, with the additional suggestion that "this report is a professional consultation and should not be shared with the client." Reports printed by the Interpretive Scoring Systems Division of National Computer Systems supplies the following caveat with reports based on the Millon Clinical Multiaxial Inventory (MCMI): "Inferential and probabilistic, this report must be viewed as only one aspect of a thorough diagnostic study . . . it should not be shown to patients or their relatives."

However, some reports have long been addressed directly to the client. The Kuder Preference Schedule (1948), indeed, is designed to be scored and profiled by student clients who are also furnished with instructions for interpreting the profile. The Strong-Campbell Interest Inventory (1974) similarly involves the client in the interpretation of his or her interest pattern. Behaviordyne makes available an MMPI report composed in the second person for personal study by the client (pp. 202–203).

Today reports written by psychologists about clients might well also be written for clients. Such a disposition was strongly represented in a 1971 APA symposium entilted "Shared Results and Open Files with the Client: Professional Irresponsibility or Effective Involvement?" A group of papers in the Fall 1972 issue of *Professional Psychology* (Brodsky, 1972) favors such an approach, as does the practice of many contemporary psychologists—for example, Craddick (1972, 1975) and Mosak and Gushurst (1972). Fischer (1970, 1972) involves the client as a coevaluator of data, as does Dorr (1981) who prepares both oral and written reports for clients (Chapter 7). Allen (1981) emphasizes the therapeutic aspect of psychological diagnosis and the need to "build a diagnostic alliance." In seeking this goal he invites the client to tell how testing might be helpful and what questions might be explored. Similar to the approach of Fischer and Dorr, Allen also invites the client to participate in test interpretation. Richman (1967) and Aranow and Reznikoff (1971) also report the sharing of test data to be therapeutically advantageous.

Wright (1981) also proposes that clients be shown their reports, but for other than therapeutic reasons. He believes that when reports contain material that the client might view as unpleasant or as blocking an opportunity (e.g., promotion, a chance for probation), the client, should he or she eventually become aware of the report content, might decide to initiate a malpractice suit. He believes that sharing findings and recommendations with the client can perhaps defuse a potentially dangerous situation. The client will not be faced with unwanted "surprises" sometime in the future and has an opportunity to digest the findings and work through reactions to them.

Regardless of the preceding opinions and practices, our actions are now governed by a number of laws that permit access to clinical reports: the Privacy Act of 1974, the "Buckley Amendment," various state laws, and PL 94–142. These laws mandate the terms under which clients and others with legitimate interests—for example, parents—may request to see records and the responsibilities of those who hold the information.

An inevitable question, then, is whether the disclosure of clinical material might be harmful to clients. "The federally appointed Privacy Protection Study Commission, after conducting extensive inquiries and holding hearings . . . has reported that 'not one witness was able to identify an instance where access to (one's own) records has had an untoward effect on a patient's condition.' " The commission further reported that ". . . clients' potential access to the files actually improved the quality of the notes, because . . . personnel were striving to enhance accuracy and exclude irrelevancies." (Plotkin, 1978).

In a study of psychiatric inpatients, Stein, Furedy, Simonton, and Neuffer (1979) report that patients who were given access to their records said that they were better informed and more involved in their treatment. Similar to what the Privacy Protection Study Commission found concerning record keeping, Stein et al. also note increased staff conscientiousness in this respect. Roth, Wolford, and Meisel (1980) permitted psychiatric patients to read their records in the presence of a staff member to explain the contents. Access to the complete record was not provided to all patients, however. Under such conditions of limited access the authors report ". . . a generally positive experience for the patients, and harm has not ensued."

How clients subjectively experience having access to their records is probably at least as important an issue as whether they are permitted access. Smith (1978) advises that reports focus on the questions raised, and that simple language—as opposed to jargon and technical language—be used. But no matter how clearly the clinician writes, it appears to be a good idea that a professional be available to explain the report. Hammitt (1982) reports on 100 consecutive admissions to Madison State Hospital who were tested for word recognition and reading comprehension. Some 54 percent of the patients scored below the seventh-grade level, from which she concluded that large numbers of state hospital patients are "functionally illiterate." However, intelligent, well-educated persons may also experience problems in understanding when their own psyche is the topic.

Confidentiality

The sharing of information with clients may be a less troublesome issue than making records available to nonclinical personnel. The danger is that of breaching confidentiality. The psychologist must be aware that records may become involved in legal proceedings, even though they were not prepared for any such purpose. He or she obviously is in a difficult position when a court orders the disclosure of information that was received with the explicit understanding that it would be held confidential.

Therefore, the psychologist should be familiar with the law as it pertains to *privileged communication* of *psychological* records—the right of the client to bar personal information given to a professional person from being made available in a legal proceeding. (Psychiatric, i.e., "medical" records may be regarded differently by the law in various jurisdictions.) The mere awareness that such records might be subpoenaed, should make the psychologist cautious.

The presence of the ubiquitous computer sounds a further note of caution. For example, information must be submitted to insurance companies as a condition of payment for psychological services. Such information routinely is stored in computers. Unfortunately, persons with no legitimate right to confidential information, have been known to gain access to computer memory.

Forensic Reports
and Expert Testimony

"I have almost invariably found the clinician's report to be a gold mine of material with which to challenge his conclusions. A careful review of the report should be done with sensitivity to omissions as well as conclusions. . . . Not uncommonly, material in one part of the report will be discrepant with material in another part." Thus writes Ziskin (1981), a psychologist-lawyer whose two-volume work addressed to lawyers is intended to serve the purpose of "destroying or diminishing the credibility of opposing mental health experts." Ziskin's is but one of several "canned attacks on psychological testimony" that are available to the legal profession (King & Leli, 1979). The psychologist who writes reports on which testimony will be based might do well to study the ways in which professional opinions can be vulnerable—or be made to appear vulnerable, which may also provide grounds for a courtroom victory. Appearances, as well as credibility of the expert witness, count heavily.

Material that the psychologist presents must therefore be convincing and within the concrete understanding of judges and jurors. Cohen (1979) quotes from the writings of no less an authority than Freud (1913/1959b) to illustrate the sort of testimony that should *not* be offered:

The first . . . chance actions of the patient . . . will betray one of the governing complexes of the neurosis. A clever young philosopher, with leanings toward aesthetic exquisiteness, hastens to twitch the crease in his trousers into place before lying down for the first sitting; he reveals himself as an erstwhile coprophiliac of the highest refinement, as was to be expected of the developed aesthete. A young girl on the same occasion hurriedly pulls the hem of her skirt over her exposed ankle; she has betrayed the kernel of what analysis will discover later, her narcissistic pride in her bodily beauty and her tendencies to exhibitionism.

Cohen suggests that an attorney would have little difficulty in successfully challenging the *credibility* of Freud were he to present such clinical insights by way of testimony.

The substance of an attorney's attack on testimony will likely not be on the psychologist's conclusions per se but more on the methods and theories that give rise to those conclusions (Schwitzgebel & Schwitzgebel, 1980). It is "scientific adequacy" that is likely to be challenged. Hence the need for the psychologist to be fully knowledgeable about the instruments used in arriving at conclusions. Such issues as validity, reliability, techniques of administration, scoring, interpretation, cultural and other bias, and behavioral norms may be raised by the cross-examining attorney, and the psychologist had better be deft in reciting current pertinent knowledge.

The well-read attorney may be expected to raise questions on quite technical matters, such as the F-K Index, the standardization of the MMPI, the validity or reliability coefficients of instruments, or the conclusions of particular studies. Ziskin, for example, cites abundant evidence from the literature that impugns the validity and legal usefulness of the psychological armamentarium of tests in general and also of a number of widely used instruments such as the WAIS, the Rorschach, the TAT, the MMPI, the Bender, and Figure Drawing. Unmentioned, of course, are those studies whose conclusions support their use or even those aspects of "negative" studies that are favorable to the instruments. The responsible psychologist will be familiar with these. Also helpful are compilations such as those by Gilbert (1978, 1980) and Ogdon (1981) that list research relating test data with possible interpretations. Although such material normally would not be recommended for inclusion in the written report, the psychologist might draw on such material in the courtroom to support the manner in which conclusions were gained.

Poythress (1980) recommends a similar defensive mode for psychologists whose opinions are challenged with "learned treatises." He cites the sort of evidence with which psychologists might be confronted and then suggests rebuttal tactics and rebuttal sources. For example, the assertion that "mental health professionals (psychiatrists or psychologists) cannot distinguish the mentally ill or insane person from the normal or sane person" likely would rest on Rosenhan's widely known study (1973). Poythress recommends "absolute denial that Rosenhan's paper has any relevance for the judgment of legal insanity" and suggests as a rebuttal source the critique of a recognized authority (Spitzer, 1976). The responsible psychologist, however, will not seek to defend indefensible positions. Regarding the issue of future dangerousness, which tends to be overpredicted by psychologists and other clinicians, if there is need to make such a prediction it should be done with appropriate qualification or be stated in probability terms. Two of Poythress' suggestions may be helpful:

> Your Honor, my clinical impression is that the defendant may be physically assaultive in the near future if not hospitalized and treated soon; however, I should warn the court that predictions in this area are highly inaccurate and there is risk of hospitalizing a nondangerous person.
> [Also,] Your Honor, while the absolute risk for suicide in this patient is low, his disorder of psychotic depression places him in a relatively high-risk group for suicides; some studies (e.g., Pokorny, 1964) indicate a suicide risk level 53 times that of the suicide risk level for the "normal person."

There are many occasions in which the psychologist must be cautious. Morse (1978) suggests that the sort of data that courts seek from mental health professionals is primarily social, moral, or legal, not scientific. Clinicians should therefore attempt to answer only those questions where they have expertise and adequately validated tools.

Matters of form demand utmost consideration. For example, Cohen (1979) advises on the importance of record keeping: "Clear, concise statements summarizing your contacts with the patient are looked upon favorably by judges and juries." Dillon and Wildman's (1979) practical guide includes the following:

> Typically, the psychologist is required to submit a written report to the court. The authors advocate the three part format advanced by McGarry (1976). The three parts are: 1. Restate the questions you have been asked to address. This should demonstrate to the officers of the court that you know what the relevant questions are. 2. Summarize your findings in a mental status type manner. This will document the clinical material you are basing your opinion on. 3. State your opinions about the legal questions asked.

In typical clinical practice such cautions as restating the questions asked would be superfluous.

In general, however, sound court practice is the same as sound clinical practice. Thus Dillon and Wildman warn that jargon should be avoided in forensic reports and that the language used be comprehensible to lay persons: "We have found it helpful to use descriptive terms as much as possible, and to try to define technical terms when they have to be used." Cohen (1979) suggests that ". . . mental health professionals would do well to supplement or, if possible, exchange their psychiatric diagnoses for clear behaviorial descriptions, complete with concrete behavioral vignettes that support their conclusions."

THE CLIENT IS AN INDIVIDUAL

In the diagnostic-treatment situation the psychologist's reason for being is to represent the client in the relevant terms of unique behavior, overt or covert. Perhaps the meaning of uniqueness as used here should be defined in terms of an orientation to human behavior. This is based largely on the idiographic approach, which stresses that each human being has a personality and behaviors that are different from those of all other persons; this individuality distinguishes relevant psychological features of one person from another as do fingerprints. Widespread traits, factors, clusters, constellations, complexes, types, pathological dispositions, and temperaments can be identified and ascribed to persons, but such descriptions must remain general and tend to omit much of what is important. Concern with these descriptions is only the first step in understanding an individual. The clinical approach, with its interest in the generally recognized human qualities, stresses that these are different in strength, in idiosyncrasies (which may be subtle but of the greatest importance), in terms of level and configuration, and in forms and occasions of expression.

In a previous publication the writer summarized some of the more common practices involved in general as opposed to individual clinical descriptions (Tallent, 1958). What is probably the most common of these is termed the *Aunt Fanny Description.* This designation seems appropriate because the report reader, on noting the characteristics ascribed to the client—what the client *has*—might well think, "So has my Aunt Fanny!" Thus, "The client has traits of immaturity," or ". . . he has dependency needs," or "has latent homosexual strivings." Such statements can hardly differentiate among people or point up what is unique—a person's specific needs, deficiencies, strengths, stresses, or implications for the treatment of a troubled person. A study by Davenport (1952) lends support to this impression held by many psychologists. This is not to say that all statements in a report need be of differentiating value in and of themselves, for even the most objective statements take on additional meaning as they are appropriately modified and integrated with other findings. For example, you don't really know much about a person when told, "Her IQ is 115." This statement is true of millions of people (or at least would be if we tested many millions of persons). The information is not sufficient to judge whether the person might make a superior teacher or regularly get lost between the bus stop and her house. However, when a statement about an individual's IQ is appropriately linked with other information—interests, attitudes, goals, defense mechanisms, formal thought processes, memory function—the contribution can become highly meaningful.

The following "psychological report" is a hoax. It was prepared by Dr. Norman Sundberg (1956) along with an accompanying explanation and is reproduced with permission. It was selected as a good example of the Aunt Fanny technique. Overlooking the fact that Fanny is a female appellation, this particular case report is, at least to a degree, applicable to many schizophrenic persons. Dr. Sundberg comments, "We had a lot of fun presenting it and discussing it at the Oregon Psychological Association meeting. It was quite impressive how it seemed to fit the case when it was actually presented."[1]

Completely Blind Analysis of the Case of A Schizophrenic Veteran
—Norman D. Sundberg

(Written before knowing *anything* about the patient except that he was a new admission to the Roseburg VAH and was to be worked up for an OPA meeting.)

This veteran approached the testing situation with some reluctance. He was cooperative with the clinician, but was mildly evasive on some of the material. Both the tests and the past history suggest considerable inadequacy in interpersonal relations, particularly with members of his family. Although it is doubtful whether he has ever had very close relationships with anyone, the few apparently close relationships which he has had were tinged with a great deal of ambivalence. He has never been able to sink his roots very deeply. He is immature, egocentric and irritable, and often he mis-perceives the good intentions of the people around him. Projection is one of his prominent defense mechanisms. He tends to be basically passive and dependent, though there are occasional periods of resistance and rebellion against others. Although he shows some seclusiveness and autistic trends, he is in fair to good contact with reality. Vocationally, his adjustment has been very poor. Mostly he has drifted from one job to another. His interests are shallow and he tends to have poor motivation for his work. Also, he has had a hard time keeping his jobs because of difficulty in getting along with fellow employees. Though he has had some affairs, his sex life has been unsatisfactory to him. At present, he is mildly depressed, although a great deal of affect is not shown. What physical complaints he has appear mainly to have a functional origin. His intelligence is close to average, but he is functioning below his full capacity. In summary, this is a long-time inadequate or borderline adjustment pattern. Test results and case history, though they do not give a strong clear-cut diagnostic picture, suggest the diagnosis of schizophrenia, chronic undifferentiated type. Prognosis for response to treatment appears to be poor.

This completely blind analysis is based on the following assumptions:

1. The veteran being referred for psychological testing is not likely to be an obvious or clear-cut diagnostic case. There is no need for testing unless there is some indecision. Consequently, hedging is to be expected on a report anyway.
2. This is a schizophrenic case. Given the general class of schizophrenia, one can work back to some of the characteristics which belong in that class and have a fair chance of being right.

[1]Personal communication.

3.   There are some modal characteristics of patients coming to VA hospitals. In placing bets on what the patient is likely to be like, the best guess would be a description of the modal personality. For instance most of the veterans coming to Roseburg are chronic cases who have not succeeded in jobs or in family life. Also, the best guess on intelligence would obviously be average intelligence, but since the person is a psychiatric patient it is likely that he is not functioning at his best.

4.   There are also certain modal behaviors of the clinical staff. They use certain words, certain jargon; they have a preference for certain diagnoses. Oftentimes, a large percentage of the cases wind up with the diagnosis of schizophrenia, chronic undifferentiated type.

5.   There are some "universally valid" adjectives which are appropriate for almost any psychiatric patients, such as "dependent," "immature," "irritable," and "egocentric."

6.   In the less clear areas where modal characteristics are not known, it is more safe to write a vague statement or one which can be interpreted in various ways. Readers can be counted on to overlook a few vague misses and to select the descriptions which jibe with their own preconception.

7.   All this is intended to say that we have much in common with the old fortune teller, and that what we need is better ways of dealing with individuality. Knowing modal personalities is very useful; it certainly adds to each of social communication; however, we are sometimes fooled into thinking that we know persons when actually all we know is our own stereotypes.

A good definition for the Aunt Fanny description might note that ". . . descriptions from tests are made to fit the patient largely or wholly by virtue of their triviality; and in which any nontrivial, but perhaps erroneous, inferences are hidden in a context of assertions or denials which carry high confidence simply because of the population base rate, regardless of the test's validity." It is, however, Meehl's (1956) definition of the *Barnum Report*. We prefer the following definition of the Barnum Report because its essence is to give the "customer" a palatable report. The use of high base rate statements is but part of the technique. The late D. G. Paterson's Barnum Report—the original Barnum Report quoted below—also sought acceptance by the use of flattery, which is not a feature of Aunt Fanny statements. If there is a real distinction between Aunt Fanny and Barnum, it is important that such distinction be recognized for the implications it might have both for research and for teaching psychological report writing. We can also sometimes note a negative Barnum Effect, as for example, when a psychiatrist or an administrator is "sold a bill of goods" to confirm a negative impression of an individual. Such a ploy might be an instance of Klopfer's (1960) *Madison Avenue Report* (p. 17).

The Barnum Report is viewed by the present writer (Tallent, 1958) as a method "to describe a personality by using a few mildly negative generalities which are quickly neutralized in a matrix of acceptable, even flattering remarks, both types of comments being apparently applicable to almost everybody." In short, a Barnum Report is readily "validated" by the subject about whom it supposedly is written. This was demonstrated, to the writer's satisfaction, when he passed out Professor Paterson's original Barnum Report to members of a college class, with the explanation that it was an individual personality analysis that the instructor had arrived at through inspections of samples of the students' handwriting. The report was unanimously accepted as accurate by all 39 class members, with the exception of two students who indicated very slight error. The potency of the evaluation was punctuated by several of the more startled (or least inhibited) students making exclamations like "Uncanny!" and "This is me all right!"

This sort of "validation" has been studied under more exacting conditions by Forer (1949), Sundberg (1955), Carrier (1963), Ulrich, Stachnik, and Stainton (1963), Manning (1968), Richards and Merrens (1971), Snyder (1974), Snyder and Larson (1972), Bradley and Bradley (1977), Snyder, Shenkel, and Lowery (1977), Greene (1977), Snyder, Handelsman, and Endelman (1978), Greene (1978), Jackson (1978), Layne (1978, 1979), Petty and Brock (1979), Shenkel, Snyder, Batson, and Clark (1979), Snyder and Cowles (1979), Layne and Ally (1980). However, it should be noted that all of the Barnum literature to date reports on studies of the acceptability of high base rate statements to the persons who supposedly are described by such stereotyped material. Still needed are studies of the extent to which clinicians accept as valid such material when it is written about their clients.

Paterson originally used the Barnum Report as a lesson to business executives on irresponsible personnel evaluation practices. Passing out copies to groups of executives, he obtained excellent results by asking how many recognized themselves in "their" personality descriptions. (Professor Paterson's report is reprinted here by permission.)

> **Abilities:** Above average in intelligence or mental alertness. Also above average in accuracy—rather painstaking at times. Deserves a reputation for neatness—dislikes turning out sloppy work. Has initiative; that is, ability to make suggestions and to get new ideas, open-mindedness.
>
> **Emotions:** You have a tendency to worry at times but not to excess. You do get depressed at times but you couldn't be called moody because you are generally cheerful and rather optimistic. You have a good disposition although earlier in life you have had a struggle with yourself to control your impulses and temper.
>
> **Interests:** You are strongly socially inclined, you like to meet people, especially to mix with those you know well. You appreciate art, painting and music, but you will never be a success as an artist or as a creator or composer of music. You like sports and athletic events but devote more of your attention to reading about them in the sporting page than in actual participation.
>
> **Ambitions:** You are ambitious, and deserve credit for wanting to be well thought of by your family, business associates and friends. These ambitions come out most strongly in your tendency to indulge in daydreams, in building aircastles, but this does not mean that you fail to get into the game of life actively.
>
> **Vocational:** You ought to continue to be successful so long as you stay in a social vocation. I mean if you keep at work bringing you in contact with people.

Just what work you pick out isn't as important as the fact that it must be work bringing you in touch with people. On the negative side you would never have made a success at strictly theoretical work or in pure research work such as in physics or neurology.

What may be called the *trade-marked* report (Tallent, 1958) has long been commented upon. This is a report that may overemphasize the psychologist's personal concerns, conflicts, interests, dynamics, or shortcomings at the expense of accurately describing the client. It is an example of eisegesis gone wild. Some psychologists are known in their organizations for always including and loud-pedaling a specific theme—hostility, heterosexual immaturity, homoerotic impulses, compensation for inferiority, presentation of a false facade, or conflict with father, mother, or authority. That this phenomenon exists seems well established (Filer, 1952; Hammer & Piotrowski, 1953; Robinson, 1951; Robinson & Cohen, 1954). Keller (1971) reports preliminary findings that there are three "types" of Rorschach interpreters: the *optimizers* who emphasize health and play down pathology, the *intrapsychic pathologizers,* and the *interpersonal pathologizers,* the latter two fitting the *prosecuting attorney* or the *maladjustment bias* stereotype (discussed below). Woody (1972) relates an anecdote of his meeting with a colleague, both psychologists having had the experience of attending workshops delivered by a certain Dr. X, but separated by a ten-year interval. The colleague tells Woody, "I attended that same workshop about ten years ago," and then proceeds to query, "Tell me, does the good Doctor X still find 'paranoid schizophrenics with latent homosexual tendencies' in every clinical record?" It is perhaps some comfort that such tendencies appear to be shared by clinicians of various disciplines. Observed at a staff conference was a nonpsychologist who appeared to interpret sex as the crucial dynamic in every case but could not seem to "see" the role of "hostility." The nonpsychologist impatiently asked a psychologist, who had just read his report, where he "got" all the hostility. The instant reply: "The same place where you 'get' all the sex."

Nonindividual reporting may also be seen in psychodynamically oriented reports in what has been called the *prosecuting attorney brief.* "Such reports are saturated with . . . negative dynamics . . . but give little or no attention to postive features, to commendable conscious strivings, socially valuable compensations, and other well-used defenses. These reports consistently reflect the motto 'always interpret at the lowest possible level of psychosexual fixation or regression.' They are prepared by psychological simians who hear no good, see no good, and report no good" (Tallent, 1958). This sort of reporting is what Klopfer (1960) calls the *maladjustment bias.* These observations, of course, refer to the extent to which reports are saturated with pathology. It goes without saying that a patient in a clinical setting does in fact have severe difficulties, impulses, and strivings that we may regard as unfortunate, and maladaptive defenses. These should be reported as they are meaningful. The point is that *appropriate* emphasis ought to be given to *relevant* positive features. But certainly all of the favorable qualities are not relevant. One probably need not write of a neurotic patient as being "in contact," as showing no thinking disorders, as having a satisfying heterosexual adjustment, or as having an IQ of 135 (if intelligence is not a factor in the person's clinical situation).

POINTS OF VIEW
ON INTERPRETATION
OF PSYCHOLOGICAL DATA

One of the major issues in the writing of psychological reports centers on the presentation of raw data or of incompletely interpreted data. If raw data are to be offered to the person who referred the case or to other team members, the next questions are: How much raw data? How shall such raw data be selected? For what purpose(s) shall raw data be utilized in the report? Or, from a different viewpoint, To what extent shall the psychologist interpret data for consumers of the report? On what basis may the psychologist decide what is to be interpreted and what not interpreted? Shall only interpreted data be reported? At the other extreme, Shall no interpreted data be offered? Does the presentation of raw data obviate the need for its interpretation, or should (or may) an interpretation be accompanied by raw data either in a supportive or illustrative role?

Before attempting to cope with these questions, a definition of raw data and the range of possible "rawness" should be considered. English and English (1958) define "data/raw" as "data not yet submitted to logical or statistical analysis." In working with an individual client, it is the logical analysis of data that concerns us. Thus the data with which the psychologist deals differ vastly in terms of how much logical analysis is required before they can be viewed as meaningful or can contribute to useful action.

At one extreme are data that require highly skilled interpretation and have to be considered only in the context of a battery protocol. What competent psychologist would offer an interpretation of 4 Rorschach M responses without considering also their form level, popularity or originality, whether "easy" or "hard" M, the cards where seen, possible associated determinants, preceding and succeeding responses, the content, the particular verbalization of the content, color usage, pathognomonic signs, intelligence level, fantasy content, and so on? At the other extreme are responses that require minimal interpretation. Such responses often occur in interview, on sentence completion tests, or on other self-report or other report forms, which are, in effect, controlled interview situations. Thus the completions "Most people I know . . . can't be trusted," and "Those I work with . . . are out to get me" are apparently quite simple matters for interpretation. Similarly with such "critical items" from a parent's responses to the *Personality Inventory for Children* (Wirt, Lachar, Klinedinst, & Seat, 1977): "The child hardly ever smiles," and "The child is usually rejected by other children." Yet even here the psychologist must utilize some logical analysis, such as judging whether the person is sincere, malingering, or otherwise trying to create an impression; how consistent the particular responses are with the full test protocol and other available information; and what significance the material might have. Data perhaps intermediate in the level of interpretive skill required are represented by statements such as "On four TAT cards the hero was depicted as in conflict with a father figure." Commonly appearing in psychological reports, statements of this sort are really descriptions of raw data, not basic raw data. To offer statements of this sort, the psychologist must use professional judgment, hence some degree of interpretation takes place. We may also speak in this vein of "incompletely interpreted data." Other statements in this class are "loose use of color," "concrete thinking," or "syncretistic thinking."

Psychologists do not generally present raw data without what they consider an adequate interpretation of such material. Thus taken from a report, "Rorschach responses such as '. . . Two wolves . . . they both have their teeth dug into some person as though they're trying to tear him apart . . . a person who has taken on the wings of a butterfuly . . . deformed embryos inside the womb . . . an infected vagina . . . a faint suggestion of evil spirits inside the womb . . . octopuses with horse's heads . . . two snakes seem to be trying to gain access to this vagina-like symbol'—are evidences of a severe formal thought disorder when personal material is involved. This is marked by primitive, symbolic and dream-like associations and percepts, and by an accompanying loss of appropriate distance from stimuli which results in his making poor judgments in terms of the total situation."

Even though there are copious amounts of such raw data in some psychological reports, psychologists tend to feel that the appropriateness of including them depends on their purpose. There is widespread feeling among this group that it is all right to present material such as in the preceding example, but for illustrative reasons only. Had the conclusions preceded the data here, it would have been more evident that they were meant to illustrate conclusions, not to carry the freight. On the other hand, themes like the following are currently taboo among many psychologists, although other team members might find them more acceptable.

> On the Object Assembly subtest, the patient seemed at a loss as to where to begin. He picked up pieces at random and attempted to fit the parts together in an unplanned fashion. Finally, he stated his inability to solve the problem and gave up the task.
>
> This patient's verbal IQ is 91 and his performance score is 105. The Comprehension score (11) is five points greater than Information (6). The high subtest score is on Object Assembly, the weighted score being 14, while his lowest is a 3 scored on Arthmetic.

A number of psychologists feel threatened by the idea that they must present such data to others presumably more qualified to make the proper interpretations. Similarly there is widespread objection to being required to support one's conclusions with data, since this procedure might also imply that other professional groups have qualifications to judge the adequacy of the psychologist's interpretation of data.

There is a case frequently presented for the use of raw data in psychological reports. Some psychiatrists point out correctly that it is traditional for the physician to coordinate findings from diverse sources—the physician's own examination, consultants' reports, laboratory findings, social history—and to reach conclusions through the integration of all such data. He or she accepts responsibility for these and for the actions stemming from them. The medical consultant therefore helps a clinician by presenting a narrative report that makes liberal reference to the data on which impressions are based. Notice by way of illustration the ratio of raw data to interpretation in the following report written by a pathologist for a surgeon:

> Specimen consists of a 2 cm. cyst lined with soft cheesy material.
>   Microscopic: Section reveals the cyst to be lined with flattened epidermis and the contents to consist of hyalinized, lamellated, desquamated, keratinized, epithelial cells.
>   Impression: Skin, sebaceous cyst.

It therefore particularly behooves the psychologist who is working in a medical setting to examine whether a departure from what physicians do is justified.

The experienced psychologist is in a position to cite a number of pertinent differences between medical and psychological consultations. Most obvious, personality-behavior is made of stuff that is patently different from physiological-anatomical variables. Meaningful findings are deduced only after hundreds of bits of discrete data are sifted and pondered, studied for consistency and the meanings of apparent inconsistencies, and all of the data units studied as they are given significance or are modified by the data of the entire protocol and other pertinent information.

The logical extreme of presenting raw data to support conclusions or to help the person who referred the case independently to reach conclusions is of course to present all of the data available on any given client. This practice would yield an unwieldy document of many pages, with little practical utility. Most psychologists would oppose such use of data, even when offered to associates highly trained in personality, contending that test data should be interpreted only by those who are expert in personality and psychological assessment methods.

A potent objection to presenting raw data so that the person who made the referral can make independent interpretations, "follow" the interpretations of the psychologist, or judge their correctness is simply that the practice is not valid. There is not a one-to-one relationship between datum and interpretation; neither is there universal symbolism that would permit translation from test material to client. The raw data on which interpretations are really made are far more extensive than test data. They include an experienced knowledge of the stimuli that elicited the data, an awareness of the relationship and effects of test stimulus and examiner stimulus, all sorts of behavioral variables, such as the person's tone of voice and facial expression, the entire context in which responses occurred, and all other relevant data.

A major factor pertinent to the question of presenting raw data—a factor that should be disconcerting to the clinician or other consumer of the psychologist's services who would use the data to draw independent conclusions or to check on the psychologist's conclusions—is that the psychologist in the presence of volumes of raw data must, of necessity, be selective. And herein lies a telling criticism of such a procedure. It is the psychologist's judgment that determines what raw data should be selected for presentation—certainly an uncontrolled procedure of questionable validity. The psychologist cannot decide on what raw data to include in the report until *after* weighing the merits of some particular data. Unfortunate selection could come about through insufficient competence or be used nefariously by one having need to present certain conclusions and to justify them.

There is considerable feeling that raw data may legitimately be used for illustrating conclusions, perhaps linking the two in such fashion that the source of the conclusion is explicit (Mayman, 1959). This procedure may often have much to recommend it and in some instances may be as close to imperative as can any rule for report writing. Particularly vivid or transparent material, judged by the psychologist to be a valid illustration of the conclusions it is intended to bolster, can be most effective—for example, "All the cards remind me of death, just sorrow and death." However, a response like "two bears with their tails cut off" may be transparent to the psychologist, particularly in the light of other data, but all readers may not reach similar conclusions. There is a danger that the use of such material may "backfire," a reader gaining quite a different conclusion from the psychologist or feeling that the illustration is not sufficient to support the psychologist's conclusion. Since the material is selective, the reader should be made aware that the illustrations are not fully supportive of the conclusions they advance.

Raw data may be required when conclusions rest largely on quantitative input, for example, in the diagnosis of mental retardation. The assessment of deficit based on neurological or other factors may also be documented with scores. Neuropsychological testing commonly generates volumes of data, and many psychologists find it helpful to put them in an appendix attached to the report.

A frequently safe and helpful procedure is for the psychologist to share raw data with an interested associate on a personal basis where the material may adequately be discussed. The central principles involved in the offering of raw data are (1) careful attention to the appropriateness of the circumstances of the procedure, with the wisdom of the illustrations used considered carefully from the standpoint of both validity and effectiveness, and (2) the inability of the psychologist ethically to relinquish responsibility for conclusions. Just as the physician, for good reason, is charged with coordinating all available clinical data and reaching conclusions based on them, the psychologist must coordinate all psychologically relevant material and reach independent conclusions.

THE FLAVOR OF THE REPORT

What may be called the "flavor" of the report comes in for a good deal of attention, from the readers if not also from the writers of psychological reports. The significance of the flavor is that it may readily influence the attitude of the reader. Such attitudes, positive or negative, may then contribute to what the reader derives. In addition, the flavor is inextricably enmeshed with such other matters as technical level and orientation, terminology, psychologist's attitude, and role concept. All of these have implications for the acceptance and effectiveness of the report.

Background, training, self-needs, and personality idiosyncrasies all may influence the flavor of the report. These contribute to reports that may be described by such adjectival expressions as "abstract," "theoretical," "academic," "intellectual," "erudite," or "learning theory oriented." Typical are reports with a concrete psychometric emphasis or reports that are more or less behavioral or psychoanalytic. There are also reports that exude an authoritative tone or are exhibitionistic. Although any of these flavors may arouse disapproval, disinterest, or antagonism in the reader, the latter two are regarded as particularly defeating professionally, not only because others are not likely to respond kindly to them, but also because such writing is incompatible with scientific tentativeness and modesty.

Styles of Reports

Psychological reports are sometimes categorized into one of three basic styles, although it would be easy to nominate others. These may be called the *clinical style,* the *scientific style,* and the *literary style*—which at the extreme may perhaps better be labeled "dramatic" or "flowery." No general agreement exists concerning the relative merits of each, but one does overhear comments, and the opinions of clinical workers may be formally surveyed (Tallent & Reiss, 1959b). For example, the following statement, intended as a specimen of literary writing of a somewhat dramatic sort, achieved significant popular support from clinical workers, yet many others did not feel that it suited their taste: "Crushed and defeated by telling setbacks, the patient feels unable to continue to fight what she sees as an oppressive environment."

The clinical style focuses upon pathology, maladjustment, deficiency, and equilibrative processes, and some would say that the report more nearly describes a case than a person. The orientation, of course, is basically medical and normative. An emphasis in this vein might make it hard to account for such behavioral variables as attitudes, sentiments, or relationships, unless these are diseased or associated with disease.

The scientific style, by partial contrast, is more closely related to the academic psychologist's discipline. This approach stresses the normative, and sometimes also the pathological. It differs from the clinical most in its relation to a conceptual scheme of personality or to a theory of assessment. This style would apparently be particularly compatible with approaching a personality through its segments or part processes and dealing with these in some detail. Here the psychologist becomes involved with what, for convenience of study, might be regarded as discrete functions—intellection, perception, emotion—or finer divisions of these—much as the physician may be concerned with units of clinical study like the cardiovascular system, the genitourinary system, or the neuropsychiatric system.

This approach is subject to attack from a number of directions. It would seem to do violence to the concept of personality unity (this most important matter is considered in Chapter Five) and may also appear to many to be overly "cold" and impersonal. This approach may cause the reader to feel there was no person present at all. We must be aware that many clinical workers, particularly those in disciplines other than psychology, do not have empathy with scientific-sounding reports. Another hazard is that a scientific presentation with an unusually strong laboratory flavor may reinforce the commonly held impression that psychology renders laboratory rather than consultant services.

The scientific emphasis of modern experimental and quantitative psychology is the basis on which many clinicians and others, in and out of psychology, argue that the psychological report is a scientific document. As such, it is thought proper that the report be exclusively concerned with the "findings," that which is factual; any mention of application, or of an emphasis on application, is regarded by some as latter-day sophistry. However, a great distinction needs to be made between science and its application to workaday purposes. The psychological report is a practical document, and when it is not designed to be effective, its very purpose may be defeated. It is understandable that the more palatable and comprehensible the report, the more usable it is. To merely present ideas or conclusions is not enough; they must be "brought home" or "gotten across" to the reader or they are lost, and the psychologist's mission is aborted. The psychologist must write in whatever style is appropriate and effective, using literary, clinical, and scientific styles in whatever combination necessary, using material that is objective, phenomenological, or whatever, again, as it appears to be effective and appropriate.

Archibald MacLeish suggests that the purpose of education is to weld the fact with the feel. The function of the psychologist is perhaps similar, the task being to present an integration of technical material with a feeling for the person. Many psychologists presumably operate on this premise. Recoiling from the scientific, they tend in the direction of, and sometimes get lost in, the literary. They sometimes fall into the methods of the previously given example of literary writing. Here and there a literary twist may help in capturing the flavor of the person, but to do this effectively, using facts to instill a feel for the person means presenting him or her as an individual. This objective is accomplished partly by the fortunate use of language, but mostly by developing the proper content, by understanding what the clinically relevant personality processes are and how these relate to one another, and finally by organizing these so that what is most vital stands out and what is less vital supports the essence of the presentation. The psychologist has to understand the person (a much bigger job than test interpretation) and then to convey that understanding to another.

The Use of "Human Interest"

We may profitably borrow from the newspaper people some methods of conceptualizing and presenting a theme. The traditional news item is a cut-and-dried affair concerned only with the "facts." Generations of cub reporters have learned their five W's—Who, What, When, Where, and Why—and the accounts of two reporters assigned to cover a fire on Main Street would probably read very much alike. Psychologists might even commend such similarity as evidence of a high degree of interobserver reliability.

But all newspaper stories are not the same; some strive for effect, for deeper understanding, or even for the development of understanding in the reader through "human interest." The latter can be valid enough, not detracting from the accuracy of the story and sometimes contributing to it.

Writing can, and often ought, to include both factual and affective elements—a point which Flesch (1949/1974) has developed well in his book on readable writing. Each field must develop its own styles. However, since the subject matter of psychology, like that of journalism, commonly involves the emotions of people, these can be incorporated in the report to describe people effectively and more realistically than when the emotions are exsanguinated in the objectivity of a specimen analysis. Even feature articles about events, new machines, or industrial processes can be "humanized." We shall see in Chapter Five how even some engineers knowingly allow the intrusion of subjectivity both to color their reports and aid them in conceptualizing their tasks. Indeed, great scientists like Einstein may rely heavily on the subjective and even the intuitive. He writes: "I very rarely think in words at

all. A thought comes, and I may try to express it in words afterwards. . .
During all these years there was a *feeling* of direction, of going straight
toward something concrete. It is, of course, very hard to express that *feeling*
in words; but it was decidedly the case and clearly to be distinguished from
later considerations about the rational form of the solution" (Wertheimer,
1945, emphasis added).

In view of the objections raised here to literary, clinical, and scientific
approaches, the reader might wonder what style would be suitable. Why not
a simple, matter-of-fact approach based on everday expository writing?
Such an approach can readily incorporate scientific information as necessary, give pathological manifestations appropriate representation, and retain the flexibility or even sedate license allowed in any creative writing. A
psychological report is, or at least should be, a piece of creative writing.
There is no logical reson why the tone may not approximate the conversa-
tional.

An overly specialized tone seems to be both a barrier to communication
and to understanding, and not infrequently antagonizes the reader. The
demand is for simplicity. This, of course, is distressing to some psychologists.
It disturbs them to consider, even if not to admit, that the complexities of
human behavior revealed by the psychologist's probing can be expressed in
something less than an involved presentation that might even be comprehensible to the psychologically unsophisticated. It is likely that large
numbers of psychologists, because of training or for reasons of conviction or
personal dynamics, cling to these views.

ORIENTATION
OF THE REPORT

An issue related to the problem of flavor is that of orientation, particularly
person-orientation versus test-orientation. The person-oriented report
deals with the functioning of the person and with such real, pertinent
matters as the outlook and recommendations that might prove helpful. The
test-oriented report, by contrast, places its emphasis on test responses, test
scores, and perhaps on relations among test scores. The first kind of report
talks about the person, the other about the person's performance on tests.

Although the test-oriented report is still quite common, there is considerable feeling that reports ought to be person-oriented. Test orientation
probably harks back to the early days of psychometrics and school psychology, when the IQ was regarded at a premium and the various successes and
failures on test items supposedly had some obvious and practical meaning.

The early days of clinical psychology in psychiatric settings again saw
"mental testers" very much concerned with scores and proficiency levels.
The orientation was essentially that of a technician, where the data were

delivered to a clinician for interpretation—an entirely unacceptable procedure in personality assessment in a contemporary psychologist's point of view. However, many psychologists have carried over from early psychometric procedures to modern instruments a propensity to talk about tests rather than about people. At worst, test talk may be used as a veil to conceal the examiner's lack of understanding of the client or lack of ability to present conclusions effectively.

THE MANNER
OF PRESENTING CONCLUSIONS

The reporting of conclusions must be from the standpoint of a psychologist who has achieved certain impressions, or has *not* achieved impressions, about areas of the client's life that are of professional interest. In any event the psychologist's report ought to concentrate on what is known, not on what is not known. It is hardly necessary that the psychologist recapitulate the agonies of weighing data, accepting conclusions, rejecting conclusions, and holding other tentative impressions in abeyance. There is no need to hedge or to be indecisive, or even to "let the reader in on" the decision-making process. The process is complicated, but the major contradiction to a democratic approach is that it would take too many pages to convey the gross and subtle data that could permit the qualified reader to retrace the psychologist's steps. (As already indicated, however, it is desirable, when the personal relationship permits, to discuss such matters with team associates.) It falls upon the psychologist to state conclusions, together with appropriate modifying terms to indicate verbally the degree of confidence with which they are offered.

Speculation

Speculation refers to tentatively held conclusions for which adequate dependable evidence does not exist. Sometimes the psychologist's basis for such conclusions is little more than "impression," which might even stem from features of one's own personality, or from one or two test responses that are interpretively equivocal. Hence speculation refers to conclusions offered at a low level of confidence. One of the greatest sins a psychologist can commit is to fail to point out what is speculation.

In perusing the thousands of negative comments made about psychological reports (some of which form the basis for Chapter 2), one might readily conclude that a major job activity of psychologists is speculating. If there is truth in such a conclusion, so much the worse for psychology. Then what is the occasion for speculating? Legitimately, speculation may be in order when few definitive data are available and an important issue requiring attention is raised by the person making the referral, or when the psychologist becomes aware of such an issue during examination of a client.

An uncertain answer may be better than none in *some* cases, particularly if it is not misleading. Blank (1965) suggests that ". . . waiting for ironclad proof [not an event occurring with great frequency] leads to a sterile report." It may be important in certain cases to speculate about such matters as suicide, homicide, antisocial sexual behavior, cerebral pathology, or rehabilitation potential. Inadequate information about such matters may suggest the need for further investigations by a social worker, a medical specialist, or another who might be able to throw light on the topic. However, speculation about matters that are not especially relevant may not be defensible. An example of this might be speculation about developmental events in a patient who is being seen in a setting where treatment is almost entirely by medication.

Transfer of Responsibility

A final comment on the manner of presenting conclusions pertains to the transfer of responsibility for conclusions from the psychologist to tests—for example, "Psychological testing reveals . . . ," "The Rorschach shows . . .," "Stories given to the TAT point up a person who. . . ." It is hardly quibbling to insist that psychological tests reveal or indicate nothing. The psychologist uses tests but reaches conclusions that involve clinical judgment (and theory) as well (Chapter 5). (Typically, in fact, conclusions are based more on a battery than on individual tests.) Sometimes quotes such as the preceding are little more than a manner of speech, but in other cases they reflect a psychologist's lack of confidence in self or in conclusion(s). The psychologist is hiding behind tests. The effect on the reader might not always be what the psychologist desired. In fact, this way of presenting conclusions might prompt referrals asking for administration of certain tests because of the sort of information they are thought to reveal. The belief of nonpsychologically trained readers—lawyers or judges, for example—that decisions affecting a person's life turn on a test (whose validity might be challenged in the literature and consequently in courts of law) rather than on a psychologist, a responsible human, may lead to some unsought outcomes. Ulrich, Stachnik, and Stainton (1963), in a study of gullibility to generalized personality interpretations, point to results that indicate ". . . the awe with which personality tests per se are viewed by the naive student or others of comparable test sophistication"—that is, many readers of psychological reports. Snyder and Larson (1972) report similar findings.

PRIMARY PRESENTATION
OF THE REPORT

The mode of primary presentation of the report may have a bearing on how it is written, although this need not be so. Many persons find it easier to absorb technical material by eye than by ear. When a report is requested for oral staff presentation or is likely to serve this purpose, special attention is necessary in the preparation. Reports heard in staff meetings may often be characterized as "involved," "complex," or "saturated," and many are difficult to understand when presented orally. However, it is often possible to derive meaning, sometimes important meaning, on reading these same reports. It would be a worthwhile objective, then, to write reports suitable both for written and oral presentation.

TERMINOLOGY
IN THE REPORT

Everyone probably agrees that a piece of writing ought to be comprehensible to its intended readers. Psychological reports are read by persons with various kinds of training and backgrounds, and it is not possible to know in advance who all of the readers might be. Terminology obviously is one of the matters related to comprehensibility, and the question of appropriate terminology has not yet been settled. Psychological terminology is viewed by many as highly technical and specialized, complex, and esoteric (Tallent & Reiss, 1959c). Is it possible to substitute something simpler?

Sargent (1951) thinks not. At least in writing for consumers familiar with psychological constructs, she observes that, in the context of relating "the degree and kind of abnormal psychological functioning . . . technical terms and concepts are . . . considered to be more economical and cogent carriers of meaning . . . than if they were to be translated into everyday language." Hammond and Allen (1953) go further. They contend that "technical vocabulary is indispensable for three reasons: first, it is precise; second, it can communicate concepts that are virtually impossible to convey in ordinary language; and third, it is economical." These writers do point out that the amount of technical verbiage used should be gauged by the ability of the intended reader(s) to understand and should be appropriate to the context, but for communicating "complex technical concepts with precision to a qualified reader," such a vocabulary is "indispensable."

A case can also be made against the use of technical terminology. Hammond and Allen themselves discuss frankly the shortcomings of such language as used in psychological reports and suggest some remedies. These writers effectively point out the difficulties the psychologist may face in the use of such words and the lack of understanding or the misunderstanding they may cause in the reader(s) of the report. Cited are variability in sophistication and orientation among the readers, the specialized meaning of certain terms, and the multiple meanings as well as technical meanings which differ from lay meanings. There is also a demonstrated tendency for professional persons to assign nonconsensual meanings to words commonly used in psychological reports. Here the work of Johnson (1945) and of Grayson and Tolman (1950) is pertinent. As an example of word ambiguity, Grayson and

Tolman classified definitions of *anxiety* contributed by psychologists and psychiatrists—a word which appears in a very high percentage of psychological reports—into no fewer than seven categories of meaning. It would seem that the psychologist must indeed step lightly!

Another meaningful study that gives some understanding of at least the current effects of using technical verbiage is reported by Davenport (1952). She found that interpretive statements taken from case reports frequently did not differentiate adequately among persons and were ambiguous, with psychoanalytic-type expressions the worst offender. This observation calls attention to a special problem about technical words—the issue of analytic terminology. Many psychologists are sharply against its use. Writing that incorporates analytic terminology is more fashionable in some quarters than in others; in some settings it seems to be the expected mode of expression. However, the inexact, nondifferentiating use to which such a vocabularly may be put has caused considerable discussion. There has been for some years now a trend away from psychoanalytic terminology, and even many dynamically oriented psychologists may find it fashionable *not* to use it.

It may be true that technical words are precise, but such precision is to be found only in a carefully defined context associated with *discrete* orientations. It would be a prodigious task to train all writers and readers of psychological reports, even those at the professional level, to accept and learn some common meanings for several hundred words. At present, report readers—teachers, administrators, legal and correctional persons, medical people, and even psychiatrists and psychiatric social workers—typically do not have a large technical *psychological* vocabulary. Further, the multitude of schools, orientations, and loyalties that abound in the psychological domain would be a telling barrier. Nor would the eclectic, whose understanding reflects a number of viewpoints and glossaries, some of them contradictory, fare any better. Indeed, the same writer may use the same word with different meanings. Freud, for example, uses *ego* in various senses. Erikson uses *identity* somewhat differently in different contexts.

What about the argument that technical words "communicate concepts which are virtually impossible to convey in ordinary language" and that they are "economical"? Hammond and Allen point up specific examples: the words *empathy, rapport,* and *subliminal.* These words are said to be "virtually impossible to express in plain English: They may, by means of a lengthy paraphrase, be approximated, but the communication thus achieved is far less complete and *satisfactory* than that produced by use of the terms themselves *when they are fully understood by the reader.*" (emphasis supplied) It does seem that paraphrased technical terms would be longer; how much longer would be determined from the context. The question is, who finds the technical terms more "satisfactory," since the study on "The Trouble with Psychological Reports" compels the belief that very large numbers of readers, and writers, do not? The crucial phrase is, "when they are fully understood by the reader." The findings of the Grayson-Tolman study are too overpowering to suggest that such conditions are readily attainable. The answer to the question of economy is, can fewer words be regarded as economical when they fail to do the job?

Technical psychological words used in a theoretical or a general context are wholly different from what is required in clinically oriented usage; even in a theoretical context such words are meaningful only when they are in a consistent, theoretical framework. Theories, by definition, deal with general phenomena. Clinically oriented psychology deals with the application of specific knowledge of general phenomena to persons. Technical names are certainly appropriate for abstract ideas or occurrences or for scientific notions or occurrences that are subjected to special study. Technical names are appropriate for many ideas or concepts or for phenomena, the understanding of which can suitably be modified with words to meet the individual instance. Individual personality study may be importantly different because of the numerous ways and occasions in which generally identified behaviors or other psychological phenomena are expressed.

Considering the example of *empathy*, to the extent our knowledge of an individual permits we may describe specific situations in which particular usages of this word are identifiable and contributory to the understanding of a unique person. We may glibly talk of an empathic person, but does the person exhibit empathy in all situations—empathy for a Hitler or for modern-day terrorists? It would be better to talk of the surface correlates of empathy, of the depth of the experience, of the kinds of situations that call forth empathic experiences, and perhaps of the kinds of situations in which the "empathic" person experiences feelings quite different from empathy. This approach to personality description is appropriate to clinically oriented psychology. Clinical description has to be specific because it is supposed to be useful, a basis for decision and action. In clinical prediction, where there may be a question of assaultive behavior or suicide, it does not help much to talk of generalized and somewhat ubiquitous psychological phenomena like sadomasochism, hostility, narcissistic wounds, or inadequate empathic development, because Aunt Fanny and perhaps her psychotherapist too may "have" these.

In the clinically oriented mission it is necessary to spell out each conclusion in terms of the occurrences, levels, nuances, and interrelationship of events with the rest of personality. Such an approach is less economical of syllables than is one that relies on technical words to transmit insights. A more careful approach, in fact, may utilize technical verbiage to help establish a set or emphasize a personality component, but not really as organic to the description. For example, "This patient is narcissistic *in the sense that . . .*" or, "He has little confidence in himself and is dominantly oriented to seeking all sorts of support, guidance, and reassurance, essentially an oral person." Notice that the ways in which the person is "oral" are spelled out. In how many ways, grossly, subtly, disguisedly, can one be "oral"? In our view words like *oral, narcissistic, masochistic, immature, compulsive,* and *schizophrenia* are often more concealing than revealing.

Technical words do not cause, but readily lend themselves to, imprecise or incomplete thinking. There is the *error of nominalism,* wherein we simply name a thing or an occurrence and think we understand something of the real world. Of course, this patient is anal, or immature, or insecure, or sadistic. But really, what is this living person, Mary Jones, *like* when she is anal, or immature, or insecure, or sadistic, and what does she *do,* overtly or intrapsychically? Do the terms differentiate, make for understanding? Cannot two persons have dominant traits of sadism, one of them awaiting capital punishment stemming from this characteristic, the other the respectable warden charged with carrying out the sentence? It may be countered that if the psychologist is careful to define the term *as it is used in a particular case,* then the term *would* differentiate among persons. However, then the term itself would become superfluous except, as suggested, that it might be used to help establish a set or emphasize a personality component. In this sense, *sadistic* may be employed as a strong word of dramatic quality to help focus on a central personality theme of personal or social significance. Too many such words obviously cannot be used in one report.

This point of view perhaps requires more evidence, although hopefully the arguments developed at least pose a real challenge to what we regard as the continued irresponsible use of technical language. Two specific questions follow from this challenge. The first is whether it would be desirable to write reports in lay language. It is criticized that such writing permits the least common denominator to set the level of the report. In a sense this is true, but since even professionals trip over technical terms, plain English would seem to meet the need for a clear understanding shared by all readers of the psychological report.

Since technical language is often presumed more scientific, it is well to note Block's (1961) rejection of this point of view and his use of lay language in a quantitative research method (Q-sort technique). He notes, "The orientation of the presently proposed descriptive language is, as Lewin would say a 'contemporaneous' one. *The subject is described as he appears and is understood by the observer at the time of observation.*"

Technical language is sometimes defended as necessary or at least useful as a "professional shorthand." If so, does it have a place in psychological reports, many of whose readers have not been trained in this shorthand? Worse still, in view of the Grayson-Tolman study, showing as it does intraprofessional variation as well as interprofessional variation in the understanding of professional terms, it becomes necessary to redefine the various symbols.

In its current stage of development, the mental health profession, considered collectively, has an appreciable tolerance for terminological looseness, and unambiguous usage of technical words is not yet the rule. It seems to cause little concern to label as *paranoid* one who is defensive and cautious in interpersonal relations, and as *compulsive* a person who is careful, conscientious, ethical, and reliable. You may even hear that all psychologists or all graduate students are *compulsive*—that one has to be in order to negotiate the curriculum.

Such loose usage raises yet an additional question. What is *technical language?* Is *compulsive* still a technical word? Or *paranoid?* Or *identity?* These terms have drifted into the language and are freely used in everyday life sometimes no more carelessly than by some psychologists. They may be used in psychological reports, if used responsibly and meaningfully as suggested in the foregoing discussion. On the other hand, *intratest scatter, critical item, cut-off whole, sex shock, position response* certainly are technical terms, test talk. They can only confuse or befuddle most readers. They have no place in most psychological reports.

There is a common-sense approach to the use of words. Words can be our servants or our master. They are supposed to stand for real phenomena, things, or ideas, and as such they can help us to conceptualize our ideas in terms of real events, or we can allow them to confuse us with generalities, vagaries, ambiguities, and imprecision. There is not necessarily a one-to-one relationship between word and referent, as *a* stands for the side of a given triangle. These facts are further complicated because many words—big words, little-known words, impressive-sounding words—have long been used by psychologists as currency and have an appeal not based on their communication value.

Having noted all this, we might as well conclude, that at least in the present state of the science and the art of psychology, and of language, our word usage is going to be something less than perfect—even as is word usage in many everyday documents. It is difficult in our field not to use at least occasionally such stock-in-trade words as *anxiety, defense,* or *affective,* even though there is inadequate consensus on their meaning. Knowing this, however, we can be careful how we use them. In-context usage well might result in less ambiguity than the out-of-context studies that identified these terms as ambiguous. We may also rationalize that we are still far from perfection in many other areas of human endeavor. Our interpretations are often not perfect either, and we are too aware of the many pitfalls that await the unwary psychologist. The responsible psychologist can produce an effective psychological report, however.

This discussion of terminology, then, is not intended to be totally proscriptive of technical terminology, but the heavily technical reports that were all but universal yesteryear (and which, alas, linger on here and there) are clearly not appropriate to most practical missions. We use some technical terms *in communicating among professionals who can be expected to know these terms* simply because there are no substitutes. In the report on Henry Dennis pp. 183–184) terms like *form constancy* and *position in space,* and the scores obtained on these, are highly meaningful to the intended reader, but the psychologist attenuates the technical psychological material in reporting to the child's physician (p. 184). It is difficult to document an organic brain syndrome (or to do without the term *organic brain syndrome*) without using some technical material. Diagnostic terminology is frequently appropriate in a psychiatric setting, school terminology in a school setting, counseling terminology in a counseling setting. Even though there is insufficient understanding of schizophrenia with accompanying semantic confusion about the term *schizophrenia,* we have no substitute (*split personality* will hardly do!).

UNFAMILIAR CONCEPTS
IN THE REPORT

The use of unfamiliar concepts or materials from the psychologist's tool box can be as great a barrier to effective communication, and evoke much the same personal reaction, as the use of unfamiliar words. Unfamiliar concepts that psychologists are prone to use, to the detriment of the clinical mission, stem from (1) theory, (2) tests, (3) statistics.

Theoretical concepts that give trouble are often carried into the report by equally troublesome words. Many readers remain unenlightened after reading about projection in the classical Freudian sense, "an inverted Oedipal complex," "unconscious fantasy," "an external super-ego," "intermittent reinforcement," the "A-B situation," or "identification with the aggressor." Simply recording test results may suggest that the reader should, but doesn't, know what is being discussed.

Other unfamiliar matter presented to the reader presupposes familiarity with the physical nature of tests and score sheets. This includes talk of the client's performance on the Object Assembly test, a particular response to Card VI (Is that the one with the butterfly?), or a clear spike on the psychopathic deviate scale which is accentuated by unusually low scores on the neurotic triad. Some thoughtful psychologists try to take the reader into consideration by a description intended to be meaningful: "on a test involving the assembly of pieces such as in a jig-saw puzzle . . ." or "on a card showing two male figures commonly seen as father and son. . . ." It is uncertain to what extent these humanitarian essays bring the reader closer to understanding.

Statistical expressions cause a certain amount of dismay, too, although this is not as widespread. Unfortunately, but understandably, reporting in terms of T-scores or percentiles would not be appreciated (Tallent & Reiss, 1959b), although from a technical standpoint these have much to commend them. These concepts can be used effectively, however, even with laypersons, in the context of an oral report if they are explained. Talking about people in terms of norms, standardization data, or standard deviations will probably not be confusing to the untrained inasmuch as such persons will not become sufficiently involved to become confused.

THE LENGTH OF REPORTS

A certain business executive likes to relate the anecdote about the occasion when he assigned a new employee to prepare a report for him. In due time a voluminous piece of writing was returned. Dismayed, the executive pointed out that the required information could be presented on one, or certainly not more than two, pages. "But sir," pleaded the young man, "I don't know that much about the matter you assigned me to."

On purely impressionistic grounds there does not seem to be a necessarily positive correlation between the length of documents and the quality of their content. Some observers insist that in the case of psychological reports, the relationship is a negative one. At any rate, report readers tend to dislike overly long reports, even when they are otherwise good.

The often-noted "length compulsion" probably has a multiple etiology. Teachers often demand long pieces of writing, probably with the idea that this will lead to coping thoroughly with the assigned task. Is it possible to assign a term paper to a college class without a hand going up and a student asking how long it must be? The present-day psychological consultation also seems to encourage long reports. The nonspecific referral is one factor; another would seem to be a defensive attitude in many psychologists which gives rise to unnecessary inclusiveness of topic coverage, heavy detailing, hedging, and superfluous qualifications that are wasteful of space. The long document may then be identified as the "exhaustive report," or, more commonly, the "shotgun report."

Some common-sense considerations might help to reduce the length of reports. But when is a report *too long? It is often too long when it is not conceptualized in terms of the mission.* It probably is too long when the psychologist is unhappy over the length of time required to write it and experiences difficulty in organizing a multitude of details for presentation. It is too long when it contains content that is not relevant or useful, when the detailing is greater than can be put to good use, when low confidence statements (speculations) are presented without an excellent rationale for their inclusion, when the writing is unnecessarily repetitious, when the organization does not evidence "tightness," and when the reader is irritated by the length or limits reading of the report to one or more smaller sections like a summary, a diagnostic impression, or a statement of recommendations.

The Ten Commandments are expressed in 297 words. It took 300 words to write the Declaration of Independence and 266 words to compose the Gettysburg Address. Surely the modern psychologist can try to approach this standard.

4

CONTENT OF THE PSYCHOLOGICAL REPORT

There is presently little consensus on the appropriate content for a psychological report. To start with, the psychologist might question the purpose to which the report will be put and the role that various items of content might play. With this orientation, how well does the "traditional" material of reports stand up to scrutiny? It should become apparent that although certain issues that are commonly discussed in reports are never appropriate, other "traditional" items of content may frequently be incorporated in the report to advantage. The choice and the appropriate emphasis of report content always depend on the case and the mission.

THE PSYCHOLOGIST IN THE ASSESSMENT ROLE is an important source of information about people. Such information, in large measure, is typically based on the interpretation of test performance and observation of the client.

Some, however, think the task of the psychologist should be merely to pass along test "findings." Such a view suggests that the process of clinical communication is a more basic matter than the issue of what to communicate. Quite to the contrary, adequate guidelines for determining what content the psychologist should communicate can be discussed only in general terms; they must be developed for each individual case in terms of specific assessment missions and the settings in which psychologists work. The products of assessment probes ought to be *selected* interpretations. This chapter scrutinizes the development of report content in relation to the mission of the psychologist.

THE MULTIPLE PURPOSE
OF REPORT CONTENT

The usage of psychological reports dictates that content be developed in accordance with (1) the needs of the immediate mission, (2) the anticipation of questions and future needs, and (3) the creation of a record.

Needs of the Mission

The immediate mission must be regarded as having the highest priority, for this is understood in relation to a felt need and is therefore the only purpose (other than research, or sometimes training) that justifies the seeking of psychological information. Unfortunately the full scope of the mission is not always easy to define, particularly when the psychologist is in the consultant role and information is not requested in specific terms. However, the request for information, even when quite specific, does not necessarily circumscribe the mission. The specific request or statement of problem may profitably be modified as a result of discussion between the psychologist and the person who has referred the case. Beyond this, the psychologist must exercise judgment and decide how to understand the case in terms of personal experience, background, and theoretical and value systems.

Anticipation of Needs

Often the psychologist might wish to increase understanding of the mission in anticipation of further immediate or short-term uses that might be made of the report, or of further questions that might arise in current work with the case. If, for example, a psychologist in a medical setting feels that a patient is likely to present problems in nursing care, these might be explained in anticipation of difficulties. Similarly problems might be foreseen in the areas of psychotherapy, rehabilitation, social behavior, or diagnosis. Suggestions might be included on the best approaches in psychotherapy, in occupational therapy, or in diagnostic interview techniques.

Creation of a Record

The final, but essential, purpose of the report is the creation of a record for long-term use. A record is valuable as a means of comparing a person's condition from one assessment period to another. The psychologist must anticipate further questions and uses, but such anticipations are more easily found in short-term considerations of the case than in projections of its uses over the long run. A person who had earlier been regarded as showing a functional reaction may, some years later, be examined for organicity, and the psychological record searched for earlier evidences or suspicions of such a disorder. Or a person who commits a crime of violence might have an earlier record consulted for an understanding of personality tendencies that might help explain such behavior. The psychologist's record may eventually be used for research, in a court case, or for its further direct contribution to a case, as in a patient's readmission to a hospital. The difficulties of anticipation may therefore appear to be great, but the discussions of relevance and appropriateness later in this chapter will hopefully make the task easier.

DEFINITION
AND CLASSIFICATION
OF CONTENT

Before delving further into the topics of *content*, we should differentiate among the various meanings of the term. Content can be thought of in a rather broad sense, or in a more limited way. In a broad sense, content is anything the psychologist writes into the report—perhaps statements on such topics as the reason for referral, why a person is under treatment, how well a child cooperated, an IQ, an F percent, a diagnostic impression, recommendations for treatment, a discussion of scatter, what the client saw on Card II, or the fact that the client had to be excused twice to go to the bathroom. In the limited sense, content refers to the conclusions that are transmitted to the person who has referred the case.

It is perhaps most useful to think of content in the limited sense as the *primary* (organic) content of the report and everything else as *secondary* content. This makes it easier to concentrate on the mission and to relegate other material that the psychologist feels ought to be transmitted to its rightful auxiliary position. Making the distinction will help to highlight the conclusions and to de-emphasize whatever else is required to make the report complete or effective.

The primary content may also be thought of as the psychological core content, since it is a basic (and original) contribution the psychologist makes to the case study. In many instances all or a substantial part of such content may be congruent with the findings of others. When this occurs, so much the better! The psychologist's contribution is original, not necessarily for the information it supplies—since psychological information may be gained in a number of ways against a number of orientations—but because conclusions derive from expertness in utilizing psychological methods for understanding the personality of individuals. It is as much a contribution when the psychologist, in agreement with a child's teacher, suggests that the child's poor classroom deportment is a desperate attempt to achieve recognition (which the teacher might make a direct effort to provide) as it is to report that a child's reading difficulty is based on brain dysfunction.

Various items of secondary content round out the report. Such material is not vital in the sense that the conclusions are so regarded. Nevertheless, the information may be important in developing and supporting the conclusions, and just as a fortunate choice of words and pleasant readability add effectiveness, so can information of secondary importance help to "put across" a report. Such nonorganic items as the date the evaluation was made and the reason for referral can have great bearing at some future time.

Orienting Data

First to be considered are orienting data. These refer to judiciously selected items of information (probably available elsewhere) that may help put the conclusions in appropriate context. For example, it may make a difference on how the conclusions are understood if the reason for referral or something of the client's social or educational background is given. A prosaic matter like the client's age may be highly relevant, since behavior or goals that are fully appropriate and expected at one age may be regarded as inappropriate, ludicrous, pathologic, or socially incongruous at another. To illustrate further, a request for vocational appraisal is often a straightforward matter, but sometimes it is not. How shall we understand the findings that might be obtained on a 35-year-old woman who appeared at the writer's office and asked for "vocational guidance testing"? Asked the nature of her vocational and educational background, she disclosed that she had just been awarded a Ph.D. in anthropology.

Illustrative and Persuasive Content

Illustrative material, the use of which has already been discussed in a more general context (pp. 74–78), may also be regarded as secondary content. At some indefinite point such matter shades into persuasive writing, which, at the extreme, is neither objective nor scientific. Some would argue that readers should be allowed to reach their own conclusions. A good thought, until we consider the process of reaching conclusions and the ingredients which go into these. The psychologist is responsible for forming conclusions, and to the extent there is confidence in them the psychologist has the responsibilty to try to be an effective contributor to the case study.

Subconclusions

Judiciously used illustrative material may be considered secondary content on a par with the necessary subconclusions that contribute to one or several of the major conclusions of the report. Major conclusions require support, not in the sense that raw data may validly support conclusions or that the psychologist's impressions are otherwise suspect, but because these conclusions are more comprehensible and useful when presented in the context of their components. It would be unthinkable, for example, to suggest, for no apparent reason, a diagnosis of schizophrenia. Mention should be made of such observed deviancies as a formal thought disorder, bizarre content, pervasive and exaggerated suspiciousness, and grossly inadequate insight. Nor would it be well to suggest that a patient is capable of destructive behavior without first pointing to such (possible) factors as severe undercontrol of thought and conduct, a tendency to projection and strong accompanying hostile ideation, and belligerence in the examination situation.

SOURCES OF CONTENT

A number of sources of content are available to the psychologist, although there is little agreement on what constitutes the proper sources of content. Three of these sources are directly available to the psychologist through examination: test data, interview material, and observed behavior. In addition, the psychologist may observe the client in nontest situations, possibly even know the person as a member of the community. Finally, there are a number of nonpsychological sources of information ordinarily available to the psychologist. These may include a social history, psychiatric and medical reports, nursing notes, staff conference proceedings, reports from various therapists, or discussion with a physician, psychiatrist, teacher, principal, lawyer, nurse, attendant, therapist, or social worker.

Some workers, generally not psychologists, do not look at all kindly upon the practice of the psychologist seeking out and using data other than that elicited through testing. Those few who hold this attitude in its most extreme form would have the psychologist do fully blind diagnoses and not see the client or know anything about the person. This position is held because psychological tests are regarded by these workers as objective tools, and the psychologist's function is seen as "testing"—a laboratory procedure where extraneous information might bias the "readings." Besides, expressing interest in the data or conclusion of others, or even in the psychologist's own interpersonal observations, to some coworkers smacks of dishonesty or calls into question the competency of the individual psychologist or the validity of testing. Presumably if it is not practicable for one psychologist to test the client and turn over the protocol to a colleague for interpretation, then at least the tester should attempt to maintain objectivity in the light of observations that might be made while testing the client.

Most psychologists flatly reject this point of view, pointing out that blind diagnosis is (1) a training device, (2) a stunt, and (3) a research method. Blind assessment can, however, supply pertinent information. Some psychologists might wish to examine the protocol in the presence of minimal data available from other sources before completing the assessment by utilizing all pertinent material. A comparison of conclusions arrived at blindly with data available from other sources may permit the psychologist to estimate the proper confidence which may be placed in various aspects of integrated conclusions based on test data *and* other material. In general, where practical decisions are to be made that may have temporary or lasting effect on a person, that person should have the benefit of being assessed by the psychologist under conditions where conclusions and recommendations are most likely to be realistic, accurate, or helpful—a matter of basic human ethics. The psychologist who functions in this manner is clearly a high-level professional, not a technician.

Recognized, but perhaps not adequately appreciated by many psychologists, is the fact that tests are merely devices to help understanding. They represent contrived samples of behavior, some of which can responsibly be regarded, with a good degree of confidence, as having meaning for more typical life situations. Others, however, are of more tenuous value. In general, and within practical limitations, the more behavioral samples observed in the psychologist's office and elsewhere, the better, and the more meaningful and responsible the conclusions. Tests help us to understand the meaning and purpose of behavior in the person's everyday life situation; knowing something of a person's life in advance adds meaning and significance to test performance, thus increasing its practical implications. Tests are predictors of significant behavior only in the sense that they show potentialities; otherwise there would be a one-to-one relationship between test response and behavior, or between test interpretation and behavior. A

Rorschach protocol may suggest a potentiality for behavioral undercontrol, but seen against a background of the person's history with regard to this variable, a more precise and practical estimate of future conduct, or an understanding of present or past conduct, may be offered. The value of testing is based only partly on tests and partly on the circumstances of testing and the collateral material available to the psychologist.

Certain cautions are necessary in using data that are or may be available elsewhere. The danger is repetition or unnecessary duplication, which is wasteful of time, increases report length, and may be offensive to those who feel that certain kinds of information, for example, clinical appearance and behavior, or social history are more properly identified with professions other than psychology. The psychologist may therefore reflect on what such material adds to the report.

What, for example, does the psychologist tell Frank's teacher that has not been observed over and over since he has been in class, the psychologist's last observation, incidentally, being the reason the child was referred?

> Frank is a neatly dressed, eight-year-old boy whose left eye constantly squints. He is courteous, perhaps overly courteous, and is most cooperative. When he doesn't know an answer, he becomes noticeably upset, sometimes appearing to be on the verge of tears.

What is added to the psychologist's contribution to the case study when the following is submitted on Patient A?

> The patient says he came to the hospital because for the last three months he has become extremely "nervous"—couldn't eat, couldn't sleep, "started hitting the jug again," has been quarreling with his wife, his boss, and fellow employees, and last Tuesday night struck his wife during an argument although he "didn't mean to do it."

This information is no doubt available from the intake or initial examination interview. What is added to the case study when a psychologist in a psychiatric hospital writes the following on Patient B?

> The patient enters the office with apparent apprehension, glances furtively about the room and asks if it is wired. She several times inquires about the examiner's purpose with questions like "What's this for?" She is guarded and evasive in responding to questions.

Isn't such material routinely noted in the psychiatrist's report? And, of course, it is usually the physician or the social worker who reports:

> The patient is the youngest in a family of five children, the four older sibs being girls. All during school he was teased by his classmates because of certain effeminate ways, and he was taunted with the name "sissy." He admits that he doesn't have much interest in girls and thinks that this is why he was rejected by

the army. He volunteers that the medical examiner asked him, "Do you go out with girls?"

There is great distinction to be made, however, between repeating or duplicating what is usually the property of others and utilizing such material *in the context of a new integration*. This sort of content can be employed for strengthening conclusions and insights suggested by tests, for understanding the practical significance of behavioral trends as indicated by test data, for showing how underlying psychological factors may relate to overt behavior which is of concern, or as illustrations for presented conclusions.

Thus, for Frank:

This child's perfectionistic strivings, if not modified, can become a way of life, crippling spontaneity and ability to relate with warmth and satisfaction. He could develop a very serious breakdown as early as adolescence. He has the feeling that catastrophe awaits him if he does not achieve at an exaggeratedly high level, that somehow such performance is expected of him. Seeking to minimize fear, he sacrifices the positive feelings and true interest in his scholarship, for being correct is what is important to him and not the meaning of the work. This child has need for warmth, kindness, and acceptance—especially when he does not know the answer. He needs to learn that he can be accepted for himself rather than for his performance. He should be involved in play therapy, particularly in contact and rough-and-tumble games where getting dirty is assured. Finger painting might also be helpful.

For Patient A:

. . . anxiety centering largely about his sex role, conflict over his adequacy as a male, and dependency needs for which he cannot secure adequate gratification is most usually not too troublesome to him because a pattern of life emphasizing order, meticulous attention to details, and achievement tends to prevent the experiencing of acute distress. However, this defensive pattern is currently not sufficiently effective to control either strong subjective responses—anxiety and tension—which are apparently evidenced in his being "nervous," in his inability to eat or sleep well, and in drinking. Similarly, rather pervasive negative feelings toward others, about which he usually has no particular awareness, are now associated with an acting out potential. He currently ascribes his own antagonistic feelings to others and perceives people as a threat to him. Though according to the information now available he has expressed hostility only verbally with the exception of one temporary lapse of control when he struck his wife, he is seen as potentially capable of serious assaultive behavior and he should be closely observed for these tendencies particularly during his period of acute upset.

It should also be pointed out that the medical data of a physician influenced the writing of this passage, although there is no direct reference to it. The "nervousness," insomnia, and eating difficulties that the patient reports could have a physiological basis, but since the medical examination was essentially negative, these symptoms may tentatively be ascribed to the psychological state with which they are consistent.

Consider the following passage written about patient B.

> . . . she ascribes these unbridled hostile impulses to others, which causes her to experience her relationships in a context of severe threat. With the loosening of ties to reality she seems to see threat everywhere and is beyond rationality in her suspiciousness, a factor which no doubt aggravates her ability to function socially. This was observed during the examination where she was guarded and evasive, queried the examiner several times with "What's this for?" and especially when she entered the office, furtively looked about the room and asked if it was wired.

This integration of test conclusions with clinical observations makes real and alive the psychological defense maneuver of hypersuspiciousness and its social consequences. The purpose here is hardly to tell that Patient B is paranoid, which everyone knows, but to present the condition in a context where it is more understandable and its severity illustrated. This presentation differs from the more common practice of noting clinical behavior prior to offering test conclusions and then reporting the latter without reference to the patient's clinical behavior, which is kept separate from these (exclusively test) conclusions. The psychologist may feel the need to put forth much effort to illustrate or support an "independent" (test-derived) conclusion that Patient B is paranoid. This may be accomplished by offering test data, the meanings of which are less obvious (and also less valid) than the overt paranoid behavior of the patient. Such overt behavior would probably lend excellent support in this instance and illustrate test-gained diagnostic material were it not regarded as out of bounds to psychologists. Thus, "on the Rorschach he sees a number of faces and the rear end of a bee; on the figure drawing there is eye emphasis, spearlike fingers, and concern is expressed over the size of the buttocks on the male figure; and one of his TAT stories depicts a character as an F.B.I. agent." This practice may be likened to determining a person's job qualifications by giving him or her an aptitude test, when actual job performance records on the subject—the sort of criteria against which the test is validated—are available.

This discussion of the source and the appropriateness of the content that the psychologist presents is to be understood in the context of an adequate, functioning team and in relation to a setting. In a traditional psychiatric setting it is not the psychologist who is usually charged with integrating the total data of the various disciplines. In other kinds of settings the psychologist, by choice or not, may do many things usually regarded as not part of the psychologist's role in traditional psychiatric teams. The pyschologist in current team practice often may be selective and utilize the contributions of others or material ordinarily available to others only as these help to round out and make more useful the basic psychological conclusions.

SELECTION OF CONTENT
IN TERMS OF RELEVANCE

The problem of what is relevant for a given psychological report often is not broached. This is because of the tendency of psychologists to see their role as reporting the "findings"—whatever their tests happen to yield, such as IQs and other raw and partially interpreted data—rather than developing and interpreting content in terms of a specific mission. What content goes into a given report may depend on any or all of the following: (1) the orientation of the psychologist, (2) the orientation of the person who makes the referral, (3) the particular immediate problem which is under consideration, (4) the anticipated use(s) for the findings, (5) habit.

The psychologist generally has the option to select content on the basis of a firm rationale and within liberal limits to be the sole judge of relevance. On the other hand, the psychologist may be subject to pressures from other team members, and the person who makes the referral may take quite an active role in the determination of relevance. If the latter is a Freudian, there may be obvious interest in getting data on such matters as psychosexual development, drives, and dynamics; the unconscious in general; the client's defensive structure and ego strength. If the orientation of the person making the referral is primarily descriptive, there may be heavy emphasis on diagnosis or classification and an expectation that the psychological report work toward these ends.

Despite the strong orientations of many readers of psychological reports, the interests of the client and the goals of the setting should receive priority. In a setting where rehabilitation is emphasized, depth evaluations often detract from the main purpose. Instead, what is probably needed is information to help the staff understand the client's personal and social skills, attitudes toward rehabilitation and attainment of greater independence, and perhaps the client's interest or the ability to learn new skills. In settings where psychotherapy is practiced, it is often desirable to learn through psychological assessment of the individual's ability to profit from this form of treatment, the nature of the defensive structure, the basic personality integrity (ego strength), and hints to the psychotherapist. Where mental retardation seems to be the problem, a detailed qualitative and quantitative evaluation of intellectual and social skills might be in order.

Because of the possibly differing orientations among psychologists and other staff members, and also because of the wide range of problems that clients may present, there may exist a difference of opinion on what might be relevant information in a given case. A conference between the psychologist and the person who makes the referral, or indeed a preliminary staff conference, might be the best way of determining what kind of data are needed. Of course, after the psychologist starts the examination, pertinent material not previously seen as important might emerge.

The determination of relevance is a very practical problem when we consider the scope and complexity of personality, to say nothing of the various ways in which we try to understand it. The full personality can hardly be approximated in a psychological report, even when the psychologist resorts to the presentation of an exhaustive list of conclusions. Nor would it be easy in practice to visualize where full or global coverage might be desirable, apart from the economic difficulties such an attempt would entail. Reports that include more content than is necessary require too much time to write and to read. They impose on the reader the task of separating that which is essential from that which is not—a duty that really belongs primarily to the psychologist to the extent that it is possible to anticipate what is needed.

What sort of conclusions should the psychologist report? There is no general answer to this question. The sort of information that might be indispensable in one case is probably superfluous or quite out of place in another. It is often appropriate to report on such matters as the self-concept, how others see the person, intellectual prowess or shortcomings, interests, life goals, frustrations, anxieties, defenses, and interpersonal and sexual adjustment factors. Frequently it is not. Sometimes it is well to discuss brain dysfunction, false notions held about the self, acting-out potentialities, self-destructive tendencies, impairments, relative skills, range and qualitative features of affective response, diagnostic category, intellectual level, or intellectual functioning, but often it is wasteful and an imposition on the reader to do so.

Fortunately it is possible to be more specific than this. Much of the remainder of this chapter discusses the sort of content often found in reports. We can assert quite definitely that certain kinds of content sometimes found in reports *never* belong there, and it is not at all likely that any particular primary content category ought to be represented in *all* reports. It is constructive to talk about the kinds of content that are frequently appropriate. Further, we often should not think about content on an all-or-none basis, but in terms of how much emphasis ought to be given to various kinds of content in specific case situations.

AN EVALUATION OF COMMON CONTENT CATEGORIES IN "TRADITIONAL" PSYCHOLOGICAL REPORTS

A systematic evaluation, specifically of psychological report content, might begin with an examination of what constitutes the "traditional" psychological report. The "traditional" report apparently came into its present form by accretion rather than by formulation and development of a rationale. This fact was of concern to Taylor and Teicher, who in 1946 noted that "clinical psychology . . . appears to have given little systematic study to the manner in which test findings are organized and formulated to provide necessary records and to render the data easily and fully understood by professional associates." Their solution to the problem was to offer a report-writing outline quite similar to the many now in existence. Apparently there was then no concern with what content is appropriate for *specific* reports, since the authors made reference only to the "test findings" and to "the data."

Many current psychological reports contain abundant "archeological" indicators of the origins of psychological practice. The early school background and the influence of the testing movement are evident in the prominent concern with matters of the intellect, and especially with the exalted position of the IQ. A more recent layer of development (1939) building on the Binet-Terman foundation is seen in the assignment of three IQs per person rather than one, and in the eager interest in which of the client's skill groupings—verbal or performance—is better. With the appearance in this country of the inkblots and the publication of the TAT, prominent new foci were what the person sees and the stories that are made up. After the association of psychology with psychiatry, Freud was welcomed into most clinics, and the emphasis shifted to personality, albeit one aspect of personality—such impalpables as the drives that trouble the individual and society, defenses, and retrospective developmental reconstructions. All of these accretions commonly make up modern reports, prominent exceptions being found in many behaviorally oriented and neuropsychological reports where, for example, analytic concepts typically are absent. Just as taxes, once enacted, are hardly ever repealed, content categories, once they find their way into a report, are likely to be with us for some time.

Test-by-Test Reporting

Content categories do sometimes change, however. In many settings emphasis has shifted from discussion of clients' performance on tests to contributions derived with the help of tests. Test-by-test reporting has lost favor. Now the battery report is utilized by most psychologists. Nevertheless, content categories based on tests still seem to exist, although not formally divided into such units. It is sometimes easy to read reports and silently observe that "now the psychologist is talking about WAIS data (the client has a good fund of information, superior vocabulary, and conceptual ability . . . her knowledge of cultural precepts is somewhat better than her ability to manipulate concrete materials, and visual-motor coordination is poorer than her verbal skills . . .)." Similarly the reader might be aware that "now the psychologist is talking about the Rorschach," even though intellectual factors are again under discussion—and even though the material appears in a section of the report so labeled as to suggest that some other content, such as "personality" or "emotional factors," is the focus (respect for reality is basically good, but there is a poverty of fantasy and creativity, the patient tending to restrict her range of interest and to understand and deal with events in simple, stereotyped terms . . .). However, the almost complete demise of the test-by-test report is at least a step in the right direction. Reports , as a result, now tend to be less test-oriented and more person-oriented.

Reporting in Terms of Part Processes

Another type of broad content categorization still finds acceptance in many settings. This is the report that focuses on part processes—for example, intellection, drives, dynamics, affective responses, defenses, or sex adjustment. Objection is raised to this kind of report usually because some readers have difficulty in reconstructing the "whole person" from the segments. This kind of reporting predetermines what categories of content are important in *all* cases, largely relieving the psychologist of the necessity of questioning which conclusions are relevant and which are not.

Content Categories in Traditional Reports

The more typical traditional reports tend to contain a number of narrow content categories and two major categories, the first major category (typically appearing first in the report) labeled something like "Intellectual Aspects," and the second "Emotional Aspects," or simply "Personality." These common content categories may serve as a stable reference point against which revised categories may be compared.

Preliminary Part of Report

The first item of a report is often a statement of the reason for assessment. This can be a valuable piece of information, since the psychologist's mission is (or should be) largely defined by some presenting problem. A statement of the reason for assessment, therefore, may orient the reader on the sort of material likely to follow. This information commonly is supplied by someone other than the psychologist, such as a clinician who refers a case to a psychologist for assessment.

Following this statement may be a section on clinical behavior, various kinds of identifying information, or social data. Sometimes these heterogeneous classes of information are combined, appearing under the same heading or the same section of the report.

What the client does or says in the psychologist's office is commonly reported under a label like "Clinical Behavior," "Behavioral Note," "Behavioral Observations," or "Clinical Observations." The length of the section ranges from a few lines up to perhaps two single-spaced pages, and the sort of material found in it may vary widely from report to report and from psychologist to psychologist. In addition to behavioral information, this section often contains identifying information (e.g., age, city of residence), descriptive information (e.g., dress, attractiveness, how make-up is used), impressions (e.g., the client has an underlying hostile attitude), matters of social history (e.g., the person ran away and got married at 16), or the reason the person is being seen in the clinic, in the counselor's office or wherever, in the individual's own words. In many instances such information is unjustifiably repetitious (e.g., the date of admission to the hospital, height, body build, or what is elsewhere conveniently available) and such data are usually raw, uninterpreted, and often of doubtful value. Thus, "The patient readily entered the examining room and took the chair assigned" (few patients are dragged in, even when they are negativistic about being examined; in a school setting, however, a child's approach to an examiner is sometimes such as to challenge the validity of intelligence test results). Another example: "He wore a loose-fitting, faded blue bathrobe" (the one issued to him) "and was unshaven" (the patient is not permitted to shave himself and is shaved by an attendant three times weekly).

The behavior commented upon may be normal behavior (the patient responded appropriately to questions, showed appropriate affect, or gave no evidence of delusions or hallucinations); pathological behavior (the patient sat staring off into space, but with some difficulty could be induced to respond); common behavior (the patient smoked four filter-tip cigarettes during the two-hour testing session); or distinctive behavior (the patient was unusually ingratiating). Verbalizations commonly appear here, too. ("He spoke at length about his war experiences: 'I can still see the way the sergeant looked with his guts hanging out.' ")

Presumably the material selected for reporting has some interpretive meaning which is best translated into clinically significant conclusions by the reader of the report. This abrogation of responsibility is, of course, out of keeping with a responsible professional role. Such practice goes so far at times that it strains the interpretive resources of even the most imaginative clinician ("the patient wore a bright red tie," or "the patient was excused during the testing period to go to the bathroom"). It should also be a matter of concern that there is no rational nor consensual basis for what should appear in this section; this becomes obvious when we consider how much irrelevant and unoriginal data are found here.

There is apparently more rationale in reporting on the client's test behavior and test attitudes (the client moved the blocks about in random fashion, sometimes forming a correct beginning for the required design, but then breaking up the pattern and starting over; or, the client usually responded overly quickly, often being in error, and then usually asked for permission to correct her answer; or, he was vehement in his objection to testing, referring to the procedure as "brain picking," and "in violation of the spirit, if not the wording, of the Fifth Amendment"). Here too, however, the psychologist is asking another to interpret data that are clearly part of psychological training and competency. It may be very wasteful of such significant data to present them uninterpreted and apart from the important conclusions to which they may contribute.

Fresh Fish Sold Here   Before proceeding further, a word of caution and logic may help reduce the sort of superfluous content that can work its way into reports. It should be a rule that the psychologist ask about each bit of content presented: "Does this contribute useful information?" Both in the preliminary section and throughout the report superfluous, totally useless material can be nipped in the bud. The psychologist is not really contributing, as a psychologist, in reporting on such matters as the client's age, number of sibs, the presence of an accent, or the amount of hair that remains on the scalp.

There is the tale of the young man who went into the fish business. He rented a store, erected a sign, FRESH FISH SOLD HERE, and acquired merchandise.

As he was standing back admiring his market and his sign, a friend happened along. Following congratulations, the friend gazed at the sign and read aloud, FRESH FISH SOLD HERE. Of course it's *here*. You wouldn't sell it elsewhere, would you? Impressed with such astuteness, the young man painted over the obviously superfluous word. The next helpful comment had to do with the word *sold*. You aren't giving it away? Again impressed, he eliminated the useless word. Seemingly that was it, but the critic then focused on the word *fresh*. You wouldn't sell spoiled fish, would you? Once more our hero bowed to the strength of logic. Finally he was relieved that he had a logic-tight sign for his business: FISH. His ever alert friend, however, audibly sniffing the air for effect, made a final observation: "You don't need a sign."

"Test Results"

Following the preliminary part of the report—such content categories as "Reason for Assessment," "Reason for Referral," "Descriptive Data," "Identifying Data," "Social Information," and "Clinical Behavior"—psychologists commonly shift gears and move to another realm of reporting that employs a sharply different flavor and vocabulary and examines the client on a wholly different level. This section of the report may be introduced by a heading such as "Test Results," "Findings," "Test Interpretation," or "Evaluation." Whereas the report up to this point made obvious reference to the client in various concrete ways, it is in this section that the consumer of the report frequently reads about matters like tests and theories, with the client an incidental, a vehicle to carry information about the psychologist's instruments and beliefs.

This broad content category is then commonly subdivided into two smaller categories. Let us call them, as they often are, "Intellectual Aspects" and "Personality" or "Emotional Factors."

"Intellectual Aspects"

Almost always found in the section on intellectual aspects is an IQ—or more usually, IQs—along with considerable discussion about the number(s) offered to the reader. Commonly it is thought important to let the reader know whether the number is truthful or not, but to report a number in any event. Thus the writer once saw a psychological report prepared on a poorly accessible patient; the obtained IQ quite obviously did not have meaning or utility in its usual sense and was no indicator of the person's potential under more fortunate circumstances. Nevertheless, the psychologist, feeling constrained to report the expected IQ, wrote, "The patient obtained an IQ of 58, which is regarded as invalid." Then why present it? Is it not like the old technique of the late comedian Jack Benny who always reported that he was 39, the humor residing in the fact that everyone understood this to be a broad falsification? (This is not to deny the pathognomonic significance of the impaired intellectual functioning.)

Also prominent in this section of the report, if one of the Wechsler scales is used, is a statement about the variability or "evenness" of intellectual functioning (scatter), about the patient's relative proficiency in the verbal and performance areas, and in certain heterogeneous skill groupings which may be subsumed under various descriptive headings, such as visual-motor function. Frequently there is no apparent rationale for the inclusion of such material, and what are presented as conclusions are more akin to raw data. Heavy scatter, for example, as determined either by inspection or by a quantitative index, is without any necessary meaning, even though there is a tendency for a high scatter index to be associated with schizophrenia (Trehub & Scherer, 1958). Nevertheless, the prudent psychologist will not conclude that a patient is schizophrenic solely on the basis of scatter; other data must also be weighed. On including a report about scatter, the psychologist must therefore consider what conclusions readers might reach from such raw datum. If a report of scatter is intended to support a conclusion, then it is also necessary to report the other main components that brought about that conclusion.

Some psychologists report in this section personality implications of intelligence test findings, matters like personality organization and factors related to adjustment. This meaningful approach, however, poses problems of content organization, since many such conclusions are less matters of the intellect than what is generally considered, report-wise, to fall under "personality." But some psychologists are not very much concerned about such matters and report *all* conclusions gained from intelligence tests under "Intellectual Aspects" and *all* conclusions derived from general tests of personality under "Personality"—even basic information on intellectual function gained through, for example, the Rorschach.

"Personality" or "Emotional Factors"

The section often entitled "Personality" or "Emotional Factors" may cause discomfort to the purist solely because of terminology. The objection is that personality is generally regarded as encompassing a larger field of study, perhaps something like ". . . the dynamic organization within the individual of those psychophysical systems that determine his unique adjustments to his environment" (Allport, 1937). To exclude what may be vital information on the role of cognition in adjustment (excluded because it is already neatly tied up in the previous section in a discussions of levels of test achievements, assets, shortcomings, and impressions about abstract heterogeneous skills) is hardly to give an adequate picture of personality. As for the term *emotional factors,* it should be obvious that much of the vital personality material described here—goals, interests, psychological characteristics of the parents, or cultural factors in the home—are not necessarily more related to emotions than is the intellect or the IQ.

The sort of content that appears in this section may vary somewhat among psychologists, but stereotypy is frequent. Commonly written about are such topics as psychopathology, unconscious drives, attitudes, conflicts, frustration, guilt, anxiety, defenses, psychosexual factors, and significant relationships. These topics may frequently be related to the mission, but often they are not. In many instances this section does not integrate significant environmental factors, the content of consciousness, and surface behavior with the deeper elements of personality.

"Diagnosis"

In many diagnostic-treatment settings the psychological report commonly gives some attention to a formal psychiatric diagnosis, usually after the discussion of "Intellectual Aspects" and "Personality," and somewhere toward the end of the report. As we have already seen (Chapter 2), the contribution is sometimes not appreciated. This objection apparently does not relate to psychologists' ability to diagnose, for it seems that they are as well qualified as are other experts in this respect (Wiener & Raths, 1959). Indeed, behavioral and neuropsychological diagnoses are almost exclusively in the realm of psychology. The issue seems rather to be one of role and of responsibility. The psychiatric diagnosis has long been considered a medical prerogative and is sometimes based on information not ordinarily available to the psychologist or on information that the psychologist cannot competently or ethically utilize (e.g., neurological findings, or a laboratory procedure such as the recently introduced dexamethasone suppression test). The official psychiatric diagnosis has traditionally been legally entrusted only to physicians. In practice, in a team setting the formal diagnosis frequently reflects the contributions of various team members.

Many psychiatrists are not offended by a psychologist's diagnostic impression or by a suggested diagnosis. It is possible to be overly obsequious in suggesting a diagnosis: "Such a pattern is commonly found in patients diagnosed as schizophrenic." This apologetic suggestion of a diagnosis may imply either (1) that the psychologist is convinced that this is a case of schizophrenia but hesitates to say so, or (2) that diagnoses stem from tests and not from psychologists. The verbal maneuver is not necessary. Some psychiatrists might be offended only when the psychologist authoritatively indicates that schizophrenia *is* the diagnosis, thus usurping what some psychiatrists consider to be their function. It is hard to know why there is so much concern over formal diagnosis, particularly since many psychologists and dynamic psychiatrists minimize, or are even critical of, this contribution to the case study.

There are obvious instances where the psychologist's reporting of classificatory material is superfluous, even in settings where diagnosis is an administrative requirement or a matter of firm orientation. One occasion of this sort is when the person presents clear-cut classificatory characteristics or is already well known or "well diagnosed." Another occasion when the psychologist's suggested diagnosis contributes minimally, if at all, is when the emphasis is on understanding some personality characteristic, for example, when it is more important to know the meaning of a symptom than to know that the client's behavior merits some particular diagnosis.

Diagnosis, assessment, and *evaluation* are terms sometimes used interchangeably, in which case *diagnosis* usually includes much more than a formal classification. In such cases the term often refers to a major evaluative conclusion. Sometimes such contributions may consider what is appropriate as a formal diagnosis in a discussion context rather than offering a clipped nosological entity. In all cases the appropriateness of this diagnostic contribution depends partly on its pertinence and partly on the psychologist's qualifications to render it. In no case is the psychologist qualified to render what is properly a medical diagnosis.

Consider the following quoted material, taken from a discussion in Sarbin, Taft, and Bailey (1960). A 17-year-old girl had been referred to a psychiatric clinic because of "hysterical manifestations" after the examining physician could find no organic basis for her complaints of abdominal pains. As part of the total evaluation process the patient was seen by a psychologist who reported, in part, "the patient's unresolved oedipal conflict is apparent in her responses to the Thematic Apperception Test. The 'abdominal pains' *are* at one and the same time an identification with her departed father and a way of getting love from her mother." (emphasis supplied) Unfortunately for the patient, and for the validity of the psychologist's diagnostic statement, she was soon found to have a far advanced cancer in the region of complaint and succumbed to this condition the day following its discovery.

Now it may be that the psychologist's psychodynamic explanation was based on a sound understanding of the person. In fact, we are told that the girl's mother reported that her daughter had always been given over to dramatizing her problems and that she had been close to her father, who died as the result of a perforated ulcer. Such collateral information about the girl is similar to what the psychologist concluded from tests, but it should have been regarded in the light of the original medical findings only as *suggestive* of the nature of the girl's ailment, what it *might* be. How much better it would have been if the psychologist had not rendered an unqualified opinion on the nature of a bodily complaint, but had offered the opinion that the findings were consistent with a functional complaint, or even, in the light of the medical conclusion, suggested that "hysteria" was a *possible* explanation of the complaint.

"Prognosis"

Prognosis often follows diagnosis, as is frequently the case in medicine. Again, the objection from some psychiatric associates rests on how the content is presented. Certainly the psychologist's understanding of an individual's personality permits the making of certain predictions about future behavior. The psychiatrist may welcome these. What the psychiatrist may object to is wording to the effect that the psychologist is charting the presumed course of a *diseased* state. When behavioral deviancy is regarded in this manner, clearly a declining point of view, the psychologist is evidently wrong. Hence the manner in which predictions are made—even the headings under which predictions are recorded—may influence the reader's perception of just what sort of content is being reported. What can seem to be subtle differences are sometimes of great practical moment.

"Recommendations"

Recommendations often appear as one of the final content categories of the report. In many settings, in schools, for example, psychological consultation is sought for the help the psychologist can give in dealing with a problem. In other settings, notably some psychiatric settings, however, there is dispute about the psychologist's offering of such content. Some psychiatrists actively solicit this kind of material whereas others denounce it as inappropriate and an encroachment upon medical function. There is no doubt that the psychologist does have information that can be translated into practical terms that have meaning for treatment, disposition, or other special considerations. And, in responding to a referral, the psychologist's purpose is specifically to present that content that meets the needs of the person making the referral. The manner of presentation, particularly the tactfulness of presentation, must be reemphasized. Thus, "Psychotherapy along with treatment directed at symptomatic reduction of depression may be beneficial" probably is a more palatable statement to most psychiatrists than "This patient ought to have psychotherapy and be started on Ludiomil 50 mg. b.i.d."

The working relationship will determine in part "just how far the psychologist should go." In the context of many relationships it is probably appropriate to write something to the effect that "the prominent and incapacitating depressive features in this patient suggest that she might respond to E.C.T." But it is doubtful that a recommendation such as ". . . the patient should be started on a course of insulin therapy with participation in group psychotherapy and occupational therapy. . . ," appearing in Garfield's (1957) textbook of clinical psychology, would be well received. Insulin treatment can have serious physiological consequences (the recommendation, incidentally, does not specify whether subcoma—"subinsulin"—is being prescribed or whether the psychologist wants the patient to have comas—"deep insulin"). Treatment with insulin requires intimate medical and nursing control, and the hazards of "deep insulin" have long since been one of the reasons for discarding its use in most settings.

"Summary"

Generally the report is concluded with a content category labeled "Summary," or sometimes "Summary and Conclusions," which may imply that new major material not dealt with in the body of the report, perhaps some diagnostic considerations or some recommendations, is being introduced. It is hard to argue against the use of summary content since this is so well entrenched in writing practice, and since many clinical workers seem to feel the need for such a statement (Tallent & Reiss, 1959a, 1959b). However, the use of a summary may often be injudicious, and it should be considered for use with discretion.

The major objection raised against the use of a summary is that it may serve with some degree of effectiveness as an antidote to an otherwise inadequate report. Such seems particularly true of reports that are inadequate because they are too long, too difficult, and too involved, the summary by comparison being readable. The reader is soon trained to ignore the report proper and to be content with the summary, even though by definition this section can hardly be expected to carry the legitimate freight of the report. The fact that a number of readers are apparently content with first perusing the summary suggests that perhaps this briefer version of a report often more closely approximates the felt requirements of report readers than does the main body.

An opposite objection to the use of a summary may be made when the summary concludes an otherwise succinct report. There is now a tendency among some psychologists to present a concise, content-loaded report, although without omitting the traditional summary. The result may appear ludicrous, at least visually if not also logically, when the length of the summary approaches the length of the report. In terms of actual measurement, one may find reports of six, seven, or eight inches in length to which is appended a summary statement of three, four, or five inches!

When a summary statement is used, Hammond and Allen's (1953) suggestion for an "opening summary"—what is sometimes called an *overview*—is well taken. This technique seems to be used effectively in journalism, particularly in feature articles, in scientific journals, and with book chapters. It is thought that presenting the essence of the material at the beginning will create in the reader the proper set needed for understanding and will entice the reader to delve into the main body of writing. By contrast, many are of the opinion that a summary at the end, when read first, tends against turning back to the text proper.

FREQUENTLY APPROPRIATE CONTENT

From consideration of the traditional report, we may profitably turn to a discussion of the kinds of psychological content commonly thought to be helpful to clinical workers. The data forming the basis for the ensuing discussion are from the survey reported on in Chapter 2 (Tallent & Reiss, 1959a). No doubt some of the expressed needs reflect familiarity with traditional reports, but many who offered advice on appropriate content had ideas of their own. All of the categories suggested with a degree of frequency are examined closely in terms of their positive and negative potentialities and with a view to their proper usage. The kinds of content mentioned are not appropriate for all reports, since each report is a highly individual matter. Nor is it implied that reports be limited to these categories, which are meant only as general guidelines. It is better to think in terms of what sort of content is *frequently* appropriate.

Clinical Behavior and Descriptive Material

Report readers are evidently interested in a broad range of behavior, both current and potential, and the reporting of the client's clinical behavior and other descriptive material continues to find favor among a number of them. This area of data, dealing as it does with overt material, presents the hazard of duplicating the contributions of other team members. Such observations are best presented—if relevant to the evaluation goal—in a unique context elicited in some special way, or one that offers some special insights (for example, in response to test stimuli or in association with unique psychological findings).

Three subcategories of such material are specifically mentioned as appropriate: appearance, general behavioral observations, and a description of the examiner-client interaction. Of these, a discussion of a client's appearance (probably noted elsewhere, particularly if highly unusual) is least likely to be fruitful. This is especially true of those aspects of appearance without apparent psychological correlates or not reliably interpretable.

General behavioral observations are frequently unique material because of the inherent differences between a psychological examination and the contacts of other workers. A psychological examination involving a full battery is, in general, more time consuming than are other examinations or the interviews carried out by the psychologist's associates. This longer period of observation offers the possibility of noting behavior that might not occur in procedures which are cursory by comparison. The length of examination also presents opportunities for noting variations in behavior, particularly when the client is seen over a period of two or more days. Unique behavior is frequently elicited because aspects of the psychological examination are ambiguous to the client. Many clients find it hard to understand the role of the psychologist, the purpose or rationale of the tools that are used, and the procedures. The psychological examination is a projective situation to which people make diagnostically useful responses.

The examiner-client interaction is a vital datum, especially to those psychologists who stress the role of interpersonal relationships in the understanding of personality. Knowledge of this interaction is regarded as valuable, as it is a sample of a role the person tends to take in certain social encounters and of some of the person's more typical behaviors. Thus the unique personality of the psychologist is as much an examination stimulus as are the various test stimuli. The client's test productions are quite reasonably regarded as based in part on the interaction between examiner and client. (Masling, 1960) This situation, skillfully understood, can contribute valuable conclusions to the case study.

From the point of view of the current presentation, all such behavior description is generally best offered as interpreted material, except where it is used for its illustrative value. Some readers of the psychological report ask for the psychologist's impressions, which are, in effect, interpreted observations. Such interpretation no doubt involves a greater subjective element than is often regarded as proper in the interpretation of test data.

Intellectual Factors of Personality

Various intellectual factors of personality continue to be of interest to clinical workers in nonschool or nonrehabilitation settings, although the specific things they want to know sometimes differ from the information found in the traditional report. Their concern with intellect often has less important consequences than does the concern of the teacher or the rehabilitation worker, for example. Yet some workers are particularly interested in learning about the intellectual assets of their patients. Such data would seem to be most valuable to school personnel, when rehabilitation measures involving training or placement are at issue, and sometimes under other circumstances, such as when forensic matters are at issue. They may be helpful, in fact, when any change in a person's life situation is contemplated, since cognitive resources are definitely a factor in adjustment.

Intellectual liabilities seem to call up interest among clinical workers, perhaps because of the "maladjustment focus" that is so often found in the diagnostic-treatment setting. Data on low intelligence, however, may help to explain the person's frustrations or other problems of significance to the case study. Planning for the future is thus facilitated. Similar interest centers about acquired intellectual deficit—various earlier resources that are no longer available to the individual. This type of difficulty may present problems, particularly vocational, academic and social adjustment problems. Of importance here are the nature and the extent of deficit and the requirements that are placed upon the person. An isolated statement of deficit may not be very valuable practically, since persons can often carry on adequately in well-practiced areas of function, sometimes even in occupations involving a fair degree of responsibility, in the presence of appreciable loss.

Information about another aspect of deficit, that of the premorbid intelligence, seems to be spontaneously requested by clinical workers far less frequently than such discussions occur in samples of psychological reports. An estimate of premorbid functioning, or of the relationship of current to premorbid functioning, is mainly of value as a crude, nonspecific index of the extent of psychopathology and is perhaps best expressed in qualitative terms. Figures presented on deficit frequently lack practical clinical meaning, particularly when they are presented out of context of the functioning personality.

The interest of many clinical workers is in some specific aspect or aspects of intellectual functioning that they feel is of importance. A psychiatrist or a social worker may wish further information on such matters as abstract ability, memory function, or the ability to learn. Such more or less specific requirements point up the desirability of specific referrals. Many workers nevertheless express a general interest, such as in the "current intellectual status." Presumably such a request gives the psychologist latitude in deciding which findings about the intellect ought to be reported.

Surprisingly, when asked about the sort of content that ought to appear in psychological reports, 58 percent of the replies from psychiatrists indicated that an IQ or the intelligence level be specified, whereas only 1 percent of the psychologists so replied. This finding is surprising because a much higher percentage of psychologists *do* apparently give this kind of datum high priority by presenting it before there is any discussion of other findings.

Is it possible that psychologists do not really believe in this generous offering of the IQ but are under the impression that it is supposed to be done? The psychiatrists' apparent eager interest in numbers purporting to tell how intelligent their patients are is also surprising, since it is often uncertain what practical use they make of this information. It may be that this interest is a residual of the great emphasis psychologists and educators had put on the IQ in an earlier era, or it may reflect the interest in intelligence emphasized in the middle-class cultural background of many psychiatrists.

Whatever the sources of differing opinions on the need for various kinds of intellectual data, it is appropriate that we reexamine the role that knowledge of the intellect plays in the appraisal of personality in practical (clinical-type) situations. There should be almost universal agreement that knowledge of the functioning of the intellect offers information on (1) skill-interest-motivational complexes of efficiencies, (2) the functioning of various personality processes, and as a special case, (3) the kinds and degrees of both functional and organic disruption of the personality.

The relatively infrequent need for detailed knowledge of efficiencies and inefficiencies, in many diagnostic-treatment settings has already been mentioned. The common use of individual intelligence tests which require over an hour to administer, score, and interpret, would hardly be justified in many cases were the main purpose to determine intellectual level. There frequently are more economical ways of obtaining such information.

On the other hand, individual intelligence tests of the Wechsler group are being used effectively to gain personality information of the sort presumably related to intellectual function but usually thought of in a noncognitive context. Information on personality, such as dependency traits, attitudes toward society, suspiciousness, impulsivity, and defense mechanisms, may be gained through intelligence tests. The manner in which such traits are intimately tied up with the client's intellectual resources often constitutes valuable datum for the person who makes the referral. Information of this sort, however, generally is best discussed along with personality features other than the client's skills and efficiencies.

An analysis of intellectual functioning is sometimes the key contribution the psychologist can make to the case study. This contribution commonly is arrived at through a study of deficits, both quantitative and qualitative. Certain quantitative deficit patterns, often considered together with observations of functioning on an intelligence test, may be identified as the effect of brain pathology. This item of information is of particular interest to many teachers, psychiatrists, and neurologists, as well as to psychologists, and is regarded as one of the more valuable contributions of the psychologist.

Psychiatrists are often interested in learning from the psychologist about the formal thought processes. The offical criteria for the diagnosis of the schizophrenic psychoses include alterations in the thought processes

(Spitzer et al., 1980), and these are often best evaluated through psychological procedures. Sometimes, in fact, this kind of malfunction is not evident in samples of well-practiced interpersonal relationships and is seen only in performance on psychological tests—intelligence tests and other psychological tests. Similarly the full effect of a neurotic process or a personality disorder often is better understood through the effects on the cognitive processes.

Nonintellectual Factors of Personality

Those personality factors generally considered nonintellectual are mentioned as proper content by large numbers of report readers, although sometimes one professional group places more emphasis on certain classes of data than do others. The separation of these data from intellectual operations is merely a habitual way of thinking, a result of the artificial dichotomization of the personality in psychological reports (or perhaps more basically of the "isolation" of intelligence from the rest of personality years ago). Many clinical workers mention as proper content a "general personality picture."

Interest in psychopathology is widespread in psychiatric settings, and there are a number of discrete areas that are often specified. These include general description of the psychopathological process, discussion of the areas of disturbed functioning, behavioral symptomatology, reality contact, and etiological information, although perhaps significantly it is primarily psychologists who seem to value such content in reports. Now that the *Diagnostic and Statistical Manual* of the American Psychiatric Association (Spitzer et al., 1980) is essentially "atheoretical," many users of the manual perhaps are also inclined to be "atheoretical" in their diagnostic formulations and do not seek etiological information. It is difficult to believe, however, that dynamically oriented psychiatrists, or others, will alter their position on the basis of the conceptual underpinnings of DSM-III.

The underlying psychological processes are regarded as an appropriate topic by all professions of the classical clinical team. Many think in terms of a partial dichotomization of evaluative function between psychologists and other team members, the former being charged with illuminating deep activities of the psyche whereas psychiatrists and social workers focus on more palpable behaviors—historical information, affect, or stream of consciousness, with some inferential penetrations into the unconscious. This view is inaccurate and unfair to all concerned. All levels of behavior are the province of psychology, and psychological examination is often invaluable in describing important but essentially overt manifestations of behavior, functions such as memory, behavioral control, the intensity of surface hostility, and the channels through which it is expressed. The psy-

chologist who seeks an integrated view of the client explores the unconscious, too, often contributing valued information. Instruments such as the
Rorschach frequently contribute to a significant advantage in subsurface
explorations, but the psychologist holds no deed on this section of the
personality.

One of the more vital content areas, in the opinion of our respondents,
is the conflicts of the patient, although for some reason psychologists and
social workers mentioned this topic far more often than did psychiatrists.
Presumably both unconscious and conscious conflicts are alluded to here,
although the unconscious conflicts are generally considered the more important ones in shaping psychopathology.

Various categories of direct adjustment variables were deemed to be
appropriate by all of the groups of our sample. The adjustment variable
most frequently suggested as proper content is the defenses, and clinical
workers are in apparent agreement on the importance of this topic in the
psychological report. The defensive structure is truly one of the major
highways leading to an understanding of personality. A knowledge of the
defenses permits one to gauge the stability of a person and may also have a
direct relationship to psychotherapeutic activity. The sort of controls exer-
cised by a person, and their effectiveness, can be of key significance. Some
think it may be advisable to discuss the appearance or the role of anxiety in
adjustment.

The motivational factors in personality also come in for a good deal of
attention. Again these would seem to be of central importance in understanding the personality and its key problems. In general, there is much
stress on the importance of drives or dynamics, but some point out the
importance of motivational elements which are largely conscious, such as the
person's interest areas and goals. It certainly would be remiss of the
psychologist not to emerge occasionally from the depths of the unconscious
to assess the molding power of forces about which the person has awareness
and which are probably significant to an individual's life.

The personality assets and liabilities of the client, aside from purely
intellectual assets and liabilities, are commonly proposed as important
psychological contributions to the case study. Interestingly the psychologists
in our sample far more frequently suggested the appropriateness of reporting on assets rather than on liabilities. This opinion contrasts with the notion
that many psychologists show a "maladjustment bias" in their reports.
Psychiatrists and social workers in particular comment on the importance of
learning from the psychologist about the person's "ego strength," an item of
information that would be especially important when psychotherapeutic
intervention is contemplated.

In our sample many of the social workers and psychologists, and some
psychiatrists, spontaneously indicated that the presentation of social variables is of importance in the psychologist's report. These data would bear

special scrutiny, particularly from the point of view of the social worker. It has already been pointed out that at least some social workers are sensitive to what they perceive as the psychologist's encroachment on their area and so could hardly be sympathetic toward reports that parallel or duplicate their own material. There is no doubt, however, that social workers advocate the importance of social data to the understanding of behavior. May it be presumed then that they would favor the thesis presented here, that social variables ought to be presented in the psycholgist's study, but only when they are integrated with other personality data?

Perhaps this does represent the view of some, but the sort of social variables mentioned also might suggest that the respondents intended these items of information to be elicited independently by the psychologist. About half of the social worker respondents suggested the appropriateness of data on interpersonal relationships, and about one quarter of this group indicated they would like to read in the psychological report about the client's relationship to significant life figures. Possibly the social worker is thinking of integrating the psycholgist's findings on this topic with social work data developed in another context. This would not, and should not, preclude the psychologist from integrating social work data with psychological findings any more than it ought to keep the psychiatrist from the long-established practice of utilizing the findings of associates to add to an understanding of the patient.

Arbitrarily separated for discussion from the topic of the person's interpersonal relationships is the matter of interpersonal perceptions. Psychologists understand that a person's perception of the environment is vastly more important than the physical facts of environment. This area of personality function appears central to adequate case study in many instances. Often of similar basic importance is the self-concept.

Diagnostic Material

The reaction of many psychiatrists to the offering of a diagnosis by the psychologist has already been presented in several contexts. It is well to note the other side of the coin, the expressed *interest* of psychiatrists in obtaining diagnostic information from the psychologist. The existence of such differences would seem to emphasize the individual focus of psychological work. Much of the diagnostic information sought is not formal or in terms of an official classification.

Approximately one-fourth of the psychiatrists responding did request that formal diagnoses be offered. The percentage of psychologists in agreement with this view was somewhat greater, whereas the proportion of social workers who expressed a desire for a psychological diagnosis was somewhat less. About one in eight of the psychiatric group would like a psychologist to suggest a differential diagnosis, where required, whereas the social workers recorded no interest at all in this matter. In many situations the psychologist will justifiably feel a need to suggest a diagnosis, if indeed such content is not routinely expected or required in the report.

Some psychiatrists would also have the psychologist render an opinion about the existence of a possible underlying psychosis. Some wish to be informed on what the psychologist thinks about the presence of an overt psychosis. The medical orientation of many psychiatrists is particularly evident in their interest in securing from the psychologist diagnostic information concerning a possible organic mental disorder. Forty-two percent of the psychiatric group indicated that the psychologist ought to give information on the presence or absence of such conditions—their requests for psychological assessment often reading "rule out organicity." It is good both that psychologists are able to deliver an informed opinion on this important topic and that psychiatrists are so much aware of this fact.

Predictive Material

The cautions mentioned with reference to the offering of diagnoses also apply to predictions. Particularly the giving of a prognosis may be a delicate matter, as already noted. Social workers, however, seem to be more accepting of such contributions than are psychiatrists, hardly a surprising finding. Social workers also emphasize the practical and the environmental in the way of predictions and ask for such information as the vocational and educational outlook. Thus the reception of various areas of prediction is an individual matter among report readers. Many are interested in several of the different forms of acting-out potential, such as homicide, suicide, or paraphilia, and others want to know about treatment prospects.

Recommendations

The objections raised to the psychologist's offering of recommendations have also been noted. Some potential strain is seen in clinical relations because psychologists in general seem to want to make recommendations more often than their team associates, particularly psychiatrists, might wish to have them. Thus 74 percent of the psychologist sample suggested that it is appropriate to offer recommendations regarding treatment, whereas only 14 percent of the psychiatric respondents spontaneously mentioned the need for such help. Teachers and others who so eagerly seek the help of psychologists must find all of this strange.

What is appropriate content for a psychological report depends, then, on the workers involved in the case, on the reasons for which the person is referred, and on the available conclusions from which the psychologist has to select.

INAPPROPRIATE CONTENT

It is far easier to make pronouncements on what is never appropriate in a psychological report than to offer opinions on what may be appropriate. The most helpful generalization is that the psychologist never renders conclusions that are outside actual or defined limits of function or competence. Admittedly the borderlines are sometimes vague and subject to personal interpretations that may be at variance with group consensus. The overall psychoevaluative competence of the psycholgist is not generally challenged, however, and at this late date is not likely to be. Yet the establishment of certain conclusions based on personality data—for example, the declaration of the legal competency of patients and the making of medical treatment decisions—are functions legally proscribed to the psychologist. Thus there exist some clear external guidelines that show what is beyond the psychologist's qualifications or functions. This observation is consistent with the fact that psychologists may be, and are, asked to contribute information or opinions to decisions which are ultimately outside their scope.

Then there are matters that are within the broad purview of psychology but that may be beyond the competence of a given psychologist. Generally the decision here is based on the psychologist's awareness of personal limitations of training and experience and on adherence to ethical principles (American Psychological Association, 1981). A psychologist not skilled in the Rorschach ought not to present conclusions based on the use of this instrument. A psychologist not enlightened or practiced in psychoanalytic usage ought not present conclusions in such a framework. Many psychologists cannot give sound direct treatment suggestions in cases of speech disability or reading disability, but psychologists who have had adequate training and experience in these areas might be specifically employed for their ability to render conclusions on such problems.

THE APPROPRIATE EMPHASIS
OF CONTENT

In report writing it is helpful to think not only in terms of what to include or exclude but also of what contents to emphasize or de-emphasize. The topics comprising the psychological report should, according to our present frame of reference, try to meet perceived and anticipated needs of the client. This requirement ought to be true of the various emphases in a report, too. If we take into consideration the different orientations held by psychologists, however, it is understandable for the psychologist to present findings in terms of a personal approach to understanding personality and behavior. This is probably not wrong *as long as the psychologist is still able to fulfill the mission as perceived.* This argument is not meant to defend the habitual emphases of a psychologist who has no clear-cut orientation or who emphasizes certain kinds of material solely because of a misguided impression of how psychological reports are supposed to be written.

We may consider, for example, emphasis on developmental content versus emphasis on contemporary content. A psychoanalytic orientation might focus on developmental stages and apparently suit the requirements that prevail in an analytically oriented setting; even here, though, the therapist will probably be more interested in the strength of the individual's defensive structure and on other issues (see the discussion on pp. 31–32). When humanistic or somatic therapies, are used, we should be aware that such treatments may deliberately be blind to the individual's developmental history. Even when traditional psychotherapy is the chosen approach, many therapists, including analytically oriented workers, now tend to believe that treatment centering about contemporary problems offers the greatest therapeutic leverage.

An emphasis on unconscious content often appears in reports to the exclusion of concern with consciously directed behavior, the content of consciousness, and surface behavior. Unconscious content is commonly related to the origins and to the deepest reaches of psychopathology. To dwell on such content may be unjustifiable in other than very dynamically oriented situations. Other significant clues to psychological problems—such as the precipitating factors and salient features of the condition, its future course, and therapeutic possibilities—can often be effectively approached through the content of consciousness and the surface behavior. The practical relevance of content may then properly dictate the emphasis. Consider, for example, the matter of drives or dynamics, or, as a specific instance of this, the term *hostility,* which appears so frequently in psychological reports. The form this ubiquitous trait takes may be central to the understanding of a particular problem—for example, "hysterical" behavior—otherwise it is often unworthy of emphasis or even of mention in a report. Much the same may be said of the common content categories of defenses and conflicts. A discussion of these topics can be crucial to the psychotherapist who wishes to strengthen a functioning personality and needs to know how well the client can cope with stress developed in the therapeutic situation. But of what value is the presentation of unconscious content to the symptomatically oriented chemotherapist?

5

CONCEPTUALIZING THE PSYCHOLOGICAL REPORT

A flexible approach makes for better psychological reports. This view, along with some ways to implement it, is offered as a contribution to the old problem of how to organize reports. Apparently the difficulties involved in this task have not been alleviated by the various general report outlines that are presently available. What is proposed here is a new schema of the assessment process together with the suggestion that the report be case-focused and conceptualized in terms of the mission. In such a report the roles of issues like content selection, theoretical orientation, and organizational form will readily take on meaning.

THE RESPONSIBILITY OF THE PSYCHOLOGIST—to the client, to the person who makes the referral, to the team, and to society—is the central theme of this discourse. The foregoing discussions have dealt with many of the elements that comprise such responsibility. This chapter ventures to round out the points already made and to suggest for them a framework to provide some additional rationale and further guidance for the effective preparation of a psychological report.

In an earlier chapter much space was given to the topic of pitfalls that, unfortunately, seem to be prevalent in psychological report writing. Additional pitfalls are exposed in the ensuing discussion, but there are differences. The pitfalls that were discussed earlier are, for the most part, of the sort that are common to poor rhetoric: inappropriate choices about what to write, insufficient self-criticalness of the writer and the consequent presentation of faulty and blurred ideas, inadequate consideration for the reader's needs, poor command of language, and the like. Only in our discussion of "Problems of Science and Profession" do we confront another sort of pitfall.

In focusing on the assessment process we reveal concern that many psychologists do not conceptualize well an adequate scheme of psychological assessment. When such is true, the development and implementation of assessment skills may be seriously impeded. The value of psychological input into the case may be in doubt.

THE EVOLUTION OF PSYCHOLOGICAL ASSESSMENT SCHEMES

The psychological report is the end product of the assessment process and a contribution to some sort of intervention in a person's life. To follow the thinking that leads to the report, we must first conceptualize a theory of the assessment process, from the development and integration of information to the emergence of pragmatic conclusions. Let us start the discussion by noting the role of the physicalistic model of assessment and then move to a model of clinical assessment that better reflects much of current practice.

Clinical psychological assessment stems from, and *incorporates* features of, the psychometric model that has so long been prominent in psychology. Thorndike's logically sequential pronouncements are the basis: "If a thing exists, it exists in some amount," and, "If it exists in some amount, it can be measured."

Such a physicalistic position, equating psychological behaviors at all levels with *things,* a position that many find conceptually flawed, nevertheless has long proved useful in making individual and group predictions. Measurement of this sort is also the basis for norms that have such a crucial role in assessment. Group testers and individual assessors differ, however, inasmuch as the individual assessor develops or utilizes normative data only as these are consistent with and amplify other highly valued data. For example, a psychologist employing the Halstead-Reitan Neuropsychological Battery may encounter a high error score on the Categories test suggestive of conceptual impairment and possible brain dysfunction in the client. But alternatively, the psychologist might be impressed that the client demonstrates good conceptual ability in other ways, or perhaps even that adequate motivation to do this rather demanding test well seemed lacking. For such reasons a diagnostic impression of brain dysfunction may be neither conclusive nor convincing.

In the routine course of clinical psychological assessment, numerous problems are encountered for which the psychometric (physicalistic) model is not adequate. A new scheme of assessment must be explicitly set forth; clinical psychologists obviously have long followed leaders other than Thorndike. But even these leaders evidence some Thorndikian influence, at least in their word usage, employing such still current expressions as *tester* and *test results.* Indeed, Ivnik (1977) points out that the term *psychodiagnosis* sometimes ". . . is primarily reserved for the use of psychological tests." There seems to be a discrepancy in that many who do not follow a physicalistic model routinely use physicalistic language.

Schafer (1949), in a research-oriented paper with broad significance for clinical practice, was, as a participant in the development of the Rapaportian tradition, among the first to contribute direction to the approach to assessment presented here. Indeed, many view his emphasis of psychologist over tests as a major distinction of modern practice:

> Scores are not meant to replace psychological thinking; they are designed to facilitate it, and as such they can be relegated to the background when this is warranted by the logic of the problem.

Also

> The alternative to considering the score the adequate meaningful micro-unit is considering the interpretation the meaningful unit. This approach recognizes that the same score can have different meanings and that the same meaning can be conveyed by different scores. It also recognizes the fact that scores in general do not adequately convey all the implications of a response or a set of responses.

Further, in the psychometric era of the 1940s, anticipating more nearly universal current trends, Schafer (1949) set forth the following as goals of psychological assessment:

"Identifying personality characteristics rather than diagnoses as clinical criteria.
Individual variations as a focus of interest along with group trends.
Blind qualitative analysis prior to statistical comparison.
Interpretation as micro-units of analysis and batteries of tests as macro-units of investigation."

Drifting further from the earlier physicalistic approach, Shectman (1979) argues that effectiveness of assessment must now consider personal characteristics of the psychologist (particularly shortcomings, covered in our earlier section called "Pitfalls") and interpersonal staff issues (see pp. 16–17). Additionally Shectman broaches the content of the referral question. With this issue the complexity of clinical psychological assessment starts to become evident.

How the clinician formulates questions to the psychologist is a related issue. The psychologist sometimes must interpret the referral source—that is, what does the referring clinician *really* want to know? Might one infer from the question as posed that the assessment psychologist is in a position to supply useful information that is *not* being requested, or is the referral question as posed impossible to answer meaningfully or usefully? Thus Shectman (1979) comments ". . . the provider who responds to the referral issues alone and not to the person making the referral repeats Freud's mistake and that of diagnosticians who respond to referral questions as if they existed in a vacuum." Freudiana surfaces again as Cohen (1980) suggests that ". . . there is a manifest and a latent content to many testing referrals." The latent content very well may pertain to interpersonal factors among clinic personnel. One example, a personal anecdote cited by Cohen, reports on a case where the real issue was a disagreement over diagnosis between psychiatrist and patient with Cohen finding himself more in the position of arbiter than of diagnostician.

Howe (1981) describes an evaluation schema that emphasizes (1) the need for meaningful referral, (2) "the differences between a diagnostic model of *testing* and dispositional assessment" (emphasis added), and (3) the need for ". . . the assessor to understand the treatment context as well as the client. . . ."

Shevrin and Shectman (1973) propose yet additional crucial features for an assessment schema. Such features are relevant, of course, in various diagnostic situations and not simply in the diagnosis of mental disorders of which the authors write: "In the diagnosis of mental disorders, the diagnostician, through the *medium of a personal relationship, elicits and observes* a range of *psychological functioning* which he considers *relevant on some theoretical grounds* for understanding the disorders so that he can make a *recommendation* which stands a good chance of being acted on as a basis for dealing with the disorders." Consideration of the personal role of the psychologist and of the psychologist's theoretical position leads to another powerful comment: "From our point of view, diagnosis is *not* the unsolicited functioning existing in a purely impersonal empirical realm unrelated to theoretical orientation and indifferent to outcome."

The Sloves-Docherty-Schneider Scientific Problem-Solving Model

A logical end point to the evolution of Thorndike's physicalistic thesis is based on Sloves, Docherty, and Schneider's (1979) adaptation of a scientific problem-solving model proposed by Comtois and Clark (1976). Such an adaptation is informed by their view that "the current state of affairs in psychological assessment is one of confusion, misconception, attack, and counterattack." The position of Sloves et al. suggests that the roots of this problem run deep:

> Much of the confusion and misconception over psychological assessment is a result of the failure to differentiate between two conceptually distinct aspects of psychodiagnosis, referred to here as psychological assessment and psychological testing. Psychological assessment is defined as a variable process of problem solving, decision making, and evaluation procedures. The goal of psychological assessment is to "yield information relevant to treatment and . . . generate decisions which will be helpful to clients" (Peterson, 1968, p. 8). Psychological testing is defined as a set of skills, tactics, and strategies subsumed under the heading of psychological methods. In this view, methods represent the technical skills used as a means of carrying out a psychological assessment. Psychological assessment is systems and problem oriented, dynamic, and conceptual; whereas psychological testing is methods and measurement oriented, descriptive, and technical.

Lack of conception of such fundamentals has, in the view of these authors, resulted in the inability of ". . . many practitioners and trainers in professional psychology to distinguish between assessment and testing." This problem, in turn, ". . . has lead to a tendency for the profession to focus its attention on the mechanistic and technical aspects of test administration and to ignore or slight the conceptual basis of the assessment process."

To counter this trend, Sloves et al. present their model in six steps:

Step one, *problem clarification,* is a reframing of the referral question. What are the needs of the referral source? To answer this seemingly simple question may require the posing of a number of additional questions and a study of the circumstances that have led to the making of a referral.

Step two is called *planning*. Responding to the statement of a problem, the psychologist forms hypotheses for testing. What might give rise to the problem and how might we establish that such is the case? Often there might be alternative explanations, and it might be wise to consider which of these apply.

Development, the third step, involves planning for implementation of the previous step. What data are requested? Will the administration and interpretation of tests in widespread use meet our purpose, or is the construction of an ad hoc tool, such as an instrument for the systematic recording of behavior, indicated?

The fourth step, *implementation*, involves all of the parameters of what usually come under the rubric of "testing" or of the making of direct observations. Such "details" as preparing clients for assessment and explaining to them their legal rights are part of this step.

The fifth step is *outcome determination*. Here the effects of the psychologist's intervention are evaluated. Was the information deemed necessary for clarifying issues forthcoming? Were the hypotheses adequately tested? Responding to these questions involves a number of considerations, such as evaluations of "the level of expertise of the assessor, the instruments used, any biases of the instruments or assessor that may have influenced the reliability and validity of the assessment, and the reactions of the persons involved in the assessment." No small order! An accomplished, well-seasoned psychologist, we would hope, can take the responsibility for such a determination. Perhaps at times the collaboration of a colleague might also be helpful at this stage of use of the problem-solving model (or at any stage, for that matter). Certainly where a trainee is involved the role of the supervisor should be particularly conspicuous.

The final step, *dissemination*, involves report writing in the broad sense that we use it here and, as such, is concerned with many of the issues dealt with in this book. The authors define this step well in terms of "the communication of *useful* information to those concerned with the assessment" (emphasis supplied).

Although the authors see some drawbacks to the use of this model, they nevertheless believe that its advantages ultimately overshadow initial difficulties and that it provides a training aid to the neophyte:

> By making the process explicit, of course, it becomes at once laborious to use and a gross simplification of the actual clinical process. However, it need only be used in this unwieldly manner until the model is internalized. The oversimplification of the model is a characteristic of any conceptual model and can actually be considered an advantage for the sake of training. Once the process is internalized, the clinician-trainee can begin to provide his or her own elaboration in practice.

An Interactional Schema of the Clinical Assessment Process

Figure 5-1, the author's concept of the assessment process, would appear to be compatible with the views formulated by Sloves et al. (1979). As these authors indicate, assessment is not a linear event, and as described here, the process is understood primarily as an interaction between the psychologist and four key categories of information: (1) the reason for assessment, (2) raw data, (3) frame(s) of reference, and (4) the psychological report. Only as the psychologist adequately develops, reacts to, and integrates the first three categories (placed at the angles of the triangle) do his or her activities lead to a set of meaningful conclusions, that when effectively presented make for an adequate psychological report.

Focusing attention on the triangle, the placement of the psychologist (Ψ) at the center emphasizes a hierarchy of importance of the interacting elements. As commonly observed, in psychological assessment the psychologist is the chief diagnostic instrument. The reason for assessment, a matter to which the psychologist should always react, is a matter of importance secondary only to the psychologist and is shown at the apex of the triangle. Without an explict and meaningful reason for assessment, an assessment needn't be carried out.

Frame(s) of reference should be considered to hold a somewhat lower position inasmuch as the reason for assessment commonly can be dealt with in the context of various frames of reference. For example, the solution to a problem may be sought in a behavioral approach, in various dynamic positions, in a humanistic or neuropsychological orientation, or perhaps even through some combination of these or through an open-ended exploration.

Similarly assessment data are in a subordinate position since these are developed by the psychologist in terms both of the reason for assessment and the frame(s) of reference. Test results may be placed in the category of

FIGURE 5-1   Psychological Assessment Schema

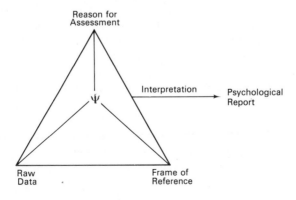

assessment data: test results are not the basic purpose of a clinical assessment and are not synonymous with the psychological report.

In the following paragraphs the components of the schema of which the psychologist is an integral part, are explicated terms of typical clinical practice. The practicum material on supervision presented in Chapter 8 is a concrete illustration of the schema in operation.

Reason for Assessment   The psychologist may carry out an assessment to provide guidelines for planning a therapeutic strategy. Or a therapist, a teacher, or an administrator may seek the help of a psychological assessor to gain understanding and an approach to working with a person. Regardless of who initiates the request for assessment, the reason for assessment in a treatment situation is always based on the recognition that some specific behavior or behaviors in a client may be changeable to the client's advantage.

Problems are most likely to arise when the referral source does not provide a reason for requesting an assessment or when the reason given appears to the psychologist to be unrealistic or not likely to yield the sort of information that might be helpful. The psychologist therefore cannot be merely the passive recipient of referrals. Often it is necessary for the psychologist to contact the referral source and clarify what sort of data should be sought in the assessment. The psychologist plays an active role in developing the consultation. The assessment procedure starts before the psychologist meets the client.

Raw Data   *Raw data* consist of all observations and other information available to the psychologist and that may be pertinent in responding to the reason for carrying out an assessment or that otherwise might be judged by the psychologist to be useful. Included are direct observation of behavior (including the client's spontaneous actions and verbalizations) plus information supplied by others, such as parents or teachers. Behavior report forms may be completed by such persons or by the psychologist. The psychologist may also administer tests from which stem such data as scores, ratios, percentages, profiles, and verbalizations. Classically such material, together with a discussion of quantitative relationships among scores and a qualitative description of test performance, have been labeled *test results*. [The author's preference is to call such material *raw data* (pp.   –   ).] Currently the term *test results* is also used by some psychologists when various interpretive comments accompany a discussion of raw data.

Frame(s) of Reference   *Frame of reference* refers to the personality theory (theories) plus the views on psychopathology and other behaviors that the psychologist holds. These, together with the reason for assessment, greatly influence the data that the psychologist seeks to gather and the means used to gather them. Shall the psychologist seek parents' and teachers' reports of a child's social behavior, for example, or is the content of the child's unconscious judged to be of greater pertinence? Is a behavioral report likely to supply the material we need, or should we look to the client's performance on projective techniques such as the Rorschach and the TAT? Finally, frame of reference determines the psychologist's recorded response (the psychological report) to the reason for assessment.

Interpretation   The translation of raw data into formulations that are meaningful and significant in terms of the reason for assessment and the psychologist's frame of reference is called *interpretation*. Such topics as why certain behavior occurs or antecedents or events associated with such behavior is part of the interpretation that is made. Implicit or explicit in the interpretation may be found suggestions for approaches to changing behavior. Interpretation always involves the relation of a client's responses to conclusions, but interpretation typically is not as simple as A (datum) = B (conclusion). The relations between test data and conclusions collected by Gilbert (1978, 1980) and Ogdon (1981) may be helpful to the neophyte psychologist but do not explicate the process of interpretation. As Levy (1963) suggests, an indefinable style may also affect whether one is a good or a poor interpreter.

Psychological Report   The *psychological report* is the end product of the assessment procedure. It consists of a series of interpretive statements plus other content as discussed in Chapter 4. Omitted are those conclusions that the psychologist judges to be not pertinent to the reason for assessment or otherwise not relevant to the needs of the client. The manner in which conclusions are presented reflect the assessment skill of the psychologist and determine the usefulness of the report.

THE RATIONALE FOR FLEXIBILITY

"There is, of course, no one way to write a report, just as there is no one form or organization that will always suffice. *Each writer's personal characteristics will determine, in part, how he will attack his problem.*" (emphasis supplied) The source of this quote is perhaps as important as the idea which it expresses. It is taken from *Technical Report Writing* by James W. Souther (1957), a guidebook prepared for engineers. Engineering, as the nontechnically trained understand it, utilizes precise methods based on the physical sciences and mathematics. The sort of things engineers write about in their reports are machines, factory or mine installations, or industrial manufacturing processes. Where should one be more systematized and objective? Yet engineers are trained to be flexible and to allow their personalities to color their reports, whereas psychologists are frequently exhorted to deny their participant-observer role, to standardize their report procedures, to be objective. We are frequently reminded from within and without our profession that the psychological report is a laboratory report or a scientific document.

General outlines for dealing with large areas of *personality* at various levels, as is typical with traditional reports, are to be regarded as Procrustean schemes, and none will be found on these pages. How can a rigid outline accommodate the protean complexities of personality and recognize the variability among people, circumstances, and practical needs? Such outlines, especially if well detailed, may be welcomed because they partly or totally relieve the psychologist of the necessity of thinking about how to organize an effective presentation. But they also force the psychologist to fit findings where they may not belong if optimal meaning and effectiveness is to be had.

When we deal with problem-oriented, prescriptive reports, the situation can be different. Here we deal with well-defined, circumscribed areas of behavior such that the psychologist is in a position to juxtapose problem areas or symptoms and plans for remediation. Such reports are of particular value in the behavior therapies. For example, Lazarus' (1981) categorization by the modalities that comprise the "Basic Id—*B*ehavior, *A*ffect, *S*ensation, *I*magery, *C*ognition, *I*nterpersonal relationships, *D*rugs/Biological factors (pp. 185–186)—exemplifies a highly functional approach. Computer reports, too, are an exception. Such reports present conclusions under predetermined categories. Thus the following main categories provide the conceptual framework for the MCMI Report (Chapter 7): Axis II (Personality Patterns), Axis I (Clinical Syndromes), Noteworthy Responses, and DSM-III Multiaxial Diagnosis. Additional information is provided under the headings Psychosocial Stressors, Severity of Disturbance, and Therapeutic Implications.

However, Souther's observation still applies. Have you ever noticed how many psychological reports start the body of the report with a statement of IQ(s) and a stereotyped discussion of intellectual functioning? Why? Is it because these are the most important findings about the client? Is it because such matters appearing later in the report after a discussion of more meaningful personality content would be anticlimactic and are thus best gotten out of the way as soon as possible? Or is it that this is the way we have been doing it for over a generation and don't really know what else to do? In any event, second (or third) generation generalized report outlines continue to place, after "Test Behavior" or "Behavioral Observations," a report of the IQ and data on intellectual functioning (e.g., Carr, 1968; Lacks, Horton, & Owen, 1969; Sturm, 1974; van Reken, (1981).

Let's look at it this way. The psychologist has a creative, custom-job to do and following an outline approaches the mechanical filling out of a standard form. Perhaps the engineers can help us again. Dr. L. B. Headrick (1956) of RCA advises, "Consider the writing of a technical paper as an engineering problem. Analysis of a problem is essential to understanding and to an organized plan of attack." Souther amplifies this point while presenting a rationale and general guide to the kind of report he proposes.

> The point of attack is always identification of the problem and analyzing the writing situation. Material must be gathered and evaluated, and the report must be designed and written. Failure and confusion often result because the writer starts in the middle of the process or overlooks major considerations. Thus the application of the engineering approach to the solution of writing problems is certain to produce more effective reports, for a report, like any other engineering product, must be designed to satisfy a particular industrial function with its own specific set of requirements. If the analysis is accurate and extensive, the investigation complete and thorough, the design detailed and purposeful, and the application careful and ordered, the report will effectively communicate to its audience, play its industrial role, and fulfill its purpose.[1]

To which a psychologist can but meekly add, "Writing, communication itself, is also a psychological problem."

HOW TO ORGANIZE REPORTS: AN OLD PROBLEM

The discussion to this point has extolled the merits of flexibility, albeit in general terms, and discouraged rigid outline schemes. "But how then are we to get help in organzing our reports?" the reader might be justified in asking. An unpublished survey of ours among student psychologists and psychologists at various levels of experience indicated that a prominent concern of report writers is difficulty in organizing their reports and that a prominent criticism of training programs is that they do not offer enough help on how to accomplish this task. (These observations in themselves would seem to imply that report-writing outlines are not felt to be satisfactory, for there certainly are enough of them to be had!) One cannot give a simple answer on how to organize the report. This depends on how the assessment function is conceptualized, which, in turn, depends on one's philosophy of the assessment function itself.

WHEN THE PSYCHOLOGIST IS A CONSULTANT

The psychologist, when serving as a consultant, is a contributing and interacting member of a professional group. Persons with psychological problems of various sorts, are, in effect, assigned to the group with the expecta-

[1]From James W. Souther *Technical Report Writing* (New York: John Wiley & Sons, Inc., 1957). Copyright © 1957 by John Wiley and Sons, Inc. and reprinted by permission.

tion that it can help, in some degree, to overcome or cope with their problems, or even that it can manage or care for them better than they can do for themselves. To accomplish one or more of these goals, different kinds of information about the person may be required.

It is the psychologist who sets the goal(s) of assessment. Others may request answers to certain questions, but the psychologist determines the means of responding to those questions. There are times when the psychologist conceptualizes a problem differently from the way it is understood by others; during the assessment process the psychologist may even come to see a problem as something other than was initially the case. Nevertheless, an attempt should always be made to respond to questions that are raised even though additional (not asked for) material be offered. Thus a client may be referred to a psychologist for assessment of the extent of depression, but the data additionally are interpreted as showing the existence of a schizophrenic process. The report should comment on both the depression and the schizophrenia.

All findings are not reported, however. The psychologist selects from a reservoir of interpretations only those that might contribute to the mission and omits those that are apparently not relevant or that add unnecessary length and confuse the issue. The presence of deep castration anxiety—with which the person will no doubt die—would not ordinarily be pertinent when a patient's emotional stability is being evaluated to help determine the advisability of hospital discharge. In fact, the busy psychologist, on spotting raw data that would apparently not contribute to the assessment goal, might not wish to develop further interpretations in this area. In addition, it may be found advisable to eliminate low confidence conclusions or perhaps to retain them with appropriate qualifications only if they relate to pertinent issues.

At this point the psychologist will resort to some sort of weighting of interpretations, placing them in a hierarchy of importance and perhaps reevaluating a few of the conclusions earlier judged not to be relevant. Again the psychologist might well ask how much confidence should be placed in the conclusions and how pertinent they seem to be. In most cases only a few key conclusions constitute the essence of the report, and the minor conclusions often are best eliminated lest they add bulk and detract from the central theme(s) of the case.

The psychologist is now ready to set pen to paper. It is here that the problem of effective presentation might seem greatest. Chapter 4 discusses the problem of what content may or may not be appropriate and also broaches the topic of emphasis of content. Only in working with a specific case, however, does the psychologist concretely face the problem of which conclusions to report, their organization, and the composition scheme that will enhance the appropriate emphases.

SOME BASIC
CONSIDERATIONS IN
ORGANIZING THE REPORT

Prior to organizing the case presentation with an eye to its effectiveness, the psychologist must review the mission. Focus should be on what is important in the case, emphasizing that which needs to be emphasized and eliminating that which is not immediately or potentially useful. Parsimony is basic to organization in addition to whatever other virtues it might have. Parsimony will not only save the time of the report writer and reader and cut down on bulk but will also eliminate some of the possible sources of confusion and misunderstanding in the report. Parsimonious writing will tend to emphasize the central problem(s) and personality issues for the psychologist and the reader, whereas shotgun reporting tends to dilute the main conclusions and place them on a par with matters of minor relevance. For example, for a patient who had been economically and socially successful but was now being evaluated for discharge following hospitalization brought about by an acute break, a recitation of the relations among intellectual skills would probably not add, and might detract from, attention to the main problem. We might similarly judge to be insignificant knowledge about psychosexual development, feeling of inadequacy as a male, fear of heterosexual contacts, or oedipal status in a patient who is being evaluated for protective institutional employment.

It is well for the psychologist to be committed to a theoretical orientation, and to be aware of biases that might enter the report. There must be concern with what the psychologist can do for a specific person with a specific problem or problems, in the particular situation where a client is being assessed and treated. Often there is a temptation to conceptualize the consultation in terms of what the psychologist regards as ideal rather than in terms of the perceived limitations of the situation. A psychologist can think, perhaps rightly so, that psychotherapy (perhaps even a certain kind of psychotherapy) is the therapy of choice, for most clients. However, it would be unrealistic to conceptualize the typical mission in terms of evaluating the indications for psychotherapy or specific recommendations for psychotherapy in a setting where the availability of this form of treatment is very limited.

The language in which the psychologist *thinks* is also a major issue, influencing as it does both the conceptualization and the presentation of the case. The inexactness and multiple meanings of jargon are well established. When the psychologist thinks in terms of these inexactitudes, can the writing be any more precise? Is it constructive to think through a case using words that are variously used and variously understood and then to *translate* these

into words that have but one meaning and are in the experience of the report reader?

The same sort of consideration applies to the theoretical constructs in terms of which the psychologist *thinks* about clients, particularly if these are complex and removed from the experience or perceived requirements of associates. The psychological report is a practical document prepared for use by persons with various amounts of psychological knowledge. Many of them are not expected to be sophisticated in psychological theory. When the psychologist conceptualizes a case in terms of theoretical constructs to communicate to the reader, practical considerations might require that conclusions be translated, simplified, or diluted. Again the question is raised whether the maneuver of translating can be accomplished satisfactorily. Simplifying or diluting the conclusions might tend to call forth a condescending attitude on the part of the psychologist. Theoretical constructs are most useful when dealing with theoretical matters, and they are often helpful, probably indispensable, in making it possible for the psychologist to understand the client. Such use of theory, often implicit, is to be distinguished from publicly conceptualizing the case in terms of theoretical constructs. The psychologist may frequently turn to personality theory or to test theory to find meaning in the data. But one cannot dwell at this level, for the needs of the client in a particular situation are sometimes far removed from even clinically derived theory.

A direct counterproposal to a formal theoretical orientation is that the psychologist think about clients in terms of a simple descriptive and operational approach (cf. Schafer's [1976] "action language"). In the interest of relevance a client may be largely described both in terms of current behavior and potential behavior. Presumptions about what the client does and might do are both likely to be important; sometimes current behavior, sometimes potential behavior is of greatest pertinence.

Relevant behavior may be found in that which is overt and that which is covert, that which is in consciousness and that which is unconscious or preconscious, the molar and the molecular. Things that the person may *do* include the entertainment, at various levels of consciousness, of goals, ideas, beliefs, or feelings; the exercise of various intellectual and social skills, and other means of manipulating the environment; and the many possible ego defensive maneuvers. Behaviors that are habitual or part of a life style would ordinarily be of greater import than occasional behaviors.

Although potential behavior may sometimes overshadow in importance current behavior, often the two need to be jointly considered. Paranoid ideation may be a factor in potential assaultive conduct, but we may also be interested in the presence or absence of such thinking because it is needed to fix a diagnosis, determine feasibility for psychotherapy, or to estimate the client's ability to adjust to a certain environment. The psychologist can often predict potential behavior, such as improvement or retrogression, or socially

significant actions when adequate indications are not otherwise available. Even though past behavior is often the most efficient predictor of future events, nevertheless, the psychologist can often point up unsuspected trends or tensions, the sort of stimuli that activate them, and perhaps even estimate the thresholds at which they are activated.

With these several considerations in mind, we may now begin to think about the problem of organization. The very wording of this proposal indicates our bias of presentation in this book, at least as far as the presentation of personality topics is concerned: personality ought to be contemplated as an organized whole, not as unorganized segments.

In this book the psychologist is exhorted to humanize reports, to think and write in simple operational terms, and to describe the client in functional language. In basic form this mode of delivering personality data approximates the manner in which one nonpsychologist describes another, without the loose methods of observing and reaching conclusions that some untrained persons employ.

Lay evaluation is organized into functional unities that focus on behaviors. Nonpsychologists concentrate, as the occasion demands, on areas of felt concern, such as an associate's intelligence, sincerity, friendliness, or "personality." They reach conclusions rather directly—come to the point and tell what sort of a person someone is. "He's the sort of feller you can trust. You can count on him when you need him. He'll go out of his way to help when you're in a jam." The narrator may then cite some empirical supporting evidence, or perhaps even intuitive knowledge. One can hardly be more succinct than the late president Lyndon Johnson who characterized a political rival as "a man who can't walk and chew gum at the same time." The nonpsychologist never segmentalizes a subject into predetermined and fixed discrete areas such as "intellect," "emotions," and "interpersonal relations." The lay listener might have difficulty in integrating such segments into some kind of a functional whole. Professional people sometimes have similar problems.

A segmentalized presentation of more or less static personality data may appear to be scientific and clinically functional because it suggests the existence of distinct, identifiable personality components that were isolated and measured, or otherwise assessed. However, we believe that personality is a functional interrelated unity, and we concur with those who believe that clinically important traits are largely specific, that a stimulus in a total situation is as relevant as the organism or its responses. A more extreme point of view holds that general traits may be invalid abstractions of transactional behavior. Even if we think in terms of psychometrically defined general traits, the personality segments ordinarily discussed in reports do not correspond closely with personality variables so established. Nevertheless, to some workers segments seem a convenient way of thinking about a person. A report composed of information on various a priori established segments may seem crisp and "scientific." It is crisp, but it is no more scientific than an integrated presentation.

The presentation of discrete segments to a report reader may be regarded as akin to presenting data having a certain degree of rawness. The whole is more than the sum of its parts, and the functionally integrated report has meaning not found in the separate information units with which the psychologist initially deals. It is logically the psychologist's duty to integrate data, if we accept that the purpose of psychological assessment is to present functional conclusions rather than mere elemental data. It is technically sound to entrust this responsibility to a psychologist who has a grasp of the data and is in a position to judge which of these should enter the report and which should be omitted. The psychologist ought to be able to formulate more meaningful psychological conclusions than can someone who has a less initimate grasp of the basic materials.

THEORETICAL CONSTRUCTS
AND THE REPORT

It is the task of the psychologist to translate the raw material of the protocol into a meaningful, useful picture of personality or behavior. This is the most difficult phase of assessment. Many theories—from Freud's to Skinner's—may be helpful; the same is true of theories of assessment and experience with assessment modalities. In general, clinically derived theories, especially Freudian psychoanalysis and its more socially oriented modifications, are pertinent to dynamically oriented psychologists, since they are concerned with human development and the major conditions of the maladjustment and readjustment processes. At the same time psychoanalysis is not particularly conversant with the assessment of skills, with many aspects of rehabilitation, or with behavior therapies, or with neuropsychology, or with current humanistic approaches. Other orientations, such as learning or conditioning theories, are also adapted to help understand human development, maladjustment, and readjustment. Increasingly a cognitive approach is recognized as very useful.

As helpful as systematic views of personality can be, they too often become unduly injected into a case and lead both the unwary psychologist and the reader astray, away from the individual and toward the generalities that characterize most persons. Personality tests can be interpreted in the framework of any number of theories. The Rorschach owes allegiance to no particular theory and is compatible with many. The Murray TAT can, of course, be interpreted according to the viewpoint on personality from which it emerged, but more often the TAT stories are assigned meanings contributed by various theorists. Responses to a psychometric procedure (e.g., the

WAIS-R) are freely interpreted as contributions to personality understanding.

Interpretation that closely follows a personality theory—for example, Freudian psychoanalysis—can be technically superb in terms of the accuracy of the insights offered, completeness and potency of presentation, and internal consistency, yet fall far short of the case requirements. A protocol thus interpreted is likely to give workers who are sophisticated in analytic theory an excellent understanding of such matters as basic drive structure, psychosexual status, and developmental factors. Unfortunately an understanding of such matters may not be very helpful in working with a particular individual, whereas other information may be much more pertinent. Knowledge of early factors in the client's emotional development can be quite beside the point when the problem is one of attempting a community readjustment or treating the individual with available modalities such as electroconvulsive therapy, occupational therapy, or antidepressants. Many modern analysts, as well as other psychotherapists, do not rely very much on information about the person's early life, preferring in many instances to deal with how the individual copes with contemporary problems.

THE CLIENT'S NEEDS
AND THE REPORT

What would seem to be required is a realistic point of view on what are the clinically important variables commonly found in the people we evaluate. The topics of concern must be established on the basis of judged relevance for each individual case, not on the basis of the topics prominent in some personality theory nor on classes of content thought to be regularly made available through the use of various tests. At the present stage of our development, this task may be accomplished independently by psychologists through both experience and theoretical orientation. Theory is sometimes to an extent implicit and based partly on personal factors in the psychologist, hence perhaps less alterable than it should be. Regardless of the reason, some workers will stress the role of hostility, social influences, the role of the mother, the oedipal status, inferiority feelings, repression, or fixation at the oral level. An a priori list of variables acceptable to all would be extremely difficult to draw up, although systematic investigation might eventually succeed with this task.

The General Topics
of the Report

Quite arbitrarily we can draw up a useful list of tentative general personality topics that could provide the basic elements around which the psychologist might conceptualize the case presentation. These may be regarded as "handles" with which the psychologist can come to grips with the mission in the presence of the mass of data accumulated about the client. Although something might be written on almost every one of these topics for every person (a systematic approach to shotgun reporting!), usually a person can be meaningfully and effectively described in skeletal form by focusing on just a few of them. In most instances the case presentation can probably be conceptualized around perhaps three to six of these topics. Occasionally seven or eight might be required, but at other times, particularly when a pointed question is asked, even one or two might suffice. The report can then be rounded out with subcategories also taken from the list.

This list of topics cannot be offered as complete, nor are all topics mutually exclusive. Each psychologist may wish to add those variables that seem to be generally pertinent.

EXAMPLES OF GENERAL PERSONALITY TOPICS AROUND WHICH A CASE PRESENTATION MAY BE CONCEPTUALIZED

Achievement	Emotional Controls
Affect	Emotivity
Aggressiveness	Fears
Antisocial Tendencies	Fixations
Anxieties	Flexibility
Aptitudes	Frustrations
Attitudes	Gender Identity
Aversions	Goals
Background Factors	Hostility
Behavioral Problems	Identity
Biological Factors	Imagery
Brain Dysfunction	Insight
Cognitive Functioning	Intellectual Controls
Cognitive Skills	Intellectual Level
Cognitive Style	Interests
Competency	Interpersonal Relations
Conative Factors	Interpersonal Skills
Conflicts	Life Style
Content of Consciousness	Molar Surface Behavior
Contingency Management	Needs
Defenses	Outlook
Deficits	Perception of Environment
Developmental Factors	Perception of Self
Diagnostic Considerations	Personal Consequences of Behavior
Drives, Dynamics	Placement Prospects
Emotional Cathexes	Psychopathology

Rehabilitation Needs
Rehabilitation Prospects
Self-concept
Sentiments
Sex
Sex Role
Significant Others
Situational Factors
Social Consequences of Behavior
Social Role
Social Stimulus Value

Social Structure
Special Assets
Subjective Feeling States
Substance Use
Symptoms
Target Behaviors
Thought Processes
Treatment Prospects
Value System
Vocational Topics

The Concept of Case-Focusing

Related to the selection of general topics on which to report is another major but more specific aspect of the conceptualization of the report. This is the matter of selecting the appropriate focus of interpretation—the kind of conclusions to be derived from the raw data. Test manuals and textbooks, good as they may be, can suggest interpretations only in the general terms of the accepted meanings of such variables as test responses, scores, or quantitative patterns. The psychologist must adapt these general interpretive meanings to the specific case and mission, determine the central and pertinent topics with which to deal, and develop the interpretations (conclusions) in these topic areas as the mission requires.

There are several differences between interpretations made in general terms and *case-focused interpretations.* First, the case-focused interpretation is derived relative to a mission. We administer selected tests and search the elicited protocol for any information related to the assessment goal. Such data are emphasized to the partial or total neglect of other material. Second, interpretations are made according to their implications for action. The psychologist bridges the gap between the general interpretation and the perceived needs of the mission; in effect, *the conclusions, with greater or lesser directness, are recommendations.* The interpretations tell the report readers as much as possible about the practical meaning gained by the psychologist's unique approach. Finally, in the case-focused interpretation the psychologist is not content with reaching conclusions solely on the basis of the restricted assessment units (e.g., tests, subtests, scores, ratios, profiles, indexes) on which validity research has been done and for which published interpretation guides are available. Following sophisticated clinical practice, whatever fortuitous data are available are appropriated. Thus the psychologist may probe the meaning of verbalizations or of symbolic productions, interpret sequences or combinations of responses or scores in a manner not authorized or explicitly set forth by the test manual. Meanings may be derived by comparing scores or responses on one test with those on another (the battery approach), or conclusions reached from any of the preceding in the light of, or in combination with, such information as that provided by direct observation, anamnesis, other self-reports, behavior reported by others, or physical examination.

Let us consider a few brief examples showing the difference between general interpretation and case-focused interpretation. For meaningful, psychological work, general interpretations are incomplete interpretations which, too often, are of the Aunt Fanny sort. The mission of the psychologist is more closely related to knowing, for example, whether the client will act out than whether he is "hostile"; whether he requires treatment rather than whether he has "anxiety."

Here is a statement from a case report:

> The patient appears to be an immature, dependent individual whose passivity and feelings of insecurity leave him with little capacity to initiate decisive action.

There are four Aunt Fanny-type statements in this example: "immature," "dependent," "passivity," "feelings of insecurity." These four sub-conclusions contribute to a final conclusion, ". . . leave him with little capacity to initiate decisive action," which may or may not have specific meaning to the reader, depending partly on what other information about the patient is available. On the basis of interview information and impressions and a social history, the referring clinician might not even know that the patient cannot initiate decisive action. Even if the conclusion is correct, this behavioral fact may not be apparent on the surface and may come as a complete surprise to the clinician. What is to be done with this conclusion? What does it mean in terms of the patient's condition? At best, if the person making the referral is given corroborating information showing that the patient cannot initiate decisive action (which would reduce the value of the psychologist's contribution, since people who cannot initiate decisive action probably are dependent, immature, passive, and insecure anyway), the information can be integrated with the psychologist's overall findings and other data and some pertinent understandings reached. The psychologist, on the other hand, has available much additional information (through tests and from other sources) that would permit the development of a fuller integrative statement of the patient's psychological make-up. Instead, the report writer seems to stay close to the test data, as if "blind" interpretation had been made. Had the psychologist been closer to the patient and drawn on all information, the above statement, drawing in part from material scattered about the report, might have been written something like this:

> The patient currently presents an apparent picture of self-assurance since he is socially deft, alert, and obviously knowledgeable. Nevertheless, an over-protective upbringing becomes apparent when he has to put forth directed and sustained effort such as evidently was required in his recent business venture

which failed and preceded by a few weeks his admission with a diagnosis of major depressive episode. His need to achieve "success" is mostly a matter of his family's aspiration for him and is not congruent with his self-needs. Thus we find a person who does not at a deep level aspire to adult standards for responsibility and achievement. He would rather receive than produce. Hence when he finds himself in a position of responsibility he becomes fearful of his ability to perform as expected. Tension, confusion, indecisiveness, and depression are the results, the patient alternating between different courses of action but unable to take definite steps.

Another general interpretive statement gleaned from a report reads:

Tension, depression, aggression, and sexual conflict are evident in the protocol.

One hundred percent Aunt Fanny!

Maybe the patient is something like this:

This patient is deeply involved with a mother figure, and mixed feelings about this relationship seem to be associated with the symptoms for which the patient seeks help at the clinic. A dependent and overly close relationship with this parent has hampered his ability to assume a male role without conflict, and his mere urges to heterosexual expression cause him to feel anxious and tense, sometimes to a degree which incapacitates him for his everyday functioning. At the same time his sexual tensions and fantasy mean to him that he is going against his relationship with the mother, a feeling which ties in with other deep negative feelings which he has for her.

But this guess might be wrong. Possibly the next piece of fiction would be more descriptive of the patient who produced the protocol. Notice, incidentally, that an Aunt Fanny "sexual conflict" may fit both sexes.

The client is in conflict over what are the proper sex mores, the family and church teachings being on the one hand, and her liberated peer group standards and pressures being on the other. She initially complained to the counselor of an "inability to concentrate," and she does in fact seem to have a degree of tension which at times may hamper her studying. But she has always apparently become anxious when in conflict, and her present struggle to readjust to the standards of her new environment is hardly the basic cause of tension. What probably really brings her to counseling is a feeling that she is "letting down" her parents (a matter of truth at a fairly deep level where she does entertain rebellious urges). The implication this has to her for a vital relationship in her life has been causing her to feel unhappy.

And another illustration:

Thinking is syncretistic.

What does this mean for a particular patient? Perhaps that—

Although the clinical impression suggests a quite good remission, psychological examination of the thought processes indicates an active psychosis, the nature of which suggests that if the patient is now returned to the community he might repeat the behavior which led to his hospitalization. It is true that the patient has better emotional controls now, but his thinking causes him to reach some unlikely, sometimes bizarre ideas because he is prone to illogically relate unrelated ideas in a manner which can cause social difficulties. It might be well to delay discharge and have this patient's thought processes restudied in three weeks or a month.

THE PROCESS OF CONCEPTUALIZATION

In conceptualizing the presentation of a case, the psychologist might first imagine being asked to "Tell me about this person with regard to *(reason for assessment)*." In responding to such a request the report writer recognizes (1) the need to be selective of the information to be conveyed and (2) the need to organize this information meaningfully.

The first task takes cognizance of the frequent observation that the various aspects of a person's existence may be understood in terms of some kind of hierarchical order, and from this structure those traits that are of "central or dominating importance" may reliably be judged (Conrad, 1932). As a result of psychological study, certain features suggest themselves as predominant in the person's psychoeconomics. In our clients we may identify, in addition to overt behaviors of interest, organizing centers or central themes, which may relate to underlying tendencies or to modes of expression. Thus we become aware of the basic role of such issues as an inadequate self-concept, an attitude of interpersonal hostility, a need for achievement, a rigid control over emotional expression, tendencies to withdrawal, conflicts over sexual goals, or a pattern of achieving self-needs through the manipulation of others. A large number of such issues may be identified in any person, although there is perhaps a relatively smaller number of recurring themes that accounts for many of the topics found to be apparently relevant in case studies.

The organization of the central themes into a report may, for discussion purposes, be regarded as involving several different tasks. What the psychologist considers most important must be made to stand out, with the other material assigned an auxiliary role for the sake of completeness. Importance is gauged in terms of consequences, which might mean that the major emphasis is not accorded to the most central feature in the person's psychoeconomics—if this can be determined. Thus a hospital psychologist, for example, must think in such practical terms as whether obtained information will give the staff the sort of understanding needed to relate more effectively to the patient. The psychologist may have determined that dependency, hostility, and a poor gender identity are the central themes. A hierarchy of emphasis for these must be established. If depression and suicidal tendencies were also identified, the practical imperativeness of this finding would dictate that it be emphasized, even though sexual conflict was basic in undermining the patient's adjustment.

There are as many means of supplying appropriate emphasis to content as literary creativity will permit. For practical use, however, the more common techniques will generally suffice. These include the order of presentation, the skillful and appropriate use of adjectives, and the use of vivid illustrative material. Less often the psychologist might resort to the use of underlining, capitalization, dramatic presentation (such as is produced by a clipped statement), or an exclamation point. Sometimes the occasion presents itself when the psychologist can state in virtually so many words what is most important: "This man is best understood through a description of his deep dependency needs and his manner of attempting to gratify these."

The skillful use of repetition can also make for effective emphasis. This is perhaps best accomplished by weaving the central theme through all or a substantial part of the report, relating subsidiary themes to that which has been selected as the main point for emphasis. The dependency theme mentioned in the previous paragraph, for example, can be related to the other prominent and clinically relevant personality themes. Suppose that a person has strong but inexpressible urges, a tendency to perceive the environment as threatening, feelings of inadequacy and depression, deep anxieties about the adequacy of core gender identity, and the objective appearance of free anxiety. All of these may be more or less directly related to the crucial dependency problem, and the dependency theme might be presented in a number of contexts.

What this amounts to is that the psychologist should practice a mild form of caricature. This was also the intent when the principle of selectivity of content was advocated. We are charged with presenting a clinically useful picture, not an exact photograph. Admittedly by eliminating certain material judged to be nonrelevant to the purpose, we produce a distortion of the whole person; yet we might as well accept the fact that we cannot present an undistorted picture of the person—the full content is simply not available to us, and we may not be entirely accurate in what we do know. The shotgun report also deletes information, but its errors are more serious because its bulk can prevent the reader from recognizing the relative importance of the various topics and can thus lead to the development of a distorted image. Test-by-test reporting, segmentalized reporting, and traditional, non-case-focused reports, for various reasons, have similar effects.

Along with seeing the case in terms of its needed emphases, the psychologist must consider the detailed attributes of the central themes to be understood and presented. Each basic theme must be seen in terms of its role in the person's economy, its unique components, its social import, and associated personality information (for example, the relationship of a central theme of inferiority feelings to a subsidiary theme of deficiencies in heterosexual functioning). It is these that make the central themes take on the action characteristic of life.

On achieving an understanding of the client and the basic tactics of case presentation in terms of the overall guiding principles discussed here, the psychologist is ready to outline a report—preferably on paper, although this might not be necessary for some seasoned psychologists. The first step in this task is to select from a population of personality topics, such as that presented in the list on pages 138–139, those that comprise the central features of the case.

Outlining a Report

Here is an example of how a case may be outlined, together with the report that emerges. The report will serve to initiate a discussion of the often troubling problem of intraparagraph and interparagraph organization.

The client, a young man in his twenties, twice in recent months had come into difficulties which led to his arrest, the first time for "bookie" activities and the second time for threatening his parents with a gun after consuming "12 or 14 beers." The psychiatrist who examined the client on direction of the court referred the case to us, with the request that we probe the meaning of the antisocial tendencies.

We determined that the client had a basic conflict centering about passivity and dependency, these being associated with what the client perceived as a harsh father, and hence a (now generalized) need to rebel was developed. No fewer than four clinically relevant defenses were erected against this conflict: (1) a denial of personal inadequacy, (2) a denial of real events, which precludes effective or constructive action, (3) a renunciation of personal goals so as to gain support (and thus perhaps to be maneuvered by "bad company"), and (4) a hostile and unrealistic fantasy life. The typical view he presented to others and the difficulties he experienced in cognitive functioning round out this picture.

The core personality topic outline might go like this:

    I.   Conflicts
   II.   Social Stimulus Value
  III.   Cognitive Functioning
   IV.   Defenses (1)
    V.   Defenses (2)
   VI.   Defenses (3)
  VII.   Defenses (4)

This preliminary outline form is both general and incomplete. Yet it presents an overall structure for the report, and the topic headings might well form the bases for paragraphs. In practice we would now simply translate these headings into more specific behavior referents, and elaborate on the content to be discussed in these paragraphs. By drawing the following additional topics from the same list that supplied the material for the core personality topic outline:

Attitudes	Interpersonal Skills
Awareness	Needs
Cognitive Skills	Outlook
Conative Factors	Perception of Environment
Content of Consciousness	Perception of Self
Deficit	Personal Consequences of Behavior
Drives, Dynamics	Psychopathology
Emotional Cathexes	Subjective Feeling States
Emotional Controls	Social Consequences of Behavior
Frustrations	Social Role
Goals	Value System
Interpersonal Relations	

The outline then becomes

    I. Conflicts
        A. Self-Perception
        B. Goals
        C. Frustrations
        D. Interpersonal Relations
        E. Perception of Environment
        F. Drives, Dynamics
        G. Emotional Cathexes
        H. Emotional Controls
   II. Social Stimulus Value
        A. Cognitive Skills
        B. Conative Factors
        C. Goals
        D. Social Role
  III. Cognitive Functioning
        A. Deficit
        B. Psychopathology
   IV. Defenses (1)
        A. Self-Perception
        B. Needs
        C. Conflicts
    V. Defenses (2)
        A. Subjective Feeling States
        B. Attitudes
        C. Deficits
        D. Personal Consequences of Behavior
        E. Insight
        F. Subjective Feeling States
        G. Insight
        H. Social Stimulus Value
        I. Social Consequences of Behavior

  VI. Defenses (3)
      A. Interpersonal Relations
      B. Needs
      C. Interpersonal Skills
      D. Emotional Controls
 VII. Defenses (4)
      A. Content of Consciousness
      B. Needs
      C. Values
      D. Needs
      E. Social Consequences of Action

. . . which now, in more lifelike terms, still highly detailed for teaching purposes, becomes

    I. Conflict centering about dependency and passivity
      A. Feelings of inadequacy
      B. Frustrated personal goals (dependency and passivity)
      C. Faulty, unsatisfying relationship with father
      D. Father seen as cold, rejecting, punishing
      E. Rebellious tendencies which are generalized
      F. Control over negative impulses out of fear
   II. How others see client
      A. Intellectual level and skills
      B. Lack of will to function at optimum
      C. Fluctuating goal for self-achievement
      D. Social irresponsibility
  III. Cognitive functioning
      A. Deficiencies under stress
      B. Psychopathological aspects of deficiencies
  IV. Denial of felt inadequacy
      A. Negative view of self
      B. Need to feel "like everybody else"
      C. Conflict over adequacy as a male
    V. Denial and nonexperience of pertinent realities
      A. Partial avoidance of depressed feelings
      B. Naive attitude
      C. Inability to assess his behavior adequately
      D. Inability to correct own behavior
      E. Inability to understand problems
      F. Depressive tendencies
      G. Lack of full experience of depression
      H. Social masking of depressed feelings
      I. Relation of inner feelings to negative social behavior
  VI. Social maneuvers to gain acceptance
      A. Receptive orientation
      B. Need for support
      C. Techniques of gaining support
      D. Control of negative impulses to retain support
 VII. Fantasy as a basic defense
      A. Value of fantasy
      B. Needs as reflected in fantasy

    C.   Deficiency of social values
    D.   Need to appear in socially favorable light
    E.   Fantasy content and deficiency of social values as a basis for unlawful activity

. . . and then, initiated by an opening summary or overview, is translated into the body of a report:

> This man is most readily understood in terms of his unusually passive, dependent approach to life and his attempts to overcome the deeply unhappy state brought about by this personality limitation.
>
> Mr. A does not feel very adequate as a person, an attitude which is developed through experiencing a continual sense of failure in terms of his own goals, and which apparently is reinforced by others. In fact, his relations with his father very likely are the basic reason for such feeling. This person is seen by the patient as cold, rejecting, punishing, and unapproachable. He has an urge to rebel and fight against this person—an urge which has been generalized to all society, but he is afraid to give vent to his impulses. Whatever emotional support he does get (got) seems to be from the mother.
>
> As others see him, he seems to have the essential capacity to do well if only he would try. He scores at the average level on a test of intelligence (IQ: 106), he is able to learn readily, when he wants to, and on occasion can perform unusually fast and effectively. Yet he does not typically follow through on this advantage. His willingness, sometimes even his desire, to do well fluctuates, so that in the long run he could not be regarded as a constructive or responsible person.
>
> Other personality deficiencies also compromise his functioning. Under stress or when faced with difficult problems he becomes blocked, confused, and indecisive. His thinking does not show sufficient flexibility to meet such situations so that he would be regarded as inadaptable and unspontaneous.
>
> Mr. A's felt inadequacy causes him to feel that he is not as good as others. By way of reassuring himself on this matter he frequently during examination makes remarks that he is "like everybody else." The feeling that he is inferior includes also the sexual area where he is quite confused about his maleness. It is likely that one or more sex problems contribute to his sense of failure, although, quite understandably, he denies this and indicates a satsifactory sex life "like everybody else."
>
> He hardly experiences the full effect of his failures, however. He protects himself by denying many events of reality, by keeping many facts about himself and others unconscious, by a general attitude of "not knowing"—an attitude of naiveness. He can hardly take corrective action about himself because he does not understand himself or his actions, or recognize the nature of his problems. Oddly enough, as already stated, this is an unhappy person, but he does not adequately recognize this fact nor does he appear to others as depressed. Yet on occasion this might be a factor in his behavior which could be personally or socially unfortunate.
>
> This man's insecurity about himself forces him into a receptive orientation to other people. He must have friends to provide support. To achieve this he presents himself in a positive, correct light, tries to say the "right" things and even to be ingratiating and obsequious. It is important that he create the "right" effect and may resort to dramatic behavior to bring this about. "Friends" are so important to him that he sometimes must take abuse in order to hold them. He must always hold back hostile expression.

But it is perhaps in fantasy where the greatest satisfaction is derived. He dreams of being a "success" (his term)—accumulating enough money by the age of 35 so he can retire and effortlessly enjoy the comforts of the world. In his fantasy he is independent of authority, can openly express the aggression he ordinarily cannot, and flout society. He has no positive feelings about social rules (although he may profess to), but is concerned when apprehended for misconduct, possibly less for the real punishment than for how it "looks" to be known for doing what he is afraid to do. It is little wonder that he is easy prey for an "easy money" scheme.

The reader will note that the sections of the outline and the paragraphs in the report contain heterogeneous and occasionally repeated content. This is intentional. A report consisting of homogeneous paragraphs would be a form of segmentalized report (although perhaps not as artificial as the kind of segmentalized reports commented on in this book) and subject to some of the same censure. The psychologist should try to relate in the report those behaviors that occur together in the functioning context of the person. If sex conflicts hamper intellectual functioning, these related facts should be mentioned as closely together as they are in this sentence, not as unconnected statements occurring in different and possibly widely separated paragraphs. In a good report the beginning of a paragraph commonly announces the integrated theme of the topics that compose it.

Arranging Findings in a Report

There is a final and most important consideration pertaining to effective organization. How are the component findings to be arranged in a report? How, for example, was the scheme for the preceding report developed?

First consider the intraparagraph organization. The intention was to take the main integrated themes emerging in response to the imaginary request to "Tell me about this person"—the brief statement of the psychologist's findings that precedes the outline (p. 144). Thus each of the four basic methods of defense the client uses has some meaningfully interrelated components. Consider the derivation of the fifth paragraph of the report. That the client feels inadequate was one of the principal conclusions of the psychologist. In fact, the client's repeated statement that he is "like everybody else" strengthens this conclusion and also suggests how he tries to adopt an attitude to deny his feeling of inadequacy. The psychologist also had strong reasons to reach the conclusion that the client had several prominent sex conflicts associated with his feelings of inadequacy—a conclusion perhaps strengthened by the client's comment (to a sentence completion item) that he has a sex life that is "like everybody else." (Notice, incidentally, the emphasis to be gained by repeating this expression closely together in different but related contexts. The topics in the fifth paragraph obviously belong together.)

Or look at the third paragraph. From observations of samples of the client's intellectual functioning, it was apparent to the psychologist that he would impress others well in this respect, at least as regards capacity. Yet it was also clear by the client's performance on a number of tests that there was a fluctuating will and a consequent lack of goal-directedness and responsibility. It was further noted that he meets many of his problems through fantasy, but this possible way of elaborating on the theme of irresponsibility and its social effects was reserved for the emphasis that can be brought about by treating a topic in a final paragraph. In the third paragraph, however, it was thought appropriate to contrast his capacity with his output, since this discrepancy suggests that people would be critical of him, an important finding in view of what rejection means to the client. The theme was not "pushed" more strongly only because the conclusion was not judged to be sufficiently firm. If it were, it could easily have been developed in this paragraph.

There is one simple rule for deciding on the contents of a paragraph: functional relatedness (what relatedness is there in the other paragraphs in the report on Mr. A?). This criterion permits the intentional repetition of items of content in different paragraphs. Beyond this, the psychologist has to decide how to arrange the several items in the paragraph and how to word thoughts for effectiveness. The limiting factor in learning this skill is probably the basic prose style of the psychologist. Nevertheless, much of the ingenuity needed for this skill can be acquired. Perhaps most important are the terms in which the psychologist thinks. If the task is conceptualized in terms of communicating "findings"—perhaps that the client has anxiety, hostility, and narcissistic wounds—such content probably is precisely what will be recorded. But if the psychologist understands the case in terms of a practical mission, conceptualization of report content and the manner in which it is expressed is likely to be more functional.

The novice can learn how to make a paragraph hang together by studying samples of effective clinical writing. Supervisors are often in a position to make relevant suggestions in training conferences based on live case material. There are any number of writing techniques that can be adapted for specific effect. For example, in paragraph three the method of contrast was used. The client's capacity was contrasted with his productivity because of the social meaning and implications such a discrepancy may have. Some of the techniques that aid in interparagraph organization might also be useful.

The organization of paragraphs in a report is possibly more complex than the organization of conclusions within a paragraph, because the report is a larger conceptual unit. Moreover, the organization of each report must have its own rationale, although certainly other reports may have a similar rationale and be organized along similar lines. How do we arrive at a rationale for organizing a report? How, for example, was the rationale for the report on Mr. A. reached?

First, Mr. A was understood in terms of an approach to life (central personality theme) that is not socially adaptive and leads to some personally unsatisfying results. The ways in which he tries to overcome some of the effects of his basic personality orientation bear rather directly on the reason for his being referred to us. By stating the central problem the client may quickly be introduced to the reader in general terms, with the understanding that the necessary details will follow.

The top priority then became the further development of the theme introduced in the first paragraph, hence the need to know about Mr. A's feelings of inadequacy. This topic led naturally to a discussion of what the client is "really" like in contrast to his misperception of himself. However, he is also objectively seen to have shortcomings, so the deficiencies mentioned in the fourth paragraph supplement those commented on in the third. So far we have presented the logically related topics of the client's perception of himself and an external evaluation of some of his qualities. All of this was thought to be pertinent to the problem for which he was referred.

The next four paragraphs are logically interrelated, since they serially disclose how Mr. A copes with his feelings about himself. First, in paragraph five, is a discussion of the basic manner by which he tries not to feel inadequate. The theme is amplified in the sixth paragraph, which suggests a very wide scope of denial and the effect this might have. The seventh paragraph shows a social maneuver he uses as a defense for the same basic problem. The final paragraph suggests an additional defense for this problem, that of a fantasy life that seems to be closely associated with his long-term antisocial activities (being a "bookie").

The overall guiding principle was to present the man in terms of his personality as this pertains to his antisocial activities. Nevertheless, the relationship between what is described in these paragraphs and his social difficulties is not mentioned in every instance. It would be logical enough to do so, but a different scheme was used in preference to cluttering the report with what in this case would be speculations. Instead, the speculations were gathered together as a "speculative note" that was appended to the body of the report. Its purpose was to attempt to relate, more directly than responsible interpretation practices permit, the basic personality of the man to his unwanted behaviors.

Speculative Note

The client's antisocial behavior appears to be related to the personality problems noted here and to his method of coping with these. His negative attitude to authority (father), of course, would seem to be a basic ingredient. His need for support is another factor, and the support of a group of persons on the other side of the law might be as meaningful as support from another source. As we have seen, he will go out of his way (engaging in illegal activities?) to retain his "friends." His fantasy life of wealth and leisure would also seem to make unlawful activities appealing. Finally, his intellectual inefficiencies and his inadaptability might tend to give trouble in more straightforward enterprises. He does not genuinely feel he is wrong.

Concerning the gun incident, the client seemed to be trying to indicate to the examining physician that the weapon was used to try forcibly to extract sympathy and support that he could not get by passive means. The gun evidently made him feel powerful, and the reasoning was childish and incomplete. Apparently the act was impulsive. The client admits to consuming 12 or 14 beers before the event and this probably loosened his usually tight control over direct hostile expression. Further acts either against himself or against others cannot be ruled out, although no specific or immediate danger is foreseen.

Schemes for Organizing Reports

There are many possible schemes suitable for organizing reports. The total number is probably limited only by the psychologist's ingenuity and the variety of case material. The following suggestions pertain to some elementary organizing schemes. In many instances one of these will not be a sufficient scheme for a whole report; several strategies will have to be combined.

Regardless of the presentation scheme, an overview statement is commonly in order. In any event a clear focus and objective must always be established in the light of the available material and its significance. Sometimes it will be most effective to present a major conclusion at the beginning (a purpose often served by an overview) and then make supporting information available. At other times the psychologist may be able to build up to the major conclusion and present it more forcefully at the end of the report. It is difficult to generalize. Most often, when the psychologist is asked to contribute a diagnosis, this matter may be dealt with at the conclusion of the report after the relevant evidence presumably has been presented. However, a diagnosis may be offered at the beginning of a report for a good reason: "This is a severely schizophrenic patient whose homicidal fantasies and inability to control her behavior could pose a serious threat to the community."

1. The simplest approach to report organization is possible when it is necessary to deal only with a limited segment of behavior, such as might be the case when dealing with a circumscribed matter. Thus when dealing with intellectual efficiency, the report considers serially the several pertinent aspects of this problem. Or if the problem is one of cognitive deficit, such as in a brain syndrome, it is necessary only to cite the related data contributing to the major conclusion—for example, that the deficit is present. Probably the relative seriousness of the signs, such as memory defect, inability to shift concepts, concreteness, confabulation, loss of mental control, confusion, and loss of orientation, will suggest a meaningful order of presentation and appropriate data groupings—for example, memory defect and confabulation would probably be closely linked.

2. With more complex material a quite simple, yet effective, approach is to present a general opening statement, an overview, or an introductory statement, followed by the necessary elaborations and whatever other pertinent information is required to round out the personality study. A report might

start: "The dominant emphasis in Ms. B's life is manipulating others in order to realize a set of strong ambitions." The nature of these ambitions, why they are important to her, and her techniques of manipulation might then be commented upon. Finally, whatever else is important, such as capacity (e.g., intellectual or social), situational frustrations, adaptability, or the effects of failure, could be woven into the theme.

3. Some reports might be essentially a buildup to a diagnosis or some major conclusion. What is required is that the psychologist present bits of evidence step by step, as these contribute to a final conclusion. A tightly reasoned report of this sort might be in order particularly when the conclusion is of far-reaching significance. Examples would occur when a diagnosis is an essential ingredient in a court decision, or when contemplated action like commitment to or release from a hospital might hinge on the psychologist's findings. Such an organization might be in order when the psychologist feels the need to convincingly present findings that are not at all apparent. Quite frequently, for example, clinical diagnosis may point to neurosis or personality disorder while psychological indicators suggest psychosis.

4. A cause-and-effect presentation can be useful when concern is with some symptom whose basis needs to be understood. Physical symptoms which are thought by a physician to be psychogenic are a common instance. This approach is also particularly valuable when a social symptom, such as misbehavior in school or criminal behavior, needs to be understood and identified with a set of dynamics or with pathology, such as a brain syndrome. It may be best at times to first explore the nature of the unwanted symptom and then to deal with its causes. At other times it may be appropriate to deal with the pertinent underlying psychological material and show how this relates to the issue of concern.

5. In many instances the order of presentation might be from periphery to center or from center to periphery, and the most effective approach can be a subjective matter. Frequently it is helpful to contrast the surface picture with what is not apparent. Reasons for doing this might be (a) to alert others to unsuspected personality features; (b) to contribute understanding as to why a person who is without evident pathology gets into difficulties; or (c) to contrast a superficial picture or facade with what a person is "really" like.

6. Sometimes it is appropriate to emphasize the subjective view of the individual if the writer feels it is important to understand the situation(s) as the client does. Contrasting the subjective picture with the external viewpoint can often contribute valuable perspective to a case. When the fantasy life, orientation, or perception of environment is particularly important, the value of this approach becomes evident.

7. Contrast can be an appropriate organizing focus of a report. The nature of a conflict may be brought out quite effectively by contrasting its elements—for example, incompatible goals. Contrast can also be functional when different layers of behavior need to be understood in relation to one another. An illustration of this might be severely hostile attitudes sublimated in one who fights for social justice. This technique is also called for when the findings of a current examination are compared with those of a previous examination. The writer sets forth the important similarities and differences uncovered in the two examinations and whatever significance these might have.

6

A WORKSHOP
ON PSYCHOLOGICAL
REPORT WRITING
How to Write Reports
and How Not to

The author's impetus for writing a book on psychological report writing relates, in part, to the large number of inferior reports that are still to be found in file cabinets. What better way to emphasize this point than to share a few of them with the reader? Fortunately, good, effective reports are also being written, and it also seems to be sound to share some of these with the reader.

REPORTS NOT TO EMULATE

Presented first in this chapter are examples of how *not* to write psychological reports. They were gathered from case folders over a period of time. Each case is followed by comments based on the principles set forth in this book.

Most of these reports were written by students, hence in general they are a better source of instructional material than are the products of practicing psychologists. Nevertheless, experienced persons often have the same difficulties as beginners do. Some of the reports, particularly those personality-oriented reports written in test-by-test fashion, were selected to illustrate an approach that is fortunately much less popular than it was some years ago. Several of the reports are of the shotgun type, harking back to a time when it was common to encourage students to include as much as possible in their reports in order to demonstrate their competence to interpret test data. Although this teaching method is still in use, we strongly encourage supervisors to teach the writing of case-focused reports. Students can demonstrate their interpretive skills in supervisory conferences and their overall qualifications as psychologists in the writing of case-focused reports.

The approach is informal, and the criticisms that are made of reports are similar to some of the observations that a supervisor might make (see Chapter 8). For self-instruction or assigned instruction, it may be profitable for students to apply the principles of the preceding chapters to the following selections or to samples of their own reports. While doing such exercises, it is well to be aware that some of the reports can be variously criticized, according to one's point of view. Thus a selection might merit the labels "academic," "theoretical," and "cold and impersonal" at the same time. Some readers will be more inclined to describe a piece of writing by one of these terms, some by another.

In most instances the reasons for referral of the cases which resulted in the following passages are not known. Most of the referrals were probably general. The overinclusiveness that is typical in the ensuing reports probably would not be much altered were the referrals specific, however. Unnecessary content is a major characteristic of many traditional reports.

The first exhibit is presented to illustrate a number of principles. It was selected also because of its uniqueness and for the question it poses: Can flexibility be overdone?

Behavior During the Examination

The patient, John C., appeared to be very alert and in good contact with his surroundings. He claimed that he was in the hospital because of his wife's threat to leave him if he did not come here and cure his chronic alcoholism. He also felt that his children would be hurt. The obvious omission in his statements is a reference to himself as having anything to do with his being in the hospital or acknowledging his desire to get well for his own sake. But the omission is understandable if we make the following assumptions: (1) He does not want to acknowledge any responsibility for himself; and (2) his problem is really his wife's problem. In support of these assumptions consider the following incident which occurred at the very beginning of the testing session between the patient and the examiner. The examiner brought an ashtray into the room. There may have been some question as to its decorative value but there really were no grounds for questioning its use as a supplement to smoking. Nevertheless, the patient asked, very timidly, if he could smoke. Now, if he knew the answer to his own question which was made all too obvious by the ashtray that the examiner had *just* brought in and placed before him, why did he ask it? Again, his behavior makes perfectly good sense if we assume that (1) he wanted the examiner to give him explicit permission for smoking, thus setting up the examiner in a judgmental role; (2) he wanted to appear inept and helpless in the situation, hoping that the examiner would then be inclined to intervene and direct him since he "obviously" could not direct himself with any measure of success if he were inept and helpless; (3) he was so self-absorbed that he was not attending to the situation and the ashtray was not in his perceptual field. However, since the question, "Can I smoke?", followed *immediately* upon the presentation of the ashtray, we may reject this assumption as not doing justice to the facts. Thus, there is a striking parallel between his expressed relation to his wife and the relationship he tried to establish with the examiner. In both cases he is told what to do ("Go to the hospital." "You can smoke."), and he disclaims responsibility for both ("I am in the hospital because of my wife." "I smoke because I have your permission.")

Consider another example in which two items of the patient's behavior which followed each other in close temporal succession *appear* absurd because they are mutually exclusive. The patient let the examiner know that he was enjoying the tests and that he found them very interesting. (We will disregard, for the moment, the rote fashion of his verbalization.) As often as he let the examiner know this, which was several times, he just as often followed it with an inquiry as to how many more tests there were left, leaving very little doubt in the examiner's mind that the patient wanted to leave and was trying to find out how much longer it would be before his "enjoyment" would be terminated. Again, certain assumptions make good sense out of what is, prima facie, an absurdity. These assumptions are that: (1) He would not permit himself to be interested in or to enjoy what he was doing, the product of a pathological predilection for discomfiture. Thus, he could not even say he was interested in what he was doing with any real conviction in his voice. But, this certainly does not explain why he should ever mention his "interest" and "enjoyment" to begin with. This brings us to the second assumption which ties together many loose ends: (2) The patient did not really mean he was interested at all as his voice, for one thing, indicated. His subsequent behavior (asking the examiner how much more time the testing would consume) gave the lie with more certainty than ever to his preceding words ("I am enjoying this"). So why did he say he was enjoying the testing? He said it strictly for the consumption of the examiner. The patient's modus operandi vis-à-vis the examiner was to act the role of a "good" testee thus entitling himself to the examiner's charity in return. "Surely the examiner will be pleased with me and relax his gimlet eye if I flatter him as a purveyor of good things." This role, we may note, was part and parcel of a pervasive obsequiousness and servility that ran through all of the patient's behavior. Possibly, at a more dynamic level, we are observing a rigid reaction formation against hostility which has lost even its pseudo-adaptive quality and culminated in a sticky sweetness which is emotionally inappropriate to the situation.

Test Findings

The patient's intellectual functioning is in the normal range (Full Scale IQ 97). His almost total failure on the Arithmetic Subtest of the Wechsler suggests a severe defect in concentration. His Performance Subtests are generally better than his Verbal, suggesting an intelligence potential in the bright normal range. An overall educational retardation is suggested if, in addition to the low Verbal and Arithmetic scores (the latter score is, of course, too low to be *only* a matter of educational retardation), one makes a qualitative evaluation of the Information Subtest where the patient shows an inability to even closely approximate the population of the United States or the distance from New York to Paris.

Personality-wise, the patient is unable to relate to people. The intimacy implied in such relationships brings the danger of his experiencing hostile impulses toward the objects of his "affection." Thus, he relates to women, whom he conceives of as mother figures, by provoking them, thus externalizing (projecting) his hostility and setting up the situation so that the hostility is directed back at him. This seems to serve the triple purpose of (1) distorting the outer world as a hostile place and reversing the source of the hostility so that the net effect is for him to disown (repress) his own hostility, yet still define his relationships within a hostile context; (2) punishing himself to serve an expiatory need based on his own completely unacceptable hostile impulses; (3) forcing other people to take an interest in him, thus temporarily putting his isolation in abeyance and making his own need for human contact seem to be the need of the other person. His chronic alcoholism in this context seems to be an attempt to be taken in hand and punished for his derelictions toward his wife and family. His social naiveté allows him to think that an apology for wrongdoing ("wrongdoing" is used here not in its moral sense but to define something the patient does which he may depend upon to provoke somebody) will bring everything back to its ante-bellum status. The "peace" is maintained until, unable to bear his isolation and loneliness, and unable to relate to people because of his hostile feelings (exaggerated all the more when he realizes his need for them) he commits a social crime, i.e., infidelity or irresponsible alcoholism, to hurt his family. The crime naturally forces the intervention of some other people to take him in hand (usually the wife in her maternal role).

The dynamics of this particular patient's pathology seem more clear-cut than is usually the case. He was placed in a home by his mother as an infant. She could not maintain him because her husband was an alcoholic and made the marital relationship impossible to endure. He did not see his mother again until, as a grown man, he accidentally located her. In all probability the mother rejected the infant not because she could not maintain the expense, but because she looked upon the child as part and parcel of the hated husband. Thus, traumatic rejection experiences in the patient's background have severely warped his whole personality development. Affectionally deprived in a most basic way, he can find affection only by twisting his human relationships in such a way that he "finds" rejection everywhere. Is this also a way of finding his parents everywhere? In the most naively impossible way he tries to gain acceptance by being apologetic, an acceptance which is doomed to be very short-lived since it amounts to nothing but an uneasy truce with none of the relevant issues even hinted at. Thus he may be assured that the rejection will be forthcoming again, symbolically reconstituting the basic relation to the rejecting parents, the paradigm of all his relationships.

A therapeutic approach which has, in this type of case, succeeded, is the so-called relationship-therapy in the style of Jessie Taft or of the Rankian School. The basic premise and whole modus operandi of such therapies are focused on just such a barrier to establishing interpersonal relationships on a realistic basis as the patient has to break through.

Summary

The patient, John C., is a 35-year-old man. Intellectually he functions in the normal range with a bright normal potential which is not reached because of a severe concentration defect and what appears to be an overall educational retardation. The patient's pathology seems focused around a severe disturbance in interpersonal relationships based on traumatic rejection experiences in infancy. Rigid reaction formations against his tremendous hostility toward people, conceived of as essentially rejecting, prevent the possibility of any but the most pseudo-adaptive adjustment. Feeling intensely lonely and isolated, his need for people grows more urgent, as does his hostility toward them because he is so completely dependent on them. However, unable to acknowledge this need, he forces other people, primarily his family, to intervene in his life by committing some social misdemeanor (infidelity or alcoholism). Rejection experiences are compulsively sought after as a way of symbolically reconstituting the basic relationship to the rejecting parents, the paradigm for all his relationships. His attempt to break this relationship by a childish apology, usually to his wife conceived of in a maternal role, is as naive and shallow as it is abortive and unworkable. Yet he persists in maintaining a Pollyannish optimism. Thus, with his pathology firmly secured, he goes his self-defeating way.

Diagnostic Impression

Chronic Alcoholism in an Emotionally Unstable Personality.

Just glancing at this report, one may wonder if it is too long. On reading it, one may be sure that it is. The relationship of length to usable content is disproportionate. Too much space is devoted to building a case, as opposed to presenting pertinent conclusions. In fact, what are the pertinent conclusions?

This question cannot be fully answered without knowing the reason for referral, which unfortunately is not available. We do know, however, that the person is in a hospital and is regarded as an alcoholic, at least by his wife. What then might have been the basis for referral? What might have been the psychologist's evaluation goal? What might he have contributed to the case? We can't be sure, of course, but a contribution to the diagnosis could be of importance. That is, is the presenting symptom secondary to some other condition—possibly a condition that might be treatable? Perhaps knowing the role alcohol plays in the patient's economy could be a therapeutic lead. Or it might be useful to know something of the patient's "ego strength," or of his motivation for therapy.

How well does the psychologist approximate goals like these? As to diagnosis, he is impressed that this is a case of "alcoholism," this is a contribution of sorts in that he implies the absence of a number of other conditions, such as schizophrenic disorder, dysthymic disorder, or generalized anxiety disorder. He does, however, link the patient's drinking with an "emotionally unstable personality."

This diagnosis, no longer current, applies when ". . . the individual reacts with excitability and ineffectiveness when confronted by minor stress. His judgment may be undependable under stress, and his relationship to other people is continuously fraught with fluctuating emotional attitudes, because of strong and poorly controlled hostility, guilt, and anxiety" (American Psychiatric Association, *Diagnostic and Statistical Manual, Mental Disorders,* 1952). The accuracy of the diagnosis can hardly be challenged at this time, but the reader of the report has no warning that it is coming. The conclusion is in no way supported, and we in fact think that the content of the report better supports another diagnosis (passive-aggressive personality?).

The psychologist does considerably better in defining the role of the symptom that led to hospital admission in the person's economy, and this information, if accurate, might be of value to a therapist. Unfortunately we do not know if the man would be a good candidate for psychotherapy. The psychologist recommends a special kind of therapy, but the early part of the report suggests that the individual does not recognize that he has a problem and that there is no motivation to change. On the other hand, the report would seem to indicate that the symptom is an aspect of the person's basic psychic structure, and that the man can be successfully treated through "relationship therapy" has to be questioned. Apparently the psychologist himself is skeptical and seems to hedge here. He speaks of success "in this type of case" but does not prophesy success in the case of John C.

Looking at the case in overall perspective again, it is well written. The composition is good, and the report reads smoothly. The organization is grammatically logical, in a sense, yet there is no apparent development of major conclusions in the interest of effectiveness. Intelligence is given priority in the discussion, although how the patient's intellectual level or his intellectual defects are related to anything relevant is not apparent.

The flavor of the writing is captured by words like "pompous," "exhibitionistic," "authoritative," "erudite," and "academic." Notice the deftness with which apparently insignificant events are made to yield their full portentousness. The reader should feel that he is being instructed in a method of clinical analysis as well as being informed. Most readers would probably also feel that the foreign expressions used in the report are a bit too show-offy for a clinical document, and the contribution about Jessie Taft and the Rankian School almost certainly is so. The reader might be self-critical for not being as smart as the psychologist, unless he or she concludes that the psychologist is now studying—or has recently studied—the various schools of psychotherapy. If the reader understands the matter this way, he or she may feel the comment to be gratuitous and more appropriate in a term paper.

The report seems to have been written by a prosecuting attorney who sees the patient, a not very honest fellow, as always up to some nefarious end. But he won't "get away" with anything. The manner of expression contributes more to this impression than does the content. How much of the jockeying for position and trying to outmaneuver the other fellow belongs to the patient and how much to the psychologist is hard to tell. This question might be easily answered, of course, if we had available other sample reports by the same psychologist. Nevertheless, how the psychologist feels about his patient is evident in talk of a "modus operandi," of receiving the "examiner's charity," and of behavior which "gave the lie." "Now I've got you, you son of a bitch," is the way Berne (1964) puts it. The patient is seen as a manipulator and a leech.

The report would seem to be patient-centered in the sense that the discussion is about the patient and only minimally (as reports go) about tests and test products, and the common Aunt Fanny stereotypy does not occur. Yet the feeling is strong that the psychologist is really more interested in juggling ideas than in meaningfully describing the patient. From the hundreds of words appearing under the title "Behavior during the Examination," we know with a good degree of confidence that "the patient appeared to be very alert and in good contact with his surroundings" (no doubt already observed by the staff), the patient's view of his hospitalization, that the patient asked for permission to smoke after an ash tray was placed before him (and presumably also before the psychologist), that the patient indicated enjoyment of testing but behaved otherwise, and that the patient's behavior involved obsequiousness and servility. With a lesser degree of confidence we learn something more about the patient, mostly on a dynamic level. With at least the same degree of confidence, we know more about the psychologist than about the patient from this passage.

The responsibility with which interpretations are made here is a matter of great concern. Near the end of the report we learn, with eager anticipation, of how clear-cut the dynamics are. Then we find that the mother placed the patient in a home while he was an infant, an event which the psychologist unhesitatingly calls a "rejection" (we would need more evidence than presented here to be able to conclude that *the patient* felt rejected). Then the psychologist guesses that the mother "in all probability . . . rejected" the infant because she saw him as "part and parcel of the hated husband."

There is no reason given why this guess was made, and there is no evidence offered that the patient's mother hated her husband, certainly not to such an extent that she also did not want their child. The fact (?) that the husband's drinking made it impossible for the marriage to endure does not necessarily indicate hatred. The mother may have had feelings of ambivalence, or possibly even some feelings of love for the man with whom she could not live. People are that way. Nevertheless, the psychologist accepts all of this without feeling the need to offer a bit of evidence, if he has it (the report writer does not impress one as being a devotee of parsimony), to make such far-reaching conclusions appear plausible and to relate them to the patient's way of life as he (the psychologist) understands it—apparently to no small extent in terms of his personal and class values. Thus unsupported events are brought together to develop one speculation; this is then accepted as a premise and another speculation built on it. The purpose of this is not certain, since the patient's "dynamics" as described are not clearly linked to the presenting problem (presumably alcoholism). We are told that his mode of life is symbolically to relive the rejection by his parents, but in the previous paragraph we find the symptom related to hostility and a means of getting himself taken care of (the opposite of seeking rejection). Quite evidently, this psychologist does not appreciate the difficulty of relating current behaviors to their distant causes, even when there seems to be an evidential link.

The responsibility of interpretation is also particularly suspect in the first sections of the report. The psychologist arbitrarily restricts the possible interpretations of the patient's behavior and then selects the ones that seem most reasonable to him. However, we can only wonder to what extent his obviously ill perception of the patient guides his interpretation.

The following text reads very much like a laboratory report.

Test Results—WAIS:

Verbal IQ	114.	Full Scale IQ	119.
Perf. IQ	121.	Classified—Bright Normal.	

The patient is presently functioning at a Bright Normal level of intelligence (IQ 119) demonstrating a Bright Normal capacity on the verbal scale and a Superior capacity on the performance scale. There was a considerable amount of scatter on the verbal scale. On the performance scale, however, scatter was minimal. There was some intra-test variability. The patient's concentration and voluntary effort was good but capacity for abstraction and psycho-motor speed was inefficient. The test did show anxiety and depressive trends as well as some schizophrenic indications.

Draw-a-Person

The results of this test indicated that the patient manifested some degree of uncertainty in handling reality situations, and that his world is but vaguely perceived. Orality, anxiety, infantile aggression and dependence and guilt feelings are also present. There are some indications that the patient is attempting to compensate for an inadequate sexuality.

Rorschach

The tests show orality, anxiety, infantile aggression, and dependence and guilt feelings are also present. Color usage exceeds human movement responses, and the F percent is high (72). He no doubt converts tension into psychosomatic complaints.

Bender Gestalt

No severe pathological indications. There is evidence, however, of infantilism and regression.

Szondi

There is an open demand for love and affection. The patient is openly accepting his emotional outbursts. He is fond of pleasure and ease and accepts things from people.

Babcock Memory Paragraph

The memory paragraph was greatly rearranged, distorted, and poorly recalled. The patient's memory is not functioning freely and efficiently; there is a definite indication of pathology.

Projective Sentence Completion

The patient balked a great deal in doing this test. He repeatedly asked if he had to fill in all of the sentences and stated that many did not refer to him. He took an unusually long time to complete the test. The results indicated insecurity, evasiveness, anxiety, dependency on mother and ambivalence toward her. The possibility of latent homosexuality was also indicated.

Word Association

Many clang associations and close reactions were given indicating a lack of flexibility of thought processes. A poor psychosexual adjustment was indicated. A good deal of orality was present. On the whole, the responses were of a regressive, infantile nature suggesting a schizophrenic process.

Object Sorting

There were many rejects, narrow, and split narrow groupings as well as many concrete and fabulatory explanations. Capacity for abstract thinking seemed to be impaired. The results indicate a schizophrenic process.

Such test-by-test reporting with a lack of integrated conclusions and only feeble, manual-type interpretations goes beyond the laboratory technician's report of findings, but not greatly. Instead of WAIS, Draw-a-Person, and Bender Gestalt, we might have: Urinalysis, Hematology, and Serology. Instead of the sort of data which appear here we can imagine under these several laboratory headings: Color-appearance—clear amber; Reaction—acid; Specific gravity—1.020; Albumin—neg.; Sugar—neg.; W.B.C.—8,'"; Neutrophils—55; Lymphocytes—42; Eosinophils—2; Basophils—1; Hemoglobin—12.8; Hematocrit—42; Kahn—neg.; Wasserman—neg. These are meaningful bits of information, not for the laboratory technician who obtained them, but for one specifically trained to interpret and apply them.

From this point of view, consider, ". . . a Bright Normal capacity on the verbal scale and a Superior capacity on the performance scale. There was a considerable amount of scatter on the verbal scale," or "Orality, anxiety, infantile aggression, and dependence and guilt feelings are also present," or "There were many rejects, narrow, and split narrow groupings as well as many concrete and fabulatory explanations." Would it not seem apparent that the writer feels less capable of interpreting this material than do the readers for whom it is intended? Or does the psychologist endow this material with an obviousness of meaning?

There is much test jargon ("rejects," "narrow and split narrow group-ings," "concrete and fabulatory explanations") and some theory-derived language (e.g., orality and latent homosexuality). Are we to assume that the readers of the report know as much about these things as does the physician about basophils, the hematocrit, or the white blood cell count?

Perhaps the writer did not fully think so, for throughout the report there are *little* interpretations, jumps from raw data to partially interpreted data that are in the nature of general, unintegrated conclusions. For exam-ple, "The patient's memory is not functioning freely and efficiently . . . ," "The results indicated insecurity, evasiveness, anxiety, dependency on mother and ambivalence toward her." We can only wonder if such material meets the needs of the team, or if the psychologist felt she had a mission other than to report what the tests yield. What is this psychologist's concept of her role? There is throughout a tendency to attribute the conclusions offered to the tests rather than to the psychologist. If errors have been made, they presumably are the fault of the tests. In any event let us feel sorry for the report reader who *cannot*, no matter how bright or learned, interpret much of the content. Who knows, for example, in the context of the information given, the meaning of ". . . a considerable amount of scatter on the verbal scale" while on the performance scale "scatter was minimal." The further contribution that "there was some intra-test variability" would not seem to help.

The report is saturated with Aunt Fanny statements. Most of us, in our more candid moments, will admit to "anxiety," "dependence and guilt feel-ings," "orality," "insecurity," perhaps even to "dependency on mother and ambivalence to her," and to having "some degree of uncertainty in handling reality situations" (although use of the word *reality* makes the statement appear sinister). Nevertheless, much of the material may sound impressive, if not meaningful, to a nonpsychologist. But we should perhaps feel ashamed to write that "He is fond of pleasure and ease and accepts things from people" because this probably is also true of the reader of the report who may be made uncomfortable by the foregoing. It is also perhaps going too far to write "The *possibility* of latent homosexuality was also indicated." (emphasis supplied) Not only may we not be enlightened to learn that the patient has latent homosexuality (because *it* is supposed to be well-nigh ubiquitous—though *it* has no meaningful, or highly consensual, frame of reference), we would have been surprised had the psychologist concluded that there were no possibility of such!

But however critical we may be of this non-case-focused report, it is probably largely accurate. With the exception of a few statements (e.g., intellectual level, mention of pathological indications, and a diagnostic impression), the report is not specific enough to be wrong. Some of the statements are not transferable into demonstrable behavioral referents. We need to alert ourselves to the specific statements when they do occur, since it is only then that we may check for irresponsible interpretations. The psychologist is able to learn from the Rorschach that the patient "no doubt" converts tension into psychosomatic complaints. Other team members will either challenge the right of the psychologist to express this opinion or get an erroneous view of the prowess of the Rorschach.

Here is another test-by-test report.

WAIS

The patient is presently functioning in the Average range of intelligence, with a full-scale WAIS IQ of 102. This measure is, however, clearly not optimal. He refused to do either the Digit Span or Arithmetic subtests, saying, "You can't touch the darn numbers, Bill." The influence of impairing factors is also seen in inconsistent function. The patient's optimal capacity is most probably in the Superior range. His tendency toward pedantry, and a careful attention to minute details indicates compulsive features in the personality. Many verbalizations are rather bizarre, and test performance in general reflects marked deterioration.

Wechsler Memory Scale

The patient refused to do more than a few items of this test. He gave his age as 34 (incorrect), and the year as 1971 or 2, but knew where he was.

Several other tests—Color Form Sorting, Memory Paragraph, Bender, Benton, and Szondi—were refused by the patient. For the Bender he said, "You can't do it Mac—I'll bet you don't believe it, it's all ended—It has to end after a while, Bill—I can't, Bill." He seemed to have difficulty in any tests which require symbolic manipulation of materials, i.e., where there weren't models or designs to be copied.

Object Sorting

The patient rejected two items on active sorting, had two somewhat loose groupings, and manifested a tendency to narrowing. Five concepts were essentially abstract in nature, two of them also reflecting functional and concrete thinking. One grouping in passive sorting was rejected, and two elicited syncretistic reasoning. One functional concept was given. The patient was able to offer abstract concepts for the remainder of the groupings, including some of the most difficult ones. Performance on this test would contra-indicate organic involvement, but the inconsistent and erratic function points to a severely pathological process, psychotic in nature.

Rorschach Examination

The large number of responses suggests an over-ideational individual, one who has emphasized intellectualization as a defense. The stereotypy and banality of content, however, indicate an impoverishment of constructive energies in the personality. In spite of the apparent productivity, constriction is a prominent characteristic. The presence of only three popular responses indicates the degree to which the content of the patient's thinking differs from usual modes. There are also signs of gross disturbance in the structural aspect of thinking, including neologisms. Reality testing in general is quite poor, although there is some residual ability to appraise the outside world.

Chronic difficulties in interpersonal relationships are suggested, with little capacity for dealing adequately with emotional stimulation. Inferiority feelings are seen in the presence of homosexual features and paranoid thinking. Compulsive signs are found, and there appears to be a depressive aspect in the personality.

While a schizophrenia is indicated by these test results, the subtype is not clear. Both paranoid and catatonic features are seen, as well as certain aspects of function consistent with simple type. In view of these intermingled aspects, the diagnostic impression is schizophrenic process, unclassified. Lastly, general test performance would contra-indicate the importance of an organic factor.

This report in some ways resembles the previous one, yet it is different. The patient's verbalizations give much more of a feeling that a live person was present. These comments are most colorful but unfortunately are not linked with conclusions that they might illustrate.

The report is inconsistent with respect to interpreting the data. There are some meaningful conclusions—for example, those about reality testing. But much material is not interpreted. What is the meaning of the discrepancy between current intellectual functioning and estimated optimal functioning, or what is the significance of the observation that the patient experienced difficulty with tests having certain characteristics, or what is the behavioral significance of the concepts demonstrated on the Object Sorting test (other than the obvious clinical fact that the patient is psychotic)? The patient evidently was confused about his age and orientation for time, giving an incorrect age and incorrectly identifying the year, yet we must read the analysis of other tests to know that he is not "organic." The psychologist felt it important to include some deviant findings, yet not tell their meaning, although loss of orientation in two of the three "spheres" is frequently an organic indicator. Who then shall make interpretations from such inherently rich material?

This report includes much in the way of concepts and jargon which are likely to be unfamiliar to the report reader. The reader is expected especially to know about the Rorschach and the Object Sorting tests and to appreciate the significance of constriction, of three popular responses (how many should there be then, and what is a popular response anyway?), of loose groupings, and of narrowing. In general the patient is presented as an individual, although a few minor Aunt Fanny comments are to be found. Here note especially references to "inferiority feelings," "compulsive signs," and a "depressive aspect in the personality." These could all be spelled out with profit, as could the information on "homosexual features" if it is of any importance in terms of the mission.

The following report on a chronic state hospital patient attempts some segmentalization of personality and also illustrates a number of other faulty practices.

Intelligence, Memory, and Organization of Perception and Thought

The patient is presently functioning toward the lower limits of the Superior range of intelligence, with a full scale WAIS IQ of 120. Qualitative analysis suggests that anxiety, mild negativisms, obsessiveness, and excessive compulsivity may have had the effect of lowering the score somewhat from an optimal measure, which would probably fall higher in the Superior range.

It appears that there are temporary periods of preoccupation that may hinder the intake of presented material, but the memory function seems to be otherwise intact. There is a tendency for verbal material to be distorted, but this is mitigated somewhat by the patient's capacity for critical self-appraisal. So, while reality-corrupting factors are present, the patient is able to exert some degree of control over them.

Basic perceptual functioning is apparently largely intact—perceived figures are drawn in quite faithful reproduction.

In the sphere of thinking, particularly as reflected in the Object Sorting test, the level is not as abstract as would be expected in an individual of superior intelligence. Groupings are mainly assembled on the basis of functional and concrete concepts. This test further reveals the patient's over-ideational nature, and the severely obsessive-compulsive character of his thinking. The looseness of thought structure which is also observed here assumes more pathological proportions in this configuration. Looseness of psychotic degree is also evident in the Word Association test, where the patient gave distant, highly personalized, clang, and even neologistic responses.

Personality

Analysis of projective material indicates a passive-dependent, insecure individual with marked feelings of rejection, inferiority, and inadequacy, and with a strong felt need to be wanted and cared for. There is also a desire, on the other hand, to be active, assertive, and masterful, with the resultant incongruence contributing to a passive-aggressive conflict.

Hostility and its expression is a problem of magnitude for the patient. He harbors a great deal of such feeling, which is variously directed toward the father figure, toward females (who are regarded as castrating, rejecting agents), and toward himself. The extrapunitive feeling arouses a considerable amount of guilt, anxiety, and fearful apprehension of morbid proportions. The intropunitively directed aggression contributes to a marked depressive feeling-tone as well as other self-preoccupations of a more malignant nature. He pictures himself as being helplessly exposed to, and buffeted by, hostile environmental forces, with consequent feelings of futility. Worse than this, there are indications of feelings of self-disintegration and decay, which smacks of the apathy of the chronic, deteriorated schizophrenic.

It appears, in fact, that the patient is struggling, almost consciously, to achieve an emotional nirvana through schizophrenic apathy, but he has not been at all successful in this attempt. There are persistent signs of high emotional responsivity and lability, inner tension and turmoil, rather intense and apparently chronic anxiety, as well as the aforementioned hostility, guilt, and fearfulness.

All of these factors threaten the integrity of the patient's personality organization, and control over them is attempted by means of diverse defenses. Obsessive-compulsive mechanisms, principally intellectualization, predominate and result in thinking which may be characterized as over-ideational, obsessional, doubt-ridden, and ambivalent. He is extremely attentive to the minutiae in his environment, attempting to figure out the meaning and significance behind the details of events. This, in company with a somewhat suspicious criticalness, lends a strong paranoid flavor to the thought content. There is excessive ambivalence concerning almost anything which the patient considers he wants, but at the same time doesn't want, likes but doesn't like, etc. Other defensive mechanisms which the patient is utilizing include strong inhibitory efforts and repression, which give an hysterical aspect to the personality picture. These, together with observed oral material and negativism, could contribute toward catatonic features in the patient's behavior.

As a result of these various regulatory mechanisms, particularly the intellectual factors, the patient can probably succeed at times in presenting a facade which may make him appear more psychologically intact than he actually is. Large areas of thinking are apparently reality-bound, but this is achieved at the expense of rather severe constriction of personality resources. The patient has retained some ability to appraise his own thinking and behavior in order to keep it consonant to a degree with reality.

That the patient's attempts at control are not adequate is most apparent in the intensity and content of his morbid, autistic preoccupations. There is a marked, malignant self-preoccupation, indicating severe withdrawal—the patient is "all wrapped up" in himself. There is an inordinate preoccupation with his sexuality, which is undifferentiated and chaotic. Homoerotic tendencies are strong, but they are not recognized or welcome—as manifested by the extent to which the patient is absorbed with heterosexual problems. There is evidence, too, of guilt concerning autoerotic behavior. The possibility of perverse sexuality should be considered. Another area of preoccupation is religion, problems of good vs. evil, etc.

The patient's apparent willingness to talk about his problems, particularly in glib psychological terminology, would seem to indicate a high degree of positive introspection and insight. Certain test indices suggest, however, that his verboseness is a means of "covering up," of talking about topics of his own choosing. In more ambiguous, non-conversational situations he is cautious, careful, and evasive, thus enabling himself to avoid traumatic topics. This suggests that introspective capacity is actually somewhat limited and insight restricted.

His attitudes toward parental figures indicate marked residuals of unresolved oedipal problems. The father is the object of strong aggressive feelings, while the patient's attitude toward the mother has more warmth, but is still intensely ambivalent due to her rejecting qualities.

In conclusion, the foregoing description indicates a chronic schizophrenic process in an individual who has, nevertheless, retained some degree of reality contact. The type of defenses predominantly employed—i.e., obsessive-compulsive—suggests that paranoid features should be most prominent. The presence of hysterical mechanisms, plus other test indices, would suggest that catatonic features should also be in evidence.

Intelligence is discussed first. It is not optimal.

In this report the headings announce that certain portions of personality are to be separated and treated apart from the rest of "Personality." The psychologist is not successful here (fortunately), for in discussing intelligence he talks about a number of "personality" features—anxiety, negativisms, obsessiveness, compulsiveness. This is quite proper if there is a rationale for discussing the intellect in this report. The same holds true of the discussion of what the psychologist describes as the memory function. It is only the headings and the averred attempt to think of personality in terms of segments that are blameworthy.

The report is exhaustive, overdetailed—a shotgun report. What else can the patient have wrong with him? A chronic case, he is schizophrenic, apathetic, deteriorated. He is depressed, paranoid, catatonic, hysterical, and obsessive-compulsive. He is oral, and anal also, no doubt, because he is obsessive-compulsive, and he didn't do very well during the oedipal period either. He has homosexual problems, heterosexual problems, autoerotic problems, and maybe some other kinds of sexual problems. He turns aggression outward and inward because he is a hostile person. He also has guilt, anxiety, fearfulness, minor tension and turmoil, outward hyperresponsivity and lability. He feels self-disintegration and decay. He is passive-dependent, has feelings of rejection, inferiority and inadequacy, with a strong need to be wanted and cared for. He hates his father and he hates females (they castrate and reject him). The environment is a hostile place.

What is the focus of all these impressions? What are the major conclusions? What is the supporting material?

All of the faults written into the report would seem to suggest that the psychologist has a jaundiced view of the patient, but possibly some of this comes from close attention to a pathologically oriented theory. The various fixations, conflicts, and problem areas discussed by Freud are also discussed by the psychologist, the patient appearing to be the vehicle by which knowledge of the theory can be demonstrated. Had Freud lived longer, the report might have been longer. In accentuating the negative, the psychologist watches the patient closely lest he present an unjustifiably favorable image. The patient talks well (though sometimes glibly) and would seem to have much positive introspection and insight. But we mustn't be fooled. He is covering up. He is evasive. Then, too, "large areas of thinking are apparently reality-bound, but this is achieved at the expense of rather severe constriction of personality resources." This patient looks better than he actually is because he presents a facade.

Because theory is is a matter of generalities, and because Aunt Fanny typifies the banal generalities of people, this report is very much of the Aunt Fanny type. To be brief, consider traits like orality, anxiety, nonoptimal intellectual functioning, oedipal problems not fully resolved, and an imperfect sexuality. This latter theme is entrenched in many psychological reports as firmly as the IQ emphasis. Psychologists, with the diligence and dedication of Diogenes, would seem to be searching for a person with a solid gender identity, complete acceptance of his or her sex role, lack of guilt or conflict over sex activities, lack of actual or fantasy indulgence in anything but true mature heterosexuality (this is wholesome and good), lack of id impulses that tend in any direction but the latter, and great enjoyment and fulfillment in coitus. Where might we find such a person?

The report has word jargon and test jargon. Terms like *intropunitiveness* and *extrapunitiveness* are not generally used clinical terms; they are associated with a test having low rank order in clinical usage. Nevertheless, the theory talk and the test talk may give the reader the impression of having been here before.

In the next report, which is shorter and contains fewer comments on pathology, the focus is somewhat clearer. At least it would seem that the patient is an intelligent schizophrenic person who is deeply troubled and has, along with several distressing problems, difficulty in controlling the expression of his feelings.

Intellectual Evaluation

Intellectual functioning is generally in the superior range (IQ 127), with very superior verbal intelligence and excellent memory, psychomotor performance, and motor learning. He shows an unusually low drop on social comprehension, however, which is out of keeping with his general performance.

Personality Organization

Objective personality data disclose a generally deviant personality profile with particular emphasis on "depression" and "psychasthenia" scales. Underlying these surface disorders one notes the presence of malignant mental processes in terms of schizophrenic, bizarre manifestations. Thus "Schizophrenia" and

"F" scales also show deviant elevations. Disturbed psychosexual functioning is indicated by the elevated "Femininity" scale. Consistent with this picture of severe schizophrenic pathology, the Rorschach and other projective data show marked inner turmoil, multiple unresolved emotional problems, and loss of control of psychotic proportions. Uncontrolled aggressive themes on the Rorschach are exemplified by his percepts of "pelvic bone removed with blood" and "Fox's face." Also his percents of "colored designs" on plates IX and X indicate reduced emotional control which is compensated by evasive defensiveness.

His thematic associations to the figure drawing suggest considerable concern about problems relating to vocational dependability and perseverence and ability to take care of one's family. His own reported difficulties of this type indicate that he is still ruminating and experiencing loss of self-esteem because of them. His sentence completions disclose other basic personal problems having to do with marital relations, attitudes and feelings about his parents, and general interpersonal relations. There are signs of continued angry depression, intropunitiveness, and reduced self-esteem.

Even though some useful conclusions are presented, the effectiveness of this report is, for several reasons, open to question.

First, there is a lot of test talk. If the reader does not have expert knowledge, or at least a working knowledge of the MMPI, what is being discussed cannot be very meaningful (but it can still be impressive). In connection with this emphasis on test performance, as partially opposed to emphasis on the patient, is the seeming transfer of responsibility for conclusions from the psychologist to the tests. "Objective personality data disclose . . . ," "His thematic associations to the figure drawing suggest . . . ," "His sentence completions disclose. . . ." The MMPI scale scores apparently give conclusions automatically, and the presence of "schizophrenic, bizarre manifestations" are backed up with mention that " 'Schizophrenia' and 'F' scales also show deviant elevations." With this bit of instruction, other team associates may feel free to reach similar conclusions in the presence of such elevations, or to question a psychologist who does not report such conclusions when there are elevations on these scales. Similarly with the interpretation of the elevated "Femininity" scale. In the discussion of intellectual functioning, there is mention of "an unusually low drop on social comprehension," but this is not interpreted. Presumably this statement has meaning in the context in which it is mentioned, and the reader will reach the correct conclusion. Finally, in reviewing the test talk we note the use of test content both to exemplify and support conclusions. Is it really apparent that "Fox's face," seen somewhere on the Rorschach, is an uncontrolled aggressive theme? Does the isolated information that the patient saw "colored designs" on plates IX and X necessarily indicate "reduced emotional control which is compensated by evasive defensiveness"? All of these observations raise questions about the responsibility of interpretation and about the impression given to associates on the way that psychologists reach conclusions.

In a passage taken from a longer report, the opposite of the battery approach is demonstrated; the findings of an individual test are summarized and a diagnostic impression is based on this one test. This is generally hazardous and unwise. In the case from which this excerpt was taken, all of the various diagnostic impressions and other conclusions were integrated in the *summary*. This procedure may seem objective, but it sometimes forces the psychologist to arrive at far-reaching conclusions from too restricted a sample of behaviors.

WAIS

On this test, this patient attained a full scale IQ of 125, giving him a classification of "Superior" general intelligence. His performance IQ of 128 also places him in the "Superior" category, and his verbal IQ of 116 in the "Bright Normal" group. This discrepancy of 12 IQ points in favor of performance is considered very significant; this pattern would ordinarily tend to point to psychopathy.

Quantitative discrepancies of the type where easy items are missed and more difficult ones of the same subtest are passed, occurred in the following instances—he misses "movies" (0) and "land in city" (0), but gets "forest" and "child labor" on the comprehension subtest. Qualitative analysis of these and other responses on the comprehension subtest reveal some tendency toward psychopathy (he would leave the theater; his only concern would be to remain calm—he does not care about the others there) and some negativism and inaccessibility (taxes—"They're very necessary"—this is an inadequate answer considering patient's age and educational background).

There are no bizarre responses such as would indicate any pathology of psychotic proportions.

A scatter analysis shows significant negative discrepancy from the mean of the subtest scores for comprehension and digit span. The extremely low digit span performance points to an anxiety laden person; this impression is heightened by the discrepancy between digits forward and backward (5 vs. 3). The digit symbol subtest reveals a pervasive insecurity and some hostility (heavy lines).

Summary of the WAIS

This 31-year-old white male patient is now functioning at a "Superior" level of general intelligence (full scale IQ,125, performance IQ 128, verbal IQ 116). This score is taken to be a fairly reliable estimate, but patient probably has capacity to function on a Very Superior level as evidenced by his performance scores; a great amount of anxiety seems to be depressing his digit span and comprehension performance with a resultant constriction of his verbal ability. There is no indication of any psychosis.

Diagnostic Impression

Neurotic anxiety with pathological personality trends.

This psychologist seems to have faith in report readers' intimate familiarity with the test under discussion—with its items, the sort of responses it yields, and something of the scoring system, too.

The report writer also appears to be giving readers some unfortunate instruction in the interpretation of psychological tests. For example, a qualitative feature of performance on the Digit Symbol subtest is interpreted as indicating the presence of Aunt Fanny traits like "pervasive insecurity" and "some hostility." The interpretation of the patient's response to the "movies" and "child labor" items do not appear to be adequately substantiated. (What was the response to child labor?) Nevertheless, the report writer seems to be building toward the conclusion that this patient is a "psychopath." Progress toward this goal is thwarted, however, when it is noted that the Digit Span score is down—the patient repeated 5 digits forward and 3 backward, a result which could be due to various causes—and by the "pervasive insecurity" already noted from performance on the Digit Symbol test. Hence the WAIS-based diagnostic impression now becomes "neurotic anxiety with pathological personality trends," an unofficial and ambiguous classification.

The strong need for a summary statement, even though the text is so brief, is interesting. It might also be noted that the summary contains a new integration of material. The meaning of the discrepancy between verbal and performance IQs was suggested in the text (—with some hedging ". . . would ordinarily tend to point to . . .") as a "psychopathic" indicator. Now, in the summary, comes a new insight. Anxiety is leading to a "constriction" of "verbal ability," and the patient is not a "psychopath" after all. The report reader, if able to follow the twisting path of this brief report, is being asked to contribute to the conclusion-making process, rather than being presented with firm conclusions.

Notice that the psychologist interprets a verbal IQ that is lower than the performance IQ as a "constriction of his verbal ability." What impression is the report reader supposed to reach? *Verbal,* in the WAIS sense, refers to tests in which the stimuli are auditory, and the responses are made through speech. It is thus a limited technical term. In the usual connotation, *verbal* has to do with linguistic function, and apparently it was not a difficulty of this sort that resulted in a verbal IQ lower than the performance IQ. But even if the test were essentially a measure of verbal ability, a score that is a standard deviation above the mean probably should not be considered as evidence of "constriction."

The final "how not to" case is necessarily abbreviated. The request for assessment was made by a neurologist who requested a neuropsychological reevaluation, the original psychological assessment having been made prior to brain surgery. Much historical data recorded in the present report repeats information that was reported by the psychologist in the original report and is also recorded in other places in the patient's clinical folder.

The abstracted material that follows is from a report that approaches six pages in length, single spaced, plus two pages of raw appended data. The "Reason for Referral," as spelled out by the psychologist, approximates a page. "Behavioral Observations" cover two-thirds of a page. "Test Results" exceed two pages. The "Summary," which is a summary of the entire clinical course of the patient, including highlights of the surgical procedure she underwent and her postsurgical condition, is two pages in length. Then come "Recommendations" that cover half a page, short by comparison. Some excerpts follow.

Reason for Referral

Alice F. is a 46-year-old right-handed female office manager with no known familial left-handedness. On 12/21/81 she underwent a resection of a right mesial temporal arteriovenous malformation. The AVM was totally removed, and seizures were controlled with Dilantin. She was left with a dense left hemiplegia with increased tone and hyperreflexia, left hemianesthesia, left lower facial weakness, and loss of the right cranial nerves III and IV causing an inability to open voluntarily her right eyelid. After the operation she became confused about where she was. . . .

Behavioral Observations

About three to four months after surgery, Ms. F.'s mood was noted to improve. She showed constructive changes in Physical Therapy, Occupational Therapy, and Corrective Therapy. . . . Several weeks later, however, she was found to have a supply of sleeping pills, and on questioning she admitted she planned to use them to "end it all." Shortly after admission she had also threatened suicide. On testing, however, she was in a very good mood. This may be due to the fact that she is now able to get about for short distances with the help of a cane. But she is changeable, and ward nursing staff reports occasional outbursts since surgery. . . . Ms. F. was somewhat of a problem during testing, telling anecdotes, jokes, and posing riddles such as "What is the difference between a psychologist and a psychiatrist? Answer: Fifteen dollars an hour."

Test Results

Ms. F. is functioning at the average level of intelligence. Her WAIS-R IQ is 102. Her Verbal IQ is 116 and her Performance IQ is 76. Information, Comprehension, Similarities and Vocabulary are all in the High Average to Superior range (See Appendix of Scores) suggesting that this was her premorbid level. On Proverbs she is concrete, tangential and circumstantial. On the Wechsler Memory Scale immediate and 20 minute delayed recall was very good and on the Rey Auditory Learning Test she had learned 14 out of 15 words on the fifth trial. Her approach to the task was based on an active and effective strategy of encoding words into a story. Left-neglect is seen on the Bender and on Performance tasks of the WAIS, on the Visual Reproductions of the Memory Scale and in copying the Rey-Osterrieth Complex Figure Test. . . .

Summary of Current Results compared with Preoperative Results

Ms. Alice F., a 46-year-old right-handed female office manager was referred for a postsurgical neuropsychological assessment following resection of a right mesial temporal arteriovenous malformation on 12/21/81. Following surgery she became depressed and then her mood improved when she was able to get about for short distances with the help of a cane. She then became depressed again over a strain in her marriage. Test results show a marked left-neglect on the Bender, on WAIS-R Performance tasks, on Visual Reproductions of the Memory Scale and in copying the Rey-Osterrieth Complex Figure Test. Cognitive processing of verbal material exceeds performance on visual-spatial material. Knowledge of Vocabulary words and cultural facts and social knowledge is superior. Logical memory and the ability to remember lists of unrelated words is excellent (14 out of 15 words by the fifth trial). . . . Such a pattern is indicative of right fronto-temporo-parietal dysfunction. . . . Compared to preoperative testing, test scores for old verbal knowledge is the same or improved. She is more impaired on tests of visual-spatial functioning since she had her CNS surgery. There was no left-neglect in preoperative testing. . . .

Recommendations

Ms. F.'s left visual-neglect impairs her reading ability, interferes with her ability to solve the visual-performance tests she was given, and impedes her ability to move around in the environment. In addition to the Corrective and Physical Therapy that is planned, she should have visual-spatial orientation therapy.

Ms. F. has a history of maladjustment with depression that dates to 1975. She has taken mood elevators and psychotherapy for this condition until she entered the hospital for her AVM problem. . . .

Severe repetitiousness, problems with organization, and test orientation are very obvious. The function to be served by the information contributed by the psychologist is not always clear. For example, the patient's neurological history and the CNS surgical procedure performed on 12/21/81 was already well documented, and dated where it should be—in her medical records, not in the psychologist's report. A psychologist in a large medical center (where patients with this sort of problem would be treated) does not have the responsibility to integrate the reports of the various specialists into a summary report. What end is served by returning to the neurologist neurological information with which he or she no doubt is thoroughly familiar? Similarly the patient's ward behaviors, certainly the material centering about suicide, is recorded precisely where one reviewing the case would look for it. Her behaviors during testing would appear to be diagnostically rich as an indicator of current psychological status, but the psychologist simply records them for the neurologist and others. The psychologist presumes that in addition to being good, out-of-context interpreters of clinical behavior, these clinicians are well-versed in the content of psychological tests and the significance of the content that they yield.

It is evident to this reviewer that valuable conclusions are mixed with a plethora of words, their volume being multiplied by repetition that has no clear rationale. In the context of all these words, then, what is omitted stands out boldly: an exploration of the patient's personality and psychopathology as opposed to a recitation of the skills she has retained and those she has lost. True, this topic was not broached in the request for assessment made by the referring neurologist, whose immediate interests may have been focused on topics of his or her specialty. The psychologist appears to have an awareness that affective disturbance and suicidal issues are of importance, but this theme is merely noted—largely by historical reference—not developed. Indeed, no testing was done to better define this obvious problem area, and no recommendations were made to deal with it. An adequate neuro-psychological report may be required to deal with more than such typical issues as the retention or loss of cognitive and other skill functions, the lateralization and localization of brain dysfunction, and observations on whether the lesion appears to be static, progressive, acute, or resolving.

SOME CASE-FOCUSED REPORTS

Regular Clinical Reports

Contrast the preceding reports with the following case-focused reports. The first is on a 40-year-old skilled worker of moderate but comfortable means. He had made three suicide attempts, the last one involving a particularly serious gunshot wound to the abdomen. All of the attempts were associated with drink. His psychiatrist referred him to us for an opinion on his readiness for hospital discharge.

Battery: Rorschach, TAT, WAIS, Bender, DAP, Sacks Sentence Completions, MMPI

Psychological Assessment: The most obvious personal and social trait of this patient is a remarkably poor tolerance for frustrating situations—a trait which is directly relatable to his multiple suicidal attempts. This man's need is for large quantities of love and acceptance, and he refuses to stand up to stress. When the going gets rough he will "pick up his marbles and go home." This type of behavior is to be understood as including suicidal attempts.

Mr. M. does not want to know the frustration of the real world. He thinks in terms of platitudes and seeks to avoid the unpleasant (even if this means killing himself). For example, he minimizes his suicidal behavior and seems to protest that such is a matter for casualness. He is clearly an alert and perceptive person (his current IQ is 108) but he is reluctant to use his intellectual powers to help him in his adjustments. It is far easier to believe that unpleasantries are always someone else's fault.

This negative social attitude in fact is a rather strong one. An attitude of hostility and impatience is always close to the surface and many life circumstances are sufficiently frustrating to him to cause these feelings to spill out in undercontrolled behavior. This may take the form of verbal aggression or of physical belligerence. As his behavior demonstrates, there is a proneness also to turn this hostility against himself (although there is reason to believe that such behavior is seen by him as self-righteous and as a punishment for others). Alcohol apparently facilitates such a reaction, so we may partially agree with him that it is the liquor which is to blame.

There are no indications suggesting any immediate suicidal threat, but there is also no reason to believe that he is inclined to eliminate self-destructive attempts from his behavioral repertoire. There are no particular evidences of depression, clinically or subclinically. Rather this patient is seen as having a probably unmodifiable characterological defect. This in combination with frustration can again lead to the sort of behavior for which he was hospitalized.

Some "full" psychological evaluations result in a report longer than this, some shorter. A report of this length is probably about right for many referrals, although the necessity for wide variability needs to be recognized.

The approach to this case was to tell what sort of person this is, and then to relate these significant aspects of his life pattern to the problem under study. In focusing on the problem this way, much about the man is left out. Much could have been made of his hostility at the level of the id, and we could call him "oral" if we wished. However, a judgment has to be made on what sort of content to include and what to exclude. This can be done only when the psychologist focuses on the mission and understands what is relevant in terms of this requirement.

The attempt was to compose the report in an integrated, easy-flowing manner, a task which becomes increasingly difficult and time-consuming as report length increases. The language is unstilted, and the intention was that the report be comprehensible to all who have need to use it, such as physicians, social workers, nurses, chaplains, and hospital aides. Words like "frustration" need no longer be regarded as technical and hopefully are used in the nontechnical sense in which most report readers probably understand them. There is no shame in using colloquialisms like "pick up his marbles and go home." Those who believe that technical words are economical and convey what cannot be communicated otherwise should be apprised of the economy and forcefulness to be found in informal expression. Such must be used with discretion, however, and never forced or employed for its own sake.

In another case a psychological evaluation was requested on Mr. O. because his need for hospitalization was questioned by his ward physician. The possibility of a deep disturbance was raised, since it was noted that this patient is a professional person, bright and alert, and without much surface evidence of distress or deviancy. He had complained of "nervousness."

Battery: Rorschach, TAT, Sacks Sentence Completions, WAIS, Bender

Psychological Assessment: The central and prominent theme of this man's life is belligerence and rebelliousness. This negativeness has contributed to turning his marriage into a stormy affair and his job into an arena of bitter dispute. Thus two of the most vital areas of his life, family and career,now are sources of heavy situational stress.

Although Mr. O. is capable of dispensing rancor in many directions, the primary focus of discharge is against authority figures. The origin of this attitude seems to be in the early father-son relationship with the father being seen as unreasonable, not understanding, and overdemanding. In response to this situation the patient has become a great self-justifier and links his rebelliousness with a belief of almost pious self-righteousness. This is true even where his rebelliousness takes the form of flouting conventionality.

Mr. O. feels very anxious and tense at times, sometimes unsuccessful and unhappy, not only because of the stress at home and work, but because of a basic conflict in his personal needs. Stemming from his early home life is an ambition for achievement and the need to be conforming, but an even deeper need causes him to secretly yearn for passivity and to wish to overthrow, the values which are a part of him but which he does not want. Accordingly, merely fulfilling the role of a responsible male member of our society is a primary source of stress for him. If he could resolve the conflict one way or the other he would feel more comfortable.

His oppositional tendencies are a continuing source of guilt for him, and there is reason to suspect that he precipitates conflict with others so that they will retaliate, punish him and thus relieve some of the guilt. If so, this maneuver is not adequately successful for it does not sufficiently relieve deep doubts which he has about his personal adequacy. These are most readily observed in his need to present himself as a superior person.

This same type of compensating maneuver is seen in his marital infidelity. His basic sense of maleness is not strong, and he is unsure of his adequacy here, hence a need to demonstrate that he is a man. Such activity, of course, is also an expression of hostility against his wife and rebellion against his family standards. He probably would not have difficulty in justifying this kind of behavior. Thus, his pervasive negative feelings cause him to feel that others also feel obliquely toward him. He is on the defensive, feels abused, jealous and suspicious. It is very likely that at one level or another he is suspect of his wife's fidelity.

This is an intellectually bright person (his current IQ is 118) and he has a certain amount of appreciation of his difficulties. He recognizes that he is an openly hostile person and that this causes him trouble, but he also believes that he is "right." He therefore is not able to use his intelligence adequately in relating to others. It is easy to visualize his interpersonal conflicts as severe and ugly, since under stress he becomes impulsive, his judgment tends to give way seriously, and he cannot fairly see the other person's point of view.

Psychodiagnostically, this patient has all the earmarks of a generalized anxiety disorder that is precipitated or aggravated by a known stressor. There are important paranoid trends, but the basic respect for reality is good and there are no disturbances of the thought processes. No psychotic process is seen.

The personality conflicts which this person has should be amenable to a degree of resolution through individual insight-giving therapy of a moderately deep level, but his stay at the hospital might not be long enough to permit adequate time to reach this objective.

It soon became apparent to the examining psychologist that his patient sought hospitalization in connection with a "personality" problem, and it was necessary to study his social stimulus value, and the underlying conflicts and adjustment processes on which this is based. An overview of the patient's (clinically pertinent) psychological self is therefore given in the first paragraph, the rest being elaboration. A formal diagnosis is part of the process of understanding the patient—that is, recognizing the extent of his anxiety and subjective stress. A diagnosis is also in keeping with the reason for referral since, as noted, the possibility of an underlying psychotic process had been entertained.

There is a fair amount of negative comment made about this patient—negative in the sense that society regards hostility as a bad thing, and much attention is focused on his hostility (more than in an Aunt Fanny shotgun report, when we say the patient is repressed, anxious, conflicted, insecure, hostile, and withdrawn, and we can't be too concerned with the observation that he is hostile). Is this a prosecuting attorney report? The report was prepared with a knowledge of the socially negative nature of this patient's personality, and it was felt that to understand him we must highlight this trait. The psychologist felt the description to be accurate and individualized. There was no hesitancy in talking about an inadequate sense of maleness in the patient, this seeming to be directly pertinent even though prosecuting attorney psychologists commonly impugn the maleness of clients. The only way we can be sure whether or not a psychologist writes prosecuting attorney briefs, however, is to look at a number of his or her reports.

In yet another case an evaluation was requested on Mr. Q. who drinks too much. He periodically finds himself hospitalized as a result. The staff has seen other alcoholics, of course, but the questions nevertheless arise, "What sort of person is this? What can we do for him?"

Battery: Rorschach, MMPI, TAT, WAIS, Sacks Sentence Completions, Bender

Psychological Assessment: This man's dominant orientation to life is characterized by a childlike passivity and dependency, with marked inadequacy in coping with the everyday stresses of life.

Mr. Q. has never really gotten into the competitive stream of life, but, without full awareness that he is doing so, inwardly wishes to be taken care of. Superficially he subscribes to the belief that a man should be responsible and productive, but his passive needs are stronger and he can readily rationalize his shortcomings. Thus he can work for only a few months at a time, then becomes unhappy and "exhausted" and finds relief in drink. He sees himself as physically weak, not having recovered from illnesses while in service, namely malaria, jungle rash, and prickly heat. Similarly, he would like to get married for the dependency gratification this might offer (his dependency needs are much more insistent than his sexual needs), but has not sought out a mate because a girl friend married another man 20 years ago and he has not yet gotten over it.

Mr. Q.'s mode of adjustment is fairly adequate except where he is required to come to grips with life physically or mentally, to put out any form of sustained effort. This is so because of his passive needs, but also because of defects in his intellectual functioning. Though of average endowment, he is very naive about life and about himself, and he is unconcerned either with the world of real everyday living or with the poor quality of his own thinking which so easily makes it possible for him to deceive himself. Beyond this, he is remarkably unsure of himself, and any external pressures to make him function responsibly would only lead to indecisiveness, tension, and no doubt drinking.

Psychodiagnostically, this patient would appear to be a case of alcoholism in association with a personality disorder. The latter is probably classifiable as Dependent Personality Disorder, but a reliable social history (the patient is not regarded as a reliable source of information about himself) could help to establish whether this is correct. It is not felt that psychotherapy can provide any real benefits, but there is a possibility that he might be helped by associating actively with Alcoholics Anonymous.

The focus is on personality description as this might be explanatory of the behavior that leads to hospitalization. It was not felt that going into the patient's problem of orality, at a psychoanalytic level, would add to this objective. Certainly it did not seem that simply to mention that he is oral would do much for the man or for the staff.

Being unable to state a precise diagnosis is not to be regarded as a deficiency. Frequently other team members contribute to the psychologist's diagnostic impression. It can be unfortunate when the psychologist feels the need to state an impression without qualification. Most people respect honesty, and the psychologist ought not contribute to a false image of omniscience.

The following report was made on Mr. T. who has an unsavory police record. In his early forties, he has been arrested 30 times in the past 15 years for drunkenness and brawling. No doubt this figure would be much higher were he not incarcerated so much of the time. He presents an appearance rather contrary to what one might expect from a person who spends so much time on the other side of the law. He was referred simply for a fuller understanding of his behavior, anything that would contribute to an understanding of why he is as he is.

Battery: Rorschach, MMPI, TAT, Bender, Sacks Sentence Completions

Psychological Assessment: Mr. T. prefers to believe, and would have others believe, that he has a "nervous" condition which is directly attributable to war service. He does in fact experience anxiety and tension—which is quite evident, for example, in a speech blockage that he refers to as stuttering—and he does have a tendency to feel quite unhappy at times. An examination of his thinking shows blocking of thought that may be seen in temporary defects in memory and temporary confusion in dealing with problems. These too are definite indications of tension, but Mr. T.'s primary difficulty is one of social maladjustment.

Mr. T. is seen as an unusually self-centered person who feels markedly inadequate and insecure in meeting the requirements of living. He really does not try very hard to function up to the usual expectations that people have of others, and he certainly does not put himself out where sustained effort and perseverance are required. Rather, he leans very heavily on others for support to the extent that he has developed some rather effective techniques for getting such help. But this does not solve the basic problems which are responsible for his difficulties. In particular, negative feelings he has toward himself—the feeling that he is an inadequate person—and his need for support by others, as already mentioned, cause him readily to sense that he is being rejected. He reacts to this with markedly hateful feelings. Initially it was his parents who he felt were unreliable, rejecting, and making difficult demands on him, but now he tends to feel this way about people in general. In fact society itself now seems to be treating him as he felt he was treated as a child. This feeling of being "let down" by others and reacting to people with hateful urges is associated with inward feelings of guilt and unhappiness. He feels bitter toward the world, distrustful of people and suspicious of their motives.

Obviously then, this is a person who has never grown up psychologically, and one of his major apparent difficulties is in relating to others. This inability to relate to people on a mature plane is seen quite clearly in the sexual area. The patient admits that he does not feel attracted to members of the opposite sex, but he does have need for a woman because of the things she can do for him. This is one of those men who might be regarded as marrying his mother.

On the surface one observes a person with what would ordinarily be sufficient mental capacity to function quite effectively (IQ 106), but he has never adequately developed his intellectual resources any more than he has been able to mature more generally as a person. He has a good understanding of what society expects from people, and he is alert and able to acquit himself well in nonstressful social contacts. But he is not the sort of person who spends much time thinking. He prefers to do things with his body, to move around physically, rather than think. He is an impulsive person whose rash behavior does not permit him to deal constructively with everyday matters. And he has a lack of mental discipline which permits him from time to time to be unrealistic in his thinking, to deal with events as if they were different from what exists in reality. He just chooses not to see the unpleasant truths of his existence. This permits him to deceive himself about his personal motives and behavior, and to some extent probably to deceive others too, at least temporarily.

Socially Mr. T. is rather smooth, glib and ingratiating. He says the "right" things, sounding sincere and convincing. He readily volunteers that he has fallen short of even his own aspirations, but this is quickly explained as due to his childhood circumstances. Mr. T. is quite proficient in behaving in such a way that others might become sympathetic and lend support. As a matter of fact, in the testing situation before the examiner had an opportunity to understand the patient more objectively, he (the examiner) was moved to ask, more out of personal curiosity than clinical curiosity, how it happens that a person like himself has such an unsavory police record. This surface behavior is regarded as a technique of relating to others, and probably also of exploiting them, but under stress or frustration this gives way and his more basic nature emerges. He is a person who must have things on his own terms. He cannot tolerate strains or tensions very long and he must live out his needs.

Often this takes the form, when he feels abused by others (possibly as a result of misunderstanding others because of his own negative attitudes), of striking back with violence. This tendency, along with his drinking, is an unfortunate combination socially.

Notice how many traits Mr. T. has in common with much of the rest of the population. He is of average intelligence, narcissistic, impulsive, dependent, anxious, depressed, insecure, a "latent homosexual," and hostile. Yet it is possible to understand all of these as they have meaning for the patient in the context of his individuality.

Notice also the participant-observer role of the psychologist. Part of the impression gained of the patient was through the effect he had on the examiner. This is not in keeping with the principles of laboratory work.

The next two reports are reproduced with the permission of Dr. Donald N. Bersoff.

Richard was almost 17 years old when he was referred by the school guidance counselor because he was making repeated, almost continual visits to the nurse's office for vague complaints that were never substantiated. The school was interested in knowing how disturbed he was emotionally and what could be done to help him (and most likely, to help the school nurse rid herself of a disturbing child although that was not given as a reason for referral).

Richard was administered the Wechsler Adult Intelligence Scale, the Minnesota Multiphasic Inventory, and the Rorschach Psychodiagnostic Test. Richard's mother was also seen, with her son, for a brief interview. (In addition, a long telephone conversation was held with the school counselor.)

Richard is an essentially normal boy with little evidence of overt, serious emotional difficulty. He does have a tendency, however, to exaggerate minor problems and embellish their significance. He then proceeds to brood, ruminate, feel all sorts of catastrophic events are about to occur and will consequently react to the perceived problem rather than to the problem as it is in reality. As his major modes of responding to problems in living are to escape rather than confront them, and to act quickly with only moderate forethought rather than to unemotionally weigh alternatives, he wants to find a workable expedient that will aid him in his escape.

He finds school aversive for several reasons: He is compared in his athletic endeavors unfavorably to his more adept brother; he is forced to comply to schedules; he is infinitely more interested in nonacademic activities and school time prevents him from engaging in those activities when he wants to; and finally, because he has little patience to work through or think through a difficult but manageable problem, he must then find a way to escape from this aversive stimulus. This he has done by, initially, finding his parents and the school infirmary vulnerable to somatic complaints. Thus, reinforced by sympathetic understanding and excuses from class, he has found the hypochondriacal route quite appropriate to his ends.

However, this behavior is quite amenable to extinction, both at home and in school. He simply needs to be refused treatment and classroom excuses (after a brief examination in case of genuine physical illness), and his "nurse-seeing" behavior will stop. There is no reason to be inhibited in doing this. As indicated earlier, he is not suffering from any severe emotional illness; he is neither psychotic nor neurotic, and most of his outpourings of grief are a histrionic display, easily eliminated. He is an intelligent boy (Full Scale IQ Score is 113—"Bright Normal" and better than 80% of the adolescents his age) and he has merely used his intelligence to find a convenient and feasible means for avoiding frustrating and challenging work. He might fuss and fume about this refusal because he does feel victimized and picked on, a sort of hapless victim of adult irrationality, but he also has a deep well of humor and is smart enough to give up when he understands that he cannot avoid limits being set. One final note of caution: he is also bright enough to try something else.

David was referred by the family physician, although a copy of the report was sent to his school. He was referred because he exhibited all the behaviors associated with those children typically labeled as "neurologically handicapped" and the doctor wanted to know if there were any psychological indications of brain damage. The boy was in the first grade and about six and one-half years old when seen.

David was administered the Stanford-Binet Intelligence Scale, Children's Apperception Test, Thematic Apperception Test, Bender Motor-Gestalt Test, Rorschach Psychodiagnostic Test and Figure Drawings. Both parents were interviewed, and a telephone conversation was held with the doctor.

David is an imaginative, talkative, active boy of high intelligence with no overt evidence of brain injury. His measured intelligence on the Stanford-Binet is 126, which places him in the "Superior" range of intellectual ability, ranking him better than 90% of the children his age. He is able to perform tasks expected of the average seven, eight, nine, and even ten year old. It is not until he is given problems appropriate for an average eleven year old that he shows consistent failure. His vocabulary, the best single indicator of intelligence and academic success, is equivalent to that of a bright eight year old.

His intellectual capacity, however, is not matched by his emotional maturity. When frustrated or overstimulated he is very likely to become hyperactive, impulsive, disorganized, and infantile. He is an intense child whose impishness can easily turn to annoying and seemingly negativistic behavior.

It appears as if general family relationships are good, but he tends to see his mother as more restrictive and punitive than his father. But, while he sees his father as protective and concerned, David is moderately angry about the fact that he is gone a great deal. At one point he responded to a picture of a little boy looking at a violin and said, "The boy isn't very happy. His Daddy won't fix his banjo because he doesn't have time." When the examiner asked what the little boy's father does for a living, David responded, "he fixes cars" (his real father's occupation). He also has been affected, more than most children by the birth of his next youngest sibling. The usual feelings of displacement and "being left out in the cold" seem to be heightened in David.

While the syndrome of hyperactivity, impulsivity, low frustration tolerance, and irritability are classically seen in the so-called hyperkinetic child and is usually associated with intracranial damage, demonstrable brain damage does not seem to be the etiological agent in this case. His visual-motor functioning is good and at least average for his age. Any deficiencies are not due to perceptual or motor disturbances but are attributable to his difficulty in sitting still or attending to many stimuli at one time. When stimulation is reduced (for instance, presenting one card at a time to copy on separate pieces of paper rather than having 8 or 9 copied all on one sheet) his performance is more controlled, accurate, and commensurate with his intellectual level. Thus, he cannot be expected, despite his high intelligence, to consistently react and behave like the average six or seven year old. It may be that high expectations both at home and school, demands made that he was physiologically incapable of fulfilling, and attempts at restraint that were doomed to failure, all served to increase his frustration and irritability beyond his control to the point where he has begun to be viewed in such negative terms as destructive, vicious, and uncontrollable.

He is controllable and will respond to discipline if a comprehensive management regimen is begun. His parents could use brief counseling of an educative nature, during which ways of reacting to him and ways of controlling his behavior can be detailed. He can be imaginative, clever, and a highly effective child both at home and school, and proper management and perception of his problem will be helpful in securing this goal.

The language in the fifth paragraph is technical, directed as it is to the referring physician. Dr. Bersoff indicates that he would have written this paragraph differently if the referral had come from a teacher.

The following is a progress report written by the psychologist in charge of a remediation program. It is addressed to the parents who may become part of the treatment team, and who have a right to know what is being done for their child and how he is progressing.

We have worked with Jeff in three areas this year: visual memory, academic subjects, and behavior modification. Jeff's progress has been extremely slow and we feel his attitude has been the chief cause of this.

Jeff has reached a satisfactory level of ability in visual memory. We feel that no further work is required here.

We worked with Jeff in the following academic areas: reading, spelling, math, and library skills. In reading we started with a review of vowel sounds and after becoming sure of these, Jeff worked on blending and syllable division. He was placed in the beginning of the Merrill Reader, Book 2. Gradually his oral reading grew smoother and his comprehension improved. Often Jeff randomly guessed at a word by its context rather than trying to sound it out. Consequently Jeff has moved very slowly through Book 2 and still has not finished it. Another academic area we worked in was spelling. We used the same list which Jeff used in school. He had difficulty in reading the words on the list. We would study as much of the week's words as Jeff could handle. Occasionally he could tackle the whole list and at other times only one or two words. Again, Jeff would prefer to guess rather than make a calculated attempt at the correct answer. In math Jeff would count on his fingers when doing multiplication or addition and subtraction problems. This slowed his responses down considerably. We worked on his remembering the multiplication tables, but Jeff was able to remember only up to the "three times" tables out of order without using his fingers. In the area of library skills we covered alphabetical order along with puzzles involving library vocabulary.

During the year we needed an increasingly more structured behavior modification program for Jeff. Toward the end of the year we gave him chips for: good work, effort, listening to directions, and for the completion of a given task. We took chips away when Jeff was late, wasting time, guessing wildly, and for failure to complete a task. We also gave him time limits for each activity and he received chips when he came within the time limits. Jeff's teacher was able to use a similar approach in the form of a "weekly report." Jeff received checks from his teacher for copying down his assignments, for correct answers, for good behavior, and he received a bonus for a perfect paper. He received minuses for bad behavior. After he accumulated a certain number of checks he was allowed to do a job in the classroom he enjoyed. We found this to be the most effective approach in encouraging Jeff to apply himself more in a learning situation.

Conclusions and Recommendations

Overall Jeff has shown only a small amount of improvement. He no longer requires tutorial assistance for his learning disability. We are concerned over Jeff's being below grade level and avoidance behavior in a learning situation. Outside counseling might help him a great deal. We feel he should continue to seek remediation at school.

It is also strongly recommended that a comprehensive behavior modification program be set up at home and at school. We would be happy to work this out with you and the school at your convenience.

The following two reports were written on the same child. The first is written for the clinic staff as a basis for advising the child's mother and the physician who referred the case. The reason for referral and pertinent history (his restlessness and distractability are considered along with current findings in making a diagnosis) are given, then the findings are disclosed, a diagnosis is made (a diagnosis that has direct implications for treatment), and a conclusion on what must be done is offered. The scores are important. They are meaningful to those who work with minimal brain dysfunction children. The scores will be available at a later date should the child be retested, hence there is a basis for measuring change.

The letter to the physician spells out the meaning of the scores and completes the picture with a description of the child's behaviors and the diagnosis. The psychologist has reason to believe that this physician knows little about MBD and its treatment, hence tactfully suggests appropriate medication together with its physiological rationale.

Re:Henry Dennis

Henry Dennis, aged 9 years, 2 months, was evaluated at the Center. Presenting problems were impulsivity, social problems, and poor school functioning. From Henry I understand he was tested at school this past year. A retest here on part of the WISC revealed Henry to have good average intelligence. He was noted to have poor attention span, concentration and memory. He was an extremely restless and distractible child. He has a history of hearing problems related to a familial pattern.

The Frostig gave the following results:

Eye-hand coordination:	5 yrs	-3
Figure-ground	8	-3
Form constancy	3	-0
Position in space	5	-6
Spatial relations	8	-3

giving the basis for severe learning disability based on perceptual handicaps. The Wide Range Achievement Test yielded the following findings:

Reading	Grade 1.9
Spelling	1.6
Arithmetic	2.6

There was no real association between sound and symbol in reading and spelling. Arithmetic is weaker than the obtained rating. For practical purposes, Henry has not really mastered the first stage of literacy. Even the personality test (Rorschach) revealed severe figure-ground problems, inability to cope with percepts and, in general, the primary finding was that associated with a minimal brain dysfunction as the core basis of Henry's problems.

Our conclusion was that he will need special help to progress in school as well as an awareness of these special problems on an emotional level in order to keep Henry from becoming demoralized and so making worse his social adjustment. Mrs. Dennis was also referred to her physician for further consultation.

Re: Henry Dennis

Dear Dr. Prinz:

You referred Henry Dennis to us last winter for evaluation.[1] Major complaints were bedwetting, soiling, stealing, impulsivity and "does not listen." Henry was seen in February and we had a family conference with mother on April 10. The school's and our testing of Henry revealed him to be of good average intelligence but with serious physical problems. From our history the difficulties became remarkable at 3 years when Henry developed high fevers, then a hearing disability. Concurrently he became over-active, difficult to manage. Psychological studies here revealed Henry to be indeed a hyperactive child, easily stimulated and perseverative. Attention span and concentration were very poor; he was highly distractible by even tiny auditory and visual stimuli. He seemed to lack the ability to differentiate figure-ground not only in paper work but in general activity. He had no sense of body orientation, which presented continuous confusions to him. Tests revealed him to be four years below his expectancy in perceptual functioning. School achievement was still at Grade 1 level instead of Grade 3. The severity of his disabilities suggests a minimal brain dysfunction which would account for much of his basic difficulties, including the inefficiency of sphincter functions. Exacerbating these problems has been very poor parental management, leading to even greater confusion and disorganization.

We have found that children such as Henry often benefit markedly from medication (dexedrine or ritalin) by increasing efficiency of neurological functioning. Parental guidance was offered by the Center but the mother did not respond. The school is being alerted to Henry's academic disabilities and to the need for special tutorial help.

Sincerely Yours,

---

[1]The recapitulation of case circumstances apparently is necessary. The referring physician would not necessarily be expected to have immediate recall of the case and cannot be counted on to review the details of the earlier psychological report.

Next is an out-of-context report prepared by Lazarus (1973).[2] In addition to the logic of approach, it is worth noting the various areas of subjective problems—indeed the subjective problems far outnumber the objective ones.

MODALITY	PROBLEM	PROPOSED TREATMENT
Behavior	Inappropriate withdrawal responses	Assertive training
	Frequent crying	Nonreinforcement
	Unkempt appearance	Grooming instructions
	Excessive eating	Low-calorie regimen
	Negative self-statements	Positive self-talk assignments
	Poor eye contact	Rehearsal techniques
	Mumbling of words with poor voice projection	Verbal projection exercises
	Avoidance of heterosexual situations	Reeducation and desensitization
Affect	Unable to express overt anger	Role playing
	Frequent anxiety	Relaxation training and reassurance
	Absence of enthusiasm and spontaneous joy	Positive imagery procedures
	Panic attacks (usually precipitated by criticism from authority figures)	Desensitization and assertive training
	Suicidal feelings	Time projection techniques
	Emptiness and aloneness	General relationship building
Sensation	Stomach spasms	Abdominal breathing and relaxing
	Out of touch with most sensual pleasures	Sensate focus method
	Tension in jaw and neck	Differential relaxation
	Frequent lower back pains	Orthopedic exercises
	Inner tremors	Gendlin's focusing methods
Imagery	Distressing scenes of sister's funeral	Desensitization
	Mother's angry face shouting, "You fool!"	Empty chair technique
	Performing fellatio on God	Blow up technique (implosion)

[2]From "Multimodal Behavior Therapy: Treating the Basic Id" by Arnold A. Lazarus, *Journal of Nervous and Mental Disease, 1973, 156, 404*–411. Copyright © 1973 by The Williams & Wilkins Co., Baltimore, and reproduced by permission of the author and publisher. See also *The Practice of Multi-Modal Therapy* by A. A. Lazarus, (New York: McGraw-Hill, 1981.)

MODALITY	PROBLEM	PROPOSED TREATMENT
	Recurring dreams about airplane bombings	Eidetic imagery invoking feelings of being safe
Cognition	Irrational self-talk: "I am evil." "I must suffer." "Sex is dirty." "I am inferior."	Deliberate rational disputation and corrective self-talk
	Syllogistic reasoning, overgeneralization	Parsing of irrational sentences
	Sexual misinformation	Sexual education
Interpersonal relationships	Characterized by childlike dependence	Specific self-sufficiency assignments
	Easily exploited/submissive	Assertive training
	Overly suspicious	Exaggerated role taking
	Secondary gains from parental concern	Explain reinforcement principles to parents and try to enlist their help
	Manipulative tendencies	Training in direct and confrontative behaviors

The following report was contributed by Dr. Paul Lapuc, following the logical approach of Lazarus. Lapuc prepared these initial progress reports, to be updated and revised as treatment is initiated and carried out.

Henry J.   Diagnosis: Schizophrenia, Chronic Undifferentiated Type

This 37-year-old separated male was admitted in an intoxicated state. A review of his history and present condition has delineated several problem areas. These, together with proposed treatment plans, are as follows:

Problem #1: Excessive drinking, blackout spells, and associated physical acting out. Through self-admission and baseline data of a week's duration, it is ascertained that the patient drinks daily between 6 and 18, 12 oz. beers.

Proposed Treatment: A written contractual agreement limiting the number of days he will drink and expected behavior demonstrated upon return to the ward. Violation of contract will lead to restriction in p.j.'s for a period of one week.

Problem #2: Tremors of hand, other unpleasant physiological sensations that disturb him, i.e., the feeling that he can't breathe, headaches, insomnia, tightening sensations in the stomach and other muscular aches.

Proposed Treatment: Relaxation training and biofeedback.

Problem #3. Tearfulness. Occurs whenever he does not get his own way or begins to feel sorry for himself.

Proposed Treatment: Nonreinforcement.

Problem #4: Affective disorders marked by feelings of being ready to explode and then being unable to control his behavior. Feelings of anger. Depression, i.e., entertaining of suicidal thoughts.

Proposed Treatment: Time projection techniques, relaxation and desensitization.

Problem #5: Cognitive disorders marked by thoughts of not being able to do the right thing; inability to accept success; thoughts of letting his family down.
Proposed Treatment: Deliberate rational disputation and corrective self-talk.
Problem #6: Intuitive dysfunctions marked by auditory hallucinations, i.e., hearing father's voice "calling my name" and "I feel that people are out to get me."
Proposed Treatment: Psychodrama and/or role playing involving images of self; rational disputation.
Problem #7: Poor interpersonal relationships marked by dependency upon others to make decisions for him, exploitiveness, submissiveness, and manipulative tendencies.
Proposed Treatment: Specific self-sufficiency assignments: corrective training and training in direct and confrontative behaviors.

The final report in this series is based on the Luria-Nebraska Neuropsychological Battery (Golden, Hammeke, & Purisch, 1980) and was contributed by Charles J. Golden and Charles Ginn. Appended are (1) Luria-Nebraska Profile Summaries, (p. 189), (2) Localization Scales (p. 190), and (3) Factor Scales (p. 191). The item scores are not shown. This report was obviously written for a neurologically sophisticated reader who is familiar with the LNNB.

The patient is a 27-year-old Caucasian male who was involved in a single car accident in October, 1980. In the accident he suffered a closed head injury, fractured ribs, and a right pneumothorax secondary to the fractured ribs. He was semiconscious on admission to the hospital and was moving all extremities. Two to three days post-trauma, a right hemiparesis developed. This was determined to be the result of a CVA resulting from left carotid artery injury secondary to hyperextension of the neck. The CVA was confirmed by CT scan and carotid arteriogram. CT with contrast showed a wedged shape area of decreased density in the left parietal region. The arteriogram indicated occlusion of the left angular artery with marked slowing of the left internal carotid circulation. At the time of the accident the patient was doing graduate work in psychopharmacology. He has an undergraduate degree in psychology.
Test Instrument: Luria-Nebraska Neuropsychological Battery administered seven months posttrauma.
Findings: Evaluation with the LNNB revealed moderate to severe deficits across a number of areas of neuropsychological function. The severity of the injury was evidenced by the high peaks on the Pathognomonic and Left Hemisphere scales. The patterns of the deficits were consistent with damage involving the areas of the brain supplied by the left middle cerebral artery. His good performance on the Rhythm scale as well as the low Right Hemisphere Lateralization score suggested that the right hemisphere had been spared damage.
The patient had greatest difficulty in the understanding of language. This was especially so in tasks where a language related concept is tied to the comprehension of another language concept or of a spatial task. He has problems understanding verbal-logical, verbal-grammatical and verbal-spatial relationships. Problems were seen when the task was given orally to him and when he had to read the material for himself.
While he was able to read and repeat phonemes and one-syllable words,

more complex reading and repetition skills were not present. Tasks involving the coordination of verbal analysis, synthesis, and output of material were very difficult for him to complete with any degree of smoothness, speed, or accuracy. This was most evident when auxiliary words conflicted with the direct connotation of the order of actions or objects. For example, when he was asked to "Point at the pencil" or "Point at the key," he was able to do so with no trouble. However, when the directions went beyond the simple nominative function of words, he was not able to do what was asked of him. When presented with the instructions "Point with the key toward the pencil" or "Point with the pencil toward the key," he merely pointed to the pencil and to the key.

Deficiencies were also seen that were related to his residual hemiparesis. Speed and fine motor coordination were all but absent in tasks involving the use of his right hand. There also exist problems with the right hand in simple tactile sensation and in the synthesis of tactile input to identify objects by touch alone. His intelligence at present would be estimated at an IQ of 88.

Conclusion: This man is obviously performing much below that which would be expected given his age and education. Continuation with graduate school is inadvisable at this time. Considerations should be given to having him begin a vocational retraining program as it is doubtful he will regain the complex language necessary to be competitive in an academic setting. The vocational program should be designed to make use of his skills related to the intact right hemisphere. Retesting in six months would also be in order. At that time, more accurate predictions as to his potential for recovery of function can be made.

Quickie Reports

That psychological reports can be too long, take too long to write, and be a burden on the reader has already been well discussed. We wish to illustrate here that reports can be designed to be effective and even shorter than the case-focused reports presented earlier in this chapter—that are themselves short when compared with the typical reports that have long prevailed. (The shortest illustration presented here consists of but 41 words, of which 4 may be considered superfluous.) Before judging any of the examples adversely, you might consider that reports that concisely summarize the key features of a case, are easy to read, and require of the seasoned psychologist as little as five minutes to write, would appear to merit consideration.

Even shorter and more quickly written, yet no less serviceable are many work-a-day progress notes. These often skimp on formality, take liberties with syntax, and may make use of incomplete sentences, abbreviations, clinical shorthand and jargon. Thus

No change.

R/O OBS.

Mrs. K. didn't feel like talking much today. Obviously depressed. Expresses a "What's the use?" attitude.

Bill angrily refused psychological testing. He said he had tests at Clearwater where the psychologist showed him "a bunch of dirty pictures" and got him excited. The patient signed a release form and I called Clearwater for his records.

LURIA—NEBRASKA PROFILE SUMMARIES
FORM I

NAME: K.T.   TEST DATE: 6-22-81
ID#:   99999   SEX: MALE   PRIM DIAG: 99-99-99
AGE: 26   RACE: CAUC   SEC DIAG: 99-99-99
EDUC: 16   HAND: RIGHT   EXAMINER: C.G.

CRITICAL LEVEL = 51
    NO. OF SCALES ABOVE CL (NOT INCL. I-MEM) = 10   NOT INCL. WRITING AND ARITHMETIC = 9

ESTIMATED IQ DERIVED FROM LNNB SCALES: VIQ= 89   PIQ= 92   FIQ= 87

	SCORES (RAW)	T
MOTOR	(30)	62
RHYTHM	(2)	35
TACTIL	(20)	73
VISUAL	(10)	53
RECEPT	(24)	79
EXPRES	(33)	76
WRITIN	(16)	77
READIN	(16)	77
ARITHM	(3)	47
MEMORY	(11)	58
INTELL	(33)	68
PATHOG	(41)	90
LEFT	(25)	90
RIGHT	(4)	42

Frieda talked today for the first time about her stepfather. She reported that she had never told anyone of his incestuous contacts with her that occurred between the ages of 10 and 13 and ended when her parents were divorced. She sobbed a good deal but said she felt better to "get it all out." I suspect that she will have a great deal of working through to do on this matter.

The matter of quickie reports has been put in perspective by Souther and White (1977). Their message is addressed to scientists and engineers:

189

TEST DATE: 6-22-81   ID#: 99999   NAME: K.T.

          LOCALIZATION SCALES

                                                                    SCORES
                                                                    (RAW)   T
  T 30   40   50   60   70   80   90   100   110   . 120

                                                              LF   (29)   70

                                                              LSM   (20)   55

                                                              LPO   (20)   66

                                                              LT   (28)   76

                                                              RF   (14)   62

                                                              RSM   (8)   47

                                                              RPO   (20)   66

                                                              RT   (22)   61

. . . in reality, aren't some kinds of writing we produce quite adequate even if they are "quick and dirty"? Some of the things we write must, of course, possess as high a quality as we can provide.

Many of the kinds of writing that we do, however, belong somewhere between these two extremes. It would be helpful if technical and scientific writers and their supervisors would discuss the degree of quality required for the different kinds of writing that the staff must produce. Definition of quality standards would do much to clarify the writing task, both for the writer and for the reviewing supervisor.

But these authors caution that the above is not a license for inferior work:

We are not suggesting, of course, that writing can be unclear, ambiguous, distorted, or sloppy.

Several quickie cases and some comments follow:

D. R., age 12½

Debbie is a twelve-and-a-half-year-old girl from a broken home (father deserted six years ago and continues to upset the family by calling to complain to Debbie's mother about his present wife.) Debbie is thought to be underachieving in school. Her teachers see her as an angry, troubled child. Debbie herself complains that schoolwork overwhelms her, tires her out. The following report seeks to achieve an understanding of Debbie as a basis for taking further action.

FACTOR SCALES

		SCORES (RAW)	T
M1	KINESTH-BASED MOV	(2)	60
M2	DRAWING SPEED	(12)	77
M3	FINE MOTOR SPEED	(6)	53
M4	SPATIAL-BASED MOV	(2)	57
M5	ORAL MOTOR	(0)	47
RH1	RHY/PITCH PERCEPT	(1)	40
T1	SIMPLE TACTILE SEN	(9)	91
T2	STEREOGNOSIS	(8)	66
V1	VIS ACUITY/NAMING	(3)	46
V2	VIS-SPATIAL ORGANIZ	(2)	51
RC1	PHONEMIC DISCRIM	(4)	54
RC2	RELATIONAL CONCPTS	(8)	85
RC3	CONCEPT RECOG	(0)	46
RC4	VERBAL-SPATIAL REL	(4)	147
RC5	WORD COMPREHENSION	(0)	47
RC6	LOGICAL GRAM RELS	(4)	86
E1	SMPL PHONETIC READING	(0)	45
E2	WORD REPETITION	(4)	66
E3	READ POLY-SYLLABICS	(4)	55
RG1	READ COMPLEX MATL	(11)	75
RG2	READ SIMPLE MATL	(3)	95
W1	SPELLING	(16)	79
W2	MOTOR WRITING	(0)	46
A1	ARITHM CALCS	(3)	47
A2	NUMBER READING	(0)	46
ME1	VERBAL MEMORY	(4)	60
ME2	VIS/COMPLEX MEMORY	(4)	56
INT1	GEN VERBAL INTELL	(18)	62
INT2	COMPLEX VERBAL ARITH	(5)	50
INT3	SIMPLE VERBAL ARITH	(4)	66

Debbie's intellectual status is above average. Her observations are accurate and there is originality of thought. She is an insecure child who has many fears. She fears the loss of her integrity, attack from others, and her own impulses. Debbie has a great need for acceptance and affection, but is inhibited by an overpowering fear of being rejected and hurt. There seems to be hostility directed to the mother. The relationship has not been mutually satisfying, often leaving Debbie frustrated. It is my impression that the mother's inconsistencies in handling the child may be a source of anger. Now she wants her own way and is conflicted about her dependency. Her attitudes to men are also unwholesome. They are seen as weak and mutilated. And she is confused about herself. She feels inadequate, and having a specific learning disability she requires more guidance and love than most children her age. However, not being able successfully to reach out to others has only left her more frustrated.

Since Debbie finds it difficult to relate to people and because her own feelings are threatening to her, she withdraws to an immature fantasy world that provides little refuge. Even her fantasy is fearful, involving aggression and fear of being injured emotionally. Debbie is a very unhappy child.

D. J. H., age 52

The patient presents a solid picture of histrionic personality disorder. The dominant defenses are denial and repression, with resultant naiveté, poor respect for reality situations, poor judgment, and a variety of socially immature behaviors. He is remarkably self-centered, employing exaggerated histrionic techniques in a continuous attempt to gain support. He is rigid, demanding, and potentially somewhat paranoid in defending what he regards to be his best interests. He thus finds himself involved in frequent interpersonal problems, particularly with those to whom he relates most closely; and low frustration tolerance, exaggerated and labile emotional response, and acting-out tendencies that he regards as "righteous" make for assaultive behaviors. He is preoccupied with sexual fantasy and somatic problems, seeking to live out the sex material in flirtatious behaviors. Marital problems are a source of stress, albeit he contributes to these problems, most recently through his flirtations. The outlook for significant change is not great.

D. J. H. was hospitalized on the "advice" of a judge after he was charged with assault and battery on his wife for the nth time during one of their battle royals. There is no "curable" condition, and (barring a minor miracle) only separation of the couple can put a stop to the presenting complaint. This report does not do justice to the polished histrionic behaviors of this man—a veritable Hollywood actor as he plays out the scenes that regularly take place in the home. But what if the report, with the investment of great effort and time, did a superb job of capturing the flavor of this actor, surely one of the most colorful people I have ever met? Would it make any difference at all?

K. C. J., age 49

This is a florid, chronic schizophrenic of the paranoid type. Delusions are unsystematized and involve ideas of influence and persecutory themes, all in a bizarre context. Thought and speech are quite loose, and neologistic expressions are noted. The outlook is guarded.

This man has been as described for a number of years, and the most promising approach would be antipsychotic medication, support, and whatever hospital programs he might fit into. It is well to document briefly the patient's status on admission as a base line against which to evaluate possible changes in the future as these might provide a basis for action. Pages detailing personality and psychopathology could be added, and we could have at least a paragraph of discussion on intelligence, but to what end? Indeed the comment on outlook is really gratuitous.

B. F. K., age 21

This is a picture of a thoroughgoing "psychopath"—an antisocial personality with a history of disturbance extending far back into childhood. He is essentially an unsocialized individual with a hostile, nihilistic view of the world, capable of dispensing hostility, including assault and physical acts of destruction in many directions. Particularly when under the influence of alcohol and/or drugs is he likely to be destructive, and he may show psychotic-like behaviors. The possibility for any degree of improvement is slim; on the other hand, he could decompensate to psychosis.

Short, if not very sweet. It's telling it like it is. Anyone who claims to have special skills in treating character disorders may volunteer to be this man's therapist. Many nonpsychologists likely would "give up" on such a person, or already have. (Following the patient's discharge, a local district court judge ruling on his most recent transgression selected jail, over the hospital, for him.) Perhaps our random selection of cases contains a disproportionate number of "losers"; at any rate this was one person not benefited by our ministrations. We must remember that although modern treatment helps many, we don't win 'em all.

M. A. B., age 27

There are two opposing sides to this personality: on the one hand there are highly conventional aspirations, on the other, a "psychopathic" side that generally triumphs. This man is remarkably hedonistic (though his marathon sexual expression has recently become "hollow, not worth the effort"), self-indulgent, impulsive, and, in the presence of particularly low tolerance for tensions at the present time, is likely to live out his impulses. He further shows tendencies to schizophrenic behavior that evidently were lived out under LSD, and have at least some potentiality for emerging in stressful situations. He may be diagnosed in terms of his presenting complaint of drug dependence. He might profit from psychotherapy addressed not only to the direction of socialization, but also to deal with problems of hostility and anxiety about sexuality. In addition, there is psychometric evidence for an organic brain syndrome. His WAIS Full Scale I.Q. is 113, his Verbal I.Q. is 121, and his Performance I.Q. is 102. His Wechsler Memory Quotient is 73, with the greatest deficiencies in the areas of logical memory and in making and briefly retaining new visual and verbal associations.

This writer is evidently more hopeful for this man than for the previous one, but not very. The prognosis is built into the character structure. Key personality features and problems are identified, although not all in clinical terms. There is, for example, implicit depression in his "hollow" sex experiences. The nature of his sex anxieties is not spelled out but would quickly become evident to a therapist. He was assessed for a possible organic brain syndrome because of severe, prolonged drug abuse, and the level and quality of his intellectual functioning could be a factor in a rehabilitation program.

7

VARIATIONS ON THE PSYCHOLOGICAL REPORT

In Chapter 1 we suggested that clinical psychological functions are changing and increasing and that the psychological report is instrumental in this development. Computer printout reports, even for such largely impressionistic instruments as the Rorschach, are a dramatic addition to the psychological armamentarium, and computer services that process protocols of both old and new instruments are being heavily used. The application of the psychological report as a therapeutic tool is also a dramatic development.

PSYCHOLOGICAL ASSESSMENT IS NOT ONLY ALIVE AND WELL, it is in the midst of exciting developments that, for the most part, are still in the first generation. The phenomenon may be conceptualized in terms of (1) the development of significant new psychodiagnostic instruments, (2) the preparation of reports by computers, some of these based on new instruments specifically designed to yield computer reports, some based on the adaptation of instruments that are almost 50 years old, or older, and (3) the conceptualization of the psychological report to play a key role in therapy—not just to provide information that might contribute to therapy.

THE MMPI

The MMPI, in use about 50 years, is an instrument that is widely submitted for computer interpretation to the various companies that provide this service.

In the opinion of this writer such interpretations are highly useful and desirable. The computer is obviously faster than the human clinician and can store many more bits of information for fast recall. At the same time, as we pointed out in Chapter 3, various computer services quite ethically, and in keeping with scientific caution, indicate that their reports should be considered as contributing to a case study rather than offering final conclusions.

Graham (1977), a supporter of the use of computerized reports, nevertheless is constrained to caution:

> Perhaps the greatest danger of computerized interpretations is that they have come to be viewed by many persons as a substitute for a skilled clinician rather than as a valuable tool to be used by an experienced clinician. As was pointed out . . . , a skilled and experienced clinician is necessary to give meaning to test data for the individual client or subject. Most clinicians use the MMPI protocol as only one piece of information about an examinee. The inferences based on the protocol are validated against other test data, history, and observation in arriving at a meaningful formulation of the case. When the computerized interpretation of the MMPI is used instead of this more complete clinical analysis, the resulting formulation is at best incomplete and at worst inaccurate and potentially harmful to the examinee. Because some of the computerized interpretation services are used by individuals who are not psychologically sophisticated, the above concerns seem to be justified.

Following are two MMPI Behaviordyne Psychodiagnostic Laboratory reports, selected from 19 available report formats developed for specialized

```
I------STATISTICS------I          PSYCHODIAGNOSTIC       I---IDENTIFICATION-----I
I SEX: FEMALE          I          LABORATORY            I            I         I
I AGE: 24              I          REPORT                I   2 6 4 1  I    2    I
I REPORT: 7      MMPI  I                                I_____I_____I
I OPTIONS: SR          I                                I___USER_____I__SUBJECT_I
I_DATE:_OCT_1981_____I
```

THIS IS A DETAILED CLINICAL REPORT FOR PSYCHODIAGNOSIS. IT IS SENT ONLY TO PSYCHIATRISTS AND CLINICAL PSYCHOLOGISTS.

THIS IS A BEHAVIORDYNE, INCORPORATED REPORT. IT IS A PROFESSIONAL CONSULTATION COMPOSED BY COMPUTER, FOLLOWING A METHOD DESIGNED BY A PSYCHIATRIST AND A CLINICAL PSYCHOLOGIST. LIKE ANY REPORT BASED ON AN INVENTORY, THIS IS SUBJECT TO ERROR. NO DECISION SHOULD BE MADE FROM THIS REPORT ALONE, BUT ONLY FROM CONSIDERATION OF THE CASE HISTORY AND ALL THE AVAILABLE EVIDENCE.

ANALYSIS OF THIS KIND CAN BE DONE FROM ANY OF SEVERAL PSYCHOLOGICAL INVENTORIES. IN THIS CASE, THE INVENTORY COMPLETED AND SUBMITTED FOR ANALYSIS WAS THE MINNESOTA MULTIPHASIC PERSONALITY INVENTORY.

TELEPHONE: (415) 857-0111

PROFILE   USER= 2641   SUBJECT=   2   FEMALE   AGE= 24

BEHAVIORDYNE 599 COLLEGE AVENUE, SUITE ONE □ PALO ALTO, CALIFORNIA 94306

------------------------------ VALIDITY AND RESPONSE ATTITUDE ------------------------------

ALTHOUGH SHE DOES NOT HOLD TO IT CONSISTENTLY, THE EVIDENCE IS THAT IN MOST WAYS SHE CHOOSES HER ANSWERS SO AS TO GIVE A FAVORABLE PICTURE OF HERSELF. SHE IS SLOW TO ADMIT LITTLE FLAWS IN HERSELF, AS JUDGED BY RATHER PERFECTIONISTIC MORAL STANDARDS. SHE TENDS TO MAKE SOME CLAIM TO PERFECTION OF MORAL CHARACTER. SHE IS AN ENTERPRISING PERSON WHO LIKES TO PUT HER BEST FOOT FORWARD. EITHER SHE IS WARM AND FRIENDLY, OR SHE LOOKS THAT WAY THROUGH TRYING TO MAKE A GOOD IMPRESSION. WHEN SHE COMES ON NEUROTIC-SOUNDING STATEMENTS EXPRESSING FEAR AND ANGER SHE TENDS TO MARK THEM FALSE. SHE CLAIMS TO BE ADVENTUROUS AND YET VIRTUOUS. SHE DENIES WORRIES. SHE DENIES ANY EVIL IMPULSES OR ANY BAD BEHAVIOR. SHE SEEMS SOMEWHAT DEFENSIVE. SHE DENIES ANY FAULTS. SHE LIKES TO PICTURE HERSELF AS WELL BEHAVED AND DEVOTED TO DUTY.

SOME OF HER ANSWERS ARE WORTH NOTING. HERE IS WHAT SHE SAID:

302. FALSE. I HAVE NEVER BEEN IN TROUBLE BECAUSE OF MY SEX BEHAVIOR.

326. TRUE. AT TIMES I HAVE FITS OF LAUGHING AND CRYING THAT I CANNOT CONTROL.

476. TRUE. I AM A SPECIAL AGENT OF GOD.

IT MAY BE WORTHWHILE TO DISCUSS THOSE ANSWERS WITH HER TO FIND OUT WHAT SHE MEANT BY THEM.

HER PERSONALITY MAKEUP IS ONE THAT IS NOT AT ALL TYPICAL OF PATIENTS SEEN BY PSYCHIATRISTS AND BY CLINICAL PSYCHOLOGISTS. SHE IS LESS ANXIOUS OR UPSET THAN ARE MOST PATIENTS. SHE DOESN'T TAKE THINGS OUT ON HERSELF AS MUCH AS MOST PATIENTS.

SHE IS A FLEXIBLE AND OBLIGING PERSON. SHE IS A RATHER CHANGEABLE, SPONTANEOUS AND UNPREDICTABLE PERSON. SHE DOES WHAT SHE HAPPENS TO FEEL LIKE AT THE TIME. HER ATTITUDE TOWARD PEOPLE IS BASICALLY FRIENDLY AND TRUSTING. SHE BELIEVES THAT THE WORLD TREATS HER FAIRLY. SHE SEEMS ABOUT AS FREE FROM DISTRESS AS THE AVERAGE PERSON. IN GENERAL SHE DOES THINGS TO ADVANCE HERSELF AND NOT TO DEFEAT HERSELF. SHE IS FAIRLY SUCCESSFUL IN LIFE, AND SHE IS REASONABLY SATISFIED WITH THE WORLD. SHE DOESN'T UNDERSTAND HERSELF VERY WELL.

SHE IS A WARM-HEARTED PERSON, SPONTANEOUS AND FRIENDLY. PEOPLE TAKE A LIKING TO HER. SHE IS THE SORT OF PERSON WHO SEEKS RESPONSIBILITY AND TAKES RESPONSIBILITY. SHE GOES OUT OF HER WAY TO UNDERTAKE RESPONSIBILITIES. SHE IS AN ACTIVE AND ENTERTAINING PERSON, OUTGOING AND SOCIABLE. SHE USUALLY PERSUADES PEOPLE TO GO ALONG WITH HER. SHE IS A GOOD LEADER. SHE CAN BE TRUSTED TO USE HER POWER NOT SELFISHLY BUT FOR THE BENEFIT OF EVERYBODY IN THE GROUP. SHE LOOKS AFTER HER FOLLOWERS, AND SHE TRIES TO TAKE GOOD CARE OF THEM.

SHE HAS BUILT HER WAY OF LIFE AROUND THE DEFENSE MECHANISMS OF DISSOCIATION, REPRESSION, DENIAL, AND CONVERSION. MANY GOOD THINGS CAN BE SAID OF HER. SHE IS ENTHUSIASTIC, IMAGINATIVE, YOUTHFUL, SOCIABLE, OUTGOING, COURAGEOUS, AND SOCIALLY FORWARD. YET SHE IS IDEALISTIC AND TAKES LIFE SERIOUSLY. MOST OF THE TIME SHE IS KIND, PEACEFUL, AND RESPONSIBLE, TOO. WHEN THINGS GO WRONG SHE TENDS TO FEEL IT CAN'T BE HELPED, AND SO SHE BLAMES CIRCUMSTANCES AND NOT PEOPLE. SHE USUALLY MANAGES TO GET ALONG SMOOTHLY WITH PEOPLE, SOMETIMES BY PLAYING UP TO THEM OR FLATTERING THEM. SHE DOES NOT FEEL TROUBLED, NOR FEEL THAT SHE HAS ANY EMOTIONAL PROBLEMS.

BUT THAT EASY FEELING COMES AT SOME COST. SHE IS GREATLY DEPENDENT ON OTHER PEOPLE, AND LEANS HEAVILY ON THEM. AT HEART SHE IS A CHILDISH, IMMATURE, NEUROTIC PERSON WITH POOR SELF-CONTROLS, WHO SPENDS HER LIFE TRYING TO TWIST AND SWAY PEOPLE TO MEET HER DEMANDS. SHE PUTS HER DEPENDENCY NEEDS INTO ACTION, AND YET STAYS NAIVELY UNAWARE OF THE DEPENDENCY PURPOSE OF HER DEEDS, AND UNAWARE THAT SHE HAS DESIGNED THEM TO INFLUENCE PEOPLE.

SHE HAS SOME UNRESOLVED OEDIPAL PROBLEMS. THESE, TOO, MAY COME OUT IN SYMBOLIC AND UNCONSICIOUSLY PURPOSEFUL ACTIONS THAT INVOLVE OTHER PEOPLE. IT IS HER UNAWARENESS OF HER MOTIVES THAT MAKES HER SEEM NAIVE. SHE IS LIKELY TO KEEP UNAWARE OF HOSTILITY, TOO, EVEN IF AND WHEN SHE LETS IT SHAPE HER DEALINGS WITH PEOPLE. SHE IS AN EMOTIONAL PERSON, AT TIMES HIGH-STRUNG, EMOTIONALLY FLUID, AND LIABLE TO LOSE HER TEMPER SUDDENLY.

BY FOCUSING ON ONE BODILY SENSATION OR ANOTHER, SHE GIVES HERSELF CONVERSION SYMPTOMS, WHICH ARE SENSORY OR MOTOR SYMPTOMS ARISING FROM EMOTIONS AND NOT FROM BODILY SICKNESS. SHE FOOLS HERSELF, HOWEVER, INTO BELIEVING THAT SHE IS PHYSICALLY SICK, AND SHE MAY FOOL OTHER PEOPLE. HER SYMPTOMS ARE LIKELY TO BE SPECIFIC AND RESTRICTED TO ONE PART OF THE BODY, AND MAY BE SYMBOLIC OF HER EMOTIONAL CONFLICT.

SHE MAY ALSO HAVE DISSOCIATIVE REACTIONS, SPELLS OF MOOD AND BEHAVIOR DIFFERING FROM HER USUAL SELF. OR SHE MAY HAVE ACUTE ANXIETY REACTIONS. HER CONVERSION, DISSOCIATION, OR ANXIETY REACTIONS SERVE THE SAME PURPOSE AS HER OTHER BEHAVIOR: TO DRAW ATTENTION, TO EXPLOIT PEOPLE, AND TO MANIPULATE AND MANEUVER PEOPLE INTO MEETING HER PERSONAL NEEDS; AND STILL SHE IS UNAWARE THAT SHE DOES SO. SHE IS AT TIMES THANKFUL AND AT OTHER TIMES UNGRATEFUL FOR THE HELP THAT SHE MAKES PEOPLE GIVE HER.

SHE IS SO LITTLE AWARE OF HER OWN MOTIVES THAT SHE SEEMS NAIVE. HER RECOLLECTION OF THE PAST IS IDEALIZED AND ROMANTICIZED. SHE BLOTS OUT MEMORY OF THINGS THAT SHE WOULD NOT LIKE TO REMEMBER. IN VIEWING WHAT GOES ON AROUND HER, SHE OPERATES BY FORMING A GENERAL IMPRESSION. SHE DOESN'T STUDY THE DETAILS; SHE DOESN'T CALCULATE OR ADD THINGS UP. SHE WORKS IN A MORE INTUITIVE WAY. SHE IS STRUCK BY THINGS THAT ARE VIVID.

AT TIMES SHE MAY SEEM THEATRICAL OR HISTRIONIC. SHE IS LIKELY TO BE AFFECTED BY OTHER PEOPLE WHO ARE DRAMATIC OR IMPRESSIVE, TOO. WHEN SHE HAS BUILT UP A ROMANTIC AND IDEALIZED EXPECTATION OF SOME SITUATION, SHE MAY BE DISAPPOINTED TO FIND IT SO COMMONPLACE.

SHE IS SUSCEPTIBLE TO PASSING INFLUENCES. SHE MAY BE LED INTO ACTION WITHOUT STOPPING TO CONSIDER THE CONSEQUENCES. AT TIMES SHE SEEMS TO PLAY GAMES WITH PEOPLE, BUT SHE DOES IT WITH AN INNOCENT AIR.

SHE IS THE SORT OF PERSON THAT GETS BODILY SYMPTOMS TO SYMBOLIZE HER EMOTIONAL CONFLICTS. THESE SYMPTOMS MAY BE WITHOUT AN ORGANIC CAUSE AT ALL, OR THEY MAY OVERLIE AN ORGANIC SICKNESS AND MAKE IT MORE DISTRESSING. THE SYMPTOMS MAY CONSIST OF WEAKNESS, ACHES, PAINS, OR ANY OTHER SENSORY OR MOTOR COMPLAINT. THEY MAY MIMIC A NEUROLOGICAL DISORDER, BUT NOT ACCURATELY.

-------------------------- EVIDENCE FOR PSYCHOSIS OR MENTAL ILLNESS --------------------------

SHE IS NOT AT ALL MENTALLY ILL; THAT IS, NOT AT ALL PSYCHOTIC. SHE SHOWS NO TENDENCY TOWARD PSYCHOSIS AT ALL.

-------------------------- BASIC TRUST, CONFIDENCE, AND SELF-ESTEEM --------------------------

SHE HAS A REASONABLE DEGREE OF OPTIMISM AND CONFIDENCE. TO A MODERATE DEGREE, SHE MAINTAINS AN OPTIMISTIC ATTITUDE BY DENYING DISCOURAGEMENT. SHE SEEMS SOMEWHAT PREOCCUPIED WITH HER BODILY FUNCTIONS. SHE TENDS TO COMPLAIN ABOUT HER HEALTH.

SHE SHOWS NO SIGN OF GUILT FEELING. SHE ADMITS LESS THAN AVERAGE TO FEELING OF SELF-CONSCIOUSNESS OR EMBARRASSMENT.

-------------------------------- DEPENDENCY PROBLEMS --------------------------------

SHE IS NEITHER CLEARLY DEPENDENT NOR CLEARLY SELF-RELIANT.

---------------------------- DEMANDINGNESS OR ORAL AGGRESSION ----------------------------

SHE IS NEITHER CLEARLY DEMANDING NOR CLEARLY UNDEMANDING.

HER PERSONALITY AND CHARACTER ARE SOMEWHAT LIKE THOSE OF PEOPLE WHO HAVE PROBLEMS WITH ALCOHOL. SHE IS SCARCELY AWARE OF HER MOTIVES. SHE DEALS WITH HER PROBLEMS BY REPRESSION AND DENIAL.

IT IS POSSIBLE THAT SHE MAY HAVE A PROBLEM WITH DRINKING. IF SHE DOESN'T HAVE ONE, THERE IS SOME RISK THAT SHE MIGHT DEVELOP ONE.

-------------------------- MASOCHISTIC DEPENDENCY AND BITTERNESS --------------------------

SHE DOES NOT SEEM BITTER. SHE DOES NOT SEEM TO FEEL ESPECIALLY SORRY FOR HERSELF. WITHIN THE AVERAGE OR NORMAL RANGE, THERE IS NO EVIDENCE OF DEPENDENT MASOCHISM.

-------------------------------- HOSTILITY AND COPING --------------------------------

SHE IS NOT A PARTICULARLY HOSTILE PERSON. SHE IS ABOUT LIKE THE AVERAGE. SHE DOESN'T BUILD RESENTMENT UP WITHIN HERSELF ANY MORE THAN THE AVERAGE, AND MAYBE LESS. SHE HARBORS MORE RESENTMENT THAN SHE IS AWARE OF.

IN GENERAL, SHE IS NOT NOTED FOR TAKING THINGS OUT ON OTHER PEOPLE, NOR FOR TAKING THINGS OUT ON HERSELF. IN THIS CASE, HOWEVER, THERE MIGHT BE OTHER CONSIDERATIONS.

SHE LIKES TO THINK OF HERSELF AS BROADMINDED AND TOLERANT. SHE EXPECTS GOOD OF PEOPLE.

-------------------------------- RESPONSE TO AUTHORITIES --------------------------------

SHE DOESN'T SEEM TO HAVE A PROBLEM IN DEALING WITH AUTHORITIES.

---------------------------- COMPULSIVE CHARACTER FEATURES ----------------------------

SHE IS AN UNSYSTEMATIC PERSON. SHE IS NOT METHODICAL. THE THINGS THAT SHE DOES ARE IN RESPONSE TO THE SITUATION THAT SHE HAPPENS TO BE IN, AND NOT IN FOLLOWING ANY SET PLAN. SHE DOES THINGS SPONTANEOUSLY, WITHOUT FEELING ANY NEED TO BE CONSISTENT. PEOPLE FIND HER UNPREDICTABLE.
SHE SEEMS TO LIKE TO CONTROL PEOPLE.

---------------------------- HYSTERICAL PERSONALITY FEATURES ----------------------------

SHE IS HYSTERICAL IN CHARACTER. SHE REPRESSES TO A HIGH DEGREE, AND REPRESSION AND DISSOCIATION ARE HER MAIN DEFENSES. SHE TENDS TO DENY TROUBLES. SHE MAKES HERSELF UNAWARE OF THOSE IMPULSES OF HERS THAT WOULD DISTRESS HER IF SHE WERE AWARE OF THEM. SHE IS NAIVELY UNAWARE OF HER SEXUAL, HOSTILE, AND DEPENDENT MOTIVES EVEN WHILE SHE IS PUTTING THEM INTO ACTION. MANY OF HER ACTIONS ARE AIMED UNCONSCIOUSLY AT ELICITING A RESPONSE FROM OTHERS. SHE IS NAIVE AND IMMATURE, AND SEEMS TO ACT YOUNGER THAN SHE IS. WHEN SHE IS IN THE RIGHT MOOD, SHE IS ENTHUSIASTIC AND FRIENDLY, AND SHE MIXES WELL. PEOPLE LIKE HER ON CASUAL ACQUAINTANCE. SHE HAS A CLASSICAL CASE OF CONVERSION REACTION. SHE USES THE DEFENSE OF CONVERSION TO A HIGH DEGREE. WHEN EMOTIONAL PROBLEMS ARE TOO GREAT FOR HER, SHE SOLVES THEM NOT ONLY BY REPRESSION, PUSHING THEM OUT OF AWARENESS, BUT ALSO BY CONVERSION, SUBSTITUTING BODILY SYMPTOMS OF THE SKELETAL MUSCLES OR SENSES. THEY MAY BE, FOR EXAMPLE: WEAKNESS, VOMITING, SMOTHERING, HEADACHES, OR OTHER ACHES AND PAINS, OR ANXIETY ATTACKS. THESE SYMPTOMS ARE A WAY OF EXPRESSING A NEED TO BE TAKEN CARE OF, WHILE DENYING THAT IT IS AN EMOTIONAL NEED FROM WITHIN, AND ASSERTING ONLY AN ACCIDENTAL EXTERNAL NEED. SHE SHOWS NO TENDENCY TO CARRY ON SEX AFFAIRS.

----------------------- IDENTIFICATIONS, IDEALS, AND RESPONSIBILITIES -----------------------

SHE IS ETHICAL ENOUGH. SHE GENERALLY DEALS FAIRLY WITH PEOPLE, AND GENERALLY RESPECTS THEIR RIGHTS.

AS WE HAVE NOTED, SHE DOESN'T DISTINGUISH BASIC PRINCIPLES FROM SHALLOW, SUPERFICIAL RULES, AND THAT'S WHY SHE FINDS IT SO HARD TO ADMIT EVEN THE SLIGHTEST FLAW. THE MORALITY THAT SHE PROFESSES IS UNREALISTIC. SHE IS ONLY FOOLING HERSELF IF SHE THINKS THAT SHE CAN LIVE UP TO IT.

ALL TOGETHER, HER CONSCIENCE AND EGO IDEAL ARE OF AVERAGE STRENGTH, AND HER CONDUCT FOR THE MOST PART IS WITHIN NORMAL LIMITS. SHE SEEMS WHOLLY LACKING IN ANY PANGS OF GUILT. SHE IS VERY SUCCESSFUL IN CONFORMING HER DEEDS TO HER STANDARDS. MAYBE HER STANDARDS ALLOW SOME ACTIONS THAT DON'T CONFORM TO THE STRICTEST SOCIAL EXPECTATIONS. HER CONTROL MECHANISMS ARE MILD, AND GIVE HER NO DISCOMFORT. THIS WAY OF WORKING IS WELL WITHIN NORMAL LIMITS. THE SITUATION DOES NOT SEEM TO CALL FOR ANY TREATMENT.

SHE TAKES INITIATIVE. SHE DOESN'T WAIT TO BE TOLD WHAT TO DO. SHE IS CAPABLE OF SPEAKING OUT, WHEN SHE IS IN THE MOOD TO DO SO. SOCIALLY, SHE IS EXTROVERTED. SHE IS FORWARD, AND SHE TAKES INITIATIVE TOWARD PEOPLE. SHE MIXES WELL IN A GROUP. SHE IS A SOCIABLE AND OUTGOING PERSON. SHE TAKES IT ON HERSELF TO DO THINGS WITH PEOPLE. SHE GETS IDEAS OF SOMETHING NEW TO DO. SHE IS A WARM-HEARTED, SYMPATHETIC, AND THOUGHTFUL PERSON. SHE CARES ABOUT PEOPLE.

BEHAVIORDYNE   599 COLLEGE AVENUE, SUITE ONE   PALO ALTO, CALIFORNIA 94306

-- WORLD OF WORK --

SINCE SHE IS 24 YEARS OLD, SHE MUST HAVE A GOOD IDEA OF WHAT CONSTITUTES CAREER WORK. BUT IF SHE IS THINKING OF TAKING A NEW JOB, OR OF MAKING SOME CHANGE IN HER LIFE WORK, IT MAY BE UP TO YOU, AS HER COUNSELOR, TO HELP HER CONSIDER HOW HER PERSONALITY JIBES WITH THE REQUIREMENTS OF THE VARIOUS KINDS OF JOB THAT MAY BE OPEN TO HER.

AT THIS TIME, DENYING ANY TROUBLES, SHE GIVES THE IMPRESSION THAT SHE HAS WHAT IT TAKES TO SUCCEED BETTER THAN THE AVERAGE IN MOST KINDS OF WORK. BUT AFTER HER DENIAL IS DISCOUNTED SOMEWHAT, IT MAY BE MORE ACCURATE TO SAY THAT SHE HAS GOOD, NORMAL ABILITY TO DO WORK. SHE CAN DO AS WELL AS ANY AVERAGE, NORMAL PERSON IN MOST KINDS OF WORK. HER ASPIRATIONS SEEM TO BE HIGH; PERHAPS HIGHER THAN HER ABILITIES. SHE DOES WELL ENOUGH IN THE PERSONAL QUALITIES THAT MAKE FOR SUCCESS AT WORK. OF COURSE, SOME KINDS OF WORKING SITUATIONS FIT HER BETTER THAN OTHERS.

HER STRONGEST POINT, THE ONE THAT CAN HELP HER THE MOST TO SUCCEED IN HER WORK, IS HER READINESS TO TRY NEW IDEAS. SHE IS A FULLY OPEN-MINDED PERSON WHO IS ALWAYS WILLING TO LISTEN TO NEW IDEAS, AND TO PUT THEM INTO ACTION IF SHE LIKES THEM. IN THIS WAY, SHE IS RESOURCEFUL; SHE IS NOT BOUND TO THE TRADITIONAL WAYS OF DOING THINGS. SHE IS VERSATILE. HER OUTLOOK IS MODERN, LIBERAL, AND BROADMINDED. SHE DOES NOT STICK TO CONVENTIONAL APPROACHES TO A PROBLEM. SHE IS NOT BOUND BY OLD-FASHIONED METHODS, NOR BY THE PREJUDICES AND BIASES OF THE PAST. THIS IS A REAL STRENGTH. SHE CAN DO VERY WELL IN A JOB THAT CALLS ON HER TO KEEP TRYING SOMETHING NEW.

ANOTHER STRONG POINT THAT CAN HELP HER IN HER WORK IS HER INITIATIVE, DOMINANCE, AND LEADERSHIP. SHE SHOWS LEADERSHIP ABILITY. SHE APPROACHES A TASK CONFIDENTLY, AND SHE PERSUADES PEOPLE TO AGREE WITH HER WAY OF GETTING THE JOB DONE.

SHE CAN DO VERY WELL IN A JOB IN WHICH SHE IS CALLED ON TO TAKE INITIATIVE, TAKE CHARGE OF A GROUP AND LEAD IT, AND PERSUADE PEOPLE.

YOU WILL BE WISE TO HELP HER CHOOSE A LINE OF WORK THAT CALLS ON HER STRONG POINTS. IN THE RIGHT LINE OF WORK, AND IN THE RIGHT WORKING CONDITIONS AND SETTING, PEOPLE WILL APPRECIATE HER FOR HER BEST QUALITIES.

ONE OF HER WEAK POINTS, SOMETHING THAT MAY HANDICAP HER IN HER WORK, IS SOME LACK OF SELF-RELIANCE IN HER WORK, AND ABILITY TO USE GOOD JUDGMENT ABOUT IT. WITHIN THE AVERAGE RANGE, SHE IS NOT ESPECIALLY NOTED FOR GOOD INDEPENDENT JUDGMENT IN HER WORK.

ANOTHER POSSIBLE DRAWBACK, A POINT THAT MAY HAMPER HER IN HER WORK, IS SOME LACK OF ABILITY TO KEEP HER EMOTIONS FROM INTERFERING WITH THE TEAMWORK THAT IS NEEDED IN A COMPETITIVE JOB. SHE IS NOT ESPECIALLY GOOD AT KEEPING HER ENERGIES HARNESSED TO THE PRACTICAL NEEDS OF THE JOB, NOR AT KEEPING PERSONAL RESENTMENTS OUT OF IT. SHE IS ONLY AVERAGE IN THIS RESPECT.

YOU WILL BE WISE TO HELP HER CHOOSE A LINE OF WORK THAT DOESN'T DEMAND SO MUCH ALONG THOSE LINES.

SHE HAS THE CAPABILITY TO RISE ABOVE HER EMOTIONAL PROBLEMS AND IGNORE THEM. SHE DOESN'T ALLOW INWARD DISTRESS TO KEEP HER FROM GIVING ATTENTION AND CONCERN TO THE PROBLEMS AND TASKS OF REAL LIFE. EVEN WHEN SHE IS UPSET, SHE IS ABLE TO EXPRESS OPTIMISM AND CONFIDENCE, TO DEAL WITH PEOPLE, AND TO WORK AT GETTING HER NEEDS MET.

----------------------------------- DIAGNOSTIC IMPRESSION -----------------------------------
CATEGORIZING A PATIENT WITH A DIAGNOSTIC JUDGMENT MUST NEVER BE DONE FROM THE RESULTS OF PSYCHOLOGICAL TESTS ALONE, NOR FROM THE REPORTS OF OTHER LABORATORY TESTS ALONE. IN MAKING YOUR DIAGNOSTIC ASSESSMENT OF THIS PATIENT, YOU WILL RELY UPON THE CAREFUL HISTORY THAT YOU HAVE TAKEN, AND UPON THE SHREWD OBSERVATIONS THAT YOU HAVE MADE OF THE PATIENT'S BEHAVIOR IN THE INTERVIEW AS WELL AS THE LABORATORY RESULTS.

INSOFAR AS WE CAN JUDGE FROM THE ANALYSIS OF THE PSYCHOLOGICAL TESTING ALONE, THE DIAGNOSTIC LABEL MOST LIKELY TO FIT THE PATIENT BEST IS:

301.5 PERSONALITY TRAIT DISORDER, DISSOCIATING (HYSTERICAL) PERSONALITY.

OTHER DIAGNOSTIC LABELS WHICH MAY BE WORTH CONSIDERING ARE AS FOLLOWS; THEY ARE ORDERED ACCORDING TO THE PROBABILITY OF APPLICATION TO THIS PATIENT:

301.5 PERSONALITY TRAIT DISORDER, DISSOCIATING (HYSTERICAL) PERSONALITY.

318. NO DIAGNOSABLE PSYCHIATRIC CONDITION. SHE FALLS WITHIN NORMAL LIMITS, PSYCHOLOGICALLY. SHE CANNOT BE FITTED INTO ANY DIAGNOSTIC CATEGORY.

SOME PEOPLE WITH SCORES LIKE HERS ON THE TEST HAVE PROBLEMS WITH DRINKING. IF SUCH IS THE CASE WITH HER, SHE WOULD BE WELL ADVISED NOT TO DRINK AT ALL. IF SHE HAS SUCH A PROBLEM, SHE IS IN AN UNCERTAIN PHASE NOW IN THIS CHRONICALLY CYCLIC PROCESS.

----------------------------- POTENTIAL FOR PSYCHOTHERAPY ------------------------------------

SHE IS NOT A CANDIDATE FOR INTENSIVE PSYCHOTHERAPY OF THE KIND THAT AIMS AT SELF-UNDERSTANDING.

THERE IS A PROBLEM IN THAT THE REPRESSION, WHICH MAKES HER UNAWARE OF THE MESSAGES THAT SHE SENDS TO PEOPLE, IS HARD TO PENETRATE. MOST LIKELY, IF PSYCHOTHERAPY WERE TRIED, SHE WOULD DEFEND HERSELF STRONGLY AGAINST GAINING INSIGHT OR LEARNING TO LABEL HER MOTIVES. EVEN IF PSYCHOTHERAPY WERE TRIED WHEN SHE IS ANXIOUS, SHE WOULD BE LIKELY TO VENTILATE HER FEELINGS AND GET REASSURANCE AND RELIEF WITHOUT LEARNING MUCH ABOUT HERSELF.

SHE IS NOT LOOKING FOR COUNSELING OR SOCIAL CASEWORK, EITHER.

-------------------------------------- SUMMARY --
THE STATEMENTS THAT CAN BE MADE MOST CLEARLY ABOUT THIS PERSON ARE AS FOLLOWS; THESE STATEMENTS ARE GENERATED FROM THE SCALE SCORES WHICH ARE MOST DEVIANT FROM 50.0:

WHEN EMOTIONAL PROBLEMS ARE TOO GREAT FOR HER, SHE SOLVES THEM NOT ONLY BY REPRESSION, PUSHING THEM OUT OF HER KEN, BUT ALSO BY CONVERSION, SUBSTITUTING BODILY SYMPTOMS OF THE SKELETAL MUSCLES OR SENSES. THEY MAY BE, FOR EXAMPLE, WEAKNESS, VOMITING, SMOTHERING, HEADACHES, OR OTHER ACHES AND PAINS, OR ANXIETY ATTACKS. THESE ARE HER FAVORITE DEFENSES AND SHE USES THEM OFTEN. WHEN SHE IS IN THE RIGHT MOOD, SHE CAN BE ENTHUSIASTIC AND FRIENDLY, AND SHE MIXES WELL. SHE IS WELL-LIKED ON CASUAL ACQUAINTANCE. SHE IS YOUTHFUL, NAIVE, AND IMMATURE, AND SHE SEEMS YOUNGER THAN SHE IS. SHE WORRIES OVER HER HEALTH. SHE WILL BENEFIT FROM VENTILATION AND REASSURANCE WITHOUT GETTING DEEP INTO PSYCHOTHERAPY.

BEHAVIORDYNE   599 COLLEGE AVENUE, SUITE ONE □ PALO ALTO, CALIFORNIA 94306

```
SHE SHOWS NO SIGN OF GUILT FEELING.

    SHE USES THE DEFENSE OF CONVERSION, RELIEVING EMOTIONAL DISTRESS BY DEVELOPING BODILY SYMPTOMS
INSTEAD.  THESE SYMPTOMS INVOLVE THE SKELETAL MUSCLES OR THE SENSES.  THEY MAY BE, FOR EXAMPLE,
HEADACHES, VOMITING, PAINS, OR WEAKNESS.

    SHE IS A FULLY OPEN-MINDED PERSON WHO IS ALWAYS WILLING TO LISTEN TO NEW IDEAS, AND TO PUT THEM
INTO ACTION IF SHE LIKES THEM.  IN THIS WAY, SHE IS RESOURCEFUL; SHE IS NOT BOUND TO THE
TRADITIONAL WAYS OF DOING THINGS.  SHE IS VERSATILE.  HER OUTLOOK IS MODERN, LIBERAL, AND
BROADMINDED.  SHE DOES NOT STICK TO CONVENTIONAL APPROACHES TO A PROBLEM.  SHE IS NOT BOUND BY
OLD-FASHIONED METHODS, NOR BY THE PREJUDICES AND BIASES OF THE PAST.

    SHE REPRESSES AND DENIES ALL HER EMOTIONAL PROBLEMS.  SHE IS NAIVELY OPTIMISTIC, LIKE
'POLLYANNA'.  SHE IS UNAWARE OF ANY HOSTILE OR UNWORTHY MOTIVES IN HERSELF OR IN OTHER PEOPLE.  SHE
IS FLEXIBLE AND ADJUSTS TO THE PEOPLE SHE HAPPENS TO BE WITH.  PEOPLE LIKE HER ON FIRST MEETING.

    SHE DESCRIBES HERSELF AS A HIGHLY ENERGETIC AND UNINHIBITED PERSON WHO GOES AFTER WHAT SHE
WANTS.

    SHE REACTS STRONGLY IN EMOTIONAL RESPONSES OF AUTONOMIC, PHYSIOLOGIC FUNCTIONS.

    SHE IS NOT AT ALL SENSITIVE.  HER FEELINGS NEVER GET HURT.

BEHAVIORDYNE   599 COLLEGE AVENUE, SUITE ONE □ PALO ALTO, CALIFORNIA 94306
```

purposes by the laboratory. Similar reports stemming from the California Psychological Inventory are also offered. For technical background the reader should consult the factorial study by Finney (1961). Input into reports is also based on the information based on specially developed MMPI scales.

Both reports are written about the same person, a 24-year-old female. The first (pp. 197–201) was prepared for clinicians. The second (pp. 202–3), designed to be read and understood by the client, is shorter and provides less information than the professional might wish to have.

THE MILLON CLINICAL MULTIAXIAL INVENTORY (MCMI)

The *Millon Clinical Multiaxial Inventory* (MCMI) (Millon, 1982) is a sophisticated modern clinical tool. The formal diagnostic orientation is based on the DSM-III, including the multiaxial format of that scheme. Of 20 clinical scales for the measurement of personality and pathology, three focus on severe pathology (e.g., psychotic thinking), six concentrate on moderate pathology (e.g., anxiety), eight measure personality styles (e.g., the schizoid and the histrionic), and three deal with the more severe personality dispositions (i.e., the schizotypal, the borderline, and the paranoid).

All 20 scales are shown in the profile that precedes the MCMI narrative report (pp. 204–6). Reading from left to right we have the scale designations, raw and base rate scores, the profile of base rate scores, and finally the diagnostic impression.

THIS IS A REPORT WRITTEN SO THAT YOU CAN READ ABOUT YOURSELF AND LEARN TO UNDERSTAND YOURSELF BETTER. WE SEND THIS REPORT TO YOUR DOCTOR OR COUNSELOR. HE OR SHE WILL HAVE ALREADY READ THIS REPORT, AND WILL DISCUSS IT WITH YOU, EXPLAINING ANY PARTS WHICH MAY NOT BE CLEAR TO YOU.

ANALYSIS OF THIS KIND CAN BE DONE FROM ANY OF SEVERAL PSYCHOLOGICAL INVENTORIES. IN THIS CASE, THE INVENTORY COMPLETED AND SUBMITTED FOR ANALYSIS WAS THE MINNESOTA MULTIPHASIC PERSONALITY INVENTORY.

NARRATIVE REPORT   USER= 2641   SUBJECT=   2   FEMALE   AGE= 24

IN MOST WAYS YOU HAVE CHOSEN ANSWERS THAT LOOK GOOD. YOU ARE SLOW TO ADMIT LITTLE FLAWS IN YOURSELF, AS JUDGED BY RATHER PERFECTIONISTIC MORAL STANDARDS. YOU TEND TO MAKE SOME CLAIM TO PERFECTION OF MORAL CHARACTER.

YOU ARE A FLEXIBLE AND OBLIGING PERSON. YOU ARE A RATHER CHANGEABLE, SPONTANEOUS AND UNPREDICTABLE PERSON. YOU DO WHAT YOU HAPPEN TO FEEL LIKE AT THE TIME. YOUR ATTITUDE TOWARD PEOPLE IS BASICALLY FRIENDLY AND TRUSTING. YOU BELIEVE THAT THE WORLD TREATS YOU FAIRLY. YOU SEEM ABOUT AS FREE FROM DISTRESS AS THE AVERAGE PERSON. IN GENERAL YOU DO THINGS TO ADVANCE YOURSELF AND NOT TO DEFEAT YOURSELF. YOU ARE FAIRLY SUCCESSFUL IN LIFE, AND YOU ARE REASONABLY SATISFIED WITH THE WORLD. YOU DON'T UNDERSTAND YOURSELF VERY WELL.

AT YOUR BEST YOU ARE SERIOUS, IDEALISTIC, KIND, PEACEFUL, AND RESPONSIBLE. YOU ARE ALSO YOUTHFUL, IMAGINATIVE, BRAVE, FORWARD, ENTHUSIASTIC, SOCIABLE, AND OUTGOING, AND A GOOD TALKER. YOU GET ALONG SMOOTHLY WITH PEOPLE.

BUT YOU ARE NAIVE AND NOT VERY MATURE. WHEN A SITUATION PUTS PRESSURE ON YOU, YOU ARE LIKELY TO MAGNIFY YOUR ACHES AND PAINS TO THE POINT OF BELIEVING THAT YOU ARE SICK OR DISABLED. OR YOU MAY HAVE ACUTE ANXIETY, OR SPELLS OF MOOD AND BEHAVIOR DIFFERING FROM YOUR USUAL SELF. PEOPLE ARE LIKELY TO RESPOND BY TAKING CARE OF YOU.

YOU ARE SO LITTLE AWARE OF YOUR OWN MOTIVES THAT YOU SEEM NAIVE. YOUR RECOLLECTION OF THE PAST IS IDEALIZED AND ROMANTICIZED. YOU BLOT OUT MEMORY OF THINGS THAT YOU WOULD NOT LIKE TO REMEMBER. IN VIEWING WHAT GOES ON AROUND YOU, YOU OPERATE BY FORMING A GENERAL IMPRESSION. YOU DON'T STUDY THE DETAILS; YOU DON'T CALCULATE OR ADD THINGS UP. YOU WORK IN A MORE INTUITIVE WAY. YOU ARE STRUCK BY THINGS THAT ARE VIVID.

AT TIMES YOU MAY SEEM THEATRICAL OR HISTRIONIC. YOU ARE LIKELY TO BE AFFECTED BY OTHER PEOPLE WHO ARE DRAMATIC OR IMPRESSIVE, TOO. WHEN YOU HAVE BUILT UP A ROMANTIC AND IDEALIZED EXPECTATION OF SOME SITUATION, YOU MAY BE DISAPPOINTED TO FIND IT SO COMMONPLACE.

YOU ARE SUSCEPTIBLE TO PASSING INFLUENCES. YOU MAY BE LED INTO ACTION WITHOUT STOPPING TO CONSIDER THE CONSEQUENCES. AT TIMES YOU SEEM TO PLAY GAMES WITH PEOPLE, BUT YOU DO IT WITH AN INNOCENT AIR.

IN GENERAL, YOU ARE NOT NOTED FOR TAKING THINGS OUT ON OTHER PEOPLE, NOR FOR TAKING THINGS OUT ON YOURSELF.

YOU ARE ETHICAL ENOUGH. YOU GENERALLY DEAL FAIRLY WITH PEOPLE, AND YOU GENERALLY RESPECT THEIR RIGHTS.

YOU TAKE INITIATIVE. YOU DON'T WAIT TO BE TOLD WHAT TO DO. YOU ARE CAPABLE OF SPEAKING OUT, WHEN YOU ARE IN THE MOOD TO DO SO. SOCIALLY, YOU ARE EXTROVERTED. YOU ARE FORWARD, AND YOU TAKE INITIATIVE TOWARD PEOPLE. YOU MIX WELL IN A GROUP. YOU ARE A SOCIABLE AND OUTGOING PERSON. YOU TAKE IT ON YOURSELF TO DO THINGS WITH PEOPLE. YOU GET IDEAS OF SOMETHING NEW TO DO. YOU ARE A WARM-HEARTED, SYMPATHETIC, AND THOUGHTFUL PERSON. YOU CARE ABOUT PEOPLE.

-- WORLD OF WORK --

FOR SOME WOMEN, MARRIAGE AND MOTHERHOOD ARE A CAREER, BUT A WOMAN SOMETIMES FINDS THAT SHE NEEDS TO SUPPORT HERSELF MOST OF HER LIFE. THEREFORE, LET'S CONSIDER HOW YOU WOULD FIT IN WITH DIFFERENT KINDS OF WORK.

YOU HAVE GOOD, NORMAL ABILITY TO DO WORK. YOU CAN DO AS WELL AS ANY AVERAGE, NORMAL PERSON AT MOST KINDS OF WORK.

YOUR STRONGEST POINT, THE ONE THAT CAN HELP YOU THE MOST TO SUCCEED IN YOUR WORK, IS YOUR READINESS TO TRY NEW IDEAS. THIS IS A REAL STRENGTH. YOU CAN DO VERY WELL IN A JOB THAT CALLS ON YOU TO KEEP TRYING SOMETHING NEW.

ANOTHER STRONG POINT THAT CAN HELP YOU IN YOUR WORK IS YOUR INITIATIVE, DOMINANCE, AND LEADERSHIP.

YOU CAN DO VERY WELL IN A JOB IN WHICH YOU ARE CALLED ON TO TAKE INITIATIVE, TAKE CHARGE OF A GROUP AND LEAD IT, AND PERSUADE PEOPLE.

BEHAVIORDYNE   599 COLLEGE AVENUE, SUITE ONE □ PALO ALTO, CALIFORNIA 94306

YOU WILL BE WISE TO CHOOSE A LINE OF WORK THAT CALLS ON YOUR STRONG POINTS. IN THE RIGHT LINE
OF WORK, AND IN THE RIGHT WORKING CONDITIONS AND SETTING, PEOPLE WILL APPRECIATE YOU FOR YOUR BEST
QUALITIES.

ONE OF YOUR WEAK POINTS, SOMETHING THAT MAY HANDICAP YOU IN YOUR WORK, IS SOME LACK OF
SELF-RELIANCE IN YOUR WORK, AND ABILITY TO USE GOOD JUDGMENT ABOUT IT.

ANOTHER POSSIBLE DRAWBACK, A POINT THAT MAY HAMPER YOU IN YOUR WORK, IS SOME LACK OF ABILITY TO
KEEP YOUR EMOTIONS FROM INTERFERING WITH THE TEAMWORK THAT IS NEEDED IN A COMPETITIVE JOB.

IT MAY BE BETTER TO CHOOSE A LINE OF WORK IN WHICH THINGS OF THIS KIND DON'T MATTER MUCH.

YOU HAVE THE CAPABILITY TO RISE ABOVE YOUR EMOTIONAL PROBLEMS AND IGNORE THEM.   YOU DON'T
ALLOW INWARD DISTRESS TO KEEP YOU FROM GIVING ATTENTION AND CONCERN TO THE PROBLEMS AND TASKS OF
REAL LIFE. EVEN WHEN YOU ARE UPSET, YOU ARE ABLE TO EXPRESS OPTIMISM AND CONFIDENCE, TO DEAL WITH
PEOPLE, AND TO WORK AT GETTING YOUR NEEDS MET.

BEHAVIORDYNE   599 COLLEGE AVENUE, SUITE ONE ☐ PALO ALTO, CALIFORNIA 94306

THE MILLON BEHAVIORAL
HEALTH INVENTORY (MBHI)

The *Millon Behavioral Health Inventory* (MBHI) (see Millon, Green, & Meagher, 1979, 1982) was developed to meet the needs of psychologists in medical settings, namely that of "fulfilling the role of medical psychodiagnosticians." More broadly, the purpose of the instrument is ". . . to provide information to clinicians—psychologists, physicians, nurses—who must make psychological assessments and treatment decisions about persons with physical health problems." The report on pages 207–9 illustrates well how the MBHI focuses on this goal. The structure of the data pattern that precedes the narrative report is on the same conceptual order as that used with the MCMI.

THE PERSONALITY
INVENTORY FOR CHILDREN
(PIC)

The *Personality Inventory for Children* (PIC) is a highly useful instrument that may be used as a basic source of psychological and social information on children or adolescents in need of help because of personality problems. The source of the information provided by a computer printout, such as in the illustrative case that follows, is someone who knows the child well, usually a parent, who answers "True" or "False" to a number of statements concerning behavior—for example, "My child tends to pity himself" or "My child has little self-confidence." The information from statements, is presented in the form of a narrative report (pp. 210–11) and is also categorized into clusters of "critical items" that might have particular significance for further investigation and understanding of the child (pp. 211–13).

Finally, a profile resembling that of the MMPI is presented along with raw scores and T scores for regular and supplemental scales which are generally different from the MMPI scales. The regular scales, reading from

```
***** MILLON CLINICAL MULTIAXIAL INVENTORY ****    DSM-III REPORT    ***FOR PROFESSIONAL USE ONLY***
* NAME: SAMPLE    FEMALE    222222 F       VALID REPORT    WEIGHT FACTOR = -7        03/23/82   *
* CODED SUMMARY= - **8 4 2 * 3 1 5 + 67 ± -    //- //A 0 **B N T * //- //                        *
                                                                                     471 0002
* SCALES   * SCOPE *              PROFILE OF BR SCORES          * DSM-III (MILLON) PARALLELS*
*          *RAW  BR*        35      60      75      85     100  *
*          11 ] 18] 71]XXXXXXXXXXXXXXXXXXXXXXXXXXXXXX ]      ]      ] SCHIZOID (ASOCIAL)        *
*          12 ] 19] 75]XXXXXXXXXXXXXXXXXXXXXXXXXXXXXXXX     ]      ] AVOIDANT                   *
* BASIC    13 ] 17] 72]XXXXXXXXXXXXXXXXXXXXXXXXXXXXXXX ]     ]      ] DEPENDENT (SUBMISSIVE)     *
*PERSNLTY 14 ] 18] 75]XXXXXXXXXXXXXXXXXXXXXXXXXXXXXXXX      ]      ] HISTRIONIC (GREGARIOUS)    *
*PATTERN  15 ] 25] 69]XXXXXXXXXXXXXXXXXXXXXXXXXXXX ]     ]      ] NARCISSISTIC                *
*          16 ] 14] 58]XXXXXXXXXXXXXXXXXXXXX]      ]      ] ANTISOCIAL (AGGRESSIVE)    *
*          17 ] 22] 51]XXXXXXXXXXXXXXXXXXX ]     ]      ] COMPULSIVE (CONFORMING)    *
*          18 ] 19] 80]XXXXXXXXXXXXXXXXXXXXXXXXXXXXXXXXXXX     ]      ] P. AGGRESSIVE (NEGATIVSTC)*
*PATHLGCL 1S ] 20] 53]XXXXXXXXXXXXXXXXXXX ]     ]      ] SCHIZOTYPAL (SCHIZOID)     *
*PERSNLTY 1C ] 19] 56]XXXXXXXXXXXXXXXXXXXX ]     ]      ] BORDERLINE (CYCLOID)       *
*DISORDER 1P ] 19] 64]XXXXXXXXXXXXXXXXXXXXXXXX ]     ]      ] PARANOID                   *
*          1A ] 23] 95]XXXXXXXXXXXXXXXXXXXXXXXXXXXXXXXXXXXXXXXXXXXXXXXXXXXY ] ANXIETY          *
*          1H ] 19] 60]XXXXXXXXXXXXXXXXXXXXXX      ]      ] SOMATOFORM                 *
*          1N ] 30] 78]XXXXXXXXXXXXXXXXXXXXXXXXXXXXXXXXX     ]      ] HYPOMANIA          *
*CLINICAL 1D ] 22] 88]XXXXXXXXXXXXXXXXXXXXXXXXXXXXXXXXXXXXXXXXXXXXXX ] DYSTHYMIA          *
*SYNDROME 1B ] 20] 84]XXXXXXXXXXXXXXXXXXXXXXXXXXXXXXXXXXXXXXXXXX XXXX] ALCOHOL ABUSE      *
*          1T ] 26] 78]XXXXXXXXXXXXXXXXXXXXXXXXXXXXXXXXXXXXXX ]      ] DRUG ABUSE         *
*          ]SS] 14] 65]XXXXXXXXXXXXXXXXXXXXXXXXX ]     ]      ] PSYCHOTIC THINKING   *
*          ]CC] 13] 63]XXXXXXXXXXXXXXXXXXXXXXXX ]     ]      ] PSYCHOTIC DEPRESSION *
*          ]PP] 8] 63]XXXXXXXXXXXXXXXXXXXXXXXX ]     ]      ] PSYCHOTIC DELUSION   *
```

MCMI NARRATIVES HAVE BEEN NORMED ON PATIENTS EXPERIENCING EITHER GENUINE EMOTIONAL DISCOM-
FORTS OR SOCIAL DIFFICULTIES AND ARE APPLICABLE PRIMARILY DURING THE EARLY PHASES OF ASSESSMENT
OR PSYCHOTHERAPY. DISTORTIONS SUCH AS GREATER SEVERITY MAY OCCUR AMONG RESPONDENTS WHO HAVE IN-
APPROPRIATELY TAKEN THE MCMI FOR ESSENTIALLY EDUCATIONAL OR SELF-EXPLORATORY PURPOSES. INFER-
ENTIAL AND PROBABLISTIC, THIS REPORT MUST BE VIEWED AS ONLY ONE ASPECT OF A THOROUGH DIAGNOSTIC
STUDY. FOR THESE REASONS, IT SHOULD NOT BE SHOWN TO PATIENTS OR THEIR RELATIVES.

THIS FEMALE PATIENT MAY HAVE BEEN OVERLY SELF-CRITICAL AND SELF-DEPRECATING IN RESPONDING
TO THE TEST ITEMS. WHILE READING THE FOLLOWING, CLINICIANS SHOULD BE AWARE THAT SHE MAY HAVE
ADMITTED TO MORE PSYCHOLOGICAL SYMPTOMS THAN OBJECTIVELY EXIST.

AXIS II: PERSONALITY PATTERNS

THE FOLLOWING PERTAINS TO THE MORE ENDURING AND PERVASIVE CHARACTEROLOGICAL TRAITS OF THIS
WOMAN THAT UNDERLIE HER PERSONAL AND INTERPERSONAL DIFFICULTIES. RATHER THAN FOCUS ON CURRENTLY
DISTINCT BUT ESSENTIALLY TRANSITORY SYMPTOMS, THIS SECTION CONCENTRATES ON HER HABITUAL, MALAD-
APTIVE METHODS OF RELATING, BEHAVING, THINKING AND FEELING.

THIS WOMAN EXPERIENCES A HIGH DEGREE OF EMOTIONAL LIABILITY, SHORT PERIODS OF IMPULSIVE
ACTING-OUT, DEPRESSIVE COMPLAINTS, AS WELL AS A GENERAL MOODINESS AND SULKING BEHAVIORS. ALSO
NOTABLE IS A HYPERSENSITIVITY TO CRITICISM, A LOW FRUSTRATION TOLERANCE, FREQUENT IMMATURE BE-
HAVIORS, SHORT-SIGHTED HEDONISM, AND AN OCCASIONAL HISTRIONIC SEEKING FOR EXCITEMENT AND
STIMULATION. IMPULSIVE AND UNMODERATED EMOTIONS MAY SURGE READILY TO THE SURFACE, CHARACTER-
IZING HER BEHAVIOR AS DISTRACTIBLE AND ERRATIC. HER MOODS TEND TO BE BRITTLE AND VARIABLE WITH
PERIODS OF HIGH EXCITEMENT AND AFFABILITY ALTERNATING WITH LETHARGY, FATIGUE, OVERSLEEPING,
OVEREATING, AND THE POSSIBLE OVERUSE OF ALCOHOL.
ON OCCASION, SHE WILL DISPLAY SHORT-LIVED AND SUPERFICIAL EMOTIONS. MOOD LEVELS ARE HIGHLY
REACTIVE TO EXTERNAL STIMULI. HER FEELINGS OFTEN SWING CAPRICIOUSLY FROM EUPHORIA TO DESPER-
ATION, AND ARE EXPRESSED MORE INTENSELY THAN JUSTIFIED BY THE SITUATION. IN A SELF-FULFILLING
PROPHECY, SHE OFTEN ANTICIPATES WRANGLES WITH OTHERS AND DISAPPOINTMENTS FOR HERSELF. IF SHE IS
CUT OFF FROM NEEDED EXTERNAL ATTENTION, SHE MAY FRANTICALLY SEARCH FOR APPROVAL AND BECOME
EASILY NETTLED AND CONTENTIOUS OR DEJECTED AND FORLORN.
FEELING MISUNDERSTOOD AND DISAPPOINTED WITH LIFE, SHE MAY BECOME CRITICAL AND ENVIOUS,
GRUDGE OTHERS THEIR GOOD FORTUNES, AND REACT IRRITABLY TO MINOR SLIGHTS. UNUSUAL PREOCCUPATION
WITH BODILY FUNCTIONS AND HEALTH, OVERREACTIONS TO ILLNESS, AND UNREASONABLE COMPLAINTS ABOUT
MINOR AILMENTS MAY BE PROMINENT. SUCH SYMPTOMS MAY BE DISPLAYED EXHIBITIONISTICALLY TO GAIN
ATTENTION AND SUPPORT.

THE MOODS OF THIS WOMAN ARE TYPIFIED BY A HIGH DEGREE OF EMOTIONAL LABILITY, IMPULSIVE AND ANGRY OUTBURSTS ALTERNATING WITH RECURRING DEPRESSIVE COMPLAINTS AND SULKING. ALSO NOTABLE ARE AN IRRITABLE HYPERSENSITIVITY TO CRITICISM, LOW FRUSTRATION TOLERANCE, SHORT-SIGHTED HEDONISM, IMMATURE BEHAVIOR, AND AN ERRATIC SEARCH FOR MOMENTARY EXCITEMENT AND STIMULATION. IMPULSIVE AND UNMODERATED EMOTIONS SURGE READILY TO THE SURFACE, CHARACTERIZING HER BEHAVIOR AS CAPRICIOUS.

AXIS I: CLINICAL SYNDROMES

THE FOLLOWING DISTINCTIVE CLINICAL DISORDERS ARE NOTABLE. THEY MAY BE OF BRIEF DURATION, ARISE IN RESPONSE TO EXTERNAL PRECIPITANTS, AND ACCENTUATE THE MORE PERSISTENT FEATURES OF HER BASIC PERSONALITY.

THIS WOMAN FEELS APPREHENSIVE AND RESTLESS AND MAY COMPLAIN OF DISTRESSFUL PHOBIAS, RECURRENT INDECISIVENESS OVER PICAYUNE MATTERS AND ACUTE PHYSICAL DISCOMFORTS, SUCH AS INSOMNIA, MUSCULAR TIGHTNESS, HEADACHES, TREMORS AND COLD SWEATING.

THIS WOMAN EXPRESSES DEJECTION AND DISCOURAGEMENT ABOUT CURRENT LIFE MATTERS AND MAINTAINS A PESSIMISTIC VIEW OF THE FUTURE. SHE REPORTS A LOSS OF EFFICIENCY AND SELF-CONFIDENCE, DIMINISHED PLEASURE IN PREVIOUSLY REWARDING ACTIVITIES, AND A PREOCCUPATION WITH MATTERS OF DEPENDENCY SECURITY. FEELINGS OF WORTHLESSNESS OR GUILT MAY ALSO BE NOTABLE.

RECURRENT EPISODES OF ALCOHOLISM ARE PROBABLE. ALTHOUGH EFFORTS MAY HAVE BEEN MADE ON HER PART TO RESOLVE THE DIFFICULTY, SHE CONTINUES TO REPORT PROBLEMS IN THIS AREA AND MAY EXPERIENCE DISTRESS OVER THEIR CONSEQUENCES IN HER FAMILY SETTINGS.

THIS WOMAN HAS RECENTLY EXPERIENCED AN UNUSUALLY ELEVATED AND EXPANSIVE MOOD, A HIGHLY RESTLESS PURSUIT OF MULTIPLE, SELF-GENERATED ACTIVITES, PRESSURED SPEECH, AND MOMENTARY BUT INTENSE IRRITABILITIES.

PERIODS OF DRUG ABUSE APPEAR PROBABLE, AS ARE DIFFICULTIES IN ACCEPTING CONVENTIONAL SOCIAL LIMITS AND A FREQUENT DISREGARD FOR FAMILY FEELINGS AND RESPONSIBILITIES. SHE DISPLAYS EITHER AN INABILITY TO ANTICIPATE AND HANDLE, OR A CARELESS INDIFFERENCE TO, THE PERSONAL CONSEQUENCES OF HER ACTIONS.

THESE SYMPTOMS INDICATE HER INABILITY TO RESTRAIN INTENSE EMOTIONS WHICH ARE EXPRESSED IN A HIGHLY UNSTABLE AND CONTRADICTORY MANNER. EMOTIONALITY SERVES TO DISCHARGE HER ANGER AND RESENTMENT TOWARD THOSE UPON WHOM SHE DEPENDS AND IS ALSO A MEANS OF SOLICITING ATTENTION AND NURTURANCE FROM THESE DEPENDENCY SOURCES. AMBIVALENCE ABOUT CONTROLLING OR EXPRESSING HOSTILE FEELINGS IS CONTINUOUSLY MANIFESTED IN AN ERRATIC FASHION.

NOTEWORTHY RESPONSES

THE FOLLOWING STATEMENTS WERE ANSWERED BY THE PATIENT IN THE DIRECTION NOTED IN THE PARENTHESES. THESE ITEMS SUGGEST SPECIFIC PROBLEM AREAS THAT MAY DESERVE FURTHER INQUIRY ON THE PART OF THE CLINICIAN.

HEALTH PREOCCUPATION
18.   LATELY, I GET BUTTERFLIES IN MY STOMACH AND BREAK OUT IN COLD SWEATS (T).
73.   I HAVE A VERY TIGHT FEELING IN THE PIT OF MY STOMACH EVERY FEW DAYS OR SO (T).
121. I VERY OFTEN FEEL A LUMP IN MY THROAT (T).

INTERPERSONAL ALIENATION
47.   I AM SO QUIET AND WITHDRAWN, MOST PEOPLE DO NOT EVEN KNOW I EXIST (T).
49.   I AM A QUIET AND FEARFUL PERSON (T).
55.   I HATE TO TALK, EVEN TO PEOPLE I KNOW (T).
83.   A LONG TIME AGO, I DECIDED THAT IT IS BEST TO HAVE LITTLE TO DO WITH PEOPLE (T).
101. I HAVE ALWAYS GONE FOR LONG PERIODS WHEN I HARDLY TALK TO ANYONE (T).
141. I AM VERY ILL-AT-EASE WITH MEMBERS OF THE OPPOSITE SEX (T).

EMOTIONAL DYSCONTROL
26.   I TEND TO BURST OUT IN TEARS OR IN ANGER FOR UNKNOWN REASONS (T).
36.   LATELY, I FIND MYSELF CRYING WITHOUT ANY REASON (T).
67.   LATELY, I FEEL JUMPY AND UNDER TERRIBLE STRAIN, BUT I DO NOT KNOW WHY (T).
151. PEOPLE HAVE SAID IN THE PAST THAT I BECAME TOO INTERESTED AND TOO EXCITED ABOUT TOO MANY
      THINGS (T).
167. LATELY, I HAVE GONE ALL TO PIECES (T).

SELF-DESTRUCTIVE POTENTIAL
59.   I HAVE GIVEN SERIOUS THOUGHT RECENTLY TO DOING AWAY WITH MYSELF (T).
79.   SERIOUS THOUGHTS OF SUICIDE HAVE OCCURRED TO ME FOR MANY YEARS (T).
115. SOMETIMES I FEEL LIKE I MUST DO SOMETHING TO HURT MYSELF OR SOMEONE ELSE (T).

PARALLEL DSM-III MULTIAXIAL DIAGNOSES

ALTHOUGH THE DIAGNOSTIC CRITERIA UTILIZED IN THE MCMI DIFFER SOMEWHAT FROM THOSE IN THE DSM-III, THERE ARE SUFFICIENT PARALLELS TO RECOMMEND CONSIDERATION OF THE FOLLOWING ASSIGNMENTS. MORE DEFINITIVE JUDGMENTS SHOULD DRAW UPON BIOGRAPHIC, OBSERVATION AND INTERVIEW DATA, IN ADDITION TO SELF-REPORT INVENTORIES SUCH AS THE MCMI.

AXIS I: CLINICAL SYNDROME: THE MAJOR COMPLAINTS AND BEHAVIORS OF THE PATIENT PARALLEL THE FOLLOWING AXIS I DIAGNOSES, LISTED IN ORDER OF THEIR CLINICAL SIGNIFICANCE AND SALIENCE.

300.02 GENERALIZED ANXIETY DISORDER.

300.40 DYSTHYMIC DISORDER.

305.02 ALCOHOL ABUSE, EPISODIC.

AXIS II: PERSONALITY DISORDER: A DEEPLY INGRAINED AND PERVASIVE PATTERN OF MALADAPTIVE FUNCTIONING UNDERLIES THE AXIS I CLINICAL SYNDROMAL PICTURE. THE FOLLOWING PERSONALITY DIAGNOSES PARALLEL THE MOST SALIENT FEATURES THAT CHARACTERIZE THE INDIVIDUAL.

```
301.84  PASSIVE-AGGRESSIVE PERSONALITY; PROMINENT AVOIDANT OR HISTRIONIC TRAITS.

COURSE:  THE MAJOR PERSONALITY FEATURES DESCRIBED PREVIOUSLY REFLECT LONG TERM OR CHRONIC TRAITS
THAT ARE LIKELY TO HAVE PERSISTED FOR SEVERAL YEARS PRIOR TO THE PRESENT ASSESSMENT.
THE CLINICAL SYNDROMES DESCRIBED PREVIOUSLY TEND TO BE RELATIVELY TRANSIENT, WAXING AND WANING
IN THEIR PROMINENCE AND INTENSITY DEPENDING ON THE PRESENCE OF ENVIRONMENTAL STRESS.

AXIS IV:  PSYCHOSOCIAL STRESSORS:  THE REPORT ON PERSONALITY TRAITS AND CURRENT SYMPTOMATOLOGY
SUGGEST THE FOLLOWING COMPLICATING FACTORS WHICH MAY BE EXACERBATING THE PRESENT EMOTIONAL
STATE.  THEY ARE LISTED IN ORDER OF PROBABLE APPLICABILITY.  THE LISTINGS SHOULD BE VIEWED AS A
GUIDE FOR FURTHER INVESTIGATION BY THE CLINICIAN AND SHOULD NOT BE ASSUMED TO BE DEFINITE
FACTORS IN THE CASE:
RECENT LIFE CHANGES
PSYCHOSOMATIC PROBLEMS; FAMILY TENSIONS

SEVERITY OF DISTRUBANCE:  ON THE BASIS OF THE TEST DATA IT MAY BE REASONABLY ASSUMED THAT THE
PATIENT IS EXPERIENCING A MODERATELY SEVERE MENTAL DISORDER.  FURTHER PROFESSIONAL STUDY IS
JUSTIFIED TO ASSESS THE APPROPRIATENESS OF CLINICAL CARE.


   THERAPEUTIC IMPLICATIONS -- THE FOLLOWING CONSIDERATIONS ARE LIKELY TO BE OF GREATER
UTILITY AND ACCURACY DURING EARLY TREATMENT PLANNING THAN IN LATER MANAGEMENT PHASES.
   BECAUSE OF HER INTENSE AMBIVALENCE AND HER DEEP MISTRUST OF OTHERS, SHE IS UNLIKELY TO
SUSTAIN A CONSISTENT THERAPEUTIC RELATIONSHIP.  MANEUVERS DESIGNED TO TEST THE SINCERITY OF THE
THERAPIST WILL PROBABLY BE EVIDENT.  BECAUSE SHE FEARS FACING FEELINGS OF UNWORTHINESS AND
SENSES THAT HER COPING DEFENSES ARE WEAK, WITHDRAWAL FROM TREATMENT BEFORE ANY REAL GAINS HAVE
BEEN MADE IS LIKELY.  THIS PATIENT NEEDS TO BE GUIDED INTO RECOGNIZING THE SOURCE OF HER FEARS
AND AMBIVALENCE ABOUT DEPENDENCY RELATIONSHIPS.  ALTHOUGH SHE MAY BE DESIROUS OF A NURTURANT
PARENTAL FIGURE, SUBMISSION POSES A THREAT TO HER EQUALLY INTENSE DESIRE TO BE ASSERTIVE AND
INDEPENDENT.  EFFORTS TO EXPLORE THESE CONTRADICTIONS AND TO REINFORCE MORE CONSISTENT ATTITUDES
AND BEHAVIORS MAY RESULT IN A SEESAW STRUGGLE, WITH PERIODS OF TEMPORARY PROGRESS FOLLOWED BY
RETROGRESSION.  GENUINE GAINS WILL REQUIRE SLOW, LABORIOUS WORK AND A BUILDING OF TRUST BY ENHAN-
CING HER SHAKY SENSE OF SELF-WORTH.


COPYRIGHT 1976, 1981 BY THEODORE MILLON.  ALL RIGHTS RESERVED.

PUBLISHED BY  -  NCS INTERPRETIVE SCORING SYSTEMS, P.O. BOX 1416, MINNEAPOLIS, MN 55440



NAME = SAMPLE  FEMALE     222222    03/23/82    471 0002
```

left to right (See "profile" on p. 214) are the L Scale (L), the F Scale (F), the Defensiveness Scale (DEF), the adjustment Scale (ADJ), the Achievement Scale (ACH), the Intellectual Screening Scale (IS), the Development Scale (DEV), the Somatic Concern Scale (SOM), the Depression Scale (DEP), the Family Relations Scale (FAM), the Delinquency Scale (DLQ), the Withdrawal Scale (WDL), the Anxiety Scale (ANX), the Psychosis Scale (PSY), the Hyperactivity Scale (HPR), and the Social Skills Scale (SSK).

For further information and instructions concerning the use of the PIC, see Wirt, Lachar, Klinedinst, and Seat (1977) and Lachar and Gdowski (1979).

THE VOCATIONAL INTEREST INVENTORY (VII)

The results of this well-normed instrument are addressed directly to the student in nontechnical language and with full explanations. Two profiles, one called simply VII Profile of Scores and one called VII College Majors Profile contribute graphic representation for what is also discussed in narrative form (pp. 216–19). In spite of the simplicity of use of the VII, it might

```
                    MILLON BEHAVIORAL HEALTH INVENTORY
                CONFIDENTIAL INFORMATION FOR PROFESSIONAL USE ONLY

 ID NUMBER:                        RELIABLE        DATE:    100281

 CODE:  6**8*5247+13'  // -**F* // -**NNMM* // PP**QQ* //

 ****************************************************************************
  SCALES       * SCORE *         PROFILE OF BR SCORES          *
               *RAW  BR*    35   60        75        85     100  DIMENSIONS
 ********+**+***+***+------+---+---------+---------+---------+******************
          1    10    8  XX                                         INTROVERSIVE
        +--+---+---+---+------+---+---------+---------+---------+---------------
          2    10   53  XXXXXXXXX                                  INHIBITED
        +--+---+---+---+------+---+---------+---------+---------+---------------
  BASIC   3    14    5  X                                          COOPERATIVE
        +--+---+---+---+------+---+---------+---------+---------+---------------
 PERSNLTY 4    25   46  XXXXXXXX                                   SOCIABLE
        +--+---+---+---+------+---+---------+---------+---------+---------------
  STYLE   5    23   71  XXXXXXXXXXXXXXXXXX                         CONFIDENT
        +--+---+---+---+------+---+---------+---------+--q------+---------------
          6    20   85  XXXXXXXXXXXXXXXXXXXXXXXXXXXXXXX            FORCEFUL
        +--+---+---+---+------+---+---------+---------+---------+---------------
          7    24   37  XXXXXX                                     RESPECTFUL
        +--+---+---+---+------+---+---------+---------+---------+---------------
          8    20   78  XXXXXXXXXXXXXXXXXXXXXXX                    SENSITIVE
 ********+**+***+***+------+---+---------+---------+---------+******************
          A    17   60  XXXXXXXXXXX                                CHRONIC TENSION
        +--+---+---+---+------+---+---------+---------+---------+---------------
 PSYCHO-  B    14   70  XXXXXXXXXXXXXXXXX                          RECENT STRESS
        +--+---+---+---+------+---+---------+---------+---------+---------------
  GENIC   C    16   58  XXXXXXXXXX                                 PREMORB PESSIMISM
        +--+---+---+---+------+---+---------+---------+---------+---------------
  ATTI-   D    15   58  XXXXXXXXXX                                 FUTURE DESPAIR
        +--+---+---+---+------+---+---------+---------+---------+---------------
  TUDES   E     4   15  XXX                                        SOCIAL ALIENATION
        +--+---+---+---+------+---+---------+---------+---------+---------------
          F    22   78  XXXXXXXXXXXXXXXXXXXXXXX                    SOMATIC ANXIETY
 ********+**+***+***+------+---+---------+---------+---------+******************
          MM   14   79  XXXXXXXXXXXXXXXXXXXXXXXX                   ALLERGIC INCLIN
 PSYCHO- +--+---+---+---+------+---+---------+---------+---------+---------------
          NN   13   81  XXXXXXXXXXXXXXXXXXXXXXXXXX                 GASTRO SUSCEPTBL
 SOMATIC +--+---+---+---+------+---+---------+---------+---------+---------------
          OO   14   69  XXXXXXXXXXXXXXXX                           CARDIO TENDENCY
 ********+**+***+***+------+---+---------+---------+---------+******************
          PP   21  100  XXXXXXXXXXXXXXXXXXXXXXXXXXXXXXXXXXXXXXXXXX PAIN TREAT RESPON
 PROG-   +--+---+---+---+------+---+---------+---------+---------+---------------
          QQ   15   77  XXXXXXXXXXXXXXXXXXXXXXX                    LIFE-THREAT REACT
 NOSTIC +--+---+---+---+------+---+---------+---------+---------+---------------
          RR    1   35  XXXXX                                      EMOTIONAL VULNER
 ********+**+***+***+------+---+---------+---------+---------+******************
```

        THIS REPORT ASSUMES THAT THE MBHI ANSWER FORM WAS COMPLETED BY A PERSON
UNDERGOING PROFESSIONAL MEDICAL EVALUATION OR TREATMENT. IT SHOULD BE NOTED
THAT MBHI DATA AND ANALYSES DO NOT PROVIDE PHYSICAL DIAGNOSES. RATHER, THE
INSTRUMENT SUPPLEMENTS SUCH DIAGNOSES BY IDENTIFYING AND APPRAISING THE
POTENTIAL ROLE OF PSYCHOGENIC AND PSYCHOSOMATIC FACTORS IN MEDICAL DISEASE.
THE STATEMENTS PRINTED BELOW ARE DERIVED FROM CUMULATIVE RESEARCH DATA AND
THEORY. AS SUCH, THEY MUST BE CONSIDERED AS SUGGESTIVE OR PROBABILISTIC
INFERENCES, RATHER THAN DEFINITIVE JUDGMENTS, AND SHOULD BE EVALUATED IN THAT
LIGHT BY CLINICIANS. THE SPECIFIC STATEMENTS CONTAINED IN THE REPORT ARE OF A
PERSONAL NATURE AND ARE FOR CONFIDENTIAL PROFESSIONAL USE ONLY. THEY SHOULD BE
HANDLED WITH GREAT DISCRETION AND NOT BE SHOWN TO PATIENTS OR THEIR RELATIVES.

                                COPING STYLE

        THE FOLLOWING PARAGRAPHS PERTAIN TO THOSE LONGSTANDING TRAITS OF THE
PATIENT THAT HAVE CHARACTERIZED MOST PERSONAL, SOCIAL AND WORK RELATIONSHIPS.
IN ADDITION TO SUMMARIZING THESE MORE GENERAL FEATURES OF PSYCHOLOGICAL FUNC-
TIONING, THIS SECTION WILL BRIEFLY REVIEW THE MANNER IN WHICH THE PATIENT IS
LIKELY TO RELATE TO HEALTH PERSONNEL, SERVICES AND REGIMENS.

        THIS PATIENT IS CHARACTERISTICALLY IRRITABLE AND UNPREDICTABLE. AT
TIMES, SHE WILL COMPLAIN OF BEING MISUNDERSTOOD AND UNAPPRECIATED, BE EASILY
OFFENDED BY TRIFLES AND QUICKLY PROVOKED INTO BEING FRETFUL, ANGRY AND TEARFUL.
THIS TOUCHINESS REFLECTS AN OVERSENSITIVITY TO THE ATTITUDES AND OPINIONS OF
OTHERS. INCLINED TO EXPECT CRITICISM AND FEARFUL OF BEING CONDEMNED BY
OTHERS, SHE OFTEN ACTS DEFENSIVELY AND ANGRILY AND, THEREFORE, FREQUENTLY
PRECIPITATES THE ANTICIPATED AND FEARED REJECTION. THESE COMPLAINING, MOODY
AND PESSIMISTIC ATTITUDES MAY CONTRIBUTE TO FREQUENT BODILY UPSETS AND DIS-
COMFORTS. IN ADDITION, UNRESOLVED CONFLICTS BETWEEN FEELINGS OF RESENTMENT
AND FEELINGS OF GUILT, WHICH CONSTANTLY SURFACE ARE LIKELY TO ADD FURTHER
STRESS AND CONTRIBUTE TO AN INCREASED PROBABILITY OF PSYCHOSOMATIC AILMENTS.

THE PATIENT WILL REACT TO SERIOUS PERSONAL ILLNESSES AS EMOTIONALLY PAINFUL. IN ADDITION TO CONCERNS OVER THE AILMENT ITSELF, THERE IS GREAT ANXIETY OVER BEING EXPOSED AND VULNERABLE TO OTHERS. IN ADDITION, REQUIRING HELP FROM OTHERS, ALTHOUGH STRONGLY WISHED FOR, IS FELT TO BE HUMILIATING, ESPECIALLY FROM PEOPLE THAT SHE MAY NOT KNOW OR TRUST. THIS IS PROBLEM ENOUGH, BUT SHE IS ALSO OVERLY CONCERNED ABOUT ILLNESS AND STRONGLY DESIRES HELP IN BEING RID OF HER AILMENT. CAUGHT IN THE BIND OF BOTH WANTING AND NOT WANTING HELP, SHE IS APT TO BECOME INCREASINGLY TENSE AND IRRITABLE. UNDER THESE CIRCUMSTANCES, SHE IS LIABLE TO ACT ANNOYED, SARCASTIC AND RESENTFUL, LOOKING TO BLAME OTHERS FOR WHATEVER DISCOMFORTS AND HUMILIATIONS SHE EXPERIENCES. THESE DIFFICULTIES MAY BE COMPOUNDED BY HER TENDENCY TO EXPECT THAT THINGS WILL NOT WORK OUT WELL. LACKING IN CONFIDENCE IN OTHERS, EASILY DISAPPOINTED IN THE CARE RECEIVED, AND DOUBTING WHETHER HEALTH CARE PERSONNEL ARE GENUINELY CARING AND INTERESTED, SHE MAY BEGIN TO MAKE DEMANDS, QUESTION THE COMPETENCE OF STAFF OR EVEN WITHDRAW FROM TREATMENT.

AS IS EVIDENT FROM THE ABOVE, SHE IS NOT AN EASY OR COMPLIANT PATIENT. RATHER, SHE IS DISPOSED TO COMPLAIN, FIND FAULT AND BE RESISTANT TO RECOMMENDED PRESCRIPTIONS. SHE MAY TAKE ACTIONS THAT LOOK SUPERFICIALLY COOPERATIVE, BUT ARE LIKELY TO UNDERMINE THE BEST OF THERAPEUTIC EFFORTS. SIGNS OF UNCOOPERATIVENESS SHOULD BE DEALT WITH DIRECTLY, SPECIFICALLY BY ASSUMING THAT HER FEARS WILL SERVE AS MOTIVATION FOR COOPERATING. IT IS IMPORTANT IN THESE CONFRONTATIONS TO MAINTAIN A PROFESSIONAL STANCE, TO AVOID THREAT OR TO TAKE A DISCIPLINARY RATHER THAN A THERAPEUTIC ATTITUDE. A STRAIGHTFORWARD, BUSINESSLIKE DISCUSSION EXPLAINING THE REASONS FOR A COURSE OF TREATMENT AND THE NEED FOR COMPLIANCE IS MORE LIKELY TO PROVE EFFECTIVE THAN ANGER OR ANNOYANCE.

PSYCHOGENIC ATTITUDES

THE SCALES COMPRISING THIS SECTION COMPARE THE FEELINGS AND PERCEPTIONS EXPRESSED BY THE PATIENT TO THOSE OF A CROSS SECTION OF BOTH HEALTHY AND ILL ADULTS OF THE SAME SEX. THE RESULTS OF THESE SCALES ARE SUMMARIZED HERE SINCE THEY MAY BE ASSOCIATED WITH AN INCREASE IN THE PROBABILITY OF PSYCHOSOMATIC PATHOGENESIS, OR WITH TENDENCIES TO AGGRAVATE THE COURSE OF AN ESTABLISHED DISEASE, OR WITH ATTITUDES THAT MAY IMPEDE THE EFFECTIVENESS OF MEDICAL OR SURGICAL TREATMENT.

THE PATIENT SEES DAILY DEMANDS OF FAMILY OR WORK AS AVERAGE AND WITHIN MANAGEABLE PROPORTIONS. SOME PRESSURES DO EXIST, BUT THEY ARE EITHER PERIODIC OR AT LEVELS EASILY TOLERATED. AS A CONSEQUENCE, THE PATIENT EXPERIENCES PERIODS OF FREEDOM FROM SELF OR EXTERNALLY IMPOSED DEMANDS. THE PERCEPTION OF A MODEST DEGREE OF DAILY STRESS INDICATES A REASONABLY LOW LIKELIHOOD OF TENSION-RELATED ILLNESS. HOWEVER, THIS WOULD NOT PREVENT THE PATIENT, GIVEN THE PERSONALITY STYLE DESCRIBED ABOVE, FROM PERIODICALLY COMPLAINING ABOUT SUCH PRESSURES AND DEMANDS.

THE EVENTS OF THE PAST YEAR ARE REPORTED AS UNREMARKABLE AND TYPICAL IN CHARACTER FOR THE PATIENT'S LIFESTYLE. PRONE TO VIEW EVENTS AS TROUBLESOME, THIS MODEST EVALUATION OF RECENT LIFE DIFFICULTIES SUGGESTS THE PATIENT HAS EXPERIENCED A MORE COMFORTABLE PERIOD THAN USUAL. THERE IS NO INDICATION, THEREFORE, THAT AN INCREASED PROBABILITY OF A MAJOR ILLNESS WILL OCCUR THIS COMING YEAR AS A CONSEQUENCE OF PERCEIVED LIFE STRESSES.

IN SPITE OF A CHARACTERISTICALLY PESSIMISTIC OUTLOOK ON LIFE, THE PATIENT RECOUNTS BOTH THE PAST AND THE PRESENT AS GOOD SOMETIMES, AND NOT GOOD AT OTHERS. THE INCLINATION TO INTERPRET EVENTS IN A REASONABLY BALANCED MANNER INDICATES THAT THE PATIENT IS LIKELY TO REACT TO AN ILLNESS EXPERIENCE IN AN UNEXCEPTIONAL MANNER.

ALTHOUGH USUALLY EXPECTING THE WORST, THE PATIENT SHOWS ONLY AN AVERAGE DEGREE OF CONCERN REGARDING FUTURE PROSPECTS. ASSUMING THAT THE OUTLOOK WILL UNFOLD IN AN UNEXCEPTIONAL MANNER, THE PATIENT IS LIKELY TO MANAGE FUTURE OR CURRENT PHYSICAL PROBLEMS WITH LESS EMOTIONAL UPHEAVAL THAN MIGHT OTHERWISE BE EXPECTED.

FAMILY AND FRIENDS ARE SEEN AS PROVIDING WARMTH AND CARING TO THE PATIENT. PERCEIVED AS SUPPORTIVE AND CONCERNED, THEY SERVE AS A POSITIVE FORCE UNDER MOST ILLNESS CONDITIONS. GIVEN A LONG TERM ILLNESS, HOWEVER, THIS SAME CONCERN AND ATTENTION MAY LEAD TO THE DEVELOPMENT OF AN INVALID ROLE, PARTICULARLY IF THE PATIENT HAS PREVIOUSLY FELT INADEQUATELY CARED FOR.

THE PATIENT'S NATURAL TENDENCY TO VIEW EVENTS IN A NEGATIVE LIGHT IS SUPERSEDED BY AN UNUSUALLY HIGH LEVEL OF CONCERN REGARDING PHYSICAL HEALTH. QUICK TO SEEK MEDICAL HELP FOR WHAT ARE OBJECTIVELY MINOR DISCOMFORTS, AND INCLINED TO OVERREACT TO THE DIAGNOSIS OF ILLNESS, THE PATIENT MAY GET CAUGHT IN A VICIOUS CIRCLE OF REAL AND SELF-CREATED AILMENTS.

PSYCHOSOMATIC CORRELATES

THE SCALES COMPRISING THIS SECTION ARE DESIGNED FOR USE ONLY WITH PATIENTS WHO HAVE PREVIOUSLY BEEN DIAGNOSED BY PHYSICIANS AS SUFFERING ONE OF A NUMBER OF SPECIFIC DISEASE ENTITIES OR SYNDROMES, E.G., HYPERTENSION, COLITIS, ALLERGY. NOTE THAT THESE SCALES DO NOT PROVIDE DATA CONFIRMING SUCH MEDICAL DIAGNOSES, NOR DO THEY INCLUDE STATEMENTS WHICH MAY BE CONSTRUED AS SUPPORTING THEM. RATHER, THE PRIMARY INTENT OF THIS SECTION IS TO GUAGE THE EXTENT TO WHICH THE PATIENT IS SIMILAR TO COMPARABLY DIAGNOSED PATIENTS WHOSE ILLNESS HAS BEEN JUDGED TO BE SUBSTANTIALLY PSYCHOSOMATIC, OR WHOSE COURSE HAS BEEN JUDGED TO BE COMPLICATED BY EMOTIONAL OR SOCIAL FACTORS.

CHARACTERISTICALLY HYPERREACTIVE, IF THE PATIENT HAS A DIAGNOSED ALLERGIC DISORDER, E.G., PRURITIS, URTICARIA, DERMATITIS, ASTHMA, THERE IS REASONABLE LIKELIHOOD THAT THE DISORDER IS LARGELY PSYCHOSOMATIC, THAT IS PRECIPITATED OR COMPLICATED BY THE PRESENCE OF EMOTIONAL STRESSORS.

IF THE PATIENT HAS A HISTORY OF CHRONIC GASTROINTESTINAL DISORDER, E.G., PEPTIC ULCER, COLITIS, DYSPEPSIA, IRRITABLE COLON, IT IS EVIDENT FROM THE MBHI SCORES THAT THE CONSTANT EMOTIONAL UPHEAVAL EXPERIENCED BY THE PATIENT CONTRI-BUTES SIGNIFICANTLY TO BOTH THE FREQUENCY AND INTENSITY OF THE PATIENT'S MEDI-CAL COMPLAINTS.

IF THE PATIENT HAS BEEN MEDICALLY DIAGNOSED AS MANIFESTING THE SYMPTOMS OF CERTAIN CARDIOVASCULAR DISORDERS, NOTABLY HYPERTENSION OR ANGINA PECTORIS, IT WOULD APPEAR THAT THE PATIENT'S CHARACTERISTIC EMOTIONAL RESPONSE TO UPSET-TING EVENTS WILL CONTRIBUTE, THOUGH MODESTLY, TO THE EXACERBATION OF THESE SYMPTOMS.

PROGNOSTIC INDICES

THE SCALES COMPRISING THIS SECTION HAVE BEEN EMPIRICALLY CONSTRUCTED TO ASSIST CLINICIANS IN APPRAISING THE IMPACT OF PSYCHOSOCIAL FACTORS WHICH CAN COMPLICATE THE USUAL PROGNOSTIC COURSE OF PATIENTS WHO HAVE A HISTORY OF EITHER A CHRONIC OR LIFE-THREATENING ILLNESS, OR WHO ARE UNDER REVIEW FOR A LIFE-SUSTAINING SURGICAL OR MEDICAL PROCEDURE.

IF THERE HAS BEEN A MEDICAL HISTORY OF A PERIODIC OR PERSISTENT PAIN DISORDER, E.G., LOW BACK PAIN, HEADACHE, TMJ, IT IS HIGHLY LIKELY THAT THE PATIENT WILL NOT RESPOND FAVORABLY TO TRADITIONAL OUTPATIENT TREATMENT. NUMER-OUS COMPLICATIONS ARE LIKELY TO ARISE DURING THE COURSE OF TREATMENT AS A FUNCTION OF EMOTIONAL RESPONSES TO BOTH THE DISORDER AND THE TREATMENT PROGRAM. A CONSERVATIVE PHARMACOLOGIC AND SURGICAL COURSE IS RECOMMENDED. SERIOUS CON-SIDERATION SHOULD BE GIVEN TO THE OPTION OF BEHAVIORAL MODIFICATION PROGRAMS AND THOSE UTILIZING OTHER PSYCHOLOGICAL TREATMENT COMPONENTS.

IF THE PATIENT IS SUFFERING FROM A CHRONIC AND PROGRESSIVE LIFE-THREATENING ILLNESS, E.G., METASTATIC CARCINOMA, RENAL FAILURE, CONGESTIVE HEART DISEASE, IT IS PROBABLE THAT THERE WILL BE SOME UNEXPECTED DIFFICULTIES IN THE COURSE OF THE ILLNESS. IT IS POSSIBLE THAT THE PATIENT MAY FARE LESS WELL THAN MIGHT BE ANTICIPATED, IN PART AS A RESULT OF A SENSE THAT NEEDED EMOTIONAL SUPPORT IS NOT AVAILABLE. COUNSELING AND SELF-HELP GROUPS MIGHT PROVE BENEFICIAL IN COUNTERING THESE NEGATIVE ATTITUDES AND MINIMIZE PROBLEMS IN TREATMENT.

IF FACED WITH MAJOR SURGERY OR A CANDIDATE FOR ONGOING LIFE-DEPENDENT TREATMENT PROGRAMS, E.G., OPEN HEART PROCEDURES, HEMODIALYSIS, CANCER CHEMO-THERAPY, IT IS UNLIKELY THAT THE PATIENT WILL SUFFER PERIODS OF EITHER SERIOUS DEPRESSION OR PSYCHOTIC DISORIENTATION.

CAPSULE SUMMARY

QUICKLY OFFENDED BY TRIFLES, THIS PATIENT TENDS TO BE IRRITABLE AND UNPREDICTABLE. A PROTRACTED OR SERIOUS PERSONAL ILLNESS WILL PROVOKE UNDUE ANXIETY. CHARACTERISTICALLY NON-COMPLICANT, HER UNCOOPERATIVENESS SHOULD BE HANDLED BY DRAWING UPON HER STRONG DESIRES TO REGAIN HEALTH.

PUBLISHED BY NCS INTERPRETIVE SCORING SYSTEMS, P.O. BOX 1416, MINNEAPOLIS, MN 55440

```
                                                          ******
                                          Date Processed: 07/17/81
Client: Not Provided    SEND TO: Ms. Margaret G. Peery  #  2055
Answer Sheet: 09448              18333 Hatteras #46
Sex: Male    Race: Black         Tarzana, CA  91356
Age: 11 Years  6 Months
School Grade: Not Provided
Informant: Female Other
```

* * * * * PIC INTERPRETATION * * * * *

This PIC interpretation is based on the systematic analysis of data
obtained in the evaluation of behaviorally disturbed children and
adolescents. This report consists of a series of hypotheses that may
serve to guide further investigation.

GENERAL ADJUSTMENT AND INFORMANT RESPONSE STYLE:

The description of this child's behavior suggests that a
psychological/psychiatric evaluation may assist in the remediation of
current problems.

Many infrequent problems and symptoms are described in this
protocol. These responses may indicate the presence of highly
disruptive behaviors that may require hospitalization for their
treatment. Similar response patterns may be obtained by informants who
exaggerate child problems or who fail to respond to Inventory items in
a conventional manner. The possibilities of exaggeration and atypical
response sets should be carefully excluded before credence is given to
other profile scale interpretations.

COGNITIVE DEVELOPMENT AND ACADEMIC PERFORMANCE:

Clinical examination and teacher observation are likely to suggest
deficits in motor coordination, language skills, or cognitive functions.
Similar children may evidence fine- or gross-motor clumsiness, or
concrete thinking beyond age expectation. In interviews, they may
display receptive or expressive aphasic symptoms. Speech may be
described as limited, immature, or may be characterized by poor
articulation. Teachers may report poor performance in physical
education activities or may observe difficulty in fine-motor
coordination, such as in drawing. Classroom performance may reflect
poor study skills, difficulty understanding instructions, or an
inability to retain and apply basic skills taught in previous grades. A
psychological examination may suggest the presence of limited
intellectual endowment and may result in specific recommendations to
school personnel.

A history of significant academic failure and an associated
negative self-image are suggested. Similar children often approach
school assignments with an "I can't do it" attitude. They give up
easily, expect failure, and may withdraw into daydreaming. Inventory
responses indicate poor academic performance, which may result in
underdeveloped reading, mathematics, spelling, or handwriting abilities,
or in limited skills in verbal expression. A deficit in concentration
and difficulty in completion of classroom assignments is likely. School
history may include retention in grade to promote skill acquisition.

PERSONALITY AND FAMILY EVALUATION:

A history of poor peer relations may lead this child to expect
criticism and rejection from others. Parents and teachers frequently
observe that similar children have few, if any, friends. Poor social
skills may be demonstrated by a failure to initiate relationships, with
resulting isolation, or by conflict with peers that reflects poor
sportsmanship and limited frustration tolerance.

Current child behavior suggests serious psychological
maladjustments, which may be characterized by unusual thoughts and
behaviors, social isolation, and emotional lability. Parents frequently
note that similar children are "confused or in a daze," and may note
excessive daydreaming. Delayed developmental milestones may be reported
for social skills, language ability, or motor coordination. Similar
children may be resistant to change in the environment, may display
rapid mood shifts, or demonstrate poor judgment. Self-destructive
behavior (such as head-banging), destruction of objects, difficulty in
getting to sleep, or early morning awakening may be present. Current
behaviors may include symptoms that are frequently associated with
severe emotional disability, such as abnormal motor behavior, echolalic
speech, or an associative thought disorder. Evaluation of this child's
interpersonal relations and thought processes may reveal a pathological
perception of reality.

This child's behavior is likely to reflect the presence of depression, anxiety, and social withdrawal. Presenting complaints may include problems with sleeping and eating, emotional lability, multiple fears, distrust of others, or excessive worry, self-blame, or self-criticism. Similar children are likely to be described as excessively shy by both parents and teachers. They play alone, avoid group activities at school, and stay away from other family members at home. Preadolescents may be unresponsive to school surroundings, and may evidence separation anxiety, while adolescents may display suicidal thought and behavior.

A disregard for rules and societal expectations is likely to be evidenced by behavior displayed at both home and school. Similar children may express a dislike for school and demonstrate a hostile, defiant response to school personnel. Current behavior is likely to reflect impulsivity, poor judgment, or unmodulated hostility. An antisocial adjustment may be suggested by symptoms such as lying, theft, association with similarly troubled children, or by an established tendency to blame others for current problems.

A history of problematic peer relations is suggested that may be characterized by poorly controlled expression of hostility, fighting, provocation and teasing, or poor sportsmanship. Current and/or past behavior may also suggest hyperactivity, distractibility, restlessness, or impulsivity. Similar children are often inattentive in class, do not complete homework assignments, and may require adult intervention to conform to stated limits. A limited frustration tolerance may be associated with temper tantrums, destruction of objects, projection of blame, direct expression or displacement of anger, or a lack of trust in others. Other problems may include excessive seeking of attention and approval, clumsiness, frequent accidents, or fire setting.

A history of marital discord, as well as subsequent separation or divorce, is suggested. One or both parents may be judged to require professional assistance to deal with their emotional instability, alcoholism, or substance abuse. Parental inconsistency in setting limits may contribute to the development of child behavior problems.

NOTE: The studies that form the foundation for the PIC REPORT are presented in two monographs published by Western Psychological Services: "Multidimensional Description of Child Personality. A Manual for the Personality Inventory for Children" (W-152G) and "Actuarial Assessment of Child and Adolescent Personality: An Interpretive Guide for the Personality Inventory for Children Profile" (W-305).

* * * * CRITICAL ITEMS * * * *

These Inventory items were answered by the informant in the direction indicated. Although too much interpretive value should not be placed on individual responses, they may suggest areas for further inquiry.

Relative frequency of item endorsement in male normative and clinic samples is indicated at the end of each statement by this notation: [normative % / clinic %].

---- DEPRESSION AND POOR SELF-CONCEPT ----

6. My child tends to pity himself.(T) [26%/38%]
56. My child has little self-confidence.(T) [18%/54%]
194. Several times my child has threatened to kill himself.(T) [2%/6%]
532. My child speaks of himself as stupid or dumb.(T) [7%/22%]

--- WORRY AND ANXIETY ---

17. My child worries about things that usually only adults worry about.(T) [15%/21%]
71. At times my child pulls out his hair.(T) [1%/3%]
115. Often my child goes about wringing his hands.(T) [1%/9%]
151. My child is afraid of dying.(T) [10%/15%]
246. My child sometimes chews his lips until they are sore.(T) [3%/8%]
298. My child won't go into the bedroom without someone else there.(T) [3%/5%]
353. Sometimes my child's muscles twitch.(T) [5%/15%]
511. Sex seems to concern my child more than others.(T) [1%/5%]

--- REALITY DISTORTION ---

26. My child sometimes thinks he is someone else.(T) [5%/6%]
101. My child sometimes hears things others don't hear.(T) [4%/7%]
161. My child sometimes feels things that aren't there.(T) [2%/6%]
379. Often my child will laugh for no apparent reason.(T) [7%/20%]

--- PEER RELATIONS ---

69. My child is usually rejected by other children.(T) [4%/26%]
90. I have found out my child has had sex play with the opposite
    sex.(T) [3%/11%]
91. My child never takes the lead in things.(T) [13%/32%]
164. My child doesn't seem to care to be with others.(T) [4%/18%]
195. My child usually doesn't trust others.(T) [5%/19%]
208. My child really has no real friend.(T) [6%/29%]
271. My child is very jealous of others.(T) [7%/17%]
322. My child would rather be with adults than with children his own
     age.
340. Other children make fun of my child's different ideas.(T) [2%/17%]
410. My child thinks others are plotting against him.(T) [2%/12%]
505. Hardly a day goes by when my child doesn't get into a
     fight.(T) [3%/15%]

--- UNSOCIALIZED AGGRESSION ---

38. At times my child has seriously hurt others.(T) [2%/12%]
44. As a child, my child hit other children on the head with sharp
    toys.(T) [5%/12%]
70. My child seems to enjoy destroying things.(T) [4%/21%]
116. My child is sometimes cruel to animals.(T) [3%/19%]
190. My child has been in trouble for attacking others.(T) [2%/16%]
229. Often my child smashes things when angry.(T) [8%/30%]
465. Many times my child has become violent.(T) [8%/30%]
540. Several times my child has threatened to kill others.(T) [2%/11%]

--- CONSCIENCE DEVELOPMENT ---

124. My child is good at lying his way out of trouble.(T) [14%/38%]
284. Several times my child has been in trouble for stealing.
     (T) [2%/29%]
307. My child has never been in trouble with the police.(F) [9%/30%]
486. My child is always telling lies.(TO) [3%/18%]

--- POOR JUDGMENT ---

186. My child can be left home alone without danger.(F) [18%/42%]
339. I always worry about my child having an accident when he is
     out.(T) [16%/33%]
467. I have a problem stopping my child from eating
     everything.(T) [9%/14%]

--- ATYPICAL DEVELOPMENT ---

131. My child has had brief periods of time when he seems unaware of
     everything that is going on.(T) [16%/33%]
215. My child could walk downstairs alone by age five years.(F) [1%/3%]
448. My child was difficult to toilet train.(T) [16%/34%]
460. I had an especially difficult time with temper tantrums in my child
     at an earlier age.(T) [11%/28%]

--- DISTRACTIBILITY, ACTIVITY LEVEL, AND COORDINATION ---

234. My child can't seem to keep attention on anything.(T) [7%/36%]
272. Five minutes or less is about all my child will ever sit at one
     time.(T) [6%/22%]

--- SPEECH AND LANGUAGE ---

149. At one time my child had speech difficulties.(T) [17%/38%]
328. My child seldom talks.(T) [2%/19%]

--- SOMATIC COMPLAINTS/CURRENT HEALTH ---

400. Skin rash has been a problem with my child.(T) [8%/12%]
420. My child has had asthma attacks.(T) [6%/9%]
447. My child doesn't seem to feel pain like others.(T) [4%/14%]
564. My child gets pneumonia almost every year.(T) [1%/2%]

Western Psychological Services • 12031 Wilshire Boulevard • Los Angeles, California 90025

--- SCHOOL ADJUSTMENT ---

81. The school says my child needs help in getting along with other children.(T) [5%/36%]
260. My child can't sit still in school because of nervousness.(T) [5%/40%]
267. Reading has been a problem for my child.(T) [23%/53%]
288. My child has never failed a grade in school.(F) [12%/44%]
294. My child is in a special class in school (for slow learners).(T) [2%/30%]
370. School teachers complain that my child can't sit still.(T) [9%/41%]
441. My child has never been expelled from school.(F) [9%/29%]
487. Recently the child's parents have argued with the school officials.(T) [0%/3%]

--- FAMILY DISCORD ---

369. The child's parents disagree a lot about rearing the child.(T) [10%/27%]
433. Several times my child has threatened to run away.(T) [10%/28%]
526. The child's father is hardly ever home.(T) [13%/18%]
583. Our marriage has been very unstable (shaky).(T) [12%/25%]

--- OTHER ---

74. I am afraid my child might be going insane.(T) [1%/6%]
172. My child often stays in his room for hours.(T) [9%/16%]
286. Neither parent has ever been mentally ill.(F) [10%/15%]
479. I have heard that my child drinks alcohol.(T) [1%/16%]

Western Psychological Services • 12031 Wilshire Boulevard • Los Angeles, California 90025

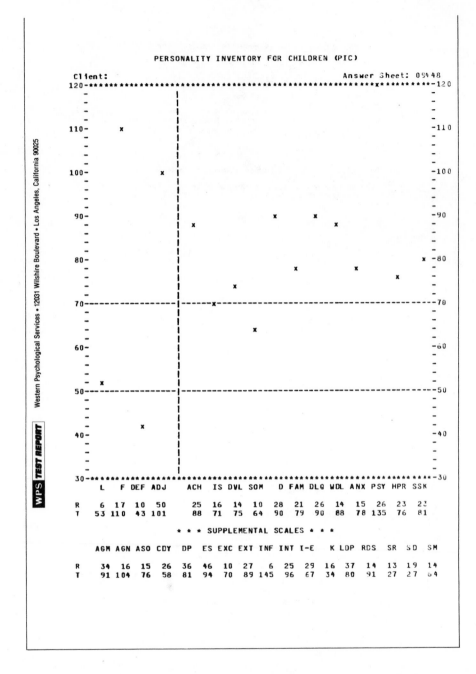

PERSONALITY INVENTORY FOR CHILDREN (PIC)

Client: Answer Sheet: 09448

	L	F	DEF	ADJ	ACH	IS	DVL	SOM	D	FAM	DLQ	WDL	ANX	PSY	HPR	SSK
R	6	17	10	50	25	16	14	10	28	21	26	14	15	26	23	23
T	53	110	43	101	88	71	75	64	90	79	90	88	78	135	76	81

* * * SUPPLEMENTAL SCALES * * *

	AGM	AGN	ASO	CDY	DP	ES	EXC	EXT	INF	INT	I-E	K	LDP	RDS	SR	SD	SM
R	34	16	15	26	36	46	10	27	6	25	29	16	37	14	13	19	14
T	91	104	76	58	81	94	70	89	145	96	67	34	80	91	27	27	64

Western Psychological Services • 12031 Wilshire Boulevard • Los Angeles, California 90025

WPS TEST REPORT

also be helpful to the student to discuss with a counselor career choices or possible areas of concentration for those who are college bound.

Further information on the VII is available in Lunneborg (1981).

RORSCHACH COMPUTER
REPORTS

Continuing with our sequence of computer printouts, we present two Rorschach interpretations that represent effective contrasts between "normal" and "abnormal" personalities. They are examples of computer-derived Rorschach interpretations as developed by Dr. Irvin H. Perline and made available by Century Diagnostics. The first (pp. 220–23) is based on a hypothetical ideal protocol of a 38-year-old female (Klopfer & Davidson, 1962). In the case of the second (pp. 224–28) we break the rule of anonymity that is applied to all of the actual case material in this book. Here the computer's conclusions on the "abnormal" case are based on the protocol of top Nazi leader Hermann Goering, who for a time was Hitler's personally selected designee to succeed to the position of Führer of the Third Reich.

Interpretation on each subject is presented in two ways, the first closely relating data with interpretation, the second taking the narrative format such as prepared by a psychologist clinician. Both experienced Rorschach workers and students are likely to have an interest in the data as well as in the Interpretive remarks. As of press time the narrative summary format is still under development.

The Goering material is particularly interesting, not only because of the subject's historical notoriety, but also because a study of the Rorschach data on which the computer conclusions are based is also readily available elsewhere (Miale & Selzer, 1975). Florence Miale is a foremost "Rorschacher," hence the extent to which her conclusions and the computer-derived conclusions are congruent is of interest to those who would assess the power of the newer interpretive technique.

What we need to watch for is not the use of identical words, but of parallel concepts. We find many. The Miale-Selzer findings stressed that Goering, although "functioning" (and at a high level at that) was "sick," "psychopathic," of primitive make-up, and heterosexually primitive. Similar findings are in the more recent report.

Why the congruence? Essentially because in some important ways the computer works like the clinician. Both are dependent on the fact that relationships exist between responses and nuances of responding, on the one hand, and various personality features on the other. The clinician, on perusing a Rorschach protocol, develops many hypotheses but is inclined to endow with credence those that are strongest and that cluster with other data of the protocol. The computer, with its enormous power of memory, facili-

NAME: WRIGHT DALE   AGE: 16
SEX: Female   ANSWER SHEET SERIAL NO.: 000490
HIGHEST GRADE COMPLETED: 10   STATED EDUCATIONAL GOAL: 4-Yr.College

INTERPRETING YOUR RESULTS ON THE VOCATIONAL INTEREST INVENTORY

The Vocational Interest Inventory (VII) is a guidance instrument to help people make post-high-school educational and vocational decisions. Your scores are compared to those of over 25,000 high school juniors who have taken the VII.

The VII measures how much interest you have in eight occupational areas which cover the entire world of work. Throughout the inventory you were asked to choose between certain occupations or activities. Now you will be able to see what your strongest interests are, as a result of the choices you made on each VII question.

The VII is easy to interpret. However, career counselors can help you to get more out of the VII. They can give you some ideas to help you make decisions about what to study in school or what kind of work is likely to be most satisfying to you.

This report is going to give you two kinds of information. First, it provides a profile of your eight VII scores with their percentile equivalents (Profile of Scores). High scores are those above the 75th percentile. Consider exploring those areas in which you have indicated the highest interest.

Second, the report gives you a profile that shows you which college graduates you are most similar to in interests (College Majors Profile). It displays the four dimensions that have been found to underlie the eight occupational interests and shows your position on each of these dimensions. This profile also shows you the average positions on each dimension of people who graduated from college in various college majors based on their VII results collected when they were in high school. This may help you in selecting among possible college majors.

You will also be encouraged to explore any occupational areas that are nontraditional for your sex if you have a score between the 50th and 75th percentiles on any nontraditional scale.

YOUR PROFILE OF SCORES

On the next page is your Profile of Scores. Identify your high scores (those above the 75th percentile) and then read the interpretation provided for you on the page following the profile. Each of the eight scores is defined in the VII Guide to Interpretation, a printed booklet that should be available with this report.

SCORE SUMMARY

	Service	Business	Organization	Technical	Outdoor	Science	Culture	Art
Percentile	97	25	34	99	98	4	35	5
T Scores	69	43	46	80	72	32	46	34

INTERPRETING YOUR PROFILE OF SCORES

The heights of the bars in the Profile of Scores on the previous page show how you compare with high school students in the relative amount of interest you have in eight basic occupational areas. The percentile number on the top of each bar tells you the percentage of students with less interest than you in that occupational area. Scores at the 75th percentile are higher than 3/4 of the other students' scores. Scores at the 25th percentile are low, since only 1/4 of the students scored lower. You may wish to explore jobs in your high interest areas. Study the descriptions of the eight occupational areas given in the VII Guide to Interpretation, a printed booklet that should be available with this report. If you were planning to go into an area for which your interest score was low, you might want to discuss this with a career counselor.

YOU HAD 3 SCORES AT OR ABOVE THE 75TH PERCENTILE

Your three highest scores at or above the 75th percentile were Service, Technical, and Outdoor. People with high Service interest are very people oriented and want to be helpful. Service means attending to the personal tastes, needs, and welfare of others through guidance, domestic, personal, or protective services. It is somewhat unique to see high Service interest together with high Technical/Outdoor interest. The reason

```
VII Report for WRIGHT DALE                                    Page 2

            VOCATIONAL INTEREST INVENTORY PROFILE OF SCORES

        -1-      -2-       -3-         -4-      -5-     -6-     -7-    -8-
 %ile Service Business Organization Technical Outdoor Science Culture Arts %ile
 ----  ------- -------- ------------ --------- ------- ------- ------- ---- ----
   -                                    99                                    -
   -                                   ****                                   -
  99-                                  ****      98                         -99
   -                                   ****    ****                           -
   -                                   ****    ****                           -
  98-   97                             ****    ****                         -98
   -   ****                            ****    ****                           -
   -   ****                            ****    ****                           -
   -   ****                            ****    ****                           -
  95-  ****                            ****    ****                         -95
   -   ****                            ****    ****                           -
   -   ****                            ****    ****                           -
  90-  ****                            ****    ****                         -90
   -   ****                            ****    ****                           -
   -   ****                            ****    ****                           -
  85-  ****                            ****    ****                         -85
   -   ****                            ****    ****                           -
   -   ****                            ****    ****                           -
  75- -****--------------------------****----****------------------------ -75
   -   ****                            ****    ****                           -
   -   ****                            ****    ****                           -
   -   ****                            ****    ****                           -
  60-  ****                            ****    ****                         -60
   -   ****                            ****    ****                           -
   -   ****                            ****    ****                           -
  50- -****------------------------- ****----****------------------------ -50
   -   ****                            ****    ****                           -
   -   ****                            ****    ****                           -
  40-  ****           34              ****    ****           35            -40
   -   ****          ****             ****    ****          ****             -
   -   ****          ****             ****    ****          ****             -
   -   ****     25   ****             ****    ****          ****             -
  25- -****----****----****----------****----****----------****---------- -25
   -   ****    ****   ****            ****    ****          ****             -
   -   ****    ****   ****            ****    ****          ****             -
  15-  ****    ****   ****            ****    ****          ****           -15
   -   ****    ****   ****            ****    ****          ****             -
   -   ****    ****   ****            ****    ****          ****             -
  10-  ****    ****   ****            ****    ****          ****           -10
   -   ****    ****   ****            ****    ****          ****    05       -
   5-  ****    ****   ****            ****    ****          ****   ****     -5
   -   ****    ****   ****            ****    ****    04    ****   ****       -
   -   ****    ****   ****            ****    ****   ****   ****   ****       -
   2-  ****    ****   ****            ****    ****   ****   ****   ****     -2
   -   ****    ****   ****            ****    ****   ****   ****   ****       -
   1-  ****    ****   ****            ****    ****   ****   ****   ****     -1
 ----  ------- -------- ------------ --------- ------- ------- ------- ---- ----
 %ile Service Business Organization Technical Outdoor Science Culture Arts %ile
        -1-      -2-       -3-         -4-      -5-     -6-     -7-    -8-
```

is that Technical/Outdoor interest means not being people oriented but
valuing, instead, tools, objects, and machines. Technical/Outdoor people
would rather use their hands in assembling and operating equipment than in
providing direct services to people. For a position at the high school
diploma level that combines the three interests on the job, you might explore fire fighter, humane officer (dog catcher), police officer, or ferry
boat crew member. Jobs with a bachelor's degree that combine Technical,
Outdoor, and Service interests are vocational agriculture teacher, building superintendent, and forester.

YOUR COLLEGE MAJORS PROFILE

        On the next page is the College Majors Profile that shows how close
you come in your interests to groups of college majors. Underlying
VII interests are four dimensions. There is a Service versus Technical
dimension, a Business Contact versus Science dimension, an Organization
versus Outdoor dimension, and an Arts versus Detailed Work dimension.
People who score high at one end of each dimension tend to score low at
the other end. For example, people with high service scores tend to have

low Technical scores; people with high Science scores tend to have low
Business Contact scores. The position of each college major group
is shown along with your position on each dimension. You will want
to pay particular attention to those dimensions where your position
is toward the top of the profile, indicating a high dimension score.
Also, read the interpretations on the page following the profile.

INTERPRETING YOUR COLLEGE MAJORS PROFILE

    Do your positions on the College Majors Profile make sense to you?
Do they correspond to what you think you would like to do? If the
results seem puzzling, look back at your Profile of Scores. High scores,
those above the 75th percentile, will be your best guide.

VII Report for WRIGHT DALE

VOCATIONAL INTEREST INVENTORY COLLEGE MAJORS PROFILE

-1- TECHNICAL	-2- BUSINESS	-3- OUTDOOR	-4- DETAILED WORK
		******YOU********	
			******YOU*******
Engineering			
		Fishery/Forest	
******YOU********	******YOU********		
	Political Sci		
Urban Planning		Art	
Fishery/Forest			
Accounting	Communications	Biological Sci	Engineering
Economics		History	Accounting
Biological Sci	History	Languages	Fishery/Forest
Art	Economics	Health Science	Political Sci
	Accounting	Nursing	Biological Sci
	Social Service	Home Economics	Health Science
Communications	Urban Planning	Social Service	Communications
	Art		
History	Home Economics	Urban Planning	History
Languages	Languages	Engineering	Home Economics
Home Economics		Economics	Urban Planning
Health Science		Political Sci	Languages
Nursing	Health Science		
Social Service			
	Engineering	Accounting	
	Fishery/Forest		Art
	Nursing		
	Biological Sci		
SERVICE -1-	SCIENCE -2-	ORGANIZATION -3-	ARTS -4-

Western Psychological Services • 12031 Wilshire Boulevard • Los Angeles, California 90025

WPS TEST REPORT

SERVICE VS. TECHNICAL

Your profile position is more toward the Technical end of this dimension. This means that when your interest in helping others is compared to your interest in working with tools, the Technical side is the stronger. You are thus more like engineering and urban planning majors than social service majors on this dimension, preferring to work with technical issues rather than to provide direct services to people.

BUSINESS VS. SCIENCE

Your profile position is more toward the Business Contact end of this interest dimension. This means that when your interest in Science is compared to your interest in Business Contact (persuading, promoting, winning people over to your view), the Business Contact side is the stronger. You are thus more like college graduates in political science and communications than like majors in biological sciences and health professions, preferring to work with people in a persuasive fashion instead of work in the sciences.

ORGANIZATION VS. OUTDOOR

You are more toward the Outdoor end of this interest dimension. This means that when your interest in outdoor activities is compared to your interest in organizing or managing people, your Outdoor interest is stronger. If this is more than a recreational interest, you are more like people in fisheries/forestry and graduates in art than like graduates in accounting, political science, and economics.

ART VS. DETAILED WORK

Your position is toward the Detailed Work end of this interest dimension, meaning that you have more of a preference for working in an orderly, detailed, and systematic way than in unstructured, artistic ways. Thus your interests would be somewhat more like engineering and accounting graduates than art majors.

tates this process. As is true of all computer hypotheses, the clinician is the final judge of how these are to be understood. The more complex the instrument, the more this is so, and the Rorschach is the most complex instrument in the clinical psychologist's armamentarium.

PSYCHOLOGICAL REPORTS IN MARITAL COUNSELING

The "report letter" on pages 229–233, written to "John and Mary Jones," exemplifies the follow-up approach used in marital counseling as developed by Dorr (1981). The function and form of such reports are quite atypical. The function is atypical in that reports are written directly to the clients as a therapeutic tool. The form is atypical not only because the report is fashioned in such a way as to provide an understandable summary of the counseling interaction, feedback, and an opportunity to contemplate and "digest" earlier clinical contacts, but also because the report writer uses the report as a means of interacting with the clients: objective appraisal alone

PATIENT ID: PROTO#1   SEX: F   AGE: 38   ACCOUNT ID: WORKSHOP
===

P A R T   I

DATA SUMMARY

===
SECTION 1   (*=Computation suggests Blocking or Shock)   CARD INFORMATION
===

CARD NUMBER	BLOCKING OR SHOCK	REACTION TIME	RESPONSE TIME	NUMBER OF RESPONSES	REJECTION NOTED
I	NO	35	40	1	NO
II	NO	20	30	2	NO
III	NO	8	15	2	NO
IV	NO	35	100	3	NO
V	NO	25	5	2	NO
VI	NO	35	40	2	NO
VII	NO	10	35	2	NO
VIII	NO	30	45	2	NO
IX	NO	20	50	1	NO
X	NO	30	120	8	NO

Average RESPONSE TIME(for 10 cards):   19.2 sec   Total RESPONSES: 25

Average REACTION TIME (I,IV,V,VI,VII)   :   28.0 sec
Average REACTION TIME (II,III,VIII,IX,X):   21.6 sec

===
SECTION 2   TABULATION
===

LOCATION		DETERMINANT		CONTENT		SPECIFIC CONTENT/RESPONSE MODE
W	7(1)	M	3	H	5	NATURE/LANDSCAPE CONTENT
D	14	FM	4	Hd	2	
d	3	m	(1)	A	5	
dd	1	K	1	Ad	3	
		FK	1	P	4	
		F	9	O	3	
		Fc	2			
		FC	3			
		CF	2			

===
SECTION 3   PERCENTAGES
===

MAIN SUM PARTS TOTAL PERCENTAGE (ADDITIONALS Not Included)

MAIN	SUM	PARTS	TOTAL	PERCENTAGE
W	W	Wx	7	28.0
D	D		14	56.0
S	S	s	0	0.0
F	F	F+ F-	9	36.0
A	A	Ad	8	32.0
P	P		4	16.0
O	O		3	12.0

===
SECTION 4   RATIOS
===

SUM C= 3.5   M:SUM C= 3.0: 3.5   (FM+m):(Fc+c+C')= 4.0: 2.0

===

P A R T   I I

INTERPRETIVE ANALYSIS

===
SECTION 1   COGNITIVE
===

****** W > 2M ******
  1. LEVELS OF ASPIRATION TOO HIGH.
  2. PRODUCTIVE RESOURCES UNDULY LOW.
  3. FOUND COMMONLY IN CHILDREN.

****** W = AVE ******
  4. NORMAL PERSONALITIES WITH BALANCED INTELLECTUAL AND PERCEPTUAL
     DEVELOPMENT.

****** W:M APPROX. 2:1 AND M >= 3 ******
  5. LEVELS OF ASPIRATION HIGH, BUT NOT EXCESSIVE.
  6. SATISFACTORY ADJUSTING.

****** D = AVE ******
  7. NORMAL ADJUSTING PERSONALITIES.
  8. CAPACITY TO DEAL WITH COMMON SENSE ASPECTS OF A PROBLEM.

220

```
******* S < AVE *******
  9. PASSIVE-DEPENDENT ORIENTATIONS, DOCILE COMPLIANCE.

******* M = AVE *******
 10. GOOD TIES WITH REALITY, FREE ACCESS TO FANTASY AND IMAGINAL
     PROCESSES WHICH ARE APPROPRIATELY USED IN CREATIVE ACTIVITY.
 11. WELL DEVELOPED EGO, BEHAVIOR PROBABLY IS IN ACCORD WITH REALISTIC
     FUNCTIONING, AND THERE IS SATISFACTORY INNER STABILITY,
     SELF-ACCEPTANCE, INCLUDING TOLERANCE OF BASIC IMPULSES
     AND FRUSTRATION, AND SATISFACTORY EMPATHIC ABILITY.

******* FM = AVE *******
 12. AWARENESS OF MODERATE IMPULSES TO IMMEDIATE GRATIFICATION.
 13. NORMAL STRENGTH OF NATURAL, UNACCULTURATED DRIVES.

******* F% = AVE *******
 14. SUFFICIENT RATIONAL OR INTELLECTUAL CONTROL OF BEHAVIOR WITH
     SATISFACTORY SPONTANEITY.
 15. ABILITY TO HANDLE SITUATIONS APPROPRIATELY IMPERSONALLY, IN A
     MATTER-OF-FACT WAY WHEN SITUATIONS REQUIRE IT.

******* P = AVE *******
 16. NORMAL PERCEPTION OF WORLD.
 17. ADEQUATE REALITY TIES.


=================================================================================
SECTION 2                                                             EMOTIONAL
=================================================================================

******* CARDS VIII + IX + X > 40% OF TOTAL RESPONSES *******
  1. EMOTIONAL OVERACTIVITY.
  2. PRODUCTIVITY STIMULATED BY ENVIRONMENTAL IMPACT.

******* FC' + C'F + C' <= 3 *******
  3. NORMALITY, THOUGH THIS IS NOT CONTRAINDICATIVE OF AN ABNORMAL
     PERSONALITY.

******* FC = AVE *******
  4. CONTROL OVER EMOTIONAL IMPACT WITHOUT LOSS OF NORMAL FLEXIBILITY;
     APPROPRIATELY MODULATED RESPONSIVENESS.
  5. SATISFACTORY INTERPERSONAL RELATIONS, INDIVIDUAL IS MAKING A
     SATISFACTORY SOCIAL ADJUSTMENT.
  6. HEALTHY, CONSISTENT ADJUSTING IN GENERAL.

******* Fc + FC > 2 *******
  7. SUGGESTS A CONTRAINDICATION OF ORGANICITY.

******* CF = AVE *******
  8. NORMAL SPONTANEITY.
  9. IN SETTINGS SUGGESTING PSYCHOPATHOLOGY, SCHIZOPHRENIA, AS
     CONTRASTED WITH NEUROSES AND CHARACTER DISORDERS.

******* FC > CF AND CF > 1 *******
 10. SATISFACTORY SOCIALIZATION OF EXPRESSED EMOTIONAL REACTIONS.
 11. WELL ADJUSTING PERSONALITIES.

******* FC > CF + C *******
 12. NORMAL PERSONS, WITH ADEQUATE CONTROL OVER EMOTIONAL IMPULSES;
     CONTRAINDICATIVE OF EXPLOSIVE ACTING OUT.
 13. ADEQUATE INTERPERSONAL RELATIONS.

******* CF + C > 0 AND C' = 0 *******
 14. SUGGEST POSSIBLE SCHIZOPHRENIC CONDITIONS.


=================================================================================
SECTION 3                                                         INTERPERSONAL
=================================================================================

******* KF + K = AVE *******
  1. NORMAL PERSONALITIES.

******* FK = AVE *******
  2. SATISFACTORY ADJUSTING.

******* Fc = AVE *******
  3. SATISFACTORY INTERPERSONAL RELATIONS, NORMAL SENSITIVITY TO
     NEEDS OF OTHERS, AND EMPATHY.
  4. NORMAL AWARENESS AND ACCEPTANCE OF AFFECTIONAL NEEDS, INCLUDING
     A REFINED DESIRE FOR APPROVAL, BELONGINGNESS, AND RESPONSE FROM
     OTHERS.
  5. APPROPRIATE CONTROL OF MOODS AND TACTFULNESS.
```

```
******* FM + m > Fc + c +C' *******
 6. INTROVERSIVE TENDENCIES NOT FULLY ACCEPTED BY THE PERSON.
 7. IF IN OPPOSITE DIRECTION OF M:SUM C, THIS POINTS IN THE
    DIRECTION THE PERSONALITY IS SHIFTING.

******* H = AVE *******
 8. EMPATHY, INTEREST IN AND SENSITIVITY TO OTHER PEOPLE.
 9. NORMAL, WELL ADJUSTING PERSONALITIES.


=====================================================================
SECTION 4                               SPECIFIC CONTENT/RESPONSE MODE
=====================================================================

******* NATURE AND LANDSCAPE CONTENT *******
 1. SUPERIOR INTELLIGENCE IN NORMAL PEOPLE.
 2. IN CHILDREN, POSSIBLE PSYCHOPATHIC TENDENCIES.


=====================================================================
SECTION 5                                BLOCKING, SHOCK OR REJECTION
=====================================================================


=====================================================================
                      P A R T   III

              SUMMARY OF KEYWORD OCCURRENCES
=====================================================================


                         KEYWORD SUMMARY TABLE
```

KEYWORD CATEGORY	MAXIMUM POSSIBLE TESTS	NUMBER POSITIVE TESTS	PERCENTAGE POSITIVE TESTS	HIGH SIGNIF. TESTS	OVERALL PERCENTAGE (weighted)
EGO STRENGTH	22	14	63.64	0	63.64
EMOT. CONTROL/LABILITY ...	18	1	5.56	0	5.56
ANXIETY	30	0	0.00	0	0.00
REPRESSION/CONSTRICTION ..	20	0	0.00	0	0.00
DEPRESSION/SUICIDE	22	0	0.00	0	0.00
PSYCHOSIS	23	0	0.00	0	0.00
ORGANICITY	11	-1	0.00	0	0.00

```
                         KEYWORD SUMMARY GRAPH

KEYWORD CATEGORY                 OVERALL PERCENTAGE (weighted)

                        0   10   20   30   40   50   60   70   80   90  100+
                        !----!----!----!-- -!--- !----!----!----!----!----!
EGO STRENGTH ...........!********************************
EMOT. CONTROL/LABILITY .!***
ANXIETY ................!
REPRESSION/CONSTRICTION !
DEPRESSION/SUICIDE .....!
PSYCHOSIS ..............!
ORGANICITY ............ !
                        !----!----!----!----!----!----!----!----!----!----!
                        0   10   20   30   40   50   60   70   80   90  100+
```

```
                    CENTURY DIAGNOSTICS NARRATIVE SUMMARY                    16AUG81

PATIENT ID: PROTO#1   SEX: F      AGE: 38              ACCOUNT ID: WORKSHOP
===============================================================================


COGNITIVE FUNCTION:
THIS INDIVIDUAL APPEARS TO HAVE BALANCED INTELLECTUAL AND PERCEPTUAL ABILITY.
SHE HAS THE ABILITY TO DEVELOP AN OVERVIEW OF SITUATIONS WHILE SIMULTANEOUSLY
DEALING WITH THE COMMON SENSE ASPECTS OF A PROBLEM.  THERE IS AN ABILITY TO REACT
TO SITUATIONS IN A ROUTINE, DISPASSIONATE, AND IMPARTIAL MANNER WHEN SUCH A RE-
SPONSE IS APPROPRIATE.  THERE ARE ADEQUATE EGO RESOURCES IN TERMS OF REALITY TEST-
ING.  POTENTIALLY, SHE SHOULD BE ABLE TO PERFORM AT A REASONABLE IMPULSE LEVEL.
THIS INDIVIDUAL HAS THE CAPACITY TO UTILIZE INNER RESOURCES IN RESPONDING TO
THE ENVIRONMENT.


EMOTIONAL FUNCTION:
THIS INDIVIDUAL IS REASONABLY SUCCESSFUL IN MEETING EMOTIONAL NEEDS IN AN ADAPTIVE,
SOCIALLY AND INTERPERSONALLY APPROPRIATE MANNER.  SHE IS ALSO CAPABLE OF EXPER-
IENCING AND EXPRESSING APPROPRIATE DEEPER AND SPONTANEOUS FEELINGS.  OVERALL THIS
INDIVIDUAL IS LIKELY TO BE SUCCESSFUL IN MEETING HER EMOTIONAL NEEDS IN A WAY
WHICH IS LIKELY TO ENHANCE INTERPERSONAL RELATIONSHIPS.


INTERPERSONAL FUNCTION:
THERE IS ADEQUATE POTENTIAL FOR MEETING AFFECTIONAL NEEDS THROUGH SOCIALLY APPRO-
PRIATE AND INTERPERSONALLY ADAPTIVE INTERACTIONS WITH OTHERS.  THIS INDIVIDUAL
IS CAPABLE OF MEETING SOME AFFECTIONAL NEEDS THROUGH DERIVED SECONDARY CHANNELS
OF GRATIFICATION, SUCH AS, RECOGNITION, ACHIEVEMENT, OR ADAPTIVE CONFORMITY. IN
ADDITION, THERE IS ADEQUATE POTENTIAL FOR DEEPER, MORE PRIMARY AFFECTIONAL RE-
SPONSIVITY, SUCH AS PHYSICAL CONTACT AND CLOSENESS.  THERE ARE INDICATIONS OF
NORMAL AWARENESS AND ACCEPTANCE OF AFFECTIONAL NEEDS WHICH IS LIKELY TO HAVE
A POSITIVE INFLUENCE ON INTERPERSONAL RELATIONSHIPS.  OVERALL, THIS PERSON
APPEARS TO HAVE ACHIEVED AN APPROPRIATE LEVEL OF SOCIALIZATION, WHEREIN SHE
SHOULD BE ABLE TO MEET HER NEEDS THROUGH SOCIALLY SATISFYING INTERACTION WITH
OTHERS.









THIS NARRATIVE SUMMARY IS BASED UPON
THE ACCOMPANYING RORSCHACH REPORT.
IT IS NOT INTENDED AS A SUBSTITUTE
FOR THAT REPORT, WHICH SHOULD BE READ
IN ITS ENTIRETY.
```

does not appear to be adequate to achieve the purpose that Dorr seeks. His personal compassion, insight, and "understanding" seem to be built into the report.

John and Mary's relationship does not exist in the best of all possible worlds, and John and Mary are not the best of all possible people—whatever that might mean. Dorr seeks to teach a couple endowed with common frailties and living in a less than perfect world how to live together. In so doing he is frank and open, yet he discusses the couple's problems in a way that is meant to be both constructive and palatable (it might be that much

PATIENT ID: GOERING   SEX: M   AGE: ACCOUNT ID: EXHIBIT
==
                              P A R T   I

                            DATA SUMMARY
==
SECTION 1   (*=Computation suggests Blocking or Shock)   CARD INFORMATION
==

CARD NUMBER	BLOCKING OR SHOCK	REACTION TIME	RESPONSE TIME	NUMBER OF RESPONSES	REJECTION NOTED
I	NO	10	OMITTED	2	NO
II	NO	5	OMITTED	1	NO
III	NO	5	OMITTED	2	NO
IV	NO	15	OMITTED	1	NO
V	NO	10	OMITTED	1	NO
VI	NO	10	OMITTED	1	NO
VII	NO *	20	OMITTED	1	NO
VIII	NO	8	OMITTED	2	NO
IX	NO	15	OMITTED	2	NO
X	NO	8	OMITTED	4	NO

Average RESPONSE TIME(for NO cards):N/A   sec   Total RESPONSES: 17

Average REACTION TIME (I,IV,V,VI,VII)   :   13.0 sec *
Average REACTION TIME (II,III,VIII,IX,X):   8.2 sec

==
SECTION 2   TABULATION
==

LOCATION		DETERMINANT		CONTENT		SPECIFIC CONTENT/RESPONSE MODE
W	5	M-	2	H	1	ANATOMY CONTENT
Wx	2	FM	3	(H)	5	EYES CONTENT
D	10	mF	(1)	A	7(1)	CONTAMINATION
S	(1)	F	7	P	6	PERPLEXITY
		FC	1(2)			
		CF	4(1)			

==
SECTION 3   PERCENTAGES
==

MAIN	SUM PARTS	TOTAL	PERCENTAGE (ADDITIONALS Not Included)
W	W Wx	7	41.2
D	D	10	58.8
S	S s	0	0.0
F	F F+ F-	7	41.2
A	A Ad	7	41.2
P	P	6	35.3

==
SECTION 4   RATIOS
==
SUM C= 4.0   M:SUM C= 2.0: 4.0   (FM+m):(Fc+c+C')= 3.0: 1.0

==
                              P A R T   II

                         INTERPRETIVE ANALYSIS
==
SECTION 1   COGNITIVE
==

******* W > 2M *******
  1. LEVELS OF ASPIRATION TOO HIGH.
  2. PRODUCTIVE RESOURCES UNDULY LOW.
  3. FOUND COMMONLY IN CHILDREN.

******* W = AVE *******
  4. NORMAL PERSONALITIES WITH BALANCED INTELLECTUAL AND PERCEPTUAL
     DEVELOPMENT.

******* D = AVE *******
  5. NORMAL ADJUSTING PERSONALITIES.
  6. CAPACITY TO DEAL WITH COMMON SENSE ASPECTS OF A PROBLEM.

******* S < AVE *******
  7. PASSIVE-DEPENDENT ORIENTATIONS, DOCILE COMPLIANCE.

******* M = AVE *******
  8. GOOD TIES WITH REALITY, FREE ACCESS TO FANTASY AND IMAGINAL
     PROCESSES WHICH ARE APPROPRIATELY USED IN CREATIVE ACTIVITY.

```
    9. WELL DEVELOPED EGO, BEHAVIOR PROBABLY IS IN ACCORD WITH REALISTIC
       FUNCTIONING, AND THERE IS SATISFACTORY INNER STABILITY,
       SELF-ACCEPTANCE, INCLUDING TOLERANCE OF BASIC IMPULSES
       AND FRUSTRATION, AND SATISFACTORY EMPATHIC ABILITY.

******* M QUALITY = - *******
   10. POOR CONTACT OR LOOSE TIES WITH REALITY.
   11. DEFECTIVE EGO ORGANIZATION.
   12. REGRESSIVE DEFENSES.
   13. LOW INTELLIGENCE OR IMPAIRED INTELLECTUAL EFFICIENCY.
   14. POSSIBLE AUTISTIC AND SCHIZOPHRENIC CONDITIONS.

******* FM = AVE *******
   15. AWARENESS OF MODERATE IMPULSES TO IMMEDIATE GRATIFICATION.
   16. NORMAL STRENGTH OF NATURAL, UNACCULTURATED DRIVES.

******* F% = AVE *******
   17. SUFFICIENT RATIONAL OR INTELLECTUAL CONTROL OF BEHAVIOR WITH
       SATISFACTORY SPONTANEITY.
   18. ABILITY TO HANDLE SITUATIONS APPROPRIATELY IMPERSONALLY, IN A
       MATTER-OF-FACT WAY WHEN SITUATIONS REQUIRE IT.

******* A% > AVE *******
   19. STEREOTYPY OF THOUGHT.
   20. LOW IQ OR MENTAL AGE.
   21. ANXIETY.
   22. PAUCITY OF INTERESTS.
   23. IMMATURITY AT ALL AGES.
   24. ELDERLY INDIVIDUALS WHO MAY BE NORMAL.
   25. REPRESSIVE, CONSTRICTIVE OR SUBMISSIVE CONFORMING DEFENSES.
   26. NEUROSES, PERHAPS OBSESSIVE-COMPULSIVE FEATURES.
   27. ORGANIC BRAIN DAMAGE.
   28. PSYCHOPATHIC, PARANOID AND HOMOCIDAL INDIVIDUALS.
   29. DEPRESSIVE CONDITIONS.

******* H + A > 2 (Hd + Ad) *******
   30. NORMALLY ADJUSTING PERSONALITIES, CONTRAINDICATIVE OF HYPER-
       CRITICAL ATTITUDES.

******* P = AVE *******
   31. NORMAL PERCEPTION OF WORLD.
   32. ADEQUATE REALITY TIES.

================================================================================
SECTION 2                                                            EMOTIONAL
================================================================================

******* CARDS VIII + IX + X > 40% OF TOTAL RESPONSES *******
    1. EMOTIONAL OVERACTIVITY.
    2. PRODUCTIVITY STIMULATED BY ENVIRONMENTAL IMPACT.

******* FC' + C'F + C' <= 3 *******
    3. NORMALITY, THOUGH THIS IS NOT CONTRAINDICATIVE OF AN ABNORMAL
       PERSONALITY.

******* FC < AVE *******
    4. MALADAPTIVE AFFECT, INADEQUATE EMOTIONAL CONTROL.
    5. POOR INTERPERSONAL RELATIONS.
    6. NEUROTIC ANXIETY CONDITIONS.
    7. IN CHILDREN, SMALL NUMBERS MAY BE NORMAL OR MAY REFLECT ANXIETY.
    8. CONVERSION HYSTERIA IN FEMALES.
    9. POSSIBLE SCHIZOPHRENIC OR ORGANIC CONDITIONS.

******* CF > AVE *******
   10. IMPULSIVENESS, EMOTIONAL LABILITY, ACTING OUT OF EMOTIONAL
       REACTION TENDENCIES AS FOUND IN EMOTIONALLY IMMATURE AND
       MALADJUSTING PERSONS.
   11. ASSAULTIVE, PERHAPS SOCIOPATHIC TENDENCIES.
   12. EXCESSIVE SENSITIVITY AND IRRITABILITY.
   13. POSSIBLE HYSTERIA.
   14. LOW IQ'S WHO ARE VERY SUGGESTIBLE AND THEREBY POTENTIAL
       DELINQUENTS.
   15. QUERULOUSLY DEMANDING PERSONS, PERHAPS NARCISSISTS.

******* CF > FC *******                              ** HIGH SIGNIFICANCE **
   16. EMOTIONAL LABILITY AND HYPOMANIA.
   17. EMOTIONAL IMMATURITY AND IMPULSIVE ACTING OUT OF EMOTIONS
       WHICH MAY BE NORMAL IN CHILDREN.
   18. WEAK AFFECTIVE CONTROL WHICH GIVES WAY UNDER STRESS RESULTING
       IN LESS COORDINATED BEHAVIOR.
   19. NEUROTIC MALADJUSTING, PERHAPS HYSTERICAL CONDITIONS.
```

```
******* CF + C > 3 AND > FC *******
  20. WEAK CONTROL OVER EMOTIONAL RESPONSES AND ACTING OUT TENDENCIES
      ESPECIALLY OF AGGRESSIVE BEHAVIOR.
  21. NARCISSISM, EGOCENTRIC IMPULSIVITY.

******* CF + C > 0 AND C' = 0 *******                    ** HIGH SIGNIFICANCE **
  22. SUGGEST POSSIBLE SCHIZOPHRENIC CONDITIONS.


=======================================================================================
SECTION 3                                                              INTERPERSONAL
=======================================================================================

******* SHADING (ACHROMATIC) SHOCK *******
   1. A SIGN OF A DEEP ROOTED PERSONALITY DISTURBANCE.
   2. FREQUENTLY ASSOCIATED WITH AWARENESS OF INADEQUACY AND
      FEAR OF EXTERNAL CONTACTS.
   3. CONTRAINDICATION OF ORGANICITY.

******* KF + K = 0 *******
   4. FREEDOM FROM PHENOMENAL ANXIETY.

******* FK < AVE *******
   5. LOW LEVEL OF AFFECTIONAL ANXIETY.
   6. LOW LEVEL OR LACK OF AWARENESS OF AFFECTIONAL ANXIETY DUE TO
      EFFECTIVE DEFENSES.

******* Fc < AVE *******
   7. REDUCED AWARENESS, REPRESSION AND/OR DENIAL OF THE NEED FOR
      AFFECTION.
   8. UNDEVELOPED NEED FOR AFFECTION, MALADJUSTING, EGOCENTRIC,
      NARCISSISTIC CONDITIONS.
   9. ANXIOUS PERSONS.

******* FM + m > Fc + c +C' *******
  10. INTROVERSIVE TENDENCIES NOT FULLY ACCEPTED BY THE PERSON.
  11. IF IN OPPOSITE DIRECTION OF M:SUM C, THIS POINTS IN THE
      DIRECTION THE PERSONALITY IS SHIFTING.

******* H < AVE *******
  12. IMPAIRMENT OR ABSENCE OF EMPATHY.
  13. SOCIAL ISOLATION, WITHDRAWAL, OR CONSTRAINT IN INTERPERSONAL
      RELATIONS.
  14. IMMATURITY WITH FEELINGS OF VULNERABILITY AND POSSIBLE
      CONFUSION REGARDING SEX ROLE.
  15. IN CHILDREN, AN EMOTIONAL DISTURBANCE, POSSIBLY SCHIZOPHRENIA.
  16. POSSIBLE SCHIZOPHRENIC CONDITIONS WITH POOR PROGNOSIS.

******* DEHUMANIZED (H) *******                          ** HIGH SIGNIFICANCE **
  17. TENDENCIES TO AVOID SOCIAL INTERACTION AND TOWARD SOCIAL
      ISOLATION.
  18. HOMOSEXUAL TENDENCIES, ESPECIALLY WITCHES OR MONSTERS TO
      CARD IX.
  19. SCHIZOPHRENIC CONDITIONS.
  20. IN CHILDREN, IMMATURITY, THOUGH MAY BE WITHIN NORMAL
      DEVELOPMENTAL PROCESSES.


=======================================================================================
SECTION 4                                              SPECIFIC CONTENT/RESPONSE MODE
=======================================================================================

******* ANATOMY CONTENT *******
   1. HYPOCHONDRIACAL TENDENCIES AND GENERAL BODY CONCERN IN ADULTS
      AND CHILDREN, AND IS SEEN IN MANY MALADJUSTING CONDITIONS,
      PARTICULARLY NEUROSES.
   2. AGGRESSIVE AND DESTRUCTIVE IMPULSES WHICH THE PATIENT MAY FEAR.
   3. INTELLECTUAL DEFENSIVENESS WITH POSSIBLE OSTENTATION.
   4. ANXIETY.
   5. CONTRAINDICATIONS OF ACTING OUT OF HOSTILITY AND DESTRUCTIVE IMPULSES.
   6. ANATOMY RESPONSES TO EIGHT OR MORE CARDS SUGGESTS SCHIZOPHRENIA.

******* EYES CONTENT *******
   7. PARTICULARLY IF 'PEERING', OR 'PIERCING', SUGGESTS PARANOID
      INDIVIDUALS INCLUDING 'SUSPICIOUS NORMALS', PARANOID
      SCHIZOPHRENICS, AND PERSONS WITH HOMOSEXUAL TENDENCIES.

******* CONTAMINATION *******
   8. ACUTE PSYCHOSIS, PERSONALITY PATHOLOGY, POSSIBLY SCHIZOPHRENIA
      WITH POOR PROGNOSIS.
   9. BIZARRE THOUGHT PROCESSES.
  10. PRIMITIVE OR ASSAULTIVE MODES OF BEHAVING.
  11. POSSIBLE ACUTE MANIC EXCITEMENT.
  12. POSSIBLE EPILEPTIC CONDITIONS.
```

13. CONTRAINDICATION OF ORGANICITY.
14. IN YOUNG CHILDREN, PERHAPS NORMALITY, BUT ALSO ASSOCIATED WITH
    SIGNIFICANT EMOTIONAL DISTURBANCES.

******* PERPLEXITY *******
15. BRAIN DAMAGE.
16. SCHIZOPHRENIC CONDITIONS WITH POOR PROGNOSIS.

```
=====================================================================================
SECTION 5                                              BLOCKING, SHOCK OR REJECTION
=====================================================================================
```

******* BLOCKING, SHOCK OR REJECTION ON CARD VII *******
1. CONSIDERED THE "MOTHER CARD," BLOCKING MAY SUGGEST VERY CLOSE,
   DIFFICULT, CONFLICTUAL RELATIONS WITH THE MOTHER OR MOTHER
   SURROGATE.
2. NEUROTIC CONFLICT REGARDING SEXUAL ACTIVITY.

```
=====================================================================================
```

                              P A R T   III

                    SUMMARY OF KEYWORD OCCURRENCES
```
=====================================================================================
```

                            KEYWORD SUMMARY TABLE

KEYWORD CATEGORY	MAXIMUM POSSIBLE TESTS	NUMBER POSITIVE TESTS	PERCENTAGE POSITIVE TESTS	HIGH SIGNIF. TESTS	OVERALL PERCENTAGE (weighted)
EGO STRENGTH	22	7	31.82	0	31.82
EMOT. CONTROL/LABILITY ...	18	4	22.22	1	27.78
ANXIETY	30	3	10.00	0	10.00
REPRESSION/CONSTRICTION ..	20	3	15.00	0	15.00
DEPRESSION/SUICIDE	22	1	4.55	0	4.55
PSYCHOSIS	23	5	21.74	1	26.09
ORGANICITY	11	0	0.00	0	0.00

                            KEYWORD SUMMARY GRAPH

KEYWORD CATEGORY   OVERALL PERCENTAGE (weighted)

```
                    0   10   20   30   40   50   60   70   80   90  100+
                    !----!----!----!----!----!----!----!----!----!----!
EGO STRENGTH ............!*****************
EMOT. CONTROL/LABILITY .!**************
ANXIETY ................!*****
REPRESSION/CONSTRICTION !********
DEPRESSION/SUICIDE .....!**
PSYCHOSIS ..............!*************
ORGANICITY ............!
                    !----!----!----!----!----!----!----!----!----!----!
                    0   10   20   30   40   50   60   70   80   90  100+
```

```
                   CENTURY DIAGNOSTICS NARRATIVE SUMMARY            1AUG81
PATIENT ID: GOERING    SEX: M    AGE:              ACCOUNT ID: EXHIBIT
=========================================================================


COGNITIVE FUNCTION:
THIS INDIVIDUAL APPEARS TO HAVE BALANCED INTELLECTUAL AND PERCEPTUAL ABILITY.
HE HAS THE ABILITY TO DEVELOP AN OVERVIEW OF SITUATIONS WHILE SIMULTANEOUSLY
DEALING WITH THE COMMON SENSE ASPECTS OF A PROBLEM.  THERE IS AN ABILITY TO
REACT TO SITUATIONS IN A ROUTINE, DISPASSIONATE AND IMPARTIAL MANNER WHEN
SUCH A RESPONSE IS APPROPRIATE.  THERE IS, HOWEVER, SOME STEREOTYPED THINKING
AND A PAUCITY OF DIVERSIFIED INTERESTS.  THERE ARE ADEQUATE EGO RESOURCES IN
TERMS OF REALITY TESTING.  POTENTIALLY, HE SHOULD BE ABLE TO PERFORM AT A
REASONABLE IMPULSE LEVEL.  HOWEVER, THERE IS A TENDENCY TOWARD DISTORTION IN
REALITY TESTING UNDER THE INFLUENCE OF EMOTIONAL IMPACT.


EMOTIONAL FUNCTION:
THIS INDIVIDUAL EXHIBITS A DEFINITE LACK IN THE ABILITY TO MEET EMOTIONAL NEEDS
IN AN ADAPTIVE, SOCIALLY APPROPRIATE MANNER.  A BREAKDOWN OF EMOTIONAL CONTROLS
IS LIKELY TO BE CHARACTERISTIC.  IMPULSIVENESS, EMOTIONAL LABILITY AND ACTING
OUT TENDENCIES ARE LIKELY TO BE CHARACTERISTIC.  THIS MAY RESULT IN INAPPRO-
PRIATE SEXUAL AND/OR AGGRESSIVE BEHAVIOR.  THE POSSIBILITY OF EXPLOSIVE OUTBURSTS
SHOULD BE CONSIDERED.


INTERPERSONAL FUNCTION:
A POOR ABILITY TO MEET AFFECTIONAL NEEDS THROUGH SOCIALLY APPROPRIATE AND INTER-
ACTION WITH OTHERS IS SUGGESTED.  INTERPERSONAL RELATIONSHIPS ARE LIKELY TO BE
VERY SUPERFICIAL.  THERE IS AN OVERALL REDUCED AWARENESS, REPRESSION AND/OR DE-
NIAL OF AFFECTIONAL NEEDS WHICH MAY RESULT IN AN ABSENCE OF EMPATHY AND IMPAIRED
INTERPERSONAL RELATIONSHIPS.










THIS NARRATIVE SUMMARY IS BASED UPON
THE ACCOMPANYING RORSCHACH REPORT.
IT IS NOT INTENDED AS A SUBSTITUTE
FOR THAT REPORT, WHICH SHOULD BE READ
IN ITS ENTIRETY.
```

more difficult to make the message constructive were it not palatable). John and Mary need to know what the significant factors in their life are. We would guess that they came to therapy knowing that they differ significantly from one another, that in some ways they are rather opposites. Yet it is possible to be encouraging: "This is not insurmountable," "This is not necessarily a problem, however." The approach seems to be to convey the message that John and Mary can maximize themselves and their relationship by realistically understanding the way they are.

December 11, 1981

Mr. and Mrs. John Jones
Street and Number
City, State, Zip

Dear John and Mary:

I hope this letter finds you well. I talked to (my cotherapists) during and
after your work with them in (another city). They informed me that you did
an enormous amount of work and appeared to be moving in a positive direction.
In this letter, I will summarize the results of the conjoint psychological
testing. I will report on each test in turn and offer some concluding remarks.

The juxtaposed Edwards profiles are appended, together with scale definitions.
You will recall that the Edwards is a psychometric instrument that is based
on Murray's needs system. The scores are reported in terms of percentiles,
hence a score at the 50th percentile is higher than about half of the
individuals in the norm group and lower than the other half.

On John's profile we see that the highest need score was for Affiliation; to
be associated with other people, to have friends, and this sort of thing.
We also see high scores on Abasement which reflects a tendency to accept
blame and to take on others' responsibilities. He was relatively high on
Nurturance which is to give nurturance to others, and his steadfastness is
revealed by the high score on Endurance. His Autonomy score was extremely
low which in some ways complements the high Affiliation score although
these scales are largely independent. He also had a relatively low
Dominance score and a low Change score. The Aggressiveness score was very
low suggesting that he avoids expression of hostility and aggression.
Overall, the profile is consistent with what I observed in the feedback
session; a quiet, retiring, gentle man who likes to avoid conflict.

Heterosexuality and Exhibitionism were the two highest scores on Mary's
scale which is consistent with the history of fashion modeling. A model
who doesn't have exhibitionistic needs probably would not do very well.
Further, Mary says that she has gotten along better with men in the past
than with women. The high Heterosexuality score reflects this. She had a
very low Affiliation need score. Very high or very low need scores usually
reflect a transitory emotional state. Mary confirmed that she is very wary
of closeness and lives as a psychological "recluse" out of fear of being
hurt or betrayed.

In comparing the two profiles I saw some possibility for conflict. For
example, the Affiliation scores deviate significantly from the norm and in
opposite directions. The absolute difference between the two scores is very
large. I am sure this would lead to conflict in marriage. Another factor
is that John has fairly high nurturance and succorance needs. Succorance
is the need to receive nurturance. Mary is not especially low on nurturance,
but in comparison to John's high succorance need, we see that John may feel
unsatisfied, unsupported, and generally unnurtured.

The juxtaposed MMPI profiles are appended together with some scale definitions.
Please remember my caution that these scales were labeled according to the
psychiatric norm group and may therefore sound overly pathological.

Mary's profile is that of a woman who hurts very much. This profile reveals
a hurt person, a cautious person, who is probably using an enormous amount of
psychological energy to protect, defend, and project, leaving little for
personal growth or joy. The repressive defenses are not working well and in
view of her accomplishments in life, her self-esteem is really quite low.
When we are hurt our basic defensive strategies tend to become exaggerated.
This is the picture we see before us. One of Mary's defenses is to be angrily
impulsive and another is to resort to externalization and projection. Hence,
we see an exaggerated elevation on the Paranoia scale. This is not exactly
clinical paranoia, but rather a kind of all-seeing, overly sensitive stance
toward life. The "feelers" are out just waiting to get stepped on. The

problem with paranoia is that it tends to feed on itself. The more sensitive
you get the more you find to feed the paranoia. Mary described herself on
the Intake Booklet as a very sensitive person. Sensitivity can be a good
personal trait. While it is desirable to be sensitive regarding other peoples
emotions we have to learn to grow some "alligator skin" around our own
personalities so that we are not easily hurt ourselves.

John's MMPI profile is "ultranormal." The MMPI does not measure normality
except in the statistical sense. Hence, the scores don't mean that he does
not have paranoid or impulsive, or other kinds of traits, it merely reveals
that these traits are closer to the statistical norm.

When comparing the two profiles, the major problem will be that John might
find it hard to empathize with his more emotional, volatile, and sensitive
spouse. This is not insurmountable. Furthermore, we know that Mary is in a
personal crisis at this time and when the crisis begins to resolve her
emotionality will settle considerably.

Now let me turn to the Rorschach. John's Rorschach was that of a man who does
his best to keep his life simple, smooth, and relaxed. Obviously, he is
extremely bright but he does not choose to exercise his mind in emotional
areas. This is not to say that he is not thoughtful. He is very sensitive and
thoughtful. However, his major strategy in life is to keep emotional reactions
under wrap. The Rorschach was consistent with the Sentence Completion
response "When the going gets rough...I get quiet."

The Rorschach suggest that while his "life strategy" helps his stability he
may be cutting himself off from psychological growth in certain areas. Is
it possible to be too stable? Perhaps. Oversimplification of life's complex
problems can lead to as many errors as overreaction. A person can be wrong
in either direction. The Rorschach would suggest that in his attempts to
maintain psychological equilibrium he may be minimally utilizing certain
internal psychological resources such that his problem-solving capability
may become stereotyped and ineffective.

Mary's Rorschach reveals a unique mind. She has an extensive associational
process and the creativity can lead her in two directions. She can either
be very original and clever in perception and problem-solving, or she may be
way "off-base." Interestingly, the Rorschach suggests that both of you may
at times be way off base in dealing with life's problems but for different
reasons; John because he may be overly constricted and Mary because she is
overly reactive.

Mary's Rorschach is that of a highly emotional individual. She has a good
reservoir of psychological strengths but these strengths are not well
organized and may not be particularly accessible to her at this time. With
continued work and treatment, of course, these strengths will become more
available.

On Mary's Rorschach I see many signs of emotional pain including depression
and anxiety. Some of the distress is clearly related to losses in life, but
also thay may be related to some erroneous assumptions about the way life is
to be. I will comment more on this later.

When I look at the Rorschachs together I see two people who are psychologically
very different. This is not necessarily a problem, however. I would suggest
to Mary that she enjoy her looseness. Looseness is not a weakness. It is a
virtue to be built on. I would encourage Mary to think like an artist. Art
is disciplined emotion. The artist must risk and then evaluate dispassionately.
As a legitimate singer, I am an artist of sorts. I am sure you know the
enormous risk of self-esteem that I face everytime that I stand up in front
of anywhere from 1 to 300 people, and wager that both sides of my brain will
work together so that I can get the words and music straight and hope that
the small pieces of gristle in my throat will work the way they did in
practice. When I go to sing I must think that I am the hottest thing going.
I must not doubt myself but when it is all over and I listen to the tape or
go back to my teacher, ego must stay outside the door. I must view the
performance dispassionately; neither being too harsh on myself (if I don't

quite sound like Robert Merrill) or unrealistic in my appraisal of my limitations. John is cautious, guarded, and also stable. While I am encouraging him to explore more the looser side of his nature, I also encourage him to rejoice in his own conservative characteristics as well.

Now let me turn to the TAT. As I mentioned the TAT interpretation is the most speculative aspect of the feedback.

On Card I (which shows the boy looking at a violin) John told a story about a little boy who had been scolded by his teacher. He settles down and doggedly goes on and becomes a very accomplished violinist. Is this the discipline that allowed John to excel? In Mary's story the little boy looked at the violin and seemed to be rather overwhelmed by the strangeness and the magnitude of the task. However, little by little he whittled the task down to something that he felt he could deal with and decided that he would at least try. This may be the way Mary views a lot of things in life. At first they are rather overwhelming but as she uses those strong psychological resources within her she begins to regain her self-confidence and go on.

Card 2 is a pastoral scene which shows a young woman in the foreground and a man plowing the background, and an older woman over on the side. John's story was about the girl in the foreground going on to continue her schooling so that she will hopefully "free her unborn sibling of the farm." The rescue theme is obvious. On the other hand, we see more gloom in Mary's story. The young girl had dreams but now merely becomes "resigned." Accepting life's reality is one thing but, to me, resignation is very depressing. I am enough of a romantic to believe that we can face certain of life's limitations and still reach for magic.

Card 4 depicts a woman clutching the shoulders of a man whose face and body are averted as though pulling away. Ninety percent of the people who respond to this card tell the story about conflict. John, however, chose to project a story in which this man and lady are friends. He is leaving and she is trying to get him to stay. There is no negative affect expressed. When asked what the people feel he responded; "Happy." There is no right answer to these stories but it struck me that John managed to duck out of the potential conflict of this story as he did in response to Card 13 MF (which shows the woman nude to the waist in bed and the man turned away). This card also "pulls" negative emotion. He started a story about a prostitute who overdosed on drugs but after the police were called John focussed on the way in which the hero "covers his eyes" because he has never seen anyone dead. Of course, the man is covering his eyes in the picture but almost no one comments on it. Am I overinterpreting in suggesting that this reflects a great reluctance to see hurt in a person. This may be a major dynamic in the marriage. Let me explain.

John met Mary when she was hurting greatly. He could satisfy his nurturance needs in playing the wonderful professional who took care of Mary's mother and Mary. He protected her and nurtured her. That sounds like a beautiful way to start a marriage but it really isn't because it starts off confirming Mary's vulnerability and weakness. Perhaps Mary has weakness and vulnerability, but she also has strength and toughness.

On the Intake Booklet John said in response to the sentence completion root "I am...what I am." But that is not really true, at least when he is around Mary. John tiptoes around trying not to get Mary mad, trying not to hurt Mary, to avoid conflict etc., etc. I believe this is done because of a genuine concern for her feelings and welfare. But in so doing he diminishes himself and also diminishes Mary. Mary is no longer a patient. John is not Mary's therapist. John has a right to be who he is and to say what he thinks and feels. As long as he continues to squelch who he is he will lessen both himself and Mary. If Mary is upset over what John is feeling that is Mary's problem, not John's. This is a matter of personal space. Mary can grow only when she is given the space to grow. If she feels that John must be this, must be that, should do this, should do that, and he allows her to continue to think that this is true Mary may not grow. He can only genuinely love her when he is honest about who he is. Then she must make a choice

whether to love the reality or not love it. But to try to be something else is
to be a phony. One cannot love an image very long.

I think Mary's response to the last blank card is the most revealing. I will
quote it verbatim.

> I had a dream--I dreamed of a world filled with beauty and love.
> The dream began as it should--or as I had pictured it would. As
> I grew older the dream began to shatter. Some things I once thought
> as beautiful were not so. The things I loved became fewer and fewer.
> Then one day I awoke and found the world could once again be beauti-
> ful and I once again could find much of the love I thought forever
> lost. With each passing year--this time--I clutched dearly the
> beautiful things and the love I at last had again. But at the last--
> even with my constant struggle to hold on dearly--the clouds started
> drifting in one by one covering the beauty and trying to draw up with
> them--the love. The ending is although I feel like it is time to
> put the dreams aside and either drift with the clouds or stay behind.
> I still struggle for my dream.

Mary let me comment on this by quoting from a paper that I am working on.

> Beth's silky black hair tumbles over her boney shoulders in
> defiance of the paralyzing depression that reigns within her.
> Her dark brown eyes plead through long, black lashes. The gaze
> is without malice or strength. Only raw need shows. The concaves
> of her scrawny body are deepened by the skin's olive hue, and its
> frailness describes her ego. Hurt Beth, child Beth, pathetic Beth.
> Her quiet scared eyes scream her loneliness. Though in years an
> adult, she is very young, vulnerable, dependent; afraid like a new
> fawn waiting quietly and anxiously in the woods for its mother to
> return with warm milk.

> Carol comes to us differently. She is arrogant, cocky, and aggressive.
> She doesn't walk, she swaggers. She is cruel, slashing and ripping all
> that crosses her path. Our reaction is to get away from her as fast
> as possible.

> Though different in style, Beth and Carol are very similar. Each is a
> part person, each is unwhole. Each possesses a personality that is
> imperfectly integrated, incomplete and static. Each is starving because
> she cannot drink the milk of love and kindness that is offered. The
> styles differ. Beth regurgitates nourishment, Carol spits it out
> petulantly. The reasons are the same and may be understood in the
> context of personality structure. Parts are split apart; they do not
> function in concert, do not speak to each other; thus they are not
> whole. Carol wrote, "even God didn't deny evil its right to existence--
> he only split it off."

> But did he? John Steinbeck says that "underneath the topmost layers
> of fraility, men want to be good and want to be loved. Indeed most of
> their vices are attempted shortcuts to love."

> God gave us what we are and it sometimes comes out as evil. Jealousy,
> hatred, spitefulness, greed are God-given drives, probably set within
> us to help us survive. To be real we must not deny these parts. Rather
> they must interact with each other.

Beth and Carol were both patients of mine. Another patient whom I will call
Sue once asked me how one attained contentment and a feeling of wholeness in
life--how one overcame the horrible feeling of loneliness that she felt
all the time. She was a pianist and we discussed music. Together we
discovered that a piece of music is only a combination of noise and time.
In its movement it becomes real.

The parts interact in time and become a new whole. To be of beauty it must
have dissonance and resolution. As an art form it must possess and stir

emotion, and not always pretty emotion. The emotion may be hate, rage, fear, sorrow, love, or compassion. There can be no body of art that is mere prettiness. It would not be wholly human, thus it would not be art. There is a place for ugliness in art because art is the reflection of the completeness of life.

But what do we do in our own lives? Do we embrace with equal zest our dull-ness and our nobleness; our stupidity and our faithfulness; our vileness and our compassion; our goodness and our badness? In my experience we do not. We float the pretty parts to the top but we sequester the not so pretty parts. We rarely know each other and thus we find it so hard to truly love each other. One cannot love a part for very long and when we show to the world only the pretty we live in constant fear that the ugly will be discovered and we will lose those whom we love. So we do not risk revealing ourselves and paradoxically we diminish ourselves and our lovers.

Let me tell you about another patient of mine whom I will call Bret. For five years Bret struggled with the terrible conflict. He wanted so badly to live in a world of beauty and gentleness and he wanted so badly to be this himself. Yet there were other parts about him that he despised. You see, the world he saw was a projection of himself, both beautiful and not so beautiful.

On the fifth anniversary of our work together he brought me a butterfly as a graduation present. He no longer needed me. The black and white butterfly was beautiful. The black symbolized what he thought was the evil--the ugly. The white symbolized what he saw as the pure and the good. What he learned was that when put together true beauty emerged. Life is beautiful in its completeness as he came to accept all parts of himself he also came to rejoice in the fullness of his universe.

Bret was very much like the little girl you told about in the TAT whose mother was reading to her. She was daydreaming about "the way she would like it to be." Bret used to think as you expressed in your response to the last TAT card--"the dream began as it should." He embraced the dream with all of his might. He "shouldered" with the tenacity of a bull dog. But when he finally let go of these myths, the true beauty of life emerged. With the butterfly he gave me a card that said "Thank you for your love, your patience, for believing in me, your friendship....but most of all for helping me become the person I am...for freedom!"

Barbara and I extend to you best wishes in your quest to achieve wholeness and true beauty in life together. If you ever wish to discuss any of this please call.

Sincerely,

Darwin Dorr, Ph.D

Darwin Dorr, Ph.D.
Director of Psychological Services

DD:lc

PSYCHOLOGICAL REPORTS AS A GROUP PSYCHOTHERAPY TOOL

Noting recent trends toward an egalitarian relationship between therapist and client, Yalom, Brown, and Bloch (1975) describe a new form of psychological report which facilitates the group psychotherapy process. Similar to the manner in which Fischer (1970), Craddick (1972, 1975), and Mosak and Gushurst (1972) share psychological data with clients, each report, consisting of a summary of the group meeting, is made available to the client prior to the next meeting. The typical report consists of three to seven pages, double spaced, of narrative and commentary. It requires 20 to 40 minutes to dictate and is done immediately following the session. The typed report is then mailed to the clients.

A number of benefits, as perceived either by the therapists or the clients, are described:

1. Revivification of the meeting. A report of the happenings of the meeting refresh the memory and make for continuity between meetings. The next meeting is likely to continue on the theme of the previous one.

2. The participant observer role. In reading the summary report the clients become observers as well as participants in the therapy process. The therapists have an opportunity to repeat interpretations they deem to be important, particularly those that clients may not have adequately attended to because of personal or sociodynamic reasons. Some interpretations are repeated because they are regarded as exceedingly important or exceedingly complex.

3. A second chance. The therapists point out what should have happened in the meeting but didn't, thus encouraging, sometimes goading clients to participate or to follow through.

4. Construction of group norms. The report is used to give structure to the group, a set of rules for the functioning of the group to maximize its effectiveness. Thus, the therapists may focus on the need for here-and-now content, or for the need of the group members to take responsibility for the conduct of the sessions. Certain practices of the group or its members may be questioned, or the members may be criticized.

5. Therapeutic leverage. Important content may be repeated and emphasized. Thus, one client evaded participation by entertaining the other group members. At one point, however, he remarked, "When you see me smiling like this in the group, it means I'm covering up pain; don't let me keep getting away with it." This crucial statement was tagged for reuse.

6. New contributions. The report provides an opportunity for the therapist to offer new observations, clarifications, or interpretations. It may be that the therapist misses certain insights during the session but arrives at them afterward. Or the timing may not have been right to make comments, or a client for various reasons may have been unreceptive. Or the introduction of cognitive material during a crucial experiential period might have been destructive.

7. Transmission of the therapist's temporal perspective. Typically the therapist has a better temporal perspective than the clients who are involved in the here and now of their own problems. The therapist must therefore become the "group historian, the time-binder." Here is what a therapist wrote into a report about a client who failed to grasp the progress she was making:

Delores described the despair she had been experiencing. In some ways it sounded almost identical to the kinds of despair Delores described in the group when she first entered—having to do with loneliness, with the feeling that she always had to ask people to be with her and do things with her, that there was no one in the world who cared about her.

However, there is an important difference in her state now and her condition at that time. Several months ago Delores presented these things as though that's the way the world *was*—that there *was* no one in the world for her. This time she has a more realistic view of it. She realizes that this is the way she is thinking right now. She feels discouraged and angry because she knows that there is so much more work to do. She is upset at the fact that her center of self-regard is not inside but still outside of herself, and that she allows others to define her, to tell her whether she is worthwhile rather than having a stable, internal sense of self-worth. In a sense then, at some level Delores recognizes that she is responsible for her bad feelings about herself, and hence can change these feelings.

8. Therapist self-disclosure. The authors feel strongly that group therapy should be demystified, that their views of the process be disclosed for the purpose of "model setting, deepening the therapist-patient relationship, demonstrating a personal belief in therapy and a trust in the group, and facilitating transference resolution." Faith healing and placebo techniques are shunned as the therapists discuss their "here-and-now feelings in the group—puzzlement, discouragement, pleasure, and annoyance." The following brief excerpt discloses some of the feelings of therapists Dave and Lena:

Dave and Lena both felt considerable strain in the meeting. We felt caught between our feelings of wanting to continue with Delores, but also being very much aware of Bob's obvious hurting in the meeting. Therefore, even at the risk of Delores's feeling that we were deserting her, we felt strongly about bringing in Bob before the end of the meeting.

9. Filling gaps. The report is helpful to clients and therapists in keeping them informed when meetings are missed because of illness or vacations. It is also the authors' impression that new patients enter the group more smoothly if given reports of the three or four previous meetings.

10. The summary as an event in the group. Individual clients react to the reports in their own idiosyncratic manners. For example, there may be paranoid distortions or feelings of rejection when attention is focused on other members of the group. The feelings aroused by the report may then be dealt with in therapy.

11. Therapist uses. The report facilitates the supervisory process as both supervisor and trainee react to the same material. More important, as in the writing of all psychological reports, the very act of writing can help us to shape and sharpen our conclusions. Writing a report—as opposed to an offhand verbal report—can force us to think more about the case. This is of particularly great importance when the writer is also the therapist.

PSYCHOLOGICAL REPORTS IN JOURNAL ARTICLES

To complete this potpourri, we present a variation of use for the psychological report rather than a new form of reporting.

The presentation of case studies in journals is a time-honored method for illustrating the conclusions of an article and sharing basic data with the reader so that the arguments can be followed. The reader acquires a "feel" for the material. Particularly in psychiatric journals is this practice common.

Psychological reports might effectively be used in this manner, yet such use is decidedly rare. Occasionally a psychologist's conclusions are quoted in an article. Generally, however, psychological data are presented on a group basis in tabular form.

The following two of the writer's reports were presented in a psychiatric journal in an article reporting on the postsurgical adjustment of cancer patients in whom colostomies had been constructed.[1] The group data summarizing the authors' conclusions and clinical case material is presented in the classical way. The psychological reports impart a feel and an understanding for the patients' adjustment that cannot quite be achieved by other means.

Illustrative Rorschach Report—No. 1

In a context of severe intellectual and emotional confusion, we see a conflict centering primarily about a life-death struggle within the self, and about bodily integrity, personality integrity, and self-identity. Things somehow do not seem "right" to him as he turns away from the outside world and focuses on himself, especially on his body and its functions. He feels mutilated, dismembered rather than whole, worthless, and as if he is a lower form of life. Specifically, there is attention directed to alimentation, elimination, the rectum, and other bodily features associated with elimination. There is also concern about sex, but its specific relation to this disordered economy is not certain. All of these difficulties, particularly as they relate to body processes are seen as the result of external assault upon him, as if others have unjustifiably done something to him and damaged him. In fact, in his current state of despair, he tends to see others as at fault and he is critical. In this manner, oppositional tendencies which are now quite strong are pushing for expression and he feels they are justifiable.

This inner state of dysphoric turbulence is seen in a loss of spontaneity, in a marked sense of insecurity, helplessness, and uncertainty, and in social relations which are characterized by tentativeness. He is overcautious. Thus, he is remarkably ineffectual and unadaptable, and unable to come to grips with problems. In novel situations or under pressure, his judgment would not be at all reliable. In a personality not comfortably defended against psychosis, the term "paranoid" intrudes itself. The possibility of further regression with depersonalization, depression, and bodily delusions has to be considered.

Illustrative Rorschach Report—No. 2

This person is existing in the context of a rigid, constricted, narrow, unspontaneous approach to daily events. It is this withdrawal from active interaction

---

[1]Illustrative Rorschach Reports 1 and 2 reprinted by permission from Orbach, Charles E., and Tallent, Norman, Modification of perceived body and body concepts following the construction of a colostomy. *Archives of General Psychiatry*, February 1965, 12, 126–135. Copyright 1965, American Medical Association.

with life which may be keeping him on this side of an active psychosis. To demand more of him undoubtedly would precipitate an actual state. His current orientation to life and his very understanding of his existence is through his bodily processes, and his comprehension of threat evidences a severe confusion on a par with the confusion which characterizes his everyday living. He seems to be groping, albeit unconstructively, for some dependable realities in life. In so doing, he constantly gravitates to primitive bodily concerns, to taking in through the mouth, the process of alimentation, elimination, and the nature of anatomical structure. Here anxiety is particularly severe and centers about a deep feeling of bodily loss which leaves him empty, without substance and without life. Sex anxieties have also come to the fore, and he also has concerns about anatomical sex differences which would suggest more the transient mental activity of a boy of 6 rather than a matter of enduring interest in a man of 60. There is the difference, however, that it is internal rather than external anatomy which is sexualized. One gets the feeling that his concern is whether the male or the female is more adequate internally.

8

SUPERVISION OF PSYCHOLOGICAL REPORT WRITING

Considerations and Guidelines for Supervisors and Students

An abundance of studies on the process of clinical supervision does not exist, and to the extent that the process has been studied and reflected upon, the focus has been on the psychotherapy situation. However, some of the conclusions of these efforts appear to have relevance for the assessment function. These are presented along with a supervisory transcript that was selected with both supervisors and students in mind.

AN INTRODUCTION TO THE WRITING OF PSYCHOLOGICAL REPORTS is often presented as an aspect of courses in clinical assessment. Quite logically, however, the important emphasis in such courses is on familiarizing students with many facets of tests—their purpose, rationale, content, administration, and scoring—and with statistical data pertaining to standardization, validity, and reliability. However, the teaching of the final phase—the practical utilization of tests, the development of interpretations, the statements or conclusions that are the substance of the psychological report—is the most demanding of time and concentrated effort.

Different tests (or batteries) require different amounts of time and commitment from a clinician who wants to become competent in deriving conclusions from their use. Klopfer and Kelley (1946) indicate that two or three years of supervised experience are necessary for those who wish to become qualified users of the Rorschach. Another essential factor in the proper interpretation of tests is skillful behavioral observation—the substance of behavior diagnosis, a very important ingredient in neuropsychological assessment and also very important in traditional clinical assessment as material to be integrated with test data.

Such requirements for the gaining of assessment skills demand supervised experience in a work setting. Students who volunteer to "take tests" from fellow students generally provide a more limited range of behaviors compared with the clinically interpretable behaviors displayed by those who are seen professionally. The student is limited largely to basing interpretations on test data or to presenting "test results." Commonly we see the workings of this approach in the format of a listing of interpretive statements with parenthetical addenda. Examples: "Reality testing is poor (F + % = 60), This person is paranoid (MMPI Pa Scale = 80), she tends to think concretely (WAIS-R Similarities = 7)." The reports are excessively test centered, and interpretations might be presented test by test.

An alternative approach might be to ask the student (1) to write a professional report that would be suitable for practical use and (2) to submit evidence, on an appended sheet or sheets, for the statements that appear in the report. The classroom demonstration of the student's ability to use test data must be sharply distinguished from the ability to write a useful, practical report. It is well to inculcate sound report-writing practices early in the course of professional education.

GENERAL GUIDELINES TO
SUPERVISION IN REPORT
WRITING

Research into the writing of psychological reports is a needed but neglected area, neglected, perhaps, because of the longstanding and widespread notion that report writing consists simply of passing along "test results" to readers. Here and there, however, there are research publications and writings related to concepts of supervision and report writing. A chapter on supervision in clinical psychology is available in Schaefer (1981) who is of the opinion that the process of supervision has not been adequately formulated. As a corollary, she observes, "More than likely, the personal and professional attributes of individual supervisors are the most important variables in characterizing supervisory relationships." Siegel and Fischer's (1981) book deals with case recording in the mental health field and might have some implications for psychological case recording. Wilson's (1980) book is addressed to the topic of supervision of social work students with respect to interview material. The approach might be helpful in supervising psychology students as they deal with interview and observational content, as well as with test data.

In contrast with the dearth of concern with research on the supervision of assessment, there has been more activity in the area of psychotherapy. Papers by Beckett (1969), Bush (1969), and Moulton (1969) conceptualize supervision in terms of psychoanalytic insights. Although their conclusions about the dynamics operating in the supervisory process pertain specifically to the supervision of students of psychoanalytic psychotherapy, they appear to hold significance as well for the supervision of students of psychological assessment. Therapy involves continuous assessment of the client in daily life, as well as of client and therapist behaviors in the therapeutic interaction. An important difference is that in most instances in the supervision of report writing, emphasis on the case may be proportionately greater than in therapy supervision where concern with student behaviors may be greater. However, both therapist and assessor "use themselves" in working with clients. There are times when some supervisors deal with issues in the assessor's personality as these appear to detract from learning or effectiveness.

According to analysts such as Beckett, Bush, and Moulton who have made observations on the supervisory process, a number of the operations that are routinely observed in therapy, such as the working (therapeutic) alliance, resistance, transference, countertransference, and identification, are of importance also in the supervisor-supervisee interaction. Historically these issues have been dealt with to the extent that they impede the student's growth as a therapist. There is also widespread belief that supervision should not be structured as personal therapy for the student. Doehrman (1976), for example, concludes from a study carried out in a psychological clinic that the supervisor should not deal with the personality of the supervisee—that is, conduct therapy. Of course, whether intentional or not, it probably is inevitable that supervision frequently has some impact on the life of the supervisee that goes beyond the gaining of technical skills. The supervisor should always be aware of the personal and interpersonal dynamics that exist in the supervisory situation, particularly since these relate to the effectiveness of learning and can have positive or negative personal effect on the student as well.

Beckett (1969), recollecting his personal experiences as a psycho-analytic candidate, spells out some reasons why the supervisor must be alert to psychological happenings in the student just as the therapist must be alert to what is happening psychologically with the client. Beckett also believes that the supervisor must have a good self-awareness since "factors which hinder the development of a working alliance in the supervisory situation may arise from sources in the supervisor or the candidate." He further notes that "transference on the part of the supervisor can also be a hazard."

Howard (1965) also turns a critical eye to the supervisor, in this case the psychological supervisor. He editorializes about a widespread appointment of supervisors who are inadequately trained in supervision or who compromise their duties by such means as failing to observe intern-patient interaction, knowing the patient instead "only through a grammatical check of a written report."

To return to Beckett and his primary focus on the candidate, he is perhaps most helpful in pointing up the role and effects of anxiety in the student. Fear of criticism by the supervisor can lead to unconstructive defensiveness. It is a ". . . mistaken impression that the 'good candidate' (like the 'good patient') has no resistances, no reservations on trust or openness, no crisis of confidence, and no doubts of his adequacy."

Beckett sets forth the hazards of both the direct and the indirect effects of anxiety thusly:

> In the supervisory situation, anxiety may be expressed indirectly through its defensive manifestations, such as competitiveness or excessive self-criticism, or in dependent demands to be directed and told what to do. The candidate's fear can be seen directly as fear of authority, fear of identification with a supervisor, or fear of taking him in, fear of exposing oneself, fear of encountering one's inadequacies or uncertainties. If the supervisor becomes identified in the candidate's mind as someone to be feared, the unexplored transference feelings will result in a climate of fear, which is inimical to learning. The student who apparently refuses to acknowledge that he is a student is like the patient who cannot acknowledge that he is a patient. Both can be regarded not as "unworkable" but as frightened. The candidate's unsureness and fear can also

be seen in his work with the patient as generalized constriction, excessive caution, or timidity in the use of himself. His preferred defensive measures (for example, obsessional concerns with detail, content, and accuracy) will be portrayed both in the treatment situation and in the supervisory sessions.

Bush (1969) also points up various unconstructive measures that the student therapist may be prompted to use and of which the supervisor should be aware. The student may be passive-aggressive or openly rebellious. Some students may display a practiced compliance. From high school and college days, some students appear to retain the maneuver of "psyching the prof."

Like Beckett, Moulton (1969) is also impressed with the destructive role of anxiety in the student and urges that the student be made comfortable. She raises a specific issue in her comment on how a student's dynamics may compromise reports:

> Another problem is that of reporting. Some students are too obsessive to be able to omit irrelevant details; they fail to get to the gist of the interaction with the patient. Other students, afraid to reveal themselves and the sources of their own anxiety in doing treatment, hide behind tapes as well as notes. The patient "comes through" to the supervisor more clearly than does the student.

Moulton views issues stemming from conflicts that many students have in relating to authority figures as a major problem: "Many have been puzzled that, even in a comparatively progressive institute, authority problems continue to interfere with learning." She is particularly concerned that what she calls the "judgmental role" of the supervisor interferes with the supervisor's role of both teacher and therapist (or model).

One may indeed wonder if the supervisory relationship is not too intimate a transaction to permit the supervisor to sit in the role of judge and report back to the authority structure of an institution where the student is in training or to the student's academic department on his or her progress and achievement. Might this requirement, in Moulton's words, lead to "interference with the learning alliance"? Might awareness of being judged in some instances be a cause of student overcompliance or "psyching the prof"?

Another way of focusing on the supervisory process is to inquire about the ways in which learning occurs in the clinical situation. Moulton proposes a triad of influence: imitation, (pedagogic) instruction, and experience. Imitation is worthy of special attention, the phenomenon of imitation learning being well established. Ekstein and Wallerstein (1958) have postulated the phenomenon of "parallel process," the supervisee relationship with the client evidencing imitation of the supervisor's conduct. Doehrman (1976) applied the concept of "mirroring" to describe findings that support the position of Ekstein and Wallerstein.

GOALS, STYLES, AND
METHODS OF SUPERVISION

Goals

Supervision, as understood in the present context, is concerned with the several phases of the assessment process, from the time the psychologist accepts commitment to a mission (1) to the delivery and follow-up of a report, or (2) to the psychologist's personal implementation of the conclusions of the assessment. The model of the process is the schema set forth in Chapter 5, pages 127–129. It is the intent that each learning experience be generalized as a means of increasing the competence of the student in all phases of the assessment and treatment process.

Styles of Supervision in Assessment and Report Writing

Supervisory style reflects a style of life; the demanding person probably becomes a demanding supervisor, the unassertive person probably becomes an unassertive supervisor. Hence students are likely to encounter a range of supervisors who differ in style of relationship as well as in subject matter skills and teaching ability. There is widespread belief that imitation of the supervisor is an important factor in learning, but such imitation likely pertains largely to technical understanding and ways of dealing with the assessment process and reaching and setting forth conclusions.

Cherniss and Egnatios (1977) identify five styles of supervision that to some extent are likely an expression of personal style. However, they also report that supervisors display variation in style. They speak of "an optimal blend of supervision styles" and are of the opinion that "the ideal supervisor probably is one who utilized all five styles depending on the current preference and need of each supervisee." This writer tends to approach a laissez-faire style as the student becomes advanced and gains in competence and confidence.

The five styles of supervision and their definitions as set forth by Cherniss and Egnatios are:

Didactic-Consultative. The supervisor offers advice, suggestions, and interpretations concerning client dynamics and clinical technique.

Insight-Oriented. The supervisor asks questions designed to stimulate the supervisee to think through and solve problems on his or her own.

Feelings-Oriented. This approach encourages the supervisee to question emotional responses to the clinical process.

Laissez-Faire. The supervisor leaves the supervisee alone most of the time and is rarely available for consultation on work problems.

Authoritative. The supervisee is told in specific terms what to do and how to do it.

Of these methods, a sample of clinical staff members interviewed by the authors preferred the *didactic-consultative,* the *insight-oriented,* and *feelings-oriented* approaches over the *laissez-faire* and the *authoritative* styles.

Mechanics of Supervision

Students may be supervised on a one-to-one basis or in small groups. When time permits, group supervision is probably the more effective teaching approach. With this method students who have not participated in the testing of a client may participate in the analysis of data and the formulation of the conclusions that are to become the psychological report. A lively interaction often develops as the supervisor and the students make comments and raise questions concerning the data and the client from whom the data were generated.

To the end that the student gain general competence, each case that is reviewed is regarded as a means for the student to learn firsthand about such matters as personality, skills of various sorts, and psychopathology. The test protocols, in addition to their use in the diagnostic-treatment process, are seen as teaching vehicles. Depending on the availability of time, the supervisor may periodically digress from case formulation to observations of a more general nature, such as test theory, the construction and use of particular instruments, dynamics, psychopathology, implications for treatment, or the history of a particular concept. Presented in the following case is a cursory review of the "wandering womb syndrome," from its apparent formulation in ancient Egypt and through Hippocrates to the present day. This brief exposition was prompted by the fact that the uterus of the patient being assessed evidently was ceaseless in its travels. At times it appears to be worthwhile to note how well a case meshes with (say) Freudian theory or with a client's reinforcement history.

There are several approaches that may be followed to initiate the student in psychological report writing. In addition to assigning the student to read about the principles of report writing and to study some effectively written reports, the supervisor may also suggest that the formulation of the case of Mr. A (pp. 144–151) be studied. The development of this case may serve as a model. The supervisor, if sufficiently comfortable in working in such a manner, and if time permits, may also be a live model, jotting down whatever outline appears to be helpful in guiding the organization of the case material and then, thinking aloud, formulate and write the report in the presence of the student.

Another more commonly used approach is the structuring of the report by the supervisor (while the student typically and busily covers a sheet with notes), suggesting what content should be covered, what content would be inappropriate, and how the report might effectively be organized. Such an approach is essentially authoritative.

The neophyte's introduction to report writing may also be laissez-faire. Particularly when the student is new to the practicum setting and has not studied the principles of report writing or read reports that might serve as models, we have a candidate for a laissez-faire approach. The student is simply asked to write a report that meets the needs of the case that has been assigned. The supervisor at the same time cautions that, as a matter of course, numerous corrections or changes will likely be needed for the revised report. This method appears to be an effective approach to learning; corrections made on the first report seldom need to be made on subsequent reports.

This writer always makes clear to the student, however, that what is being "corrected" follows indications based on a particular orientation to psychological report writing. Other supervisors might have different outlooks. The student ultimately will adapt or adopt the approach that seems to make the most sense, to be most workable, and to meet whatever organizational guidelines, local or national, that are in vogue or prescribed at any given time.

CASE SUPERVISION PRACTICUM

The following material exemplifies this writer's approach to case supervision.

The case under study is the first to be assigned to a newly arrived intern at a medical center. The patient, a 64-year-old woman who had been a practicing registered nurse for a number of years, was referred for psychological assessment for help in "clarification of the psychopathological condition." The referring psychiatrist indicated that the patient disclosed a long history of overdependency on family members and a pattern of generally poor adjustment characterized by difficult, often stormy interpersonal relationships and alcohol abuse (all-day wine drinking on a daily basis). The patient further reported to the psychiatrist that during the past five years her television set has been talking to her [personally]. For example, if the commercial message is to buy X Brand laundry detergent she immediately goes to the store and purchases the product. On admission she was inaccessible to interview or testing for two days. From time to time she screamed so loudly that she could be heard throughout the ward, the content of her screams including such remarks as "Keep away from me," "Stop doing it to me," and "It's awful, it's awful." At other times, she sat wide-eyed in front of the TV screen evidencing no response to what was being shown. The psychiatrist agreed to withhold medication for these behaviors; instead she was talked to sympathetically by ward personnel, which seemed to have a calming effect on her.

On the third day following admission the intern, who had been apprised of this information, approached the patient and found her to be quiet, friendly, and cooperative, even seductive. He administered to her over three sessions a battery based on discussion with the supervisor on what instruments are most likely to be convenient to use and to elicit the sort of data needed to respond to the referral source.

Following testing, the intern scored the tests, requiring some help with the Exner system (1974) to which he had been introduced at his university. The tests were then reviewed with the supervisor in terms of data that might be pertinent to the presenting problem. The intern was then asked to write a report which the supervisor reviewed with him and followed up with suggestions for revision. The revised version of the report required changes too minimal to concern us here.

The supervisory transaction that follows is a pieced-together abstraction taken from a tape. In addition profiles of the patient's MMPI and WAIS-R and her Bender reproductions are presented to make it easier to follow the case. Sufficient of her Rorschach and TAT are quoted to support the interpretations to which they contributed.

Review of Tests and Behavior

SUP.: Well, you have an interesting first case. What do you think of Mrs. J.?

INT.: She asked me to call her Jennifer. Everybody says she's paranoid schizophrenic. The television talks to her. Also, in restaurants she thinks that people must be talking about her because she smokes and she drinks. Dr. Herrold says she has delusions of reference and influence. And all that irrational screaming!

SUP.: We certainly want to consider that diagnosis. We want to look at her personality. What do you find in her test protocols, her clinical behaviors, including your reaction to her, her history? Why don't you start with clinical behavior?

INT.: It's strange. There are a number of strange things about her. Just a couple of days ago she was screaming as though everybody was persecuting her. She wasn't terribly neat, looked like maybe she was coming off of a drunk, her hair wasn't combed. But her son who is staying with her got rid of all the wine about a month ago and kept a close watch on her. He is certain she hasn't had a drink in that time. Now suddenly she is brightened up, has on make-up.

SUP.: How does she relate to you?

INT.: O.K. Nothing psychotic I can see. Very friendly.

SUP.: Ingratiating?

INT.: Yes, definitely.

SUP.: How?

INT.: Her whole manner, body posture, the way she tilts her head to look super attentive. Her speech manner especially. Like the way she would draw out her words, like Yes-s-s?, as though to ask me how she could be more accommodating.

SUP.: Anything else about her?

INT.: Uh, her eyes mainly. Often I would make the most innocuous comment, and she would look at me, wide-eyed, incredulous. Like a child hearing something for the first time that seemed profound. Real childlike. And her eyelids. The way she kept blinking. She didn't look like she could see anything. Her lashes were fluttering like the wings of a hummingbird.

SUP.: Maybe she's had lots of practice. Any other pertinent observations?

INT.: Well, that takes us into the tests. I felt I had to inquire about some of her responses, expecially some of her sentence completions.

SUP.: Good! More interns sin by underinquiring than by overinquiring, to put it mildly. Our test protocols have so many signs pointing to paths of needed information, but too often they just aren't followed. Sentence completions, like many of our instruments, may be considered just an interview anyway. What grabbed your eye?

INT.: Well, maybe I'm a bit voyeuristic. It had to do with sex . . .

SUP.: (Interrupting) That's O.K. Many of us think that clinical psychology, psychiatry, psychoanalysis, in fact the various health fields, are peopled by voyeurs. So apologies out of the way, what did she say about sex?

INT.: Well, mainly . . . well, first she finished the sentence, "When I think of men. . ." with "I feel ashamed." Then the item, "My sex life. . . ." she completed "I don't remember any sex life." That blew my mind. She had mentioned that she had been married and had a son. In fact she made reference to her son on the sentence completion test. So I asked her about it. I asked her, "How is it possible that you were married and had a child with no sex relations?" "I don't know. . .," she said softly with an extended pause at the end. I believed her. She seemed innocent as a young child. I didn't ask her any more questions. Do you suppose she might have a memory problem due to organicity?

SUP.: She might. We certainly should look at the other material with that in mind. That's why I suggested she have a basic brain battery—WAIS, Wechsler Memory Scale, Bender. She is a drinker. (pause) Would you buy repression as a predominating feature? (without waiting for an answer) While we're on the sentences, why don't we see what else she tells us about herself, if she shows other personality features that go with a repressive style? (picks up sentence completion form, rapidly peruses the items, then hands the completions to the intern) Any other indicators of repression?

INT.: In the item about married life she says, "I don't remember it."

SUP.: Quite a problem with memory! What else doesn't she remember?

INT.: About her father she says, "I don't remember him now." About her childhood, "I forget when I was a child."

SUP.: Highly repressed people seem to put out of awareness—quote—bad things. They see no evil, hear no evil, speak no evil. Good replaces bad. Notice how to her a real friend "is just great," how the people over her are "wonderful," how her teachers were "wonderful." It catches my eye fast when I start seeing "great," "wonderful," and other superlatives. Conventional attitudes? Many of her completions deal with the wrongness of smoking and drinking; always she indicates that her behavior is proper, that she strives to be proper and is regretful when she falls short. She indicates that when she has sex relations,—quote—"I feel guilty about it." Some inconsistency in her responses. Now she remembers and she has suffered an acute excacerbation. Return of the repressed? What else is noteworthy about her?

INT.: Well, she seems to be overconscious of appearance. She indicates feeling ashamed—a word she uses quite a bit—of her figure. Not a bad shape, though. Not bad, especially for a 64-year-old woman.

SUP.: Any other outstanding features suggested by this test?

INT.: Dependency. "Someone helps me" is the way she completes the sentence "When the odds are against me. . ."

SUP.: I'm increasingly getting a strong hysterical flavor from the material we've covered so far. I suggest you read Schafer's *Clinical Application of Psychological Tests.* It's on the reading list I gave you a couple of days ago. I suspect that as we review the additional tests we'll see how they relate to Schafer's formulation of hysteria.

INT.: Hysteria? That diagnosis wasn't covered in my studies.

SUP.: No. Neither is "psychopath," but we still frequently use the term. "Hysteria" and "psychopath," once respectable diagnostic terms—before the advent of the DSMs—now are unofficial, orienting terms to classes of psychopathology. When we clearly identify them, we are perhaps in the right church—the right section of DSM-III—but we still have to find the right pew in terms of the client's presenting behavioral criteria, current and historical. "Hysteria" refers to a particular constellation of behaviors, a constellation that has for thousands of years impressed many workers as a useful entity. The Egyptians used it to refer to the emotional symptoms in women that they attributed to the effects of a wandering womb. Hippocrates later adapted the diagnosis which incorporated the Greek name for uterus—*hystera.* Freud was given a hard time early in his career when, following Charcot, he described hysteria in men before the Vienna Medical Society. His medical colleagues were incredulous, one old surgeon challenging his reasoning—or his knowledge of anatomy. How could a man, who doesn't have a uterus, be hysterical? I suspect that "hysterics"—and "psychopaths"—will be around for a long time.

INT.: But what about the schizophrenia, the paranoia?

SUP.: We'll be looking for these things—even though the apparent age of onset of what might be schizophrenic behavior is sixty. We'll be looking for indications of thought disorder. We might even find it appropriate to use two diagnoses to summarize in a few words the condition of this woman—or three. What shall we look at next?

INT.: I need a lot of help with the MMPI. I never saw one like this in school.

SUP.: No, I wouldn't think you'd be likely to obtain such a profile in a setting not dealing with severe psychopathology. It is patently a pathological pattern that we have. Of course, that is our business. . . . Some of the scores on this profile tend to be more extreme than what we found in a number of controlled studies. Typically we find the MMPI pointing in the same direction as that of the rest of the battery and of other data and we prefer to use the instrument in a battery context rather than in isolation. Why not make a stab at what the profile shows?

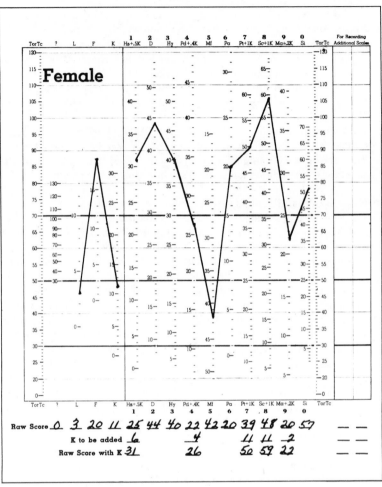

					1	**2**	**3**	**4**	**5**	**6**	**7**	**8**	**9**	**0**		For Recording
TorTc	?	L	F	K	Hs+.5K	D	Hy	Pd+.4K	Mf	Pa	Pt+1K	Sc+1K	Ma+.2K	Si	TorTc	Additional Scales

Female

	TorTc	?	L	F	K	Hs+.5K	D	Hy	Pd+.4K	Mf	Pa	Pt+1K	Sc+1K	Ma+.2K	Si	TorTc
			L	F	K	1	2	3	4	5	6	7	8	9	0	
Raw Score	0	3	20	11	25	44	40	22	42	20	39	48	20	57	—	—
K to be added				6				4			11	11	2		—	—
Raw Score with K				31		26					50	59	22		—	—

INT.: Some of the scales are extreme. The F is the only validity scale that is out of line. There are high psychotic and neurotic scores, and social introversion is high and Mf is extremely low.

SUP.: It is possible, just possible, that the F invalidates the record. Her F-K—9 points—also suggests that she might be faking bad. But we see lots of high Fs here, and they are usually indicative of severe pathology. It is not that infrequent to score Fs that go crashing through the ceiling of the profile. And almost invariably these people are *really* sick. F rises together with 6 and 8, and I don't drop my teeth when 8 pokes through 120 either. In this particular case, looking at the F, 6 and 8, as well as the neurotic triad (pointing), I see a poorly integrated, unstable, readily disorganized person—low ego strength—maybe psychotic, maybe not. She would appear to be highly anxious and depressed (pointing to the triad and 7). Health issues, maybe somatization tendencies, might be part of the psychological picture. If she is hysterical, I wouldn't look for conversations as part of the picture. I would expect probably less depression with conversion, perhaps a "conversion V."

INT.: What about the low Mf—uh—Scale 5?

SUP.: It certainly is exaggerated. A dozen or more characteristics have been related to high or low 5s, but in general we may consider the original meaning, that of how closely the person shows culturally stereotyped male or female patterns. When I see that deeply plunging V in a male profile, the first question that arises is—is this a "macho dip"? Typically it is. I've been at a loss as to what to call the same pattern in a female, but just last week I showed a similar pattern to Ann Marie [another intern], and she suggested "femme fatale." Maybe that's an aspiration that Jennifer has, but in so exaggerated a form, and with all the evident pathology on the profile—and elsewhere— I'm inclined to see Scale 5, too, in a pathological light. She well might view herself as helpless, long-suffering, abused, putting herself down as well as setting herself up to be knocked down—a masochist.

TABLE OF SCALED SCORE EQUIVALENTS*

Scaled Score	Information	Digit Span	Vocabulary	Arithmetic	Comprehension	Similarities	Picture Completion	Picture Arrangement	Block Design	Object Assembly	Digit Symbol	Scaled Score
19	—	28	70	—	32	—	—	—	51	—	93	19
18	29	27	69	—	31	28	—	—	50	41	91-92	18
17	—	26	68	19	—	—	20	20	50	—	89-90	17
16	28	25	66-67	—	30	27	—	—	49	40	84-88	16
15	27	24	65	18	29	26	—	19	47-48	39	79-83	15
14	26	22-23	63-64	17	27-28	25	19	—	44-46	38	75-78	14
13	(25)	20-21	60-62	16	26	24	—	18	42-43	37	70-74	13
12	23-24	18-19	55-59	15	25	23	18	17	38-41	35-36	66-69	12
11	22	17	52-54	13-14	23-24	22	17	15-16	35-37	34	62-65	11
10	19-21	15-16	(47-51)	12	21-22	(20-21)	(16)	14	31-34	32-33	57-61	10
9	17-18	(14)	43-46	11	19-20	18-19	15	13	27-30	30-31	53-56	9
8	15-16	12-13	37-42	10	(17-18)	16-17	14	11-12	23-26	28-29	48-52	8
7	13-14	11	29-36	(8-9)	14-16	14-15	13	8-10	20-22	(24-27)	44-47	7
6	9-12	9-10	20-28	6-7	11-13	11-13	11-12	(5-7)	14-19	21-23	(37-43)	6
5	6-8	8	14-19	5	8-10	7-10	8-10	3-4	(8-13)	16-20	30-36	5
4	5	7	11-13	4	6-7	5-6	5-7	2	3-7	13-15	23-29	4
3	4	6	9-10	3	4-5	2-4	3-4	—	2	9-12	16-22	3
2	3	3-5	6-8	1-2	2-3	1	2	1	1	6-8	8-15	2
1	0-2	0-2	0-5	0	0-1	0	0-1	0	0	0-5	0-7	1

RAW SCORE — VERBAL TESTS / PERFORMANCE TESTS

*Clinicians who wish to draw a profile may do so by locating the subject's raw scores on the table above and drawing a line to connect them. See Chapter 4 in the Manual for a discussion of the significance of differences between scores on the tests.

SUMMARY

	Raw Score	Scaled Score	
VERBAL TESTS			
Information	*25*	*13*	
Digit Span	*14*	*9*	
Vocabulary	*49*	*10*	
Arithmetic	*9*	*7*	
Comprehension	*18*	*8*	
Similarities	*20*	*10*	
Verbal Score		*57*	
PERFORMANCE TESTS			
Picture Completion	*16*	*10*	
Picture Arrangement	*7*	*6*	
Block Design	*12*	*5*	
Object Assembly	*24*	*7*	
Digit Symbol	*39*	*6*	
Performance Score		*34*	

	Sum of Scaled Scores	IQ
VERBAL	*57*	*100*
PERFORMANCE	*34*	*93*
FULL SCALE	*91*	*96*

Ψ **THE PSYCHOLOGICAL CORPORATION**
HARCOURT BRACE JOVANOVICH, PUBLISHERS

9-991829

INT.:   That Si doesn't go with a picture of belle of the ball.

SUP.:   Perhaps in fantasy, but in her social withdrawal her fantasies might also focus unkindly on others. And when she loses control . . . (glances at Bender reproductions).

INT.:   I don't know much about that.

SUP.:   I don't, either. Sometimes we get lots of valuable gratuitous information, but generally I prefer to hold down speculation. I prefer to be conservative, let's say, sticking close to description and generalizing to life circumstances when it seems justified. Do you see evidence for brain dysfunction there?

INT.:   I don't think so.

SUP.:   No constructional dyspraxia?

INT.:   It looks more like carelessness to me.

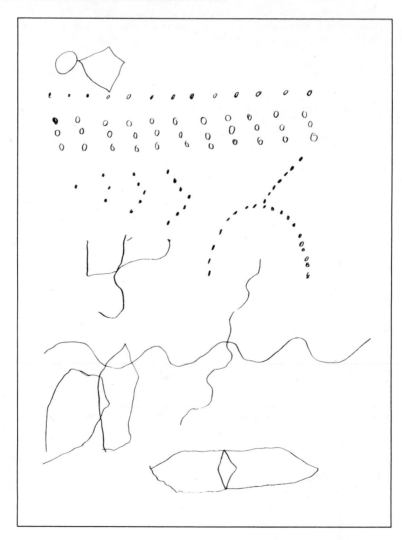

SUP.:   I agree. She runs figures together, substitutes circles or dashes for dots. I'd say the problem is one of impulse control. I'd like to see a testing of limits.

INT.:   How do you test the limits with the Bender?

SUP.:   Just ask her to do it over again with the added instruction, *"This time make the designs just as exact as you can. Make them just like they are on the cards I show you."* I might even ask her to arrange them in a more orderly manner. Sometimes you might wish to try the approach with individual designs, like Figures A and 7 which are distorted. I think she would improve her performance, that she would want to please. I don't think she appreciates the extent of the dyscontrol she exhibited here. (pause) Well, maybe we'll find some evidence for organicity on the WAIS-R and/or the memory scale. And we can also watch for verbalizations or other clues to pathology or personality. Then we can go on to the projectives and tie this case up.

INT.:   From the WAIS profile I think she could be organic.

SUP.:   I think she *could*, too. What's your reasoning?

INT.:   The discrepancy between verbal and performance is almost half a standard deviation. Not necessarily significant but . . . oh oh, I didn't look up the age-corrected scores. Well, she could, but . . . it's not conclusive.

SUP.:   Right. Any deviant or otherwise significant verbalizations?

INT.:   I don't think so.

SUP.:   No, I wouldn't say idiosyncratic. She does think that there are 96 senators, but I wouldn't think it would be hard for her to overlook the addition of two states. She has forgotten events of a more intimate nature. Particularly of an intimate nature. Let's look at the memory scale.

INT.:   An MQ of 86. That could be significant.

SUP.:   What scores or items would you point to?

INT.:   She doesn't know the mayor of Boston. She lived there all her life, and she came here directly from home.

SUP.:   But she knows who the President is, and also the previous President. Could be a matter of selective interest.

INT.:   Logical memory is lousy—only 3 out of 24 memories on the first passage, and one out of 22 on the second.

SUP.:   That is lousy. You should write out the story as related rather than just circling the memory units. Anything significant in the verbalizations?

INT.:   No. The visual reproductions are incomplete, though. She doesn't seem to be able to learn them. The same with associate learning. She can get only one hard association by the third trial. She might be organic.

SUP.:   She might be. It's more or less equivocal. There could be alternative reasons for the failures you point out. But I see nothing that would suggest an organic explanation for all the forgetting in her personal life. I wouldn't think to suggest that we are dealing with an organic amnestic syndrome.

INT.:   I agree.

SUP.:   I look for the Rorschach to help us to clarify, support, refute, or amplify our impressions. (Extends hand and intern passes to him the response sheets, location blots, and scoring summary. Supervisor peruses these for several minutes.) Very interesting. Does the Rorschach suggest psychosis?

INT.:   I wouldn't say so. F+ % is 100. Twenty-seven responses, and it's easy to see all of them.

SUP.:   Yes, 8 populars. What else is outstanding?

INT.:   Her memory problem again. She sees perfectly good responses and on Inquiry says things like "I don't remember saying that." She sees the butterfly on III, and on Inquiry I have to remind her and she just looks blank and responds, "I don't know anything about a butterfly."

SUP.:   No psychosis, I agree, and the hysteria hypothesis is hitting me again. What else in the Rorschach makes me think that?

INT.:   All the flowers?

SUP.:   She does see lots of flowers—seems to lose some distance from the cards as she comments on their prettiness—their display value. She goes into great descriptive detail. Good FC, no CF. Incidentally she is not showing the dyscontrol that she shows on the Bender, for example, and certainly not the dyscontrol that characterized her ward behavior a couple of days ago. But she appears to be paying a price for that by way of bottled-up tension and constriction. An F% of 60, the stretched hide. But do you see an emotional safety valve, any suggestion of her emotional dyscontrol?

INT.:   Not in the responses, but in her initial comments. Like on a number of cards she seemed overwhelmed and blurted out, "O, my goodness," before she could get to the task of giving responses.

SUP.:   Yes, although much of the content seemed to have inherent appeal to her, not stressful. The stereotyped feminine interests we saw on the MMPI, particularly the esthetic element, comes through. Lady slippers, budding flowers. The latter response has been noted in the literature to be related to depression related to a sense of lost youth, a girlhood she cannot recapture and I think she would be ambivalent about doing so. If you recollect the sentence completions she said that when she was younger she was better, but she also reports that she has forgotten her childhood. Her mother, she reports, "was so good to me," and she indicates her dependency in other ways, too, but that only cultivates a good head of hostility. Why do we always say "hostility"? "Hatred" is to the point. To return to the esthetic and her feminine, or should we say hyperfeminine, orientation. Note that on III she does not report that the figures look like women, but rather that they look feminine. On the center D of I she can't quite make out the woman—speculatively because of the sexual connotation and the so frequently reported hips—but she is attracted to the hourglass waist which becomes an hourglass.

INT.:   There are male symbols, too. The cigar on VII and the candle on IX.

SUP.:   Yes, both are hot at the tip. The cigar on VII is inside the female genital area. I don't think she could find any depictions of actual genitals, male or female, if we offered her a good money reward—but we're not going to test the limits there in any manner. It could be upsetting. I'll bet you a nickel that on Card 13MF of the TAT there is no sex scene.

INT.:   I didn't see some of these things and make some of the connections you make.

SUP.:   There is more, but I'm not sure it relates to the mission. I was taken by her three quality M, and I think without all that repression she would also have been able to see the woman on I. Her A% is 65—stereotyped intelligence—and her organizational ability is not much. She falls far short of realizing her intellectual potential. She seems to be paying a heavy price for her repression, her defense of not knowing, not experiencing. What about the TAT? We don't have to take the cards in order. Let's turn to 13MF to see how I make out on that nickel bet.

INT.:   You win. No sex, sickness instead. Wanna hear it?

SUP.:   Sure.

INT.:   Here it is: "O, my goodness. He came into the room and found her on the bed very sick. He can't stand it, doesn't know what to do. She's his sweetheart. Can't stand it. Calls the doctor and gets her help. And she recovers. And they marry and live happily ever after."

SUP.:   It figures. That's her. Helpless, panic, can't stand it, can't face reality. And then they live happily ever after. "Wishing will make it so" is the theme song of hysterics. Sexless, childlike. Does she start every story with an exclamation?

INT.:   No. Let's see. Card 1: Oh; 2: Oh; 3BM: Oh my; 4: Oh; 18GF: Oh my goodness. No introduction to 6GF, 6BM, or the blank card, Card 16.

SUP.:   Why don't you read 16?

INT.:   "I see a beautiful landscape and flowers and trees and children playing. Playing in the sun. And this day the children are very happy playing all the day. They live in a beautiful house and this beautiful yard that they are playing in. They have a beautiful house and a beautiful car. And they all are very happy."

SUP.:   O, to be a child again! Retrogressive fantasy, ambivalence or no ambivalence. Great, wonderful, beautiful. Wishing will make it so. . . . (pause) It's getting close to lunch. May I glance at the other stories? Let's see. On Card 1 the little boy picks up the violin and plays it after she expresses a wish that he play it *for her*. Card 2 reminds her of her childhood. They are a happy family, ". . . they love the land, they love the house, and they all look nice and healthy." There is a happy ending: ". . . and they'll all be happy." 3BM has its tribulations: ". . . Something awful happened. He got in trouble, doesn't know what to do, has no one to help him. I don't think he can do anything for himself so he is sitting there thinking." Someone comes in and helps him, of course, (glances through the several remaining stories) Just variations on a theme—as we so frequently find on the TAT. It would be busywork to review the rest of the productions and redundant to interpret each story.

Summing Up . . .
and Structuring the
Psychological Report

(Note: This is the intern's first case. Supervision is fairly authoritative, although it is also in part *didactive-consultative* and *insight-oriented*. Later reports tended to be increasingly *laissez-faire*. These terms follow Cherniss and Egnatios [1977] and are defined on page 244.)

SUP.:   Let's see if we can pull the case together. We want to present our findings as cogently as possible. We'll have to deal pointedly with the issue of diagnosis because in this case it makes a big difference in treatment if we are dealing with a hysteric as opposed to a schizophrenic. It is a strong point then that Jennifer is in good reality contact—at least now she is—and shows no current loosening of the thought processes. We will have to deal with her apparent delusions, of course, which seem to be the conforming responses of an overly conventional person, an obedient child, if you will—purchasing products as the TV instructs her to do. Her rigid conscience makes her very fearful that others are aware of her obvious smoking and drinking. She does have an intellectual problem, of course, no doubt of long standing, but that is something else. With so much repression she just doesn't have available the resources to deal effectively with matters. Often she can't adequately gain a comprehension of situations, with accompanying inappropriate behaviors—overly passive and conforming, or else undercontrolled. Forgetting, not knowing, not experiencing, is convenient to one of her make-up.

What I'm saying is that we have to deal with this woman's personality if we are to make sense out of her behaviors and be able to set forth convincingly just what is wrong with her and what treatment she needs. We have to show that she is naive, childlike, helpless, and ineffectual; that she is prone to panic; and that she is very dependent and help seeking. She therefore emphasizes conforming behaviors in her quest for support. This tends to build socially negative impulses that are waiting to burst forth when her frustration tolerance is exceeded. We saw some of that in exaggerated form.

Her more usual behaviors are more benign. She emphasizes appearance, seeks to display a soft, helpless, esthetic, feminine self. So we see a soft-spoken, eyelash-fluttering woman who seeks to be seductive, who is self-conscious about her figure, while at the same time adopting an asexual—or even antisexual—stance. She must be—quote—good, must externalize her sense of evil. She does have sexual promptings—deeply repressed.

She is poorly integrated, readily disorganized—behaviorally obvious features. But we mustn't overlook her subjective state. She is anxious, she is depressed. She hasn't the gratifications either of a child—which she yearns to be and cannot, really—or of a woman.

You should make some recommendations. I don't think she needs medication. Look at the response she has made in a couple of days without any. What does she need?

INT.:   She did well with interpersonal support. I think that's basic.

SUP.:   Yes, including guidance, which is essentially a supportive measure. The idea of growth sounds good, but I think that any significant growth, if not beyond her grasp, would be difficult to attain. Maintenance and stability seem to be more realistic goals, at least in the short run.

Do you think you can get all this down on paper, a little better organized than my—uh—after-lunch, off-the-cuff ramblings?

INT.:   I think so. But what about her psychotic behavior? Shall we list that as part of the diagnosis, have a dual diagnosis?

SUP.:   I don't think that's necessary. Hysterical behavior can be pretty disorganized, bizarre and seemingly incomprehensible. In trying to make the point for hysteria, I have overlooked the formal diagnosis. It is *histrionic personality disorder*. The gospel according to Saint Robert [Spitzer] recognizes that transient psychotic symptoms may occur in people who are given this diagnosis. After a while a clinician in a setting such as this feels more comfortable with—quote—three-day schizophrenias. I think before you start your report it would be good to read up on the histrionic personality in the DSM. (hands manual to intern) . . . Oh, I almost forgot. The question of organicity—that we raised. I think we should mention it though it is equivocal. This issue might be a matter of future—if not present—concern.

Don't try to be perfect. I don't expect it. I expect I'll be asking you to make some changes—that's par for the course. And the changes I will propose are based on my own frame of reference. Another psychologist might not see fit to make the changes I suggest, but might ask for different changes.

The Psychological Report

October 25, 1982

Battery: Rorschach, TAT, Sacks Sentence Completions, MMPI, Bender, WAIS-R, Wechsler Memory Scale, I

Clinical Behavior

Jennifer, a 64-year-old divorced, Caucasian female who was admitted to this hospital on October 18, 1982, coming here directly from her home in Boston where she has been living with her only child, a 44-year-old widower, was referred for clarification of her psychopathological condition. A registered nurse who has not been employed for many years, Jennifer was born and raised in Boston, the third of seven children, and she has lived there all her life. On admission she was very paranoid and was disorganized and screaming for several days. She was quite calm and cooperative when I approached her for testing, however. She is rather attractive for her age, well built, and wearing make-up. At times when I was not interacting with her for the moment, she looked straight ahead, wide-eyed, with an appearance of incredulity (or confusion?). At other times her eyelashes went into a rapid flutter as she looked at the examiner. She was very cooperative, ingratiating, and seeking to please. This was seen in affected speech with drawn out words like Yes-s-s-s. . . .

Intellectual Aspects

Jennifer is of average intelligence, which represents below optimal functioning. Her WAIS-R Full Scale IQ is 96, her Verbal IQ is 100, and her Performance IQ is 93. There is much scatter. She has a good fund of information, but her ability to do arithmetic tends to be poor. Most of her other verbal abilities are average. She is poor in understanding novel situations, in visual-motor learning, and in grasping abstract designs.

Personality

Jennifer is a very immature, naive, dependent, childlike person who resists growing up. She accomplishes this through the heavy use of repression which leads to forgetting, helplessness, and poor ability to understand situations. These results of repression in turn lead to ineffectual behaviors and sometimes to inappropriate behaviors. She would rather live in a fantasy world while presenting to others a facade of conventionality and conformity. Typically she appears to be very "feminine"—as she understands femininity—that is, passive, nonassertive, soft, helpless, esthetic, and attractive, a "good," "decent" person who "properly" finds sex repugnant, and, with the help of repression, literally unthinkable. This defense covers deep, hostile feelings that at times are under-controlled. This was evident in the frequent shouting which occurred during her first two days of hospitalization, and was the expression of an emotionally unstable, readily disorganized person.

Her outward behaviors are an expression of a disturbed inner state. She is wrestling with strongly experienced sexual urges that she cannot recognize nor acknowledge because of repression. She is also distressed over her inability to attain meaningfulness or gratification either as a woman or from her infantile role in life. She experiences much anxiety and depression. She would want to resolve the problem of being neither woman nor child by fully returning to childhood, but she has mixed feelings about this solution that she senses is impossible. She will have to continue to indulge her childhood strivings in fantasy.

Jennifer's response to the TV are like those of a hypersuggestible and obedient child. Her impression that others talk about her smoking and drink-ing, which are "bad" behaviors in her frame of reference, seem to be prompt-ings of her sense of remorse. But she does not appear to be at all distressed by these experiences. Nor does she appear to be particularly concerned about her memory problems. These do not appear to be due to organicity which, if present, is a mild and minor factor. Her memory problems more likely are a hysterical phenomenon. She does not exhibit a schizophrenic pattern at all.

Diagnostic Impression

Histrionic Personality Disorder

Recommendations

This woman needs sympathy and guidance. Supportive psychotherapy is rec-ommended, at least in the short run. The achievement of stability and subse-quent maintenance are necessary. To seek to effect growth probably is not realistic.

Supervisory Review of the Report

SUP.:   How did it go?

INT.:   O.K. My biggest problem was getting it to hang together.

SUP.:   (Reads the report) You appear to have treated the essential content well. With an integrated approach and the dropping of some nonessential detail, I think we will have an effective, hard-hitting report, somewhat shorter and easier for the reader to deal with. The bulk of my comments pertain to the early part of the report—it gets better as it goes along. A few of my comments will be rather minor, perhaps only a matter of personal preference. For example, reference to the patient as "Jennifer." I know she asked you to address her that way, but for a formal record . . . she's not a child.

With an integrated report you could do away with separate headings for the diagnostic impression and the recommendations, but that's O.K. as is—they logically follow from the body of the report.

The section on clinical behavior includes more than clinical behavior. There is personal information such as age and the fact that she is Caucasian. There is historical data, where she was born and raised, her appearance, and so forth. Much of this is duplication. Her age, for example, is recorded in many places throughout the clinical folder—in fact it is already on the consultation sheet on which your report will be typed. It is well known that Jennifer is female and Caucasian. How information about where she was born and raised, her living circumstances, her profession might be useful, particularly as the *psychologist's* contribution, is not clear. It is the psychologist's function to contribute in the role of psychologist unless in the role of another professional, as one who takes the history or prepares an integrated summary, for example—in which case the psychological report should still stand as a psychological report. Any material certainly is fair game if it contributes to the psychological understanding of the person. For example, if age or race or the city where born contributes to this objective, it should be integrated into the report—just as some of the material at the end of the section on clinical behavior has contributed to your report. The fact that she is wearing make-up might be a very significant observation. Very depressed or regressed and disorganized women may neglect the application of make-up. I recollect a drug ad in a psychiatric journal several years ago showing a woman sitting on a hospital bed, the legend reading, "Today she put on make-up for the first time."

All in all, this section provides me with a déjà vu experience.

I get a déjà vu experience also from the section labeled "Intellectual Aspects." Very stereotyped format and approach to content. I'm not sure how her intelligence level or relative strengths and weaknesses as measured by the WAIS contributes to our understanding or treatment of the patient's pathology. I know that neither Dr. Herrold nor anyone else on the ward team will make anything out of the test talk. We administered the WAIS primarily to help to determine whether brain dysfunction might play a significant role in the patient's problem.

I find little to criticize in the remainder of the report. It's to the point. This largest section well might be headed "Psychological Report"—which would include as much about intellectual functioning as might be pertinent. Reported here, of course, would also be noncognitive aspects of personality and behavior as inferred from intellectual functioning. I would suggest that most of the behavioral material at the end of the section on "Clinical Behavior" would be valuable if integrated with your conclusions by way of illustration.

How does that sound?

INT.:   O.K. They told me you like reports that are shorter, more compact, and better integrated than what we usually see.

The Revised Psychological Report

October 26, 1982

Battery: Rorschach, TAT, Sacks Sentence Completions, MMPI, Bender, WAIS-R, Wechsler Memory Scale, I

Psychological Report

Ms. J. is a very immature, naive, dependent, childlike person who resists growing up. This orientation comes about through the heavy use of repression which leads to forgetting that with which she is unable to cope. She presents herself as helpless with poor ability to understand her situation. Impressing as a child in many ways, her childlike stance is frequently expressed in a wide-eyed stare of incredulity (or confusion?). Such results of repression in turn lead to ineffectual, and sometimes inappropriate behaviors. She lives in a fantasy world while seeking to present a facade of conventionality and conformity.

I find Ms. J. to be very cooperative, ingratiating, and seeking to please. Her conforming tendencies are seen in an unusual way in a manner that is very cooperative and ingratiating, especially in affected speech with a solicitous tone. Thus, the drawing out of certain words, such as Yes-s-s-s . . . on first approaching her with "Ms. J.?"

Typically she appears to be very "feminine." An unusually rapid eyelash flutter as she looks at me is carried to the point of dramatic caricature. She is passive, nonassertive, "soft" in manner and speech, helpless, esthetic, and striving to be attractive, a "good," "decent" woman who "properly" finds sex repugnant and, with the help of repression, literally unthinkable.

This public self covers deep, hostile feelings that at times become under-controlled and very public. The frequent and loud shouting observed during her first two days of hospitalization exemplifies such tendencies. Such behavior is the expression of an emotionally unstable, readily disorganized person. However, for the time being she appears to have reconstituted somewhat. She expresses concern over her appearance and is wearing freshly applied make-up.

Ms. J.'s response to the TV may be compared to the behavior of a hypersuggestible and obedient child. Her impression that others talk about her smoking and drinking, which are "bad" behaviors in her frame of reference, seem to be the promptings of a sense of remorse. But she currently does not appear to be distressed by these experiences. Nor does she appear to be particularly concerned about her memory problems. These do not appear to be due to organicity, which, if present, is a mild and minor factor. Her memory problems more likely are a hysterical phenomenon. She does not exhibit a schizophrenic pattern at all.

Diagnostic Impression: Histrionic Personality Disorder

Recommendations: This woman needs sympathy and guidance. Supportive psychotherapy is recommended, at least in the short run. The achievement of stability and subsequent maintenance is indicated. To seek to effect significant growth probably is not realistic.

APPENDIX A

A Guide to Checking
the Report

The following Quality Check of the Psychological Report is based on the cardinal principles of report writing that are set forth in the text. It may be used by the student independently as an approach to reviewing the adequacy of reports. It may also be used by the supervisor and the student together as an instructional tool.

The items are worded in a general or inclusive way. Different discrete shortcomings may point up problems in particular aspects of report writing. It should also be pointed out that judgment based on experience is helpful in responding to the items. Some clinical acumen is needed, for example, in deciding whether a report meets ethical and legal responsibilities, or whether it is too speculative.

FIGURE 8-4   Quality Check of the Psychological Report

	Yes	No
Does the report meet all responsibilities, ethical and legal, to the client, and to the community, and, as applicable, to other professionals and agencies?	☐	☐
Is the completion of the report timely?	☐	☐
Is the report properly focused in terms of the reason for assessment, data on the client, and a frame of reference?	☐	☐
Does the content unnecessarily duplicate that of others? (Is there encroachment on the established role of other professions?)	☐	☐
If raw data are presented, is the material also interpreted or used for illustration?	☐	☐
Is all appropriate illustrative material presented?	☐	☐
Is all of the content relevant and significant?	☐	☐
Is content presented with appropriate emphasis?	☐	☐
Are diagnoses, prognoses, and recommendations given as necessary?	☐	☐
Is all other essential material included?	☐	☐
Is interpretation sufficiently focused (not too general, differentiating among clients)?	☐	☐
Are conclusions adequately supported by data?	☐	☐
Is speculation within reason?	☐	☐
Is speculation properly labeled as such?	☐	☐
Are all interpretations within acceptable levels of responsibility?	☐	☐

	Yes	No
Is the report written so as to be meaningful and useful?	☐	☐
Are exhibitionistic, authoritative, or similarly offensive statements avoided?	☐	☐
Is the report client oriented rather than test oriented?	☐	☐
Are concepts that are too theoretical or too abstract avoided?	☐	☐
Is word usage appropriate (absence of jargon, stereotyped, esoteric, overly technical, or complex language)?	☐	☐
Is the language used clear and unambiguous?	☐	☐
Is the report too long (padded, redundant, rambling, unfocused, offering useless content, or in the manner of a "shotgun approach")?	☐	☐
Is the style appropriate for the mission, the setting, and for those who may read it?	☐	☐
Is the report logically and effectively organized?	☐	☐
Are the conclusions of the report set forth without hedging?	☐	☐
Is the report adequately persuasive in terms of needs and forcefulness of the data?	☐	☐

APPENDIX B

RECOMMENDED READINGS

Adjunctive text and reference works may be assigned by the instructor or supervisor as helpful in learning the assessment–report writing function. The author has found the following titles of value for the purpose, but other works might also be appropriate.

General Reference Works

AMERICAN PSYCHIATRIC ASSOCIATION. *Diagnostic and Statistical Manual of Mental Disorders (DSM-III)*. Washington, D.C.: American Psychiatric Association, 1980.

DSM-III is *the* official diagnostic classification used in psychiatric settings and by psychiatrists in private practice. It is also widely recognized outside the psychiatric profession. Psychologists who render services in collaboration with psychiatrists or where psychiatric authority is recognized must be familiar with the classification and be able to use it with facility.

CAMPBELL, R. J. (Ed.). *Psychiatric Dictionary* (5th ed.). New York: Oxford University Press, 1981.

This dictionary is the leading source of technical definitions used by psychiatrists and allied professionals whose work is related to psychiatry. Psychologists use many psychiatric terms, and overlap in the vocabularies of psychologists and psychiatrists makes a good psychiatric dictionary a valuable reference work for psychological report writers.

CHOCA, J. *Manual for Clinical Psychology Practicums*. New York: Brunner/Mazel, 1980.

"The purpose of this *Manual* is to provide practical and easily understandable guidelines." Presented in outline form, there is an abundance of information on such topics as basics of clinical practice, diagnosis, record keeping, and treatment. The student psychologist might occasionally consult the manual when "working up" a case.

ENGLISH, H. B., & ENGLISH, A. C. *A Comprehensive Dictionary of Psychological and Psychoanalytic Terms*. New York: D. McKay, 1958.

Obviously, a quarter century brings many changes in scientific and professional terminology. But what this work loses in obsolescence it more than compensates for in scholarliness that often provides information and shades of meaning not to be found in any other current psychological dictionary.

PARASHAR, O. D. *Dictionary of Special Education*. Freeport, N.Y.: Educational Activities, Inc., 1977.

This dictionary is most likely to be useful to school psychologists and others working with handicapped children. Definitions are clear and minimally technical. In addition to psychological terms there are numerous entries pertaining to handicapped children, terms concerned with such matters as medical and neurological disorders.

WILKENING, H. E.   *The Psychology Almanac.* Monterey, Calif.: Brooks/Cole, 1973.
Containing a broad spectrum of psychological information, the approximately 150 pages of psychological terms contain numerous scholarly, authoritative entries.

WOLMAN, B. B. (Ed.).   *Dictionary of Behavioral Science.* New York: Van Nostrand Reinhold, 1973.
"The motto of the Dictionary is *Concision and Precision.*" Involving the collaboration of almost a hundred distinguished behavioral scientists and covering such diverse areas as genetics, psychopathology, educational psychology, industrial psychology, and psychiatry, we are inclined to expand the motto to include *comprehensive.*

And . . . A good dictionary of the English language.

Assessment

BARLOW, D. H. (Ed.).   *Behavioral Assessment of Adult Disorders.* New York: Guilford, 1981.
"This book, unlike most of its predecessors, is not a book on how to do behavioral assessment, listing the various procedures available at this time and the philosophies underlying them. The purpose of this book is to provide an up-to-date, state-of-the-art description of the assessment procedures and strategies for the most common adult clinical problems. . . ."

BECK, S. J.   *Rorschach's Test, Vol. 3: Advances in Interpretation.* New York: Grune & Stratton, 1952.
Beck first presents his views on personality as gained from clinical observation and experience with the Rorschach. He then illustrates the functioning of actual persons as seen in the Rorschach. Whether or not one is working in the context of Beck's "system," to follow this expert's interpretation of data can be nothing but an enriching experience. His approach can be considered a model.

BECK, S. J.   *Rorschach's Test, Vol. 1: Basic Processes* (3rd ed.). New York: Grune & Stratton, 1961.
Administration of the Rorschach is presented following Hermann Rorschach's view of his test as an *experiment* or *experimental procedure.* The remainder of the book sets forth and explicates Beck's scoring system.

CONE, J. D., & HAWKINS, R. P.   *Behavioral Assessment: New Directions in Clinical Psychology.* New York: Brunner/Mazel, 1977.
The focus of this book is on concepts, principles, and issues in behavioral assessment and is in contrast to books centered about specific assessment approaches and their application to problem areas that may be behaviorally assessed.

CRONBACH, L. J.   *Essentials of Psychological Testing* (3rd ed.). New York: Harper & Row, Pub., 1970.
An excellent basic text covering the principles and applications of testing. Much information is given on a number of selected instruments. Professionals, as well as students, might have occasion to consult this work.

DAHLSTROM, W. G., WELSH, G. S., & DAHLSTROM, L. E.   *An MMPI Handbook: Clinical Interpretation, Vol. I* (Rev. ed). Minneapolis: University of Minneapolis Press, 1972.
This book is a comprehensive guide to the clinical use of the MMPI, with considerable attention given to administration, scoring and profiling, procedures for coding and configural analysis, interpretative considerations, and

questions of validity. Various of 15 appendixes may from time to time be useful.

EXNER, J. E., JR.   *The Rorschach: A Comprehensive System.* New York: John Wiley, 1974.

EXNER, J. E., JR.   *The Rorschach: A Comprehensive System, Vol. II: Current Research and Advanced Interpretation.* New York: John Wiley, 1978.

This integrated system as set forth in this and the previous listing, in the words of Exner, draws on the "best of the Rorschach," i.e., on the contributions of a number of distinguished workers, particularly Beck, Klopfer, Hertz, and Piotrowski. Emerging is a new system of scoring and interpretation that has won wide acceptance even though this has meant considerable homework for instructors schooled in one of the earlier systems. A number of useful tables are included.

GILBERT, J.   *Interpreting Psychological Test Data, Vol. 1: Test Response Antecedent.* New York: Van Nostrand Reinhold, 1978.

Test performance, scores, and relationships among scores are listed along with possible interpretations on the basis of cited research. Instruments for which data are reported are the Bender-Gestalt, human figure drawing, the WAIS, and the Rorschach.

GILBERT, J.   *Interpreting Psychological Test Data, Vol. II: Behavioral Attributes Antecedent.* New York: Van Nostrand Reinhold, 1980.

Personality characteristics and behaviors are associated with test performance, scores, and relationships among scores on the basis of cited research. Instruments for which data are reported are the Bender-Gestalt, human figure drawing, the WAIS, and the Rorschach. The presentation is the reverse of the arrangement of test data to interpretation which is the format of Gilbert, Vol. I (see preceding).

GOLDEN, C. J., HAMMEKE, T. A., & PURISCH, A. D.   *A Manual for the Luria-Nebraska Neuropsychological Battery* (Rev. ed.) Los Angeles: Western Psychological Services, 1980.

This very practical work holds the complete instructions for administration of all 269 items of the battery. The chapter on interpretation deals with rationale and offers specific guidelines to the clinical diagnosis of brain dysfunction.

GRAHAM, J. R.   *The MMPI: A Practical Guide.* New York: Oxford University Press, 1977.

The title of this book sums up its content and its goals, which it meets nicely. A student unfamiliar with the MMPI who studies this book will gain a working knowledge of the instrument, from its format and content through administration, scoring, profiling, and interpretation. Special features include discussions of a number of research scales and the use of computerized reports.

HUTT, M. L.   *The Hutt Adaptation of the Bender-Gestalt Test* (3rd ed.). New York: Grune & Stratton, 1977.

Hutt's work shows how "The Bender," a test of developmental level, can also be used effectively to gain data on a wide variety of personality features. Useful information concerning psychotic disorganization, depressed mood, elevated mood, anxiety, compulsivity, impulsivity, and negativism commonly is disclosed. The instrument frequently can be used as an aid to the diagnosis of brain dysfunction.

LEZAK, M. D.   *Neuropsychological Assessment.* New York: Oxford University Press, 1976.

Lezak writes, "I have tried to make *Neuropsychological Assessment* the kind of comprehensive sourcebook in neuropsychology that psychologists and clinicians in the neurosciences need for training students for *communicating about the*

psychological aspects of brain dysfunction and for their practice and research."
(emphasis supplied) A practically oriented text, the author deals with basic
neuropsychological concepts, with neuroanatomy and the relation of brain to
behavior, with diagnostic issues, and with a number of the instruments used in
neuropsychological assessment.

LURIA, A. R. [*The Working Brain: An Introduction to Neuropsychology*] B. Haigh,
(trans.). New York: Basic Books, 1973.

The contributions of this distinguished psychologist linking brain to behavior provide a basis for the enlightened practice of neuropsychology.

MASH, E. J., & TERDAL, L. G. *Behavioral Assessment of Childhood Disorders.* New
York: Guilford, 1981.

Following an extensive introduction to behavioral assessment of childhood
disturbance are 15 chapters addressed to the assessment of classes of disorder.
These are grouped under four general headings: "Externalizing Disorders"
(e.g., hyperactivity, conduct disorders), "Internalizing Disorders" (e.g., anxiety
and depression), "Developmental Disorders" (e.g., autism, learning disabilities,
psychosexual problems), and "Health-Related Disorders" (e.g., obesity, seizure
disorders, elimination problems).

MATARAZZO, J. D. *Wechsler's Measurement and Appraisal of Adult Intelligence* (5th
ed.). New York: Oxford University Press, 1972.

Although Matarazzo's discussion of the Wechsler-Bellevue and the WAIS
are not fully pertinent to the WAIS-R, certain features retain their value (e.g.,
content of the newer instrument is similar to that of its predecessors and the
implications for understanding personality functioning to be gained from the
W-B, the WAIS, and the WAIS-R are also similar). Matarazzo's views on
intelligence and its assessment provide a good background for understanding
the intellect of one's clients.

MILLON, T. *Disorders of Personality: DSM-III, Axis II.* New York: John Wiley, 1981.

Personality disorder is one of the several major categories of psychopathology recognized in DSM-III. To comprehend Millon's discourse is to
master, to a significant degree, the concept of personality, its function and its
dysfunction. Such basic insights are also helpful for understanding other
classes of disorder. Covering the topic of personality disorder in much greater
detail than the DSM, which is essentially atheoretical, adynamic, and not
focused on developmental issues, this book presents views on all of these topics.

MILLON, T. *Millon Clinical Multiaxial Inventory.* Minneapolis: National Computer
Systems, 1982.

This manual provides valuable information to those who use reports based
on the Millon Clinical Multiaxial Inventory (MCMI).

OGDON, D. P. *Psychodiagnostics and Personality Assessment: A Handbook* (2nd ed.). Los
Angeles: Western Psychological Services, 1981.

Test performance, scores, and relationships among scores are related to
possible interpretations on the basis of cited research. Instruments reported on
are the Wechsler scales, the Rorschach, projective drawings, and the Bender-
Gestalt.

RAKOFF, V. M., STANCER, H. C., & KEDWARD, H. B. *Psychiatric Diagnosis.* New
York: Brunner/Mazel, 1977.

This book is *about* psychiatric diagnosis rather than a definitional approach
such as is found in the DSM. Psychologists and students in psychiatric settings
are better equipped to make assessments in the psychiatric idiom when they are
familiar with the problems that are involved.

RAPAPORT, D., GILL, M. M., & SCHAFER, R. *Diagnostic Psychological Testing*
(Rev. ed., R. R. Holt, Ed.). New York: International Universities Press, 1968.

In what has been called a "labor of love," Holt has revised and made more usable the 1945 (Vol. I) and 1946 (Vol. II) work that laid the basis for a tradition and orientation in psychological assessment. Particularly helpful are approaches to the uses of such tests as the Rorschach, the TAT, and the adult Wechsler scale (Rapaport et al. used the then-extant Wechsler-Bellevue Scale, but their manner of using this instrument is applicable to the WAIS-R).

REITAN, R. M., & DAVISON, L. A. (Eds.).   *Clinical Neuropsychology: Current Status and Applications*. Washington, D.C.: V. H. Winston, 1974.

This book, covering both general and specific topics in neuropsychology, may serve as a textbook and as a reference source. Much of the book is focused on issues of brain dysfunction in children. Some specific problems addressed are the application of neuropsychological techniques to mentally retarded and epileptic patients. Tests and batteries are discussed in an appendix.

RUSSELL, E. W., NEURINGER, C., & GOLDSTEIN, G.   *Assessment of Brain Damage: A Neuropsychological Key Approach*. New York: John Wiley, 1970.

The focus of this book is the Halstead-Reitan Neuropsychological Battery. In 100 pages the authors deal with description and rationale of the battery, validation, and the neuropsychological keys—i.e., a key for localizing brain damage and indicating the degree of lateralization of brain damage, and a "process" key to determine the *type* of brain damage. The latter key sorts assessment results into four categories: (a) no brain damage, (b) acute brain damage, (c) static brain damage, and (d) congenital brain damage. Norms and procedures for scoring brain dysfunctional behaviors are supplied.

SCHAFER, R.   *The Clinical Application of Psychological Tests: Diagnostic Summaries and Case Studies*. New York: International Universities Press, 1967.

Originally published in 1948, this book will remain invaluable for the foreseeable future. The diagnostic labels used do not accord well with current nomenclature, the Bellevue Scale (W-B,I) that is much discussed is the grandfather of the WAIS-R, and the Sorting Test that he routinely included in his battery is not one of our leading instruments today, but the grasp of psychopathology and the approach to understanding it that Schafer displays point up a savoir-faire and a paradigm that can serve the modern psychological assessor well.

SHAPIRO, D.   *Neurotic Styles*. New York: Basic Books, 1965.

Disregard the publication date of this book. Its topic is *neurosis*, a term that does not receive high billings in DSM-III but that is very much entrenched in clinical practice and in cultural lore. The several neuroses with which Shapiro deals have very real referents both in clinical symptoms and in everyday behavior. He focuses on four neurotic "styles": the obsessive-compulsive, the paranoid, the hysterical, and the impulsive. His formulations can be a solid contribution to insight into many problems of assessment.

SMALL, L.   *Neuropsychodiagnosis in Psychotherapy* (Rev. ed.). New York: Brunner/Mazel, 1980.

Small alerts the reader to the prevalence—possibly widespread prevalence—of brain dysfunction in clients who are being treated with psychotherapy. Often the relationship between brain dysfunction and the presenting symptom may be inferred only from "soft signs." Although treatment of neuropsychological symptoms is not far advanced, the assessor's determination that brain dysfunction is contributing to a psychological problem may have implications for making recommendations for *psychotherapy*.

WEBB, L. J., DI CLEMENTE, C. C., JOHNSTONE, E. E., SANDERS, J. I., & PERLEY, R. A.   *DSM-III Training Guide*. New York: Brunner/Mazel, 1981.

The neophyte in clinical assessment is not the only one in need of training in formal ("official") diagnosis. Seasoned clinicians, too, sometimes are confused, and many have been sent scurrying to such training guides as that produced by Webb et al. This work contributes to understanding the DSM-III system, which is a sharp departure from the two earlier DSMs. The focus is on practical application. It is endorsed by Robert Spitzer, the chief architect of DSM-III.

WIRT, R. D., LACHAR, D., KLINEDINST, J. K., & SEAT, P. D.   *Multidimensional Description of Child Personality.* Los Angeles: Western Psychological Services, 1977.

This manual provides valuable information to those who use reports based on the Personality Inventory for Children (PIC).

REFERENCES

ABEL, G. G., & BLANCHARD, B. B.   The role of fantasy in the treatment of sexual deviation. *Archives of General Psychiatry*, 1974, *30*(4), 467–475.

AFFLECK, D. C., & STRIDER, F. D.   Contribution of psychological reports to patient management. *Journal of Consulting and Clinical Psychology*, 1971, *37*(2), 177–179.

ALEXANDER, F.   The dynamics of psychotherapy in the light of learning theory. *American Journal of Psychiatry*, 1963, *120*, 440–448.

ALLEN, F. H.   *Psychotherapy with children.* New York: W. W. Norton & Co., Inc., 1942.

ALLEN, J. G.   The clinical psychologist as a diagnostic consultant. *Bulletin of the Menninger Clinic*, 1981, *45*(3), 247–258.

ALLPORT, G.   *Personality: A psychological interpretation.* New York: Holt, 1937.

AMERICAN PSYCHIATRIC ASSOCIATION.   *Diagnostic and statistical manual, mental disorders.* Washington, D.C.: American Psychiatric Association, 1952.

AMERICAN PSYCHIATRIC ASSOCIATION.   *Task force report no. 5: Behavior therapy in psychiatry.* Washington, D.C.: American Psychiatric Association, 1973.

AMERICAN PSYCHIATRIC ASSOCIATION.   *Diagnostic and statistical manual of mental disorders* (3rd ed.) (DSM-III). Washington, D.C.: American Psychiatric Association, 1980.

AMERICAN PSYCHOLOGICAL ASSOCIATION.   Shared results and open files with the client: Professional irresponsibility or effective involvement? Annual Meeting, Washington, D.C., September 1971.

AMERICAN PSYCHOLOGICAL ASSOCIATION.   Ethical principles of psychologists. *American Psychologist*, 1981, *36*(6), 633–638.

ANONYMOUS.   Encounter group change measured by POI and CPS. *Educational and Industrial Testing Service Research and Development*, 1973, *1*(8), 1–4.

APPELBAUM, S. A.   Science and persuasion in the psychological test report. *Journal of Consulting and Clinical Psychology*, 1970, *35*(3), 349–355.

APPELBAUM, S. A.   Psychological mindedness: Word, concept, and essence. *International Journal of Psychoanalysis*, 1973, *55*, 35–46.

APPELBAUM, S. A.   *The anatomy of change.* New York: Plenum, 1977.

ARANOW, E., & REZNIKOFF, M.   Application of projective tests to psychotherapy: A case study. *Journal of Personality Assessment*, 1971, *35*(4), 379–393.

ARAOZ, D. L.   The thematic apperception test in marital therapy. *Journal of Contemporary Psychotherapy*, 1972, *5*, 41–48.

AUGER, T.J.   Mental health terminology—A modern Tower of Babel? *Journal of Community Psychology*, 1974, *2*(2), 113–116.

BARLOW, D. H. (Ed.).   *Behavioral assessment of adult disorders.* New York: Guilford, 1981.

BECK, S. J.   *Rorschach's test, Vol. 3: Advances in interpretation.* New York: Grune & Stratton, 1952.

BECK, S. J.   *Rorschach's test, Vol. I: Basic processes* (3rd ed.). New York: Grune & Stratton, 1961.

BECKETT, T.   A candidate's reflections on the supervisory process. *Contemporary Psychoanalysis*, 1969, *5*(2), 169–179.

BERNE, E.   *Games people play.* New York: Grove Press, 1964.

BERSOFF, D. N.   Professional ethics and legal responsibilities on the horns of a dilemma. *Journal of School Psychology,* 1975, *13*(4), 359–376.

BLANK, L.   *Psychological evaluation in psychotherapy: Ten case histories.* Chicago: Aldine, 1965.

BLOCK, J.   *The Q-sort method in personality assessment and psychiatric research.* Springfield, Ill.: Chas. C Thomas, 1961.

BONJEAN, C. M., & VANCE, G. G.   A short form measure of self-actualization. *Journal of Applied Behavioral Science,* 1968, *4*(3), 299–312.

BRADLEY, G. W., & BRADLEY, L. A.   Experimenter prestige and feedback related to acceptance of genuine personality interpretations and self-attitude. *Journal of Personality Assessment,* 1977, *41*(2), 178–185.

BREGER, L.   Psychological testing: Treatment and research implications. *Journal of Consulting and Clinical Psychology,* 1968, *32*(2), 178–181.

BRODSKY, S. L. (Chair).   Shared results and open files with the client. *Professional Psychology,* 1972, *3*(4), 362–364.

BROWN, E. C.   Assessment from a humanistic perspective. *Psychotherapy: Theory, Research and Practice,* 1972, *9*(2), 103–106.

BROWN, E. C., & SMITH, W. H.   Measurement of existential mental health: Further exploration. *Journal of Individual Psychology,* 1968, *24,* 71–73.

BUGENTAL, J. F. T.   Humanistic psychology: A new break-through. *American Psychologist,* 1963, *18*(9), 563–567.

BUGENTAL, J. F. T.   Psychodiagnostics and the quest for certainty. *Psychiatry,* 1964, *27*(1), 73–77.

BUSH, G.   Transference, countertransference and identification in supervision. *Contemporary Psychoanalysis,* 1969, *5*(2), 158–162.

CAMPBELL, R. J. (Ed.)   *Psychiatric Dictionary, 5th ed.* New York: Oxford University Press, 1981.

CARR, A. C.   Psychological testing and reporting. *Journal of Projective Techniques and Personality Assessment,* 1968, *32*(6), 513–521.

CARRIER, N. A.   Need correlates of "gullibility." *Journal of Abnormal and Social Psychology,* 1963, *66*(1), 84–86.

CARTER, L. T., CARUSO, J. L., LANGUIRAND, M. A., & BERARD, M. A.   *The thinking skills workshop: A cognitive skills remediation manual for adults.* Springfield, Ill.: Chas. C Thomas, 1980.

CAUTELA, J. R.   Behavior therapy and the need for behavioral assessment. *Psychotherapy: Theory, Research and Practice,* 1968, *5*(3), 175–179.

CAUTELA, J. R., & UPPER, D.   A behavioral coding system. *Presidential address presented by Dr. Cautela at Annual Meeting of the Association for the Advancement of Behavior Therapy,* Miami, December, 1973.

CAUTELA, J. R., & UPPER, D.   Behavioral analysis, assessment, and diagnosis. *Proceedings of the Fifth Annual Brocton Symposium on Behavior Therapy, April 22, 1974.* Nutley, N.J.: Roche Laboratories, 1974.

CERNEY, M. S.   Use of the psychological test report in the course of psychotherapy. *Journal of Personality Assessment,* 1978, *42*(5), 457–463.

CHERNISS, C., & EGNATIOS, E.   Styles of clinical supervision in community mental health programs. *Journal of Consulting and Clinical Psychology,* 1977, *45*(6), 1195–1196.

CHOCA, J.   *Manual for clinical psychology practicums.* New York: Brunner/Mazel, 1980.

CIMINERO, A. R., CALHOUN, K. S., & ADAMS, H. E.   Chapter 1. Behavioral assessment: An overview. In *Handbook of Behavioral Assessment.* New York: John Wiley, 1977.

CLEVELAND, S. E.   Letter to VA Director of Mental Health and Behavioral Science Service. *Newsletter of Association of VA Chief Psychologists*, Nov. 12, 1980.

COHEN, L. J.   The unstated problem in a psychological testing referral. *American Journal of Psychiatry*, 1980, *137*(10), 1173–1176.

COHEN, R. J.   *Malpractice: A guide for mental health professionals*. New York: Free Press, 1979.

COLE, J. K., & MAGNUSSEN, M. G.   Where the action is. *Journal of Consulting Psychology*, 1966, *30*(6), 539–543.

COMTOIS, R. J., & CLARK, W. D.   A framework for scientific practice and practitioner training. *JSAS Catalog of Selected Documents in Psychology*, 1976, *6*, 74 (Ms. No. 1301).

CONE, J. D., & HAWKINS, R. P.   *Behavioral assessment: New directions in clinical psychology*. New York: Brunner/Mazel, 1977.

CONRAD, H. S.   The validity of personality ratings of preschool children. *Journal of Educational Psychology*, 1932, *23*, 671–680.

CRADDICK, R. A.   Humanistic assessment: A reply to Brown. *Psychotherapy: Theory, Research and Practice*, 1972, *9*(2), 107–110.

CRADDICK, R. A.   Sharing oneself in the assessment procedure. *Professional Psychology*, 1975, *6*(3), 279–282.

CRONBACH, L. J.   *Essentials of psychological testing* (3rd ed.). New York: Harper & Row, Pub., 1970.

CUADRA, C. A., & ALBAUGH, W. P.   Sources of ambiguity in psychological reports. *Journal of Clinical Psychology*, 1956, *12*, 108–115.

DAHLSTROM, W. G., WELSH, G. S., & DAHLSTROM, L. E.   *An MMPI handbook: Clinical interpretation, Vol. I* (Rev. ed.). Minneapolis: University of Minnesota Press, 1972.

DAILEY, C. A.   The practical utility of the psychological report. *Journal of Consulting Psychology*, 1953, *17*, 297–302.

DANA, R. H.   Eisegesis and assessment. *Journal of Projective Techniques*, 1966, *30*(3), 215–222.

DANA, R. H., HANNIFIN, P., LANCASTER, C., LORE, W., & NELSON, D.   Psychological reports and juvenile probation counseling. *Journal of Clinical Psychology*, 1963, *19*(3), 352–355.

DAVENPORT, B. F.   The semantic validity of TAT interpretation. *Journal of Consulting Psychology*, 1952, *16*, 171–175.

DE COURCY, P.   The hazard of short-term psychotherapy without assessment: A case history. *Journal of Personality Assessment*, 1971, *35*, 285–288.

DENGROVE, E.   Practical behavioral diagnosis. In Lazarus, A. A. *Clinical behavior therapy*. New York: Brunner/Mazel, 1972.

DILLON, C. A., & WILDMAN, R. W., II.   The psychologist in criminal court. *The Clinical Psychologist*, 1979, *32*(2), 16–18.

DOEHRMAN, M.J.G.   Parallel processes in supervision and psychotherapy. *Bulletin of the Menninger Clinic*, 1976, *40*, 9–104.

DOLLARD, J., & MILLER, N. E.   *Personality and psychotherapy*. New York: McGraw-Hill, 1950.

DOLLIN, A., & REZNIKOFF, M.   Diagnostic referral questions in psychological testing. *Psychological Reports*, 1966, *19*, 610.

DORR, D.   Conjoint psychological testing in marriage therapy: New wine in old skins. *Professional Psychology*, 1981, *12*(5), 549–555.

EKSTEIN, E. R., & WALLERSTEIN, R. S.   *The teaching and learning of psychotherapy*. New York: Basic Books, 1958.

ENGLISH, H. B., & ENGLISH, A. C.   *A comprehensive dictionary of psychological and psychoanalytical terms.* New York: Longmans, Green and Co., 1958.

EXNER, J. E., JR.   *The Rorschach systems.* New York: Grune & Stratton, 1969.

EXNER, J. E., JR.   *The Rorschach: A comprehensive system.* New York: John Wiley, 1974.

EXNER, J. E., JR.   *The Rorschach: A comprehensive system, Vol. II: Current research and advanced interpretation.* New York: John Wiley, 1978.

FARBER, S. D.   *Neurorehabilitation: A multisensory approach.* Philadelphia: W. B. Saunders, 1982.

FEE, F. A., ELKINS, G. R., & BOYD, L.   Testing and counseling psychologists: Current practices and implications for training. *Journal of Personality Assessment,* 1982, *46*(2), 116–118.

FEIN, L. G. (Ed.).   Current status of psychological diagnostic testing in university training programs and in delivery of service systems. *Psychological Reports,* 1979, *Monograph Supplement* 2-V44, *44*, 863–879.

FENSTERHEIM, H.   The initial interview. In A. A. Lazarus, *Clinical behavior therapy.* New York: Brunner/Mazel, 1972.

FILER, R. N.   The clinician's personality and his case reports. *American Psychologist,* 1952, 7, 336.

FINNEY, J. C.   The MMPI as a measure of character structure as revealed by factor analysis. *Journal of Consulting Psychology,* 1961, *25,* 327–336.

FISCHER, C. T.   The testee as co-evaluator. *Journal of Counseling Psychology,* 1970, *17*(1), 70–76.

FISCHER, C. T.   Paradigm changes which allow sharing of "results" with the client. *Professional Psychology,* 1972, *3*(4), 364–369.

FLESCH, R.   *Say what you mean.* New York: Harper & Row, Pub., 1972.

FLESCH, R.   *The art of readable writing* (25th anniversary ed.). New York: Harper & Row, Pub., 1974. (Originally published, 1949.)

FLOYD, W. A.   The use of the MMPI in marital counseling and research. *Journal of Family Counseling,* 1974, *2,* 16–21.

FORER, B. R.   The fallacy of personal validation: A classical demonstration of gullibility. *Journal of Abnormal and Social Psychology,* 1949, *44,* 118–123.

FOSTER, A.   Writing psychological reports. *Journal of Clinical Psychology,* 1951, *7,* 195.

FRENCH, T.   Interrelations between psychoanalysis and the experimental work of Pavlov. *American Journal of Psychiatry,* 1933, *12,* 1165–1203.

FREUD, S.   [On beginning the treatment. Further recommendations in the technique of psycho-analysis.] In E. Jones, & J. Riviere (Trans.), *Collected Papers, Vol. II.* New York: Basic Books, 1959. (Originally published, 1913.)

GARFIELD, S. L.   *Introductory clinical psychology.* New York: Macmillan, 1957.

GARFIELD, S. L., HEINE, R. W., & LEVENTHAL, M.   An evaluation of psychological reports in a clinical setting. *Journal of Consulting Psychology,* 1954, *18,* 281–286.

GILBERT, J.   *Interpreting psychological test data, Vol. I: Test response antecedent.* New York: Van Nostrand Reinhold, 1978.

GILBERT, J.   *Interpreting psychological test data, Vol. II: Behavioral attribute antecedent.* New York: Van Nostrand Reinhold, 1980.

GLASER, R.   The future of testing: A research agenda for cognitive psychology and psychometrics. *American Psychologist,* 1981, *36*(9), 923–936.

GOLDEN, C. J, HAMMEKE, T. A., & PURISCH, A. D.   *A manual for the Luria-Nebraska Neuropsychological Battery* (rev. ed.). Los Angeles: Western Psychological Services, 1980.

GOLDFRIED, M. R., & KENT, R. N.   Traditional vs. behavioral personality assessment: A comparison of methodological and theoretical assumptions. *Psychological Bulletin*, 1972, *77*, 409–420.

GOLDFRIED, M. R., & POMERANZ, D. M.   Role of assessment in behavior modification. *Psychological Reports, 1968, 23,* 75–87.

GOLDSTEIN, G.   Some recent developments in clinical neuropsychology. *Clinical Psychology Review,* 1981, *1* (2), 245–268.

GOODKIN, R.   Some neglected issues in the literature on behavior therapy. *Psychological Reports,* 1967, *20,* 415–420.

GRAHAM, J. R.   *The MMPI: A practical guide.* New York: Oxford University Press, 1977.

GRAYSON, H. M., & TOLMAN, R. S.   A semantic study of concepts of clinical psychologists and psychiatrists. *Journal of Abnormal and Social Psychology,* 1950, *45,* 216–231.

GREENE, R. L.   Student acceptance of generalized personality interpretations: A reexamination. *Journal of Consulting and Clinical Psychology,* 1977, *45,* 965–966.

GREENE, R. L.   Can clients provide valuable feedback to clinicians about their personality interpretations?: Greene replies. *Journal of Consulting and Clinical Psychology,* 1978, *46*(6), 1496–1497.

GREENSPOON, J., & GERSTEN, C. D.   A new look at psychological testing from the standpoint of a behaviorist. *American Psychologist,* 1967, *22*(10), 848–853.

HACKER, S. L., GAITZ, C. M., & HACKER, B. C.   A humanistic view of measuring mental health. *Journal of Humanistic Psychology,* 1972, *12*(1), 94–106.

HAMMER, E., & PIOTROWSKI, Z. A.   Hostility as a factor in the clinician's personality as it affects his interpretation of projective drawings (H-T-P). *Journal of Projective Techniques,* 1953, *17,* 210–216.

HAMMITT, K. B.   Does your patient understand? The implications of functional illiteracy. *Frontiers of Psychiatry,* 1982, *12*(1), 14.

HAMMOND, K. R., & ALLEN, J. M.   *Writing clinical reports.* Englewood Cliffs, N.J.: Prentice-Hall, 1953.

HARROWER, M., VORHAUS, P., ROMAN, M., & BAUMAN, G.   *Creative variations in the projective techniques.* Springfield, Ill.: Chas. C Thomas, 1960.

HARTLAGE, L. C., FREEMAN, W., HORINE, L., & WALTON, C.   Decisional utility of psychological reports. *Journal of Clinical Psychology,* 1968, *24*(4), 481–483.

HARTLAGE, L. C., & MERCK, K. H.   Increasing the relevance of psychological reports. *Journal of Clinical Psychology,* 1971, *27,* 459–460.

HEADRICK, L. B.   From W. O. Hadlock, Engineer as author. *RCA Engineer,* August-September, 1956.

HERSEN, M.   Complex problems require complex solutions. *Behavior Therapy,* 1981, *12,* 15–29.

HINKLE, J. E., NELSON, S. E., & MILLER, D.   Psychological test usage by psychologist psychotherapists in private practice. *Psychotherapy: Theory, Research and Practice,* 1968, *5*(4), 210–213.

HOLT, R. R.   Diagnostic testing: Present status and future prospects. *Journal of Nervous and Mental Disease,* 1967, *144*(6), 444–465.

HOLTZMAN, W. H.   Recurring dilemmas in personality assessment. *Journal of Projective Techniques and Personality Assessment,* 1964, *28*(2), 144–150.

HOLZBERG, J., ALLESSI, S. L., & WEXLER, M.   Psychological case reporting at psychiatric staff conferences. *Journal of Consulting Psychology,* 1951, *5,* 425–429.

HOWARD, A.R.   Training is the best teacher. *Journal of Clinical Psychology,* 1965, *21* (2), 231–232.

HOWE, H. E., JR.   Description and application of an evaluative scheme for assessment from a decision-making perspective. *Journal of Clinical Psychology*, 1981, *37*(1), 110–117.

HUTT, M. L.   *The Hutt adaptation of the Bender-Gestalt test* (3rd ed.). New York: Grune & Stratton, 1977.

IVNIK, R. J.   Uncertain status of psychological tests in clinical psychology. *Professional Psychology*, 1977, *8*(2), 206–213.

JACKSON, D. E.   The effect of test taking on acceptance of bogus personality statements. *Journal of Clinical Psychology*, 1978, *34*(1), 63–68.

JOHNSON, W.   The degree of extensional agreement among twenty psychologists in their use of the labels "hypothesis," "theory," and "law." *Iowa Academy of Science*, 1945, *52*, 255–259.

JONES, N.   *Letter to the Membership of the Society for Personality Assessment*, Nov. 30, 1978.

KANFER, F. H., & PHILLIPS, J. S.   *Learning foundations of behavior therapy.* New York: John Wiley, 1970.

KELLER, C. W.   *Characteristics of Rorschach interpreter types: An exploratory study.* Unpublished doctoral dissertation, Texas Tech University, 1971.

KELLY, E. L.   Clinical psychology—1960; A report of survey findings. *Newsletter, Division of Clinical Psychology of the American Psychological Association*, 1961, *14*, 1–11.

KING, R. D., & LELI, D.   Teaching mental health and law: A reply to Goldenburg. *Professional Psychology*, 1979, *10*(6), 771–772.

KLOPFER, B., & DAVIDSON, H. H.   *The Rorschach technique: An introductory manual.* New York: Harcourt Brace Jovanovich, 1962.

KLOPFER, B., & KELLEY, D. M.   *The Rorschach technique: A manual for a projective method of personality diagnosis.* New York: Collins Publishers, 1946.

KLOPFER, W. G.   Principles of report writing. In B. Klopfer, M. D. Ainsworth, W. G. Klopfer, & R. R. Holt (Eds.), *Developments in the Rorschach techniques, Vol. I: Technique and theory.* New York: Collins Publishers, 1954.

KLOPFER, W. G.   *The psychological report.* New York: Grune & Stratton, 1960.

KLOPFER, W. G.   The blind leading the blind: Psychotherapy without assessment. *Journal of Projective Techniques and Personality Assessment*, 1964, *28*(4), 387–392.

KORNER, I. N.   Test report evaluation. *Journal of Clinical Psychology*, 1962, *18*, 194–197.

KOTCHEN, T.   Existential mental health: An empirical approach. *Journal of Individual Psychology*, 1960, *16*, 174–181.

KUBIE, L. S.   Relation of the conditioned reflex to psychoanalytic technique. *Archives of Neurology and Psychiatry*, 1934, *32*, 1137–1142.

KUBIE, L. S.   Critique and comment: Pavlov, Freud and Soviety psychiatry. *Behavioral Science*, 1959, *4*, 29–34.

KUDER, G. F.   *Kuder Preference Record.* Chicago: Science Research Associates, 1948.

LACEY, H. M., & ROSS, A. O.   Multidisciplinary views on psychological reports in child guidance clinics. *Journal of Clinical Psychology*, 1964, *20*(4), 522–526.

LACHAR, D., & GDOWSKI, C. L.   *Actuarial assessment of child and adolescent personality: An interpretive guide for the personality inventory for children profile.* Los Angeles: Western Psychological Services, 1979.

LACKS, P. B., HORTON, M. M., & OWEN, J. D.   A more meaningful and practical approach to psychological reports. *Journal of Clinical Psychology*, 1969, *25*, 383–386.

LAMBLEY, P.   The dangers of therapy without assessment: A case study. *Journal of Personality Assessment*, 1974, *38*(3), 263–265.

LAYNE, C.   Relationships between the "Barnum Effect" and personality inventory responses. *Journal of Clinical Psychology*, 1978, *34*(1), 94–97.

LAYNE, C.   The Barnum effect: Rationality versus gullibility? *Journal of Consulting and Clinical Psychology*, 1979, *47*(1), 219–221.

LAYNE, C., & ALLY, G.   How and why people accept personality feedback. *Journal of Personality Assessment*, 1980, *44*(5). 541–546.

LAZARUS, A. A.   Multimodal behavior therapy: Treating the "basic id." *Journal of Nervous and Mental Disease*, 1973, *156*, 404–411.

LAZARUS, A. A.   *The practice of multimodal therapy*. New York: McGraw-Hill, 1981.

LEVY, J., & EPSTEIN, N. B.   An application of the Rorschach test in family investigation. *Family Process*, 1964, *3*, 344–376.

LEVY, L.   *Psychological interpretation*. New York: Holt, Rinehart, & Winston, 1963.

LEZAK, M.   *Neuropsychological assessment*. New York: Oxford University Press, 1976.

LOVELAND, N. T., WYNNE, L. C., & SINGER, M. T.   The family Rorschach: A new method for studying family interaction. *Family Process*, 1963, *2*, 187–215.

LUNNEBORG, P. W.   *Vocational Interest Inventory (VII), Manual*. Los Angeles: Western Psychological Services, 1981.

LURIA, A. R.   [*The working brain: An introduction to neuropsychology*] (B. Haigh, Trans.). New York: Basic Books, 1973.

McGARRY, A. L.   Proof of dangerousness—Medical or legal burden? Paper read at "Who is Competent? Who is Responsible?" Sponsored by the University of Louisville, Clarkesville, Indiana, April, 1976.

MANNING, E. J.   "Personal validation": Replication of Forer's study. *Psychological Reports*, 1968, *23*, 181–182.

MARMOR, J.   Dynamic psychotherapy and behavior therapy. *Archives of General Psychiatry*, 1971, *24*, 22–28.

MASH, E. J., & TERDAL, L. G.   *Behavioral assessment of childhood disorders*. New York: Guilford, 1981.

MASLING, J.   The influence of situational and interpersonal variables in projective testing. *Psychological Bulletin*, 1960, *57*(1), 65–85.

MATARAZZO, J. D.   Postdoctoral residency program in clinical psychology. In Conference Committee. *Preconference materials prepared for the Conference on the Professional Preparation of Clinical Psychologists*, pp. 71–73, American Psychological Association, Washington, D.C., 1965.

MATARAZZO, J. D.   *Wechsler's measurement and appraisal of adult intelligence* (5th ed.). New York: Oxford University Press, 1972.

MATARAZZO, J. D.   Obituary: David Wechsler (1896–1981). *American Psychologist*, 1981, *36*(12), 1542–1543.

MAY, R., ANGEL, E., & ELLENBERGER, H. F.   *Existence*. New York: Basic Books, 1958.

MAYMAN, M.   Style, focus, language and content of an ideal psychological test report. *Journal of Projective Techniques*, 1959, *23*, 453–458.

MEEHL, P. E.   Wanted—A good cookbook. *American Psychologist*, 1956, *11*, 263–272.

MEEHL, P. E.   The cognitive activity of the clinican. *American Psychologist*, 1960, *15*, 19–27.

MIALE, F. R., & SELZER, M.   *The Nuremberg mind*. New York: Quadrangle/The New York Times Book Co., 1975.

MILLER, E.   Psychological intervention in the management and rehabilitation of neuropsychological impairments. *Behavior Research and Therapy*, 1980, *18*, 527–535.

MILLON, T.   Disorders of personality: DSM-III, Axis II, New York: John Wiley, 1981.

MILLON, T.   *Millon Clinical Multiaxial Inventory*. Minneapolis: National Computer Systems, 1982.

Thanks!

KDE/Tgb

MILLON, T., GREEN, C. G., & MEAGHER, R. B., JR.   The MBHI: A new inventory for the psychodiagnostician in medical settings. *Professional Psychology,* 1979, *10*(4), 529–539.

MILLON, T., GREEN, C. G., & MEAGHER, R. B. JR.   *Millon Behavioral Health Inventory.* Minneapolis: National Computer Systems, 1982.

MINTZ, J.   Survey of student therapists' attitudes toward psychodiagnostic reports. *Journal of Consulting and Clinical Psychology,* 1968, *32*(4), 500.

MISCHEL, W.   *Personality and assessment.* New York: John Wiley, 1968.

MOORE, C. H., BOBLITT, W. E., & WILDMAN, R. W.   Psychiatric impressions of psychological reports. *Journal of Clinical Psychology,* 1968, *24*(3), 373–376.

MORSE, S. J.   Law and mental health professionals: The limits of expertise. *Professional Psychology,* 1978, *9*(3), 389–399.

MOSAK, H. H., & GUSHURST, R. S.   Some therapeutic uses of psychologic testing. *American Journal of Psychotherapy,* 1972, *26*(4), 539–546.

MOULTON, R.   Multiple dimensions in supervision. *Contemporary Psychoanalysis,* 1969, *5*(2), 146–150.

MUSSMAN, M. C.   Teachers' Evaluation of psychological reports. *Journal of School Psychology,* 1964, *3*(1), 35–37.

NATIONAL ASSOCIATION OF SCHOOL PSYCHOLOGISTS.   *Principles for professional ethics,* 1974. (Mimeo)

ODOM, C. L.   A study of the time required to do a Rorschach examination. *Journal of Projective Techniques,* 1950, *14*, 464–468.

OGDON, D. P.   *Psychodiagnostics and personality assessment: A handbook* (2nd ed.). Los Angeles: Western Psychological Services, 1981.

OLIVE, H.   Psychoanalysts' opinions of psychologists' reports: 1952 and 1970. *Journal of Clinical Psychology,* 1972, *28*(1), 50–54.

ORBACH, C. E., & TALLENT, N.   Modification of perceived body and body concepts following the construction of a colostomy. *Archives of General Psychiatry,* 1965, *12*, 126–135.

OXFORD ENGLISH DICTIONARY   (compact edition). New York: Oxford University Press, 1971.

PAOLINO, T. J.   Analyzability: Some categories for assessment. *Contemporary Psychoanalysis.* 1981, *17*(3), 321–340.

PARASHAR, O. D.   *Dictionary of special education.* Freeport, N.Y.: Educational Activities, Inc., 1977.

PAUL, G. L.   Strategy of outcome research in psychotherapy. *Journal of Consulting Psychology,* 1967, *31*, 109–119.

PETERSON, D. R.   *The clinical study of social behavior.* New York: Appleton-Century-Crofts, 1968.

PETTY, R. E., & BROCK, T. C.   Effects of Barnum personality assessments on cognitive behavior. *Journal of Consulting and Clinical Psychology,* 1979, *47*(1), 201–203.

PLOTKIN, R.   Through the looking glass: Clients' access to their own records. *APA Monitor,* December 1978, p. 10.

POKORNY, A. D.   Suicide rates in various psychiatric disorders. *Journal of Nervous and Mental Disease,* 1964, *139*, 499–506.

POYTHRESS, N. G.   Coping on the witness stand: Learned responses to "learned treatises." *Professional Psychology,* 1980, *11*(1), 139–149.

RAKOFF, V. M., STANCER, H. C., & KEDWARD, H. B.   *Psychiatric Diagnosis.* New York: Brunner/Mazel, 1977.

RAPAPORT, D., GILL, M. M., & SCHAFER, R.   *Diagnostic Psychological Testing* (Rev. ed., R.R. Holt, Ed.). New York: International Universities Press, 1968.

RHOADS, J. M., & FEATHER, B. W.   The application of psychodynamics to behavior therapy. *American Journal of Psychiatry*, 1974, *13*(1), 17–20.

RICHARDS, W. S., & MERRENS, M. R.   Student evaluation of generalized personality interpretations as a function of method of assessment. *Journal of Clinical Psychology*, 1971, *27*(4), 457–459.

RICHMAN, J.   Reporting diagnostic test results to patients and their families. *Journal of Projective Techniques and Personality Assessment*, 1967, *31*, 62–70.

RITCHIE, G. C.   The use of hypnosis in a case of exhibitionism. *Psychotherapy: Theory, Research and Practice*, 1968, *5*(1), 40–43.

ROBINSON, J. T.   *Some indications of personality differences among clinical psychologists as revealed in their reports on patients*. Unpublished master's thesis, Duke University, 1951.

ROBINSON, J. T., & COHEN, L. D.   Individual bias in psychological reports. *Journal of Clinical Psychology*, 1954, *10*, 333–336.

ROGERS, C. R.   *Client-centered therapy*. Boston: Houghton-Mifflin, 1951.

ROGERS, C. R.   *Counseling and psychotherapy*. Boston: Houghton-Mifflin, 1942.

ROSEN, M.   Alice in Rorschachland. *Journal of Personality Assessment*, 1973, *37*(2), 115–121.

ROSENHAN, D. L.   On being sane in insane places. *Science*, 1973, *179*, 250–258.

ROSENWALD, G. C.   Psychodiagnostics and its discontents. *Psychiatry*, 1963, *26*(3), 222–240.

ROTH, L. H., WOLFORD, J., & MEISEL, A.   Patient access to records: Tonic or toxin? *American Journal of Psychiatry*, 1980, *137*(5), 592–596.

RUCKER, C. N.   Technical language in the school psychologist's report. *Psychology in the Schools*, 1967, *4*, 146–150.

RUSSELL, E. W., NEURINGER, C., & GOLDSTEIN, G.   *Assessment of brain damage: A neuropsychological key approach*. New York: John Wiley, 1970.

SARBIN, T. R., TAFT, R., & BAILEY, D. E.   *Clinical inference and cognitive theory*. New York: Holt, Rinehart & Winston, 1960.

SARGENT, H. D.   Psychological test reporting: An experiment in technique. *Bulletin of the Menninger Clinic*, 1951, *15*, 175–186.

SCHAEFER, A. B.   Clinical supervision. In C. E. Walker (Ed.), *Clinical practice of psychology*. Elmsford, N.Y.: Pergamon Press, 1981.

SCHAFER, R.   Psychological tests in clinical research. *Journal of Consulting Psychology*, 1949, *13*, 328–334.

SCHAFER, R.   *Psychoanalytic interpretation in Rorschach testing*. New York: Grune & Stratton, 1954.

SCHAFER, R.   *A new language for psychoanalysis*. New Haven: Yale University Press, 1976.

SCHWITZGEBEL, R. L., & SCHWITZGEBEL, R. K.   *Law and psychological practice*. New York: John Wiley, 1980.

SHAPIRO, D.   *Neurotic styles*. New York: Basic Books, 1965.

SHAW, F.   A stimulus-response analysis of repression and insight in psychotherapy. *Psychological Review*, 1946, *53*, 36–42.

SHECTMAN, F.   Problems in communicating psychological understanding: Why won't they listen to me?! *American Psychologist*, 1979, *34*(9), 781–790.

SHENKEL, R. J., SNYDER, C. R., BATSON, C. D., & CLARK, G. M.   Effects of prior diagnostic information on clinicians' causal attributions of a client's problems. *Journal of Consulting and Clinical Psychology*, 1979, *47*, 404–406.

SHEVRIN, H., & SHECTMAN, F.   The diagnostic process in psychiatric evaluations. *Bulletin of the Menninger Clinic*, 1973, *37*(5), 491–494.

SHIVELY, J. J., & SMITH, A. E.   Understanding the psychological report. *Psychology in the Schools*, 1969, *6*, 272–273.

SHOBEN, E. J., JR.   Psychotherapy as a problem in learning theory. *Psychological Bulletin,* 1949, *46,* 366–392.

SIEGEL, C., & FISCHER, K. (Eds.).   *Psychiatric records in mental health care.* New York: Brunner/Mazel, 1981.

SISKIND, G.   Change of attitude? *The Clinical Psychologist,* 1967, *20*(4), 158. (a)

SISKIND, G.   Fifteen years later: A replication of "a semantic study of concepts of clinical psychologists and psychiatrists." *The Journal of Psychology,* 1967, *65,* 3–7. (b)

SLOANE, R. B.   The converging paths of behavior therapy and psychotherapy. *American Journal of Psychiatry,* 1969, *125,* 877–885.

SLOVES, R. E., DOCHERTY, E. M., & SCHNEIDER, K. C.   A scientific problem-solving model of psychological assessment. *Professional Psychology,* 1979, *10*(1), 28–35.

SMALL, L.   *Neuropsychodiagnosis in psychotherapy* (Rev. ed.). New York: Brunner/Mazel, 1980.

SMITH, W. H.   Ethical, social, and professional issues in patients' access to psychological test reports. *Bulletin of the Menninger Clinic,* 1978, *42*(2), 150–155.

SMITH, W. H., & GABBARD, G.   Psychological testing and the psychiatric resident. *Bulletin of the Menninger Clinic,* 1980, *44*(6), 647–652.

SMYTH, R., & REZNIKOFF, M.   Attitudes of psychiatrists toward the usefulness of psychodiagnostic reports. *Professional Psychology,* 1971, *2*(3), 283–288.

SNYDER, C. R.   Acceptance of personality interpretations as a function of assessment procedures. *Journal of Consulting and Clinical Psychology,* 1974, *42*(1), 150.

SNYDER, C. R., & LARSON, G. R.   A further look at student acceptance of general personality interpretations. *Journal of Consulting and Clinical Psychology,* 1972, *38*(3), 384–388.

SNYDER, C. R., SHENKEL, R. .J., & LOWERY, C. R.   Acceptance of personality interpretations: The "Barnum Effect" and beyond. *Journal of Consulting and Clinical Psychology,* 1977, *45*(1), 104–114.

SNYDER, C. R., HANDELSMAN, M. M., & ENDELMAN, J. R.   Can clients provide valuable feedback to clinicians about their personality interpretations? A reply to Greene. *Journal of Consulting and Clinical Psychology,* 1978, *46*(6), 1493–1495.

SNYDER, C. R., & COWLES, C.   Impact of positive and negative feedback based on personality and intellectual assessment. *Journal of Consulting and Clinical Psychology,* 1979, *47*(1), 207–209.

SOUTHER, J. W.   *Technical report writing.* New York: John Wiley, 1957.

SOUTHER, J. W., & WHITE, M. L.   *Technical report writing.* New York: John Wiley, 1977.

SPITZER, R. L.   More on pseudoscience in science and the case for psychiatric diagnosis: A critique of D. L. Rosenhan's "On being sane in insane places" and "The contextual nature of psychiatric diagnosis." *Archives of General Psychiatry,* 1976, *33,* 459–470.

SPITZER, R. L. (Chairperson).   *Diagnostic and statistical manual of mental disorders* (3rd ed.) (DSM-III). Washington, D.C.: American Psychiatric Association 1980.

STEIN, E. J., FUREDY, R. L., SIMONTON, M. J., & NEUFFER, C. H.   Patient access to medical records on a psychiatric inpatient unit. *American Journal of Psychiatry,* 1979, *136*(3), 327–332.

STRONG, E. K., JR., & CAMPBELL, D. P.   *Strong Vocational Interest Blank.* Stanford, Calif.: Stanford University Press, 1974.

STURM, I. E.   Toward a composite psychodiagnostic report outline. *Newsletter for Research in Mental Health and Behavioral Science,* 1974, *16*(3), 6–7.

SUGARMAN, A.   Is psychodiagnostic assessment humanistic? *Journal of Personality Assessment,* 1978, *42*(1), 11–21.

SUNDBERG, N. D.   The acceptability of "fake" versus "bona fide" personality test interpretations. *Journal of Abnormal and Social Psychology,* 1955, *50,* 145–147.

SUNDBERG, N. D.   Completely blind analysis of the case of a schizophrenic veteran. Presented at Oregon Psychological Association Meeting, January 14, 1976.

TALLENT, N.   An approach to the improvement of clinical psychological reports. *Journal of Clinical Psychology,* 1956, *12,* 102–109.

TALLENT, N.   On individualizing the psychologist's clinical evaluation. *Journal of Clinical Psychology,* 1958, *14,* 243–244.

TALLENT, N.   *Report writing in special education.* Englewood Cliffs, N.J.: Prentice-Hall, 1980.

TALLENT, N., KENNEDY, G., SZAFIR, A., & GROLIMUND, B.   An expanded role for psychiatric nursing personnel: Psychological evaluation and interpersonal care. *Journal of Psychiatric Nursing and Mental Health Services,* 1974, *12*(3), 19–23.

TALLENT, N., & RAFI, A. A.   National and professional factors in psychological consultation. *British Journal of Social and Clinical Psychology,* 1965, *4,* 149–151.

TALLENT, N., & REISS, W. J.   Multidisciplinary views on the preparation of written clinical psychological reports: I. Spontaneous suggestions for content. *Journal of Clinical Psychology,* 1959, *15,* 218–221. (a)

TALLENT, N., & REISS, W. J.   Multidisciplinary views on the preparation of written clinical psychological reports: II. Acceptability of certain common content variables and styles of expression. *Journal of Clinical Psychology,* 1959, *15,* 273–274. (b).

TALLENT, N., & REISS, W. J.   Multidisciplinary views on the preparation of written clinical psychological reports: III. The trouble with psychological reports. *Journal of Clinical Psychology,* 1959, *15,* 444–446. (c)

TALLENT, N., & REISS, W. J.   A note on an unusually high rate of returns for a mail questionnaire. *The Public Opinion Quarterly,* Winter 1959–1960, *23*(4), 579–581.

TAYLOR, J. L., & TEICHER, A. A.   A Clinical approach to reporting psychological test data. *Journal of Clinical Psychology,* 1946, *2,* 323–332.

THORNE, F. C.   *Clinical judgment: A study of clinical errors.* Brandon, Vt.: Journal of Clinical Psychology, 1961.

TOWBIN, A. P.   When are cookbooks useful? *American Psychologist,* 1960, *15,* 119–123.

TREHUB, A., & SCHERER, I. W.   Wechsler-Bellevue scatter as an index of schizophrenia. *Journal of Consulting Psychology,* 1958, *22,* 147–149.

ULRICH, R. E., STACHNIK, T. J., & STAINTON, N. R.   Student acceptance of generalized personality interpretations. *Psychological Reports,* 1963, *13,* 831–834.

VAN REKEN, M. K.   Psychological assessment and report writing. In C. E. Walker (Ed.), *Clinical practice of psychology.* Elmsford, N.Y.: Pergamon Press, 1981.

VERNON, W. H. D.   Diagnostic testing and some problems of communication between psychiatrists and clinical psychologists. *Bulletin of the Maritime Psychological Association,* Spring 1955, 12–29.

WACHTEL, P.   *Psychoanalysis and behavior therapy: Toward an integration.* New York: Basic Books, 1977.

WEBB, L. J., DI CLEMENTE, C. C., JOHNSTONE, E. E., SANDERS, J. L., & PERLEY, R. A.   *DSM-III training guide.* New York: Brunner/Mazel, 1981.

WECHSLER, D.   The psychologist in the psychiatric hospital. *Journal of Consulting Psychology*, 1944, *8*, 281–285.

WEITZMAN, B.   Behavior therapy and psychotherapy. *Psychological Review*, 1967, *74*(4), 300–317.

WERTHEIMER, M.   *Productive thinking.* New York: Harper & Row, Pub., 1945.

WIEDEMANN, C., & MINTZ, J.   Student therapists' assessment of diagnostic testing. *Journal of Personality Assessment*, 1974, *38*(3), 203–214.

WIENER, D. N., & RATHS, O. N.   Contributions of the mental hygiene clinic team to clinic decisions. *American Journal of Orthopsychiatry*, 1959, *29*, 350–356.

WILKENING, H. E.   *The psychology almanac.* Monterey, Calif.: Brooks/Cole, 1973.

WILLI, J.   Joint Rorschach testing of partner relationships. *Family Process*, 1969, *8*, 64–78.

WILLIAMS, T.   Family resemblance in abilities: The Wechsler scales. *Behavior Genetics*, 1974, *5*, 405–409.

WILSON, S. J.   *Recording: Guidelines for social workers.* New York: Free Press,1980.

WIRT, R. D., LACHAR, D., KLINEDINST, J. K., & SEAT, P. D.   *Multidimensional description of child personality: A manual for the personality inventory for children.* Los Angeles: Western Psychological Services, 1977.

WOLMAN, B. B. (Ed.).   *Dictionary of behavioral science.* New York: Van Nostrand Reinhold, 1973.

WOLPE, J.   *Psychotherapy by reciprocal inhibition.* Stanford, Calif.: Stanford University Press, 1958.

WOLPE, J.   The experimental model and treatment of neurotic depression. *Behavior Research and Therapy*, 1979, *17*, 555–565.

WOODY, R. H.   Toward a rationale for psychobehavioral therapy. *Archives of General Psychiatry*, 1968, *19*, 197–204.

WOODY, R. H.   *Psychobehavioral counseling and therapy: Integrating behavioral and insight techniques.* New York: Appleton-Century-Crofts, 1969.

WOODY, R. H.   The counselor-therapist and clinical assessment. In R. H. Woody, & J. D. Woody, *Clinical assessment in counseling and psychotherapy.* New York: Appleton-Century-Crofts, 1972.

WRIGHT, R. H.   What to do until the malpractice lawyer comes: A survivor's manual. *American Psychologist*, 1981, *36*(12), 1535–1541.

WYATT v. ADERHOLT,   503 F. 2nd 1305(1974), *Federal Reporter*, 2d Series, 1311–1312.

YALOM, I., BROWN, S., & BLOCH, S.   The written summary as a group psychotherapy technique. *Archives of General Psychiatry*, 1975, *32*(5), 605–613.

YATES, A. J.   *Behavior therapy.* New York: John Wiley, 1970.

YATES, A. J.   Behavior therapy: Past, present, future—imperfect? *Clinical Psychology Review*, 1981, *1*(3), 269–291.

ZISKIN, J.   *Coping with psychiatric and psychological testimony* (3rd ed., 2 vols.). Venice, Calif.: Law and Psychology Press, 1981.

AUTHOR INDEX

SUBJECT INDEX